# CRIMINAL JUSTICE

## PROCEDURE

# 7th
## EDITION

RONALD L. CARLSON, J.D., LL.M.
Fuller E. Callaway Professor of Law
The University of Georgia School of Law

 LexisNexis®

 anderson publishing
A member of the LexisNexis Group

**Criminal Justice Procedure, Seventh Edition**

**Library of Congress Cataloging-in-Publication Data**

Carlson, Ronald L., 1934-
    Criminal justice procedure / Ronald L. Carlson--7th ed.
       p. cm.
     Includes bibliographical references and index.
      ISBN 1-59345-961-0 (softbound : alk. paper)
      1. Criminal procedure--United States. I. Title.
    KF9619.C37 2005
    345.73'05--dc22
                                          2005009197

Cover design by Tin Box Studio, Inc.
Photo © Mel Curtis/Photonica

EDITOR Elisabeth Roszmann Ebben
ACQUISITIONS EDITOR Michael C. Braswell

# Preface

Terrorism concerns gripped the country in the early years of the twenty-first century. Courts responded by addressing cases involving the detention of people classified as "enemy combatants." In one notable decision, the United States Supreme Court ruled that when such a person's case is heard, he is entitled to counsel, including an appointed attorney if he is without funds, to assist him. Justice O'Connor's 2004 opinion explained why the extension of rights in this situation is valuable. "It is during our most challenging and uncertain moments that our nation's commitment to due process is most severely tested; and it is in those times that we must preserve our commitment at home to the principles for which we fight abroad."

The text provides added detail on the challenge of dealing with terrorist suspects within the framework of our justice system. Along with these modern concerns, the problems of "standard" crimes at home are not neglected. Drug, homicide, assault and robbery offenses continue, and the legal system continues to respond. Under federal and many state codes, the response has been to increase prison terms. Legislation imposes mandatory life sentences on felons convicted of a third violent crime under federal law. Drug sentences have been enhanced for those in possession of narcotics, with life terms for those in possession of saleable quantities of certain drugs. Federal provisions have expanded the federal death penalty.

The drive to hold convicted felons in prison for longer periods is placing a strain on existing prison space, adding impetus to the drive to construct new prisons nationwide. Courts throughout the land struggle under the weight of vast caseloads.

They also struggle with complex legal questions that face students of criminal justice as well as the courts. In criminal cases, search and seizure issues continue. For example, how long must officers wait after they knock and announce their authority and purpose when executing search warrants? That question is answered in Chapter 2. Added to such concerns are legal issues related to new legislation like the USA PATRIOT Act. Under it, enhanced wiretap and electronic surveillance are permitted. So are "sneak and peek" search warrants, which allow federal agents to make physical entry into private premises without the owner's permission or knowledge. This text traces the debates between law enforcement authorities versus civil libertarians when police power is expanded in legislative measures such as these.

The debate over the solution to America's crime and drug problem is complicated by the fact that most states with large urban areas suffer from heavy backlogs in their court systems. In addition, there is a severe shortage of jail and prison space. Incarceration for crimes of many kinds has overloaded our correctional facilities. This text will deal with prosecution of a wide range of offenses, from charges of murder to mail fraud. It details the explosion in jail populations as the criminal justice system endeavors to deal with the modern crime challenge while retaining civil rights and liberties for our citizens.

These liberties are the product of the checks and balances that operate when one is accused of a crime. The value of these checks and balances in a system of criminal justice cannot be overstated. A notable component of our democratic system is the right to trial by jury. Another is the right to be presumed innocent until the government establishes an individual's guilt beyond a reasonable doubt.

Effective processing of a criminal case through the varied and sometimes intricate stages of this system requires a clear understanding of its parts. A case is far from over once the arrest is made, no matter how careful the preliminary investigation nor how meticulous the officer's seizure of evidence. Many prosecution witnesses can testify to the rigors of a scorching defense cross-examination once the case reaches the courtroom. Intensive cross-examination of this kind is a characteristic feature of American criminal trials, which proceed under an adversary (or contest) theory of justice to arrive at the truth in a given case. Defense witnesses are also exposed to potentially searching questions by the prosecutor. It is for the jury, which observes these witnesses, to weigh the evidence and make the final decision in every case—guilty or not guilty.

This volume explores our adversary system of criminal justice, tracing the various steps that precede trial, as well as the trial process itself. Positive suggestions for citizens who appear as witnesses are set forth. Rules controlling post-trial proceedings, including appeals, habeas corpus hearings, and the probation and parole processes are clarified.

Every major project involves several important component parts, and the Seventh Edition of this text is no exception. Research assistance was provided by Amanda Bates, Ramsey Henderson, and Jen McDowell of the 2005 graduating class at the University of Georgia School of Law. Acknowledged also is the creative and affirmative atmosphere encouraged at the school by Dean Rebecca White. Mary Fielding prepared the manuscript, a task which she has ably accomplished with this edition, as well as most of the prior editions, of the book. At the publisher's level, Elisabeth Ebben provided appreciated editorial oversight.

Responsible administration of the criminal laws, as well as constructive revision of the criminal justice system, requires an effective knowledge of the subject. To that end this work is aimed and dedicated.

RONALD L. CARLSON
Professor of Law

Athens, Georgia
January 2005

# Table of Contents

Chapter 3
# Bail                                                                    **75**

Chapter 7
# Sentencing, Crime and Corrections

## Chapter 8
## Appeals and Habeas Corpus                                        261

## Chapter 9
## Special Problems:
## Location of Trial and Double Jeopardy                            285

# Selected Provisions of the United States Constitution

## AMENDMENT I [1791]

Congress shall make no law respecting an establishment of religion, or prohibiting the free exercise thereof; or abridging the freedom of speech, or of the press; or the right of the people peaceably to assemble, and to petition the Government for a redress of grievances.

## AMENDMENT II [1791]

A well regulated Militia, being necessary to the security of a free State, the right of the people to keep and bear Arms, shall not be infringed.

## AMENDMENT III [1791]

No Soldier shall, in time of peace be quartered in any house, without the consent of the Owner, nor in time of war, but in a manner to be prescribed by law.

## AMENDMENT IV [1791]

The right of the people to secure in their persons, houses, papers, and effects, against unreasonable searches and seizures, shall not be violated, and no Warrants shall issue, but upon probable cause, supported by Oath or affirmation, and particularly describing the place to be searched, and the persons or things to be seized.

## AMENDMENT V [1791]

No person shall be held to answer for a capital, or otherwise infamous crime, unless on a presentment or indictment of a Grand Jury, except in cases arising in the land or naval forces, or in the Militia, when in actual service in time of War or public danger; nor shall any person be subject for the same offence to be twice put in jeopardy of life or limb; nor shall be compelled in any criminal case to be a witness against himself, nor be deprived of life, liberty, or property, without due process of law; nor shall private property be taken for public use, without just compensation.

## AMENDMENT VI [1791]

In all criminal prosecutions, the accused shall enjoy the right to a speedy and public trial, by an impartial jury of the State and district wherein the crime shall have been committed, which district shall have been previously ascertained by law, and to be informed of the nature and cause of the accusation; to be confronted with the witness against him; to have compulsory process for obtaining witnesses in his favor, and to have the Assistance of Counsel for his defence.

## AMENDMENT VII [1791]

In Suits at common law, where the value in controversy shall exceed twenty dollars, the right of trial by jury shall be preserved, and no fact tried by jury, shall be otherwise re-examined in any Court of the United States, than according to the rules of the common law.

## AMENDMENT VIII [1791]

Excessive bail shall not be required, nor excessive fines imposed, nor cruel and unusual punishments inflicted.

## AMENDMENT IX [1791]

The enumeration in the Constitution, of certain rights, shall not be construed to deny or disparage others retained by the people.

## AMENDMENT X [1791]

The powers not delegated to the United States by the Constitution, nor prohibited by it to the States, are reserved to the States respectively, or to the people.

## AMENDMENT XIII [1865]

Section 1. Neither slavery nor involuntary servitude, except as a punishment for crime whereof the party shall have been duly convicted, shall exist within the United States, or any place subject to their jurisdiction.

Section 2. Congress shall have power to enforce this article by appropriate legislation.

## AMENDMENT XIV [1868]

Section 1. All persons born or naturalized in the United States, and subject to the jurisdiction thereof, are citizens of the United States and of the State wherein they reside. No State shall make or enforce any law which shall abridge the privileges or immunities of citizens of the United States; nor shall any State deprive any person of life, liberty, or property, without due process of law; nor deny to any person within its jurisdiction the equal protection of the laws.

Section 5. The Congress shall have power to enforce, by appropriate legislation, the provisions of the article.

# Case Citation Guide

The following list provides an explanation of case citations used in Criminal Justice Procedure, Sixth Edition, for readers who may be unfamiliar with how court decisions are cited.

U.S.
: United States Reports. Published by the United States government, this is the official source of United States Supreme Court decisions. It reports only United States Supreme Court decisions.

S. Ct.
: Supreme Court Reporter. Published by Thomson/West, this publication reports United States Supreme Court decisions.

L. Ed./L. Ed. 2d
: United States Reports, Lawyers' Edition, First Series/Second Series. Published by LexisNexis, this publication reports United States Supreme Court decisions.

F.2d/F.3d
: Federal Reports, Second Series/Third Series. Published by Thomson/West, it reports decisions of the Federal Courts of Appeals.

F. Supp.
: Federal Supplement. Published by Thomson/West, this reports decisions of the Federal District Courts.

# Sample Case Citations

*Gideon v. Wainwright,* 372 U.S. 335 (1963). This case is located in volume 372 of the United States Reports, beginning on page 335. It was decided in 1963.

*Gideon v. Wainwright,* 83 S. Ct. 792 (1963). Gideon v. Wainwright is published in volume 83 of the Supreme Court Reporter, beginning on page 792.

*Gideon v. Wainwright,* 9 L. Ed. 2d 799 (1963). Gideon v. Wainwright is also published in volume 9 of Supreme Court Reports, Lawyers' Edition, Second Series, beginning on page 799.

*Phillips v. Perry,* 106 F.3d 1420 (9th Cir. 1997). This case is located in volume 106 of Federal Reports, Third Series, beginning on page 1420. It was decided by the Ninth Circuit Court of Appeals in 1997.

*Galen v. County of Los Angeles,* 322 F. Supp. 2d 1045 (C.D. Cal. 2004). This case is located in volume 322 of *Federal Supplement,* beginning on page 1045. It was decided in 2004 by the Federal District Court for the Central District of California.

# An Overview of Criminal Justice in America

# 1

## Chapter Outline

Section

## Key Terms and Concepts

| | |
|---|---|
| adversary theory of justice | grand jury |
| appeal | habeas corpus |
| arraignment | hearings |
| arrest | indictment |
| arrest warrant | information |
| bind over | jury |
| booking a suspect | jury instructions |
| charge | magistrate |
| closing argument | motion |
| common law | motion to suppress |
| constitutional law | motion to vacate judgment |
| conviction | plea |
| coram nobis relief | post-conviction remedy |
| cross-examination | preliminary examination |
| custody | probable cause |
| defendant | prosecution |
| diversion | prosecutor |
| double jeopardy | right to counsel |
| evidence | screening |
| exclusionary rule | statutory law |
| felony | trial |

Chapter 1 is an overview chapter. Many of the terms and concepts introduced here will be covered in more depth in subsequent chapters.

## § 1.1 Preliminary Considerations: Crime, Police, and Courts

The issues of crime and its control are urgent concerns for Americans today. The public often registers these concerns when voting, and the impact of crime on public consciousness is seen in recurring opinion polls, which rate it at or near the top of "major unresolved problems in America." The criminal justice system and its processes are presented to most Americans via television's police and courtroom dramas. The courts are where society's criminal laws are enforced, and the popular view focuses on courtroom proceedings. However, the processing of criminal cases entails significantly more than a trial in criminal court,[1] the trial stage presents an apt opportunity to open discussion of the American justice system. While this text provides a comprehensive study of criminal trials, it also reviews the multiple steps in a criminal prosecution from arrest through sentencing, appeals, and habeas corpus.

---

[1] This point is discussed in § 1.4 of this chapter and in succeeding chapters of the text.

3

## Sources of Rights

The rules governing criminal proceedings in the United States have four basic sources: constitutions, statutes, case law, and court rules.

### Constitutions

Federal　　　　The U.S. Constitution contains the most basic and important rights available to accused persons in its first 10 amendments, known as the Bill of Rights.

The amendments most applicable in criminal justice procedure and the rights they ensure are listed below.

FIRST AMENDMENT
- freedom of religion
- freedom of speech
- freedom of the press
- freedom of assembly
- freedom to petition the government for redress of grievances

SECOND AMENDMENT
- right to keep and bear arms

FOURTH AMENDMENT
- right against unreasonable search and seizure and arrest

FIFTH AMENDMENT
- right to a grand jury indictment for capital or other serious crime
- right against double jeopardy
- right against self-incrimination
- prohibition against the taking of life, liberty, or property without due process of law

SIXTH AMENDMENT
- right to a speedy and public trial
- right to an impartial jury
- right to be informed of the nature and cause of the accusation
- right to confront the witness
- right to summon witnesses
- right to have assistance of counsel

EIGHTH AMENDMENT
- right against excessive bail
- right against cruel and unusual punishment

FOURTEENTH AMENDMENT
- right to due process
- right to equal protection

*State*      Each of the 50 states has its own state constitution. These constitutions must comply with the provisions set out in the U.S. Constitution, although they may provide more protection than the federal Constitution allows.

**Statutes**      Federal and state statutes frequently cover the same rights mentioned in the U.S. Constitution but in more detail. Some rights not constitutionally required, such as the right to a lawyer during probation revocation or the right to a jury trial in juvenile cases, may be given by state law.

**Case Law**      Many laws are based on the doctrine of stare decisis, which literally means "let the decision stand" and refers to the fact that law is built through legal principles that develop as cases are decided in the courts. Thus, precedent is the decision of a court that furnishes authority for an identical or similar case that arises subsequently. The prior decision of a court is binding on that court and the inferior courts (those lower in hierarchical judicial structure) of that particular judicial system. Thus, a decision of the U.S. Supreme Court on questions of federal law is binding on all lower federal courts (courts of appeals and district courts). Likewise, the decisions of the highest court of each state are binding on the inferior state courts. However, a decision of the Supreme Court of Illinois is not precedent for a California court. The California court may follow the Illinois precedent voluntarily due to its persuasiveness, but it is not bound to do so. This unwritten law becomes accepted until challenged and changed by subsequent case law.

Case law differs from common law, which is based on the unwritten laws of England and was transplanted to America through English colonization. Although it served as the basis for laws of the United States, it was adapted to the needs of this country.

**Court Rules**      The supervisory power of the courts over the administration of criminal justice has resulted in rules of the courts that have been established and have the force and effect of law. These rules may cover details not included in other sources, such as state codes. State and federal rules of criminal procedure provide examples of such court rules, as do the Federal Rules of Evidence.

Source: Adapted from Rolando V. del Carmen (1998). *Criminal Procedure: Law and Practice*, Fourth Edition, Wadsworth Publishing Company, pp. 12-15 and John W. Palmer (1997) *Constitutional Rights of Prisoners*, Fifth Edition, Anderson Publishing Co., pp. 1-5.

## § 1.2   Adversary System of Justice

American criminal trials proceed under the **adversary (or contest) theory of justice** to arrive at the truth in a given case.[2] One characteristic feature of this system is intensive **cross-examination** of both defense and prosecution witnesses. In a jury trial it is for the **jury**, which observes these witnesses, to weigh the evidence and make the ultimate decision in every case—guilty or not guilty.

For this reason an experienced police officer recognizes that a case is far from over once he or she makes an arrest, no matter how careful the preliminary investigation or how meticulous the officer's seizure of evidence.

## § 1.3   Constitutional Right to Jury Trial

Whether the adversary **trial** of a criminal case will be heard by a jury or a judge frequently depends upon the seriousness of the crime involved. The United States Constitution gives every person accused of a serious criminal offense (carrying a punishment in excess of six months) the right to be tried in front of a jury. This right belongs to an accused person whether the trial is in a state or federal court.[3] Of course, even in serious cases, many courts give the defendant the option of waiving a jury trial, and a major case is sometimes tried before a single judge, if the defendant so desires.

## § 1.4   Steps in a Criminal Prosecution

While the right to have a jury trial is guaranteed under our Constitution, numerous pretrial court procedures have evolved over the years as a result of practice and statute, as opposed to constitutional development. Beginning with the **arrest** and presentment of the **defendant** before a **magistrate**, various pretrial steps will be sketched to provide a summary overview of the criminal justice system prior to in-depth treatment of various phases later in this text.

In prosecutions for the more serious criminal offenses (felonies and high misdemeanors), the following stages mark the process.[4]

---

[2]   The strengths and weaknesses of this method for resolving such questions are reviewed in depth in the concluding chapter of this text. See Chapter 11, The Adversary System.

[3]   Duncan v. Louisiana, 391 U.S. 145, 88 S. Ct. 1444, 20 L. Ed. 2d 491 (1968).

[4]   Ordinary or petty misdemeanors are tried differently than the description provided here. For the separate method of disposing of these inferior grade offenses, *see* Chapter 10 of this text, which treats misdemeanor trials.

## 1. Arrest

It has been estimated that approximately 20 to 30 percent of all arrests are made on **felony** charges.[5] Some of these arrests are based upon arrest warrants signed by a judge or magistrate. The **warrant** is a written order directing a peace officer (frequently any officer in the state) to take a person into **custody** on a designated **charge**. The warrant is issued in the name of the state, and prior to issuance the magistrate must decide whether the facts known to the police reasonably support a conclusion that the person sought to be arrested committed the crime.

Many arrests are made without a warrant. While a few of these arrests are made by private citizens, almost all are initiated by police. To make a warrantless felony arrest, a law enforcement officer must have reasonable grounds to believe that a crime has been committed and that the defendant committed it.[6] This constitutes **probable cause**.

Following arrest, the suspect will usually be **booked**, a procedure that takes place shortly after his or her arrival at police headquarters. The suspect's name is entered on the police blotter or arrest book, as well as the time of arrest and the criminal charge. The suspect may be fingerprinted and photographed.[7]

When police officers approach a person on the street and ask him or her questions, does this process constitute a formal arrest? Unless the encounter involves more intrusive police conduct, such actions are not tantamount to arrest. The constitutional liberties of the target of the inquiries are not infringed upon. A 2004 decision by the United States Supreme Court enumerates the rights of the parties in this situation. In *Hiibel v. Sixth Judicial District Court of Nevada*,[8] the Court affirms the right of law enforcement officers to approach a person on the street or in another public place and ask him to identify himself. In many states the person who is approached may respond to the officer's inquiry or may choose to simply walk away without penalty. However, a number of jurisdictions have statutes allowing the arrest of those who refuse to identify themselves in the face of a law enforcement request. Such statutes are constitutional, says the Court in *Hiibel*.

When a person answers police questions and the answers given by the individual or other circumstances arouse a reasonable suspicion of criminal activity, the case of *Terry v. Ohio*[9] authorizes a limited search of the individual: Pat-down searches are justifiable under the Fourth Amendment if there is articulable suspicion that a person has committed or is about to commit a crime. In the *Terry* case, a stop and frisk for weapons was found unexceptional. The stop and frisk process is dealt with in more detail in § 2.1 of this text.

---

[5]　A felony is typically defined in state law as an offense punishable by death or imprisonment for a term exceeding one year.

[6]　Searches for weapons and evidence-gathering procedures, including interrogations, frequently follow arrest. The constitutional guidelines controlling these procedures are discussed in § 2.2 (searches) and § 6.3(2) (confessions, lineups).

[7]　KAMISAR, LAFAVE & ISRAEL, MODERN CRIMINAL PROCEDURE 18 (10th ed. 2002).

[8]　124 S. Ct. 2451 (2004). More discussion of this area of the law appears in § 2.1(4) *infra*.

[9]　392 U.S. 1, 88 S. Ct. 1868, 20 L. Ed. 2d 889 (1968).

## 2. Prosecution or Diversion

Not all arrested persons are fully prosecuted. A suspect may be released without the filing of a formal charge, perhaps because the police believe there is insufficient evidence to hold him. In addition, a defendant may be released to a diversion program. **Diversion** characteristically involves a discretionary decision on the part of an official that there is a better way to deal with a defendant than to prosecute him. Thus, police or prosecutors may decline to proceed with criminal **prosecution** in the first instance, or they may exercise discretion to terminate an ongoing case if they conclude that prosecution is inappropriate.

Usually the decision to divert is accompanied by an accused person's promise to take certain rehabilitative steps in his or her own behalf.[10] The authorities may discontinue prosecution of a person arrested for public drunkenness, for example, if the accused complies with certain conditions, such as treatment in a detoxification center or participation in a similar program. Juveniles may be diverted from the juvenile justice process by police who conclude that justice is better served by counseling and releasing youths to their parents or to a community agency. In lieu of formal court proceedings, aged or mentally retarded persons who have committed nonviolent offenses are frequently diverted from criminal prosecution when it is thought that another person or agency is well suited to assume responsibility for future conduct. "Although most police diversion cases involve the informal disposition of juvenile matters, some other occasions arise where certain individuals should not be subjected to the criminal process. . . . Police experience has shown that certain types of conduct, such as that manifested by the mentally ill, alcoholics, and juveniles, may be dealt with best by diversion from the criminal or juvenile justice system at any stage of the process."[11]

Diversion often involves a discretionary decision on the part of an official that there is a better way to deal with a defendant than to prosecute him or her. It characteristically uses the potential threat of a temporarily suspended criminal process to encourage rehabilitative conduct by the accused. Diversion often takes place after arrest but before a defendant goes to court (as suggested in the chart at the end of this chapter). However, diversion of offenders into noncriminal programs may take place later in the process, occurring at any stage of the prosecution prior to **conviction**. Several commentators take the view that any action after conviction is not diversion, because by this time the criminal prosecution has run to conclusion.[12]

---

[10]  In NIMMER, DIVERSION (1974), diversion, or "early diversion" as it is often called, is defined as the disposition of a criminal complaint without a conviction, the noncriminal disposition being conditioned on the performance of specified obligations by the defendant, or his participation in treatment.

[11]  WORKING PAPERS, NATIONAL CONFERENCE ON CRIMINAL JUSTICE p. 106 (1973).

[12]  National Advisory Commission on Criminal Justice Standards and Goals, COURTS 27 (1973).

Screening is a separate concept. Sometimes the case against a defendant is dropped completely. On the other hand, when several charges are brought against a defendant, some may be dismissed while others are maintained.

**Screening** out the charges in this manner has been described as the decision to abandon part or all of a criminal prosecution. Where police or prosecutors dismiss a charge (perhaps because of inadequate evidence), a screening decision has been made. The process operates at several levels. Arresting officers may exercise judgment in determining whether to formally charge a suspect. An officer may make an arrest, but at the station house the officer's superiors may decide to release the suspect or charge him or her with a non-criminal ordinance violation. Insufficient evidence is one primary reason for disposing of a case without plea or trial. The police officer who makes an investigatory stop and decides not to arrest is screening, just as the prosecutor who washes out a case on the eve of trial is screening.[13]

Thus, through screening or diversion a case may be evaluated and disposed of without trial at various stages in the prosecution.

### 3. First Appearance on the Charge

In a typical case in which court processing is appropriate, the arrested person is taken before a magistrate. The Federal Rules of Criminal Procedure require any federal officer who makes an arrest with or without an arrest warrant to take the arrested person before the nearest available federal magistrate without unnecessary delay. The magistrate must inform the defendant of the charge against him or her, of the individual's **right to counsel**, and of his or her right to have a **preliminary examination**. With certain exceptions, the magistrate sets bail and can release the defendant on bail. Statutes and court rules in most states contain provisions similar to those in the Federal Rules.[14]

### 4. Preliminary Hearing

If the defendant does not waive preliminary examination or hearing, the government must demonstrate that there is probable cause to believe that an offense has been committed and that the defendant committed it. Police officers are frequently called as witnesses at preliminary hearings to provide sufficient evidence to bind over the defendant to a court of higher jurisdiction. At the hearing, the magistrate may: find evidence of probable cause and hold the accused to answer in the trial court; find evidence of probable cause and hold the accused to answer in the trial court; or dismiss the charge and order the defendant to be released from custody.

---

[13]   Working Papers, note 11 *supra* at Ct.-7. There may be instances where a prosecutor declines to prosecute notwithstanding evidence to support a conviction, as when a defendant is not a threat to the community and suitable alternatives to prosecution are available. See National Advisory Commission, note 12, *supra* at 20.

[14]   Fed. R. Crim. P. 5.

## 5.  Indictment or Information

If the magistrate holds the defendant to answer in trial court, it becomes essential for the prosecutor to make an important decision: whether to advance the case into felony court. When the prosecutor determines to do so, he or she may proceed to the grand jury with the case. There, the **grand jury** can decide whether to issue an **indictment** or to terminate prosecution (at least for the time being) of the defendant.

Some jurisdictions allow the prosecutor to move a felony case forward without a grand jury indictment. While federal prosecutors and those in many states are bound by the grand jury requirement, other jurisdictions permit felony prosecutions upon a prosecutor's accusation, which is termed an "**information**." This document sets forth in formal legal terms the violation allegedly committed by the accused. In many "information" states, this formal charge must be approved by a trial judge.

## 6.  Arraignment in the Court of Trial

If an indictment or information is filed against the defendant, he or she is required to appear before a judge of the court that has jurisdiction to hear and dispose of the case. The purpose of this appearance, called an **arraignment**, is to apprise the defendant of the formal charge filed against him or her and to obtain his or her **plea** to this charge. If the defendant pleads not guilty, the case will be set for trial.

## 7.  Suppression Hearings

When the defendant elects to go to trial on his or her case, special **hearings** are frequently held between the time of the arraignment and the trial to deal with evidentiary matters. If incriminating items of physical evidence were seized from the defendant or the environs when he or she was arrested, or if a confession was obtained from him or her, the police officers who secured such evidence may have to defend their actions in special pretrial hearings. Hearings of this nature are occasioned when the defense lawyer files a **motion** (a legal document asking the judge to take certain action) requesting the court to prevent the government from introducing the seized items into evidence upon trial of the defendant. When unconstitutional methods of seizure were used, an **exclusionary rule** operates to bar this evidence.[15]

**Motions to suppress** evidence are used to exclude a defendant's confession. After a crime is discovered, a confession may result when a suspect is arrested and interrogated. The defendant may later claim that the police used unconstitutional means to make the defendant confess. A judge will decide. He or she may uphold the validity of the confession; on the other hand, if the defendant's rights were violated, the confession will be thrown out.

---

[15]   See §§ 2.2, 6.3(2).

Before a confession is taken, a defendant must be told of his or her constitutional protections. The defendant then can exercise his or her rights and the interrogation must cease, or he or she can decide to answer questions. The defendant must make clear his or her desire to have counsel present. The defendant's right to ask for a lawyer during questioning was not violated in one 1994 case. The defendant, a member of the U.S. Navy, was suspected of murdering another sailor. When interviewed by the authorities, he was told of his constitutional rights but elected to talk anyway. About an hour and a half into the interview, the sailor said: "Maybe I should talk to a lawyer." Everything stopped while the point was discussed. The defendant then concluded: "No, I don't want a lawyer." The interview then continued for an hour, and the defendant made damaging admissions.

The issue for the Supreme Court was whether the questioning should have stopped when the suspect made a brief reference to talking to a lawyer. Were his rights violated, and did the incriminating statements made thereafter by the defendant comport with the requirements of law? The Court held that in order for the questioning to stop "the suspect must unambiguously request counsel." In the case at hand, the subject's mood bounced back and forth. He did not clearly signal his desire for counsel, and his subsequent statements, which contributed to his guilt, were not excluded. The Court observed: "Although a suspect need not 'speak with the discrimination of an Oxford don,' he must articulate his desire to have counsel present sufficiently clearly that a reasonable police officer in the circumstances would understand the statement to be a request for an attorney."[16] That sort of request did not happen here, in the view of the Court.

When the case goes the other way and the trial judge grants the defendant's motion to suppress his or her confession or other damaging admissions, the jury does not hear the confession. Nor may a police officer or other government witness refer to the fact that a defendant confessed to the crime if the police procedures used in obtaining the confession are deemed to have been illegal.

## 8. Trial

Eighty percent or more of all defendants plead guilty in criminal cases. Of those who plead not guilty and then go to trial, the majority are tried before a jury. In a substantial number of criminal trials, however, the accused will waive his or her constitutional right to a jury trial and elect to be tried by the judge alone. Such waiver is possible in most states; however, a small minority of jurisdictions require jury trials in serious criminal cases notwithstanding the wishes of the defendant.

Whether the case is tried to the judge or a jury, the production of **evidence** on the issues of guilt or innocence frequently leads to vigorous exchanges between the prosecutor and defense attorney. Evidence may be presented

---

16  Davis v. United States, 512 U.S. 452, 114 S. Ct. 2350, 129 L. Ed. 2d 362 (1994). When the right to consult with counsel is violated, however, a defendant's statements or confession will be thrown out. Arizona v. Roberson, 108 S. Ct. 2093 (1988).

through various means, including testimony of the parties and witnesses, records, documents, exhibits, and objects. Scientific evidence issues are hotly contested in modern trials. DNA testing has taken center stage in a number of cases, with a body specimen such as blood or semen taken from the crime scene being matched to the defendant's genetic makeup.[17] Polygraph testimony may form another basis for controversy. Whether "lie detector" test results constitute proper criminal case evidence is often debated, and the United States Supreme Court entered the fray in 1998. The issue was presented in *United States v. Scheffer*.[18] The Air Force accused an airman of using an illegal drug. He submitted to a polygraph test given by the Air Force, and passed. Notwithstanding, he was tried for the drug offense. At his military trial, the polygraph results were denied admission into evidence, and the Supreme Court reviewed that decision. It approved exclusion of the polygraph proof, citing doubts about reliability.

2004 jurisprudence from the high Court emphasized that a defendant has a constitutional right to cross-examine the prosecution's witnesses. Documents or statements from government witnesses cannot simply be read to the jury by the prosecutor. The author of the document must come to the trial, testify, and be cross-examined. Without this step, the words of the witness will not be heard. In *Crawford v. Washington*,[19] a witness gave police a statement, and when she did not testify against the defendant at trial, the prosecutor played the witness's tape-recorded police statement for the jury. This procedure violated the defendant's right of **cross-examination**.

**Closing arguments** mark the end of a trial, after which, in jury trials, jurors are instructed in the law via **jury instructions**. They proceed to deliberate, applying the law to the facts, after receiving the judge's instructions. During closing arguments, each attorney attempts to persuade. To keep the persuasion within proper bounds, legal rules have grown up that restrict what the lawyers are permitted to say. These rules are reviewed in § 6.28 of the text.

Just as the lawyers must exercise care in making their remarks, the judge must observe legal standards when supplying instructions to jurors. In these directives to the jury, the judge will guide them on the elements of the offense or offenses at issue in the trial. Only if these are proved by evidence that establishes guilt beyond a reasonable doubt will the jury convict the accused.

After the instructions, the jury deliberates and reaches a verdict. If the verdict is "guilty," sentencing of the defendant is the next step in the process.

While sentencing in death penalty cases falls upon the shoulders of a jury, passing sentence in other crimes is the responsibility of the presiding judge.

Whether the defendant is charged with drunk driving or a different crime, sentencing by the trial judge is an important aspect of the justice process. Sentencing in the criminal case may travel one of several roads: suspended sen-

---

[17]   Scientific evidence of this kind is discussed in § 6.12(2) of this text.
[18]   118 S. Ct. 1261 (1998).
[19]   124 S. Ct. 1354 (2004).

tence, probation, monetary fine, a term of years in the penitentiary or a reformatory, or the death penalty in special cases in capital punishment states.

### 9. Hearings After Trial

If a defendant is found guilty, he or she may file a motion requesting the trial judge to set aside the conviction and enter a verdict in his or her favor, or in the alternative to give the defendant a new trial. Jury verdicts are overturned in only a few cases, however.

Subsequent to a defendant's conviction and sentencing by the trial judge, a major post-trial hearing in which the police officer might be involved as a witness is the hearing to revoke probation or parole. In some cases defendants commit new and separate offenses while free on probation, and the police officer who investigates the new offense may be called upon to testify at a probation revocation hearing. The officer's evidence may be crucial in deciding whether a probationer has violated the terms of his or her conditional freedom.

### 10. Appeals and Habeas Corpus

Methods are available under our law whereby convicted persons may seek review of their convictions by judges other than the trial judge who presided over the original trial. The most used of these review methods include appeals and habeas corpus proceedings. Although reliance on these measures is more often unsuccessful than victorious, a large number of prisoners seek new trials through appeals or habeas corpus every year. **Appeals** are taken directly from a conviction in the trial court to an appellate court of the state, and such appeals must be pursued by the defendant within a specified number of days following entry of the judgment convicting him. On direct appeal, a 1990 study found that a convict's chance of winning did not vary much by type of crime. "Overall, about 80 percent of criminal convictions were affirmed."[20] **Habeas corpus** is called a **post-conviction remedy**, and prisoners in state or federal penitentiaries may attack their convictions several years after the original conviction in habeas corpus proceedings. There is generally no requirement that habeas corpus be pursued within a certain time after the trial, as is the case with an appeal. Applications for **coram nobis relief** and **motions to vacate judgment** are two other forms of post-conviction remedies that may be available, depending on the jurisdiction.

### 11. Double Jeopardy

After completing a trial in which a defendant wins an acquittal, he or she cannot be tried again for the same crime because it would place him or her in **double jeopardy**. The state is not allowed to make repeated attempts to con-

---

[20]    Marcotte, *Few Reversible Errors*, 76 A.B.A.J. 30 (Sept. 1990).

vict an individual for an alleged offense. In fact, whether acquitted or convicted, the defendant is not tried again unless he succeeds in setting aside his conviction upon motion or appeal. The rule against multiple convictions for the same crime has been reviewed many times by the courts, and surfaced again in a 1996 Supreme Court decision. Suppose a defendant is charged under two separate state statutes in the same trial, and convicted of both statutory violations. Two convictions result. However, close examination discloses that it is exactly the same criminal conduct that is proscribed by both statutes. Supreme Court decisions prohibit this. Where two separate criminal convictions are involved, even if they come under two distinct statutory provisions, double jeopardy bars double convictions unless each statutory provision requires proof of a fact that the other does not. Where the underlying conduct for which defendant is punished is exactly the same under both statutes, one of the convictions must be vacated.[21]

---

[21]    Rutledge v. United States, 116 S. Ct. 1241 (1996), applying Blockburger v. United States, 284 U.S. 299 (1932) (two statutes define different offenses only if "each provision requires proof of a fact which the other does not"). Double jeopardy is discussed in this text at § 9.5.

## § 1.5   Diagram of the Felony Case Process

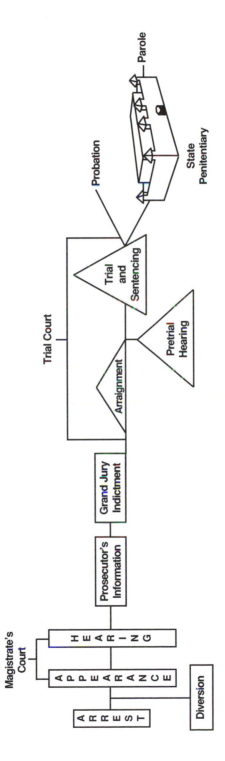

# Arrest, Appearance and Preliminary Hearing

## Chapter Outline

## Key Terms and Concepts

abandoned property doctrine
arraignment
arrest
arrest warrant
bail
citation
complainant
complaint
consent searches
contemporaneous searches
derivative evidence
exclusionary rule
exigent circumstances
felony
Fifth Amendment
Fourth Amendment
"fruit of the poisonous tree"
    doctrine
good faith exception
grand jury
hearsay evidence
hot pursuit
in the officer's presence
indictment
information

"knock-and-announce" rule
leave of court
*Miranda* warning
misdemeanor
"no-knock" statutes
plain view doctrine
preliminary hearing
pretrial discovery
probable cause
reasonable grounds
release on own recognizance
search warrant
searches incident to lawful arrest
Seventh Amendment
"silver platter" doctrine
Sixth Amendment
sneak-and-peek warrant
standing
stop-and-frisk
subpoena
summons
suppression hearing
"totality of circumstances" test
USA PATRIOT Act

## § 2.1   Arrest

The law of **arrest** comprises an exhaustive body of details that fills many volumes. The aim of this text is not to catalogue every case in this field, but rather to provide an overview of arrest procedure and to give the reader a very careful, yet concise and practical understanding of the law of arrest.

Arrests fall into two categories, those made with and those made without **arrest warrants**. While many arrests are made under the authority of warrants, the majority are warrantless arrests.

### 1. Arrest Without a Warrant

Arrests may be made for serious offenses without an arrest warrant when the law enforcement officer has **reasonable grounds** to believe that a felony has been committed and that the defendant committed it. Thus, even if the officer is wrong and no felony has actually been committed, the officer has nonetheless proceeded legally if his or her belief was reasonable. When the arrest is for a minor misdemeanor, a few jurisdictions provide latitude to the officer making a warrantless arrest similar to that applied in the case of felonies. Other jurisdictions, however, require the misdemeanor actually to have been committed. Reasonable belief alone in the latter class of cases is insufficient.

State statutes are where the authority for warrantless arrest is characteristically lodged under state law. In one such statute,[1] arrest without a warrant may be made under the following conditions: (1) where a public offense is committed or attempted in the officer's presence; (2) where a public offense has been committed in or out of the officer's presence and the officer has reasonable grounds for believing that the arrestee has committed it; (3) where the officer has reasonable grounds to believe that a felony has been committed and has reasonable grounds to believe that the person to be arrested has committed it;[2] (4) where the officer has received from the state department of public safety or other appropriate agency an official communication informing him that a warrant has been issued and is being held pending apprehension of the suspect on a designated charge;[3] and (5) where the officer believes domestic abuse has occurred and has reasonable grounds for believing the arrestee committed it.

Two terms run through state and federal arrest provisions that merit explication. These are "in the officer's presence" and "reasonable grounds." The term **"in the officer's presence"** in statutes like those noted in the preceding paragraph often has been given a liberal reading, and an offense may be committed a considerable distance from an officer and still be "within his or her presence" if she is able to see what happened. By some decisions, the offense takes place in the officer's presence if it is made known to the officer by another of his or her senses. For example, if an officer outside a residence hears the screams of a woman inside being beaten, the assault is committed in the officer's presence. The smell of illegal whiskey being brewed has been held to authorize police entry into a building to make a warrantless arrest of the violators.

The second term requiring exploration is "reasonable grounds." This term, employed in state and federal law, is virtually synonymous with the phrase "probable cause."[4] What are the boundaries of this critical concept? In the

---

[1]  Iowa Code § 804.7 (2004).

[2]  The reader should note two distinct levels of reasonable belief contained in this felony formulation: the officer may proceed on the reasonable belief that an offense has been committed, and on the reasonable belief that the defendant committed it.

[3]  *See* Whiteley v. Warden, 401 U.S. 560, 91 S. Ct. 1031, 28 L. Ed. 2d 306 (1971), which discusses arrest based on a state police bulletin.

[4]  Draper v. United States, 358 U.S. 307, 79 S. Ct. 329, 3 L. Ed. 2d 327 (1959), overruled on other grounds by United States v. Chadwick, 433 U.S. 1 (1977).

final analysis, **probable cause** depends upon the reasonableness of the officer's belief. The factual nuances of each case make impossible a four-cornered delineation of the concept that encompasses all situations. It is preferable to articulate the established probable cause standards, with factual application best left to case-by-case development. Basically, mere suspicion alone is insufficient to authorize a peace officer to make an arrest. It must be reasonable suspicion—that is, a suspicion based upon grounds sufficient to induce a reasonably prudent person to believe the arrestee guilty of the crime for which the arrest is made or to cause a person to believe there is likelihood of such guilt.[5] This reasonable belief may emanate from what the officer sees, taken in the totality of circumstances, or from credible information supplied by others. The representation by a credible person that a felony has been committed by a particular individual may well be sufficient to create a reasonable belief in his or her guilt. Two cases are illustrative:

> Information received by an officer from a friend that a tall, slim man driving a Ford coupe, with a tan top, bearing license number 988-216, had been "sticking up oil stations," gave the officer reasonable ground for believing that a person answering that description and driving that car was implicated in one or more robberies. And an officer who saw two persons running at night, one pursuing the other and calling "stop thief," had reasonable ground to believe the one in the lead had committed a felony.[6]

Other examples from modern cases dealing with reasonable grounds for arrest may be helpful.

a.  A Florida police officer on routine patrol in an unmarked squad car observed a Cadillac with New York license plates weave three or four times across the center line of a city street. When occupants of the Cadillac looked back and saw the squad car, the Cadillac went across the roadway and behind a grocery store, then headed south on another city street. The Florida police officer turned on his flashing lights and pulled the car over to the side of the road. When, upon request, the driver of the Cadillac could not produce a driver's license, he was placed under arrest for failure to have the license in his possession. A search of the arrestee's person disclosed marijuana cigarettes in a cigarette box, and the defendant was subsequently convicted of unlawful possession of marijuana. On the question of whether there was probable cause to stop the vehicle in the first instance, the Florida Supreme Court held that there was a reasonable suspicion that the driver was intoxicated, which justified stopping the vehicle. On review by the United States Supreme Court, it was held that probable cause to arrest existed when the police officer learned "that petitioner did not have his license in his possession."[7]

---

[5]  Perkins, *The Law of Arrest*, 25 IOWA L. REV. 201, 238 (1940). Information supplied by a reliable citizen is probably enough to found reasonable belief; if the information is from a criminal informant, the state must be prepared to establish the reliability of the informant on the basis of past experience.

[6]  Perkins, note 5 *supra* at 240.

[7]  State v. Gustafson, 258 So. 2d 1 (Fla. 1972), *aff'd*, Gustafson v. Florida, 414 U.S. 260, 94 S. Ct. 488, 38 L. Ed. 2d 456 (1973).

b. When a police officer lawfully stopped a motorist for speeding, the officer asked the driver to produce his vehicle registration. The driver opened the glove compartment, and there was a large roll of cash in the compartment. The driver consented to a full search of the car, which was occupied by the driver and two other men. When the officer discovered bags of cocaine hidden in the vehicle, all three men denied knowledge of the drugs and the money. The officer arrested all three men for possession of cocaine. The Supreme Court of the United States upheld the arrest of a defendant named Pringle, who was the front seat passenger. When this car passenger challenged the validity of his arrest for cocaine possession, the Court observed that "[t]o determine whether an officer had probable cause to arrest an individual, we examine the facts leading up to the arrest." The Court unanimously approved the arrest of Pringle. "Here we think it was reasonable for the officer to infer a common enterprise among the three men."[8]

c. *Draper v. United States*[9] is a landmark United States Supreme Court case involving arrest. An informer reported to a federal narcotics agent that Draper had gone from Denver, Colorado, to Chicago to get drugs, and that he would return to Denver by train with three ounces of heroin. The informer described the clothes Draper would be wearing and said he would be carrying "a tan zipper bag." The narcotics agent met the incoming Chicago train and saw a person matching the described physical appearance and carrying the bag described by the informer. Thus, the agent had verified every facet of the information given by the informer. There was probable cause to stop, arrest, and search the defendant, which turned up two envelopes containing heroin. The informer in the case had been a "special employee" of the Bureau of Narcotics for about six months; from time to time he gave information about narcotics for which he was paid small sums, and there was testimony that his information had always proved reliable. The continuing vitality of the *Draper* rule was affirmed in a 1983 Supreme Court decision when *Draper* was relied upon to find probable cause in another drug smuggling case.[10]

d. In New York, a warrantless arrest was made by federal narcotics agents upon information supplied by an informer previously unknown to police and of untested reliability. However, on his first visit with federal agents the informer gave very specific information, including the fact that a particular defendant was engaged in the distribution of heroin and that the defendant had a prior narcotics conviction. The informer supplied the defendant's address and the make and license number of his car. The address of the apartment of the defendant's girlfriend, claimed to be the base of the defendant's operations, was also given. Except for the ultimate fact of actual sale, all of these background facts, including prior nar-

---

[8]  Maryland v. Pringle, 124 S. Ct. 795 (2004).

[9]  358 U.S. 307, 79 S. Ct. 329, 3 L. Ed. 2d 327 (1959), overruled on other grounds by United States v. Chadwick, 433 U.S. 1 (1977).

[10] *See* Illinois v. Gates, 462 U.S. 213, 103 S. Ct. 2317 (1983), describing *Draper* as "the classic case on the value of corroborative efforts of police officials."

cotics convictions of the defendant, were verified by the authorities. Thus, when the defendant brought drugs to the girlfriend's apartment two weeks later, the informer's tip to this effect justified the agent's entry to arrest those trafficking in narcotics. Because the federal agents had corroborated so many of the facts supplied by the informer and then observed the defendant's car outside his girlfriend's apartment on the day of the reported narcotics transaction, the level of probable cause was held to be substantial.[11]

State statutory provisions also play an important role when an arrest without a warrant is made for a misdemeanor. In contrast to arrests for more serious offenses, some statutory formulations permit misdemeanor arrests only if a misdemeanor has actually been committed. Misdemeanors generally are not as dangerous as felonies, and pose less of a threat to public peace and order. For this reason, certain state codes require actual commission thereof to justify arrest in the absence of a warrant, and reasonable belief alone is insufficient. Arrests for felonies, however, may proceed on the reasonable belief of the officer that such offense was committed.

A variation of this rule which may be applied in misdemeanor cases, allows arrest without a warrant only for misdemeanors committed in the officer's presence. In *United States v. Watson*[12] the Supreme Court, citing the Model Code of Pre-arraignment Procedure, observed that there is a traditional approach to arrests without a warrant: "[A]n officer [may] take a person into custody if the officer has reasonable cause to believe that the person to be arrested has committed a felony, or has committed a misdemeanor or petty misdemeanor in his presence."

In addition to probable cause and/or commission of an offense in an officer's presence, there are other requirements for a valid arrest. Statutory provisions typically require the officer making the arrest to identify himself or herself as a police officer, and to inform the arrestee of the officer's intention and the cause of arrest. If arresting under the authority of a warrant, the officer must so indicate, and should exhibit the warrant if the arrestee so requests.[13]

---

[11]  United States v. Manning, 448 F.2d 992 (2d Cir.), cert. denied, 404 U.S. 995 (1971).

[12]  423 U.S. 411 (1976). The Model Code referred to in the main text provides for warrantless misdemeanor arrests where the officer reasonably believes the misdemeanant will not be apprehended unless immediately arrested, will cause injury to himself or others (or damage property), or where the misdemeanor is committed in the officer's presence.

[13]  E.g., FED R. CRIM. P. 4(c)(3)(A). When the person to be arrested is engaged in the commission of or attempt to commit an offense, such as when a robbery is in progress, a recitation of all the above requirements is often properly dispensed with.

## 2. Arrest Warrants

An arrest warrant is a written order issued by a judicial officer and directed generally to peace officers of the state, commanding the arrest of a designated person, such person to be brought before a court or magistrate to answer specified charges.[14]

Arrest warrants must be based upon probable cause. Thus, the magistrate or other judicial authority should examine the **complainant** under oath, and should carefully review any written application or affidavits supporting the request for an arrest warrant. "The arrest warrant procedure serves to insure that the deliberate, impartial judgment of a judicial officer will be interposed between the citizen and the police, to assess the weight and credibility of the information which the complaining officer adduces as probable cause."[15] Accordingly, unless an **exigent circumstances** or **hot pursuit** situation exists, police may be required to obtain an arrest warrant to enter a private residence, especially in cases that require forced entry to effect a "routine" felony arrest.[16]

What constitutes probable cause for an arrest warrant? In *Henry v. United States*[17] the Supreme Court observed that "[p]robable cause exists if the facts and circumstances known to the officer warrant a prudent man in believing that the offense has been committed." Probable cause necessary for an officer to make a warrantless arrest is substantially equivalent to the probable cause needed to secure an arrest warrant. In the arrest warrant situation, the judgment of the magistrate or other judicial officer is designed to insure that this probable cause requirement is satisfied.

When making an arrest at the subject's residence, the officer armed with an arrest warrant has legal advantages over the officer who does not seek a warrant.[18] The unfavorable consequences for law enforcement personnel who have probable cause but neglect to obtain an arrest warrant when entering a home to make an arrest were underlined in a 1990 Supreme Court opinion. There was an armed robbery of a Minnesota gasoline station. The station manager was fatally shot. When the person who was suspected of being the gunman was captured, leads were discovered suggesting that the driver of the getaway car was staying in the upper unit of a duplex. The female occupant of the duplex was called by police who had information that the driver was inside. The detective heard a male voice say "tell them I left." Without seeking permission and with weapons drawn, the police entered the duplex and found the suspect hiding in a closet. Subsequently, the defendant Olson made an inculpatory statement. Defendant's efforts to suppress this statement were

---

[14] VARON, 1 SEARCHES, SEIZURES AND IMMUNITIES 203 (2d ed. 1974).

[15] Wong Sun v. United States, 371 U.S. 471, 83 S. Ct. 407, 9 L. Ed. 2d 441 (1963).

[16] Payton v. New York, 445 U.S. 573 (1980).

[17] 361 U.S. 98, 80 S. Ct. 168, 4 L. Ed. 2d 134 (1959). *See* Beck v. Ohio, 379 U.S. 89, 85 S. Ct. 223, 13 L. Ed. 2d 142 (1964) which explores probable cause where the officer has knowledge that the accused has a criminal record.

[18] *See* Payton v. New York, 445 U.S. 573 (1980) (arrest warrant founded on probable cause implicitly carries with it the limited authority to enter a dwelling in which the suspect lives).

met with the argument that because he was not the owner of the duplex he lacked standing to attack the search. The Minnesota Supreme Court ruled that the defendant had a sufficient interest in the duplex to challenge the validity of his warrantless arrest there, that the arrest was illegal because of the absence of a warrant, and that the defendant's statement was tainted by the illegality. "Because the admission of the statement was not harmless beyond reasonable doubt, the [Minnesota] court reversed Olson's conviction and remanded for a new trial."

The United States Supreme Court affirmed the Minnesota court's ruling in favor of the defendant in the case of *Minnesota v. Olson*.[19] A suspect should not be arrested in his house without an arrest warrant, even though there is probable cause to arrest him.

However, not all evidence taken after a warrantless entry will necessarily be suppressed. If a confession is later taken at a station house, there is a possibility the evidence will be approved. Evidence seized at the dwelling may also be admissible, if police had probable cause to enter (albeit with no arrest warrant) and emergency circumstances were present.

Were exigent circumstances present in *Olson* sufficient to justify a warrantless entry into the home for the purpose of either arrest or search? There was no hot pursuit of a fleeing felon nor imminent destruction of evidence. Nor was there a need to enter without a warrant to prevent escape. Finally, risk of danger to the police or to other persons was not as great as might be thought because Olson "was not known to be the murderer but thought to be the driver of the getaway car." In the view of the Court, the police knew there was no suggestion of danger to other occupants of the duplex, and it was evident that the suspect was going nowhere. The United States Supreme Court decided not to disturb the state court's judgment that the acts did not add up to exigent circumstances.

*Olson* follows a line of cases protecting dwellings above other locations as it pertains to application of rights accorded the occupants thereof. Statements made by an accused when police enter a dwelling without a warrant, consent, or probable cause are excluded under a number of cases, including *Payton v. New York*.[20] The rule in *Payton* was designed to protect the physical integrity of the home. However, evidence gathered by police away from a dwelling is sometimes looked upon differently than that gathered in the home, even assuming an initial warrantless premises arrest. *Payton* does not always grant criminal suspects protection for statements made outside their premises where police had probable cause to make an arrest, as was held by the Supreme Court in *New York v. Harris*.[21]

In *New York v. Harris* the police found the body of a murder victim and had probable cause to believe that Harris had killed her. Three police officers went to Harris's apartment, displayed their guns to him, entered, and read him

---

[19]     495 U.S. 91, 110 S. Ct. 1684, 109 L. Ed. 2d 85 (1990).

[20]     445 U.S. 573 (1980). See KLOTTER, KANOVITZ AND KANOVITZ, CONSTITUTIONAL LAW § 3.12(D) (10th ed. 2005).

[21]     110 S. Ct. 1640, 109 L. Ed. 2d 13 (1990) (warrantless arrest in apartment, subsequent statement at station house).

his *Miranda* rights.[22] He reportedly admitted killing the victim. Later, he signed a written statement at the station house. In addition, a videotaped statement was taken. The focus of the Supreme Court's opinion was the written (second) statement because the trial judge suppressed Harris's first and third statements. It approved the evidence. The Court distinguished cases in which evidence was obtained when the police lacked probable cause. It also distinguished cases in which statements were taken in the home.

### 3. Citation and Summons

The use of a "citation" is a practice of relatively recent origin. A **citation** is a written notice to appear in court at a stated time and place to answer for an offense charged in the citation. The issuance of a citation is not an arrest; it is an alternative for an arrest. One author has appropriately characterized it as a "courtesy" substitute for an arrest. Essentially, what the citation does is to give an individual who might otherwise be arrested, an opportunity to appear in court voluntarily. Many states have enacted specific statutes authorizing the use of a citation for certain types of offenses. For example, the Kentucky Revised Statutes provide as follows:

> A peace officer may issue a citation instead of making an arrest for a misdemeanor committed in his presence, if there are reasonable grounds to believe that the person being cited will appear to answer the charge. The citation shall provide that the defendant shall appear within a designated time. (emphasis added) Ky. Rev. Stat. § 431.015

As a general rule the citation does not enlarge the officer's authority to make a warrantless arrest for a misdemeanor. An officer can issue a citation only if he or she had authority to make an arrest in the first instance.

Although the citation is used primarily in traffic cases, there is no good reason it cannot be employed for other types of offenses. Where the facts indicate a high probability that the offender will honor the citation and appear in court, the citation is a good procedure to follow. However, where the violator indicates that he or she will not respond to the citation, or where he or she is intoxicated, disorderly, or dangerous to the public, a physical arrest should be made.

The issuance of a **summons** by a judicial officer involves similar considerations, but the mechanics of issuance are distinct. While a citation may be given by a police officer, a summons is usually issued by a judge or other court official. Rule 4 of the Federal Rules of Criminal Procedure, provides that in federal practice the judge must issue a summons instead of an arrest warrant when requested by the prosecutor. The rule's guidelines for form of the warrant and the summons, as well as the manner of serving the summons, are reprinted below:

---

[22] *Miranda* rights, see § 2.1(4).

**Rule 4. Arrest Warrant or Summons on a Complaint**

**(b) Form.**

   **(1)** *Warrant.* A warrant must:

      (A) contain the defendant's name or, if it is unknown, a name or description by which the defendant can be identified with reasonable certainty;

      (B) describe the offense charged in the complaint;

      (C) command that the defendant be arrested and brought without unnecessary delay before a magistrate judge or, if none is reasonably available, before a state or local judicial officer; and

      (D) be signed by a judge.

   **(2) Summons.** A summons must be in the same form as a warrant except that it must require the defendant to appear before a magistrate judge at a stated time and place.

**(c) Execution or Service, and Return.**

   **(B)** A Summons is served on an individual defendant:

      ( i) by delivering a copy to the defendant personally; or

      (ii) by leaving a copy at the defendant's residence or usual place of abode with a person of suitable age and discretion residing at that location and by mailing a copy to the defendant's last known address.

   **(C)** A summons is served on an organization by delivering a copy to an officer, to a managing or general agent, or to another agent appointed or legally authorized to receive service of process. A copy must also be mailed to the organization's last known address within the district or to its principal place of business elsewhere in the United States.

## 4. Stops that Do Not Amount to Arrest

Stop-and-frisk cases have made headlines as well as substantial Supreme Court law. It is important to recognize that there are two distinct parts to the process, the stop as well as the frisk. These are discussed next.

### *The Nonarrest: Stopping Persons on the Street*

One authority makes the point that four requisites are involved in an arrest: (1) a purpose to take the person into custody, (2) under authority, (3) resulting in an actual or constructive seizure or detention of the person, (4) so understood by the arrestee.[23] An arrest is made by the actual restraint of the person or by submission to the custody of the officer. Can there be a temporary detention of a person for questioning without the procedure constituting an arrest? An officer in the performance of his or her duties has a right to contact people

---

23    Perkins, note 5 *supra* at 208.

who may be witnesses or suspects, and to ask them questions. The officer may ask them questions on the street, and may call upon them at their home for such purposes. Merely asking a person to voluntarily answer questions without detention of the person normally does not constitute an arrest.

Merging with the law of arrest in this area are decisions of the United States Supreme Court concerning interrogation of suspects. Chief among these is *Miranda v. Arizona*,[24] which requires that specific constitutional warnings be given a suspect prior to any interrogation "after a person has been taken into custody or otherwise deprived of his freedom of action in any significant way." Prior to questioning, the suspect must be warned that he or she has the right to remain silent, that anything the person says can and will be used against him or her in a court of law, that the suspect has the right to the presence of an attorney, and that if he or she cannot afford an attorney one will be appointed for him or her if so desired.

Can the police avoid giving constitutional warnings to a person they have taken into custody simply by refraining from placing him or her under formal arrest? Can *Miranda* be limited only to cases in which people who are placed under police authority are also told: "You are under arrest"? In determining whether an individual is "in custody" and thus is entitled to full **Miranda warnings** before police question him, the following inquiry controls: Was there a formal arrest, or at least a restraint of the suspect's freedom of movement to that degree normally associated with a formal arrest? If so, *Miranda* applies,[25] and this is true whether or not police say to the confined suspect: "We are placing you under arrest."

Does stopping a person for brief questioning on the street constitute an arrest or in-custody interrogation within the meaning of the *Miranda* rule? Under one view, reasonably brief questioning on the street does not. While debate concerning the full implications of street stops continues, it is noteworthy that the Court stated in *Miranda* that confessions remain a proper element in law enforcement, and further asserted that police may conduct on-the-scene questioning of citizens.

The point is summarized by one commentator: "[T]he four cases consolidated in the *Miranda* decision all involved a process of interrogation in the incommunicado atmosphere of the police station. Thus, the decision should not be read as prohibiting threshold interrogations outside the confines of the police station, because the possibility of potential coercion is greatly reduced."[26]

Where brief investigative questioning occurs, does the citizen have to cooperate? Must he or she answer the officer's questions? If he or she refuses, does such lack of cooperation constitute a separate crime? The Supreme Court has dealt with these issues in a recent decision.[27] The case involved a police

---

[24]  384 U.S. 436, 86 S. Ct. 1602, 16 L. Ed. 2d 694 (1966).
[25]  Stansbury v. California, 114 S. Ct. 1526 (1994).
[26]  *Comment*, 52 IOWA L. REV. 752, 757 (1967). For further details on *Miranda*, see § 6.3(2)(b) of this text.
[27]  Hiibel v. Sixth Judicial Dist. Court of Nev., 124 S. Ct. 2451 (2004).

request to a man in suspicious circumstances that he identify himself. "After continued refusals to comply with the officer's request for identification, the man began to taunt the officer by placing his hands behind his back and telling the officer to arrest him and take him to jail. This routine kept up for several minutes: the officer asked for identification 11 times and was refused each time. After warning the man that he would be arrested if he continued to refuse to comply, the officer placed him under arrest."

This dispute arose in Nevada, which has a statute allowing the arrest of those who refuse to identify themselves in the face of a law enforcement request. More than 20 states have such a law. The defendant in the Nevada case was convicted of a misdemeanor, and the United States Supreme Court affirmed the conviction. The Court remarked upon the validity of "stop and identify" statutes: "Although it is well established that an officer may ask a suspect to identify himself in the course of a *Terry* stop [*Terry* is explained more fully in the next text section], it has been an open question whether the suspect can be arrested and prosecuted for refusal to answer. . . . A state law requiring a suspect to disclose his name in the course of a valid *Terry* stop is consistent with Fourth Amendment prohibitions against unreasonable searches and seizures."

Accordingly, in a number of states, citizens who refuse to give their names to police can be arrested, even if they have done nothing else wrong. What about the slight majority of jurisdictions where no such statutes exist? Although brief questioning by police constitutes reasonable police conduct in such places, refusal of the person to identify himself is not a crime.

## The Nonsearch: Frisking the Suspect

A distinction exists between temporary detention for questioning and a frisk of the person "on the street." The laws of numerous states authorize the police to stop and question persons in suspicious circumstances. This detention is not viewed as an arrest. However, if the officer reasonably believes that he or she is in danger of life or limb, he or she may frisk the person for weapons as an appropriate safety measure. In some jurisdictions there is specific statutory authority for such procedure; in others, courts have recognized the power to **stop and frisk** for dangerous weapons, often confining the authority to "patting down" the garments of the subject.

In 1968 the Supreme Court granted certain leeway to police officers to approach pedestrians in suspicious situations and ask them questions as to identity and destination. When the pedestrian's response or other circumstances give the officer reason to believe that the person is armed, the officer may do an outer garment "pat down" or frisk. Items seized as a result may be introduced into evidence, whether weapons or items of evidence found in the reasonable pursuit of a weapon.[28] As stated in *Terry v. Ohio*:[29]

> Our evaluation of the proper balance that has to be struck in this type of case leads us to conclude that there must be a narrowly drawn authority to permit a reasonable search for weapons for the protection of the police officer, where he has reason to believe that he is dealing with an armed and dangerous individual, regardless of whether he has probable cause to arrest the individual for a crime. The officer need not be absolutely certain that the individual is armed; the issue is whether a reasonably prudent man in the circumstances would be warranted in the belief that his safety or that of others was in danger. . . .

> We merely hold today that where a police officer observes unusual conduct which leads him reasonably to conclude in light of his experience that criminal activity may be afoot and that the persons with whom he is dealing may be armed and presently dangerous, where in the course of investigating this behavior he identifies himself as a policeman and makes reasonable inquiries, and where nothing in the initial stages of the encounter serves to dispel his reasonable fear for his own or others' safety, he is entitled for the protection of himself and others in the area to conduct a carefully limited search of the outer clothing of such persons in an attempt to discover weapons which might be used to assault him.[30]

Later Supreme Court opinions reaffirm the point that *Terry* frisks are justified only for protective reasons. They are to check for weapons, and an intrusive search for evidence is not permitted under *Terry*. In a 1993 case, an officer first conducted a proper stop and pat-down. He did not find a weapon, nor did the officer feel an object that he thought was a weapon. Rather, he squeezed an object that he believed to be crack cocaine. The officer then pulled the lump of crack from the defendant's pocket. Had there been an arrest of the defendant based upon probable cause followed by a full search, such arrest and subsequent search pursuant to a full-custody arrest might give the officer authorization for seizure of the crack; a *Terry* frisk does not. The officer's seizure was deemed to be improper: "[T]he officer's continued exploration of respondent's pocket . . . amounted to the sort of evidentiary search that *Terry* expressly refused to authorize, and that we have condemned in subsequent cases." While an officer may seize nonthreatening contraband detected during a protective pat-down search for weapons, the Fourth Amendment does not permit charges to be maintained when they are based on the seizure of a lump of cocaine encountered in a pocket that the officer already

---

[28]    There is judicial language to the effect that only those items which appeared to the officer's senses of sight and touch to be weapons may be seized, i.e., a hard object that might be a gun or knife. Once a weapon is found and the suspect arrested, a more complete search may be made.

[29]    392 U.S. 1, 88 S. Ct. 1868, 20 L. Ed. 2d 889 (1968).

[30]    392 U.S. at 27, 30.

knew contained no weapon.[31] Seizure of incriminating items or contraband when such items might easily be confused for a weapon remains a viable possibility, however.

### Summary

In consequence of *Terry* and companion stop-and-frisk cases, numerous legislative and judicial proposals have been drafted to provide guidelines for police "stop-and-frisk" practices as well as related procedures. The Council of Judges, in their Model Rules of Court on Police Action from Arrest to Arraignment, Rule 2, suggested one possible approach to stopping and questioning people, and that proposal is presented here:

#### Stopping Persons

An arrest is the taking of a person into custody in order that he may be held to answer for committing a crime. For an arrest to be lawful, the officer must have a warrant of arrest or reasonable grounds to believe that the person arrested had committed or was committing a crime.

A police officer may stop a person and detain him briefly to request him to identify himself and explain his presence and may investigate his possible criminal behavior if a person of reasonable caution would be warranted in the belief that the action taken was appropriate under the circumstances even though he may not have grounds for an arrest. However, after this brief detention the officer must release the person if he does not arrest him.

## 5. Private Arrests

Thus far the discussion has concentrated on arrests by police. Arrests may also be made by private individuals. These are generally restricted to public offenses committed or attempted in the presence of the arresting person. However, some state codes authorize citizen arrests for felonies in cases in which a felony has actually been committed and the citizen has reasonable grounds to believe that the arrestee has committed it. It is apparent that under state laws and statutes, arrests by a private person are much more limited than official arrests. A reasonable belief by the person that an offense has been committed is usually insufficient; actual commission of an offense, misdemeanor or felony, appears essential under state formulations. In addition, many states restrict to felony situations alone the citizen's right to arrest a person on the reasonable belief that he or she perpetrated the offense.

---

[31]　Minnesota v. Dickerson, 113 S. Ct. 2130 (1993). *Terry* stops and flight, *see* Illinois v. Wardlow, 528 U.S. 119 (2000) (sudden flight from police in high-crime area creates reasonable suspicion justifying *Terry* stop). Informer's tips, *see* Florida v. J.L., 529 U.S. 266 (2000) (anonymous tip that a person was carrying a gun does not justify *Terry* stop).

Sometimes the citizen who accomplishes the arrest makes a search,[32] and when there is such a search, different rules frequently control the private search in contrast to searches by police. The Fourth Amendment prohibitions governing search and seizure are directed against the government. Accordingly, there is authority that the fruits of private searches may be admissible in evidence in which there is no official collusion, even though the same search would be deemed unreasonable had it been conducted by a law enforcement officer.[33]

## § 2.2  Search

As with the prior coverage of the law of arrest, the intent of this text is to give the reader a useful overview of practical search problems, not to explore exhaustively every case in the field. As a fundamental principle of freedom, the **Fourth Amendment** to the United States Constitution provides:

> The right of the people to be secure in their persons, houses, papers, and effects, against unreasonable searches and seizures, shall not be violated, and no Warrants shall issue, but upon probable cause, supported by Oath or affirmation, and particularly describing the place to be searched, and the persons or things to be seized.

The **exclusionary rule** enforces this constitutional provision by excluding from the trial of a case any evidence that has been secured by the government through means that violate the Fourth Amendment. Through the early and mid-1900s the exclusionary rule barred illegally seized evidence from federal trials. Then, in 1961, the case of *Mapp v. Ohio*[34] applied the exclusionary rule to state courts, and as a result federal supervision of state unreasonable search-and-seizure cases increased markedly. The evolution of related rules is traced in this passage:

1.  EXCLUSIONARY RULE. The exclusionary rule operates as a bar to the use of evidence obtained as a result of an illegal arrest, search, or seizure. *Weeks v. United States*, 232 U.S. 383, 58 L. Ed. 652, 34 S. Ct. 341 (1914). It was this important principle that the *Mapp* case made binding on state as well as federal courts.

2.  DERIVATIVE USE OF ILLEGALLY SEIZED EVIDENCE. The *Weeks* case dealt with evidence obtained during illegal search and seizure, but did not speak directly to the problem of leads and other real evidence located by virtue of the initial tainted "find." Whether **derivative evidence**, the

---

[32]  *See* United States v. Viale, 312 F.2d 595 (2d Cir. 1963) ("The rationale that justifies searches incident to lawful arrests . . . would seem to apply with equal force whether the arrest is made by an officer or a private citizen." This case explains New York law on private arrest).

[33]  *See* Burdeau v. McDowell, 256 U.S. 465 (1921).

[34]  367 U.S. 643 (1961). On the pros and cons of the exclusionary rule see § 6.3(3). Damage suits in lieu of the exclusionary rule are discussed in § 10.18.

**"fruit of the poisonous tree,"** is also barred was determined *in Silverthorne Lumber Co. v. United States*, 251 U.S. 385 (1920) and *Wong Sun v. United States*, 371 U.S. 471 (1963). These decisions established that where the primary illegality of the evidence is established, derivative evidence is likewise inadmissible. Although the "fruit of the poisonous tree" doctrine applies with full force when a physical object or document is illegally seized, it has no application to leads derived from *Miranda*-tainted confessions. *United States v. Patane*, 124 S. Ct. 2620 (2004).

3. SILVER PLATTER. After the exclusionary rule was applied in federal courts, and prior to the *Mapp* case, state officers who conducted illegal searches for state crimes and discovered evidence of federal crimes regularly turned such evidence over to federal authorities. Although federal officers were barred by the exclusionary principle of *Weeks v. United States* from convicting the accused on evidence they themselves had illegally seized, it was assumed that federal courts could use the evidence turned over by state officers on a "silver platter." *Elkins v. United States*, 364 U.S. 206, 4 L. Ed. 2d 1669, 80 S. Ct. 1437 (1960) ended this practice, the Court rejecting the **"silver platter" doctrine** under its supervisory power over the administration of justice in the federal courts.

4. PLAIN VIEW. The exclusionary rule has an important impact on police searches. To determine whether the rule applies in a particular case, an initial problem involves situations that do not constitute a search. The **plain view doctrine** provides an important example. Under it, the mere observation by an officer of things open to view (as looking through a car window from a public street) is not a police search. In 1983, the United States Supreme Court held that using scent-detecting dogs did not constitute a search. An officer's observations led him to reasonably conclude that a traveler's luggage contained narcotics, and the Court observed: "[E]xposure of respondent's luggage, which was located in a public place, to a trained canine did not constitute a 'search' within the meaning of the Fourth Amendment."[35] In 1989, the Supreme Court extended this principle to surveillance of yards and greenhouses by helicopters looking for marijuana. Acting on a tip, a Florida sheriff's deputy circled over property in a helicopter. The officer's observation, with his naked eye, of the interior of a partially covered greenhouse in the residential backyard from the vantage point of a helicopter circling 400 feet above did not constitute a "search" for which a warrant was required. "[T]here was no violation of the Fourth Amendment."[36] The Court, per Justice White, stated: "We agree with the State's submission that our decision in *California v. Ciraolo*, 476 U.S. 207, 106 S. Ct. 1809, 90 L.

---

[35] Texas v. Brown, 103 S. Ct. 1535 (1983). *See* Arizona v. Hicks, 480 U.S. 321 (1987); South Dakota v. Opperman, 428 U.S. 364 (1976); Coolidge v. New Hampshire, 403 U.S. 443, 91 S. Ct. 2022, 29 L. Ed. 2d 564 (1971). It is not a search, within the meaning of the Fourth Amendment, to observe things in open view in a public place, and this principle has application to things seen by officers lawfully present on private premises.

[36] Florida v. Riley, 109 S. Ct. 693 (1989). Plain view rules are reviewed in Horton v. California, 110 S. Ct. 2301 (1990); United States v. Gori, 230 F.3d 44 (2d Cir. 2000).

Ed. 2d 210 (1986), controls this case. There, acting on a tip, the police inspected the backyard of a particular house while flying in a fixed-wing aircraft at 1,000 feet. With the naked eye the officers saw what they concluded was marijuana growing in the yard. A search warrant was obtained on the strength of this airborne inspection, and marijuana plants were found.

5. ABANDONED PROPERTY. The **abandoned property doctrine** applies to seizure of evidence that is outside Fourth Amendment protection. When seizing a gun, knife, or a package of drugs, a search and seizure normally implies the dispossession of a physical object from its place of possession or custody. When an item is discarded in a trash can or dumpster, no such personal dispossession is involved. Thus, an officer is empowered to pick up property dropped on the street by a suspect or otherwise abandoned, examine it, and retain it as evidence if it appears to be useful.[37] Such situations do not require application of the exclusionary rule.

In true search situations, a general requirement of the law commands that searches and seizures must be made with proper and valid search warrants. For the officer on the street, two major exceptions to the search warrant principle exist: (1) searches incident to lawful arrest, and (2) searches made with consent.

## 1. Searches Incident to Arrest

Search of the defendant immediately following an arrest may be made whether the arrest took place with or without a warrant. The reader's attention is specifically called to the fact that we are now dealing with the authority to make a warrantless search, as opposed to the previously treated topic of warrantless arrest. Assuming a valid arrest (with or without an arrest warrant), the right to make an immediate search arises. Such a search of the arrestee, including search of the arrestee's near vicinity, is justified: (1) by the need for self-protection of the officer (the seizure of weapons that may be close by and used by the suspect to effect his escape is thus proper); and (2) by the general right to seize items connected with the crime.[38] When such items are seized incident to an arrest, the exclusionary rule will operate to bar their use in evidence against a defendant unless the arrest was lawful.[39]

---

[37] Abel v. United States, 362 U.S. 217, 80 S. Ct. 683, 4 L. Ed. 2d 668 (1960). Evidence of narcotics use was uncovered by searching trash and garbage, search approved in California v. Greenwood, 486 U.S. 35 (1988).

[38] Washington v. Chrisman, 455 U.S. 1 (1982); New York v. Belton, 453 U.S. 454 (1981). Three distinct justifications for the search are: (1) protection of the officer, (2) prevention of escape, and (3) preservation of evidence.

[39] Agnello v. United States, 269 U.S. 20, 46 S. Ct. 4, 70 L. Ed. 145 (1925).

*Scope of Search*

How broadly may a search extend and still be considered reasonable? If the suspect is arrested in his or her car, may the trunk be searched? If the suspect is arrested in his or her house, may the officers search an unconnected garage located in the backyard without a warrant?

First, the arrested person may be searched as well as items in his or her possession. This includes things in the pockets of the accused,[40] a purse that is clutched by the person who is arrested, or the contents of a suitcase carried by the suspect. Beyond the suspect's person, a permissible search extends to things under control of the suspect.[41] Court decisions have established the guideline that a valid search may be made after arrest if made within the "immediate vicinity" of where the arrest took place.[42]

The leading Supreme Court decision interpreting the term "immediate vicinity" is *Chimel v. California*.[43] It narrows significantly the perimeter of a lawful search made incident to an arrest. Under the older case of *Harris v. United States*,[44] a premises search could spread through all of the rooms on the same level of the house or apartment where the arrest of the suspect was made. Under the *Chimel* case, a premises search made incident to arrest and without a search warrant must be restricted to the room of the house in which the arrest is made, in the absence of a most pressing circumstance that might justify a more extended search. The key language that provides the applicable guideline is reflected in *Chimel* as follows:

> When an arrest is made, it is reasonable for the arresting officer to search the person arrested in order to remove any weapons that the latter might seek to use in order to resist arrest or effect his escape. Otherwise, the officer's safety might well be endangered, and the arrest itself frustrated. In addition, it is entirely reasonable for the arresting officer to search for and seize any evidence on the arrestee's person in order to prevent its concealment or destruction. And the area into which an arrestee might reach in order to grab a weapon or evidentiary items must, of course, be governed by a like rule.
>
> A gun on a table or in a drawer in front of one who is arrested can be as dangerous to the arresting officer as one concealed in the clothing of the person arrested. There is ample justification, therefore, for a search of the arrestee's person and the area "within his immediate control"—construing that phrase to mean the area from within which he might gain possession of a weapon or destructible evidence.

---

[40]  Michigan v. Summers, 101 S. Ct. 2587 (1981); Gustafson v. Florida, 414 U.S. 260 (1973).
[41]  Carroll v. United States, 267 U.S. 132, 45 S. Ct. 280, 69 L. Ed. 543 (1925).
[42]  Florida v. Royer, 460 U.S. 491, 103 S. Ct. 1319 (1983); Vale v. Louisiana, 399 U.S. 30 (1970); Preston v. United States, 376 U.S. 364, 84 S. Ct. 881, 11 L. Ed. 2d 777 (1964).
[43]  395 U.S. 752, 89 S. Ct. 2034, 23 L. Ed. 2d 685 (1969).
[44]  331 U.S. 145, 67 S. Ct. 1098, 91 L. Ed. 1399 (1947).

There is no comparable justification, however, for routinely searching rooms other than that in which an arrest occurs—or, for that matter, for searching through all the desk drawers or other closed or concealed areas in that room itself. Such searches, in the absence of well-recognized exceptions, may be made only under the authority of a search warrant. The "adherence to judicial processes" mandated by the Fourth Amendment requires no less.[45]

Search of a home beyond that counseled in *Chimel* is appropriate where a neutral and detached magistrate has issued a search warrant for the entire home, upon probable cause. There is also another justification for a wider search in arrest situations than *Chimel* generally permits. This is in the instance of multiple offenders, cases in which a key suspect is first arrested in the house and other perpetrators are reasonably suspected to be hiding in the premises. In *Maryland v. Buie*,[46] the Supreme Court held that "[t]he Fourth Amendment permits a properly limited protective sweep in conjunction with an in-home arrest when the searching officer possesses a reasonable belief based on specific and articulable facts that the area to be swept harbors an individual posing a danger to those on the arrest scene." Justice White observed that a protective sweep "is narrowly confined to a cursory visual inspection of those places in which a person might be hiding." In this case an arrest warrant was properly issued on Buie based on the belief that he participated in a robbery along with another man. One robber had worn a red running suit. When the warrant was executed at Buie's house, a police officer ordered anyone in the basement to come upstairs. Buie did so. He was placed under arrest. Another officer then went down to the basement to see if anyone else was there. In the basement he found a red running suit in plain view. This was properly seized evidence, in the view of the Court, because the officer's presence in the basement was an appropriate adjunct of Buie's arrest.

Felony arrests inside the suspect's home or apartment may have to be effected by arrest warrants in order to validate attendant searches. Absent exigent circumstances, *Payton v. New York*[47] indicates that "routine" felony arrests inside private residences (as opposed to streets or public places) are controlled by the arrest warrant requirement. This is especially the case where the premises are entered by force. Six officers went to Payton's apartment in the Bronx, intending to arrest him. They had not obtained a warrant. Crowbars were used to break open the door. No one was there, but a 30-caliber shell casing was observed, seized, and admitted into evidence at Payton's murder trial. Because no arrest warrant was obtained, Payton's murder conviction was reversed.

Applying scope-of-search principles to vehicle searches, if a person is arrested in or very near his or her automobile, many courts have held that the open cavity of the vehicle may be searched,[48] and this probably includes the

---

[45]   395 U.S. at 762-763, 89 S. Ct. at 2040, 23 L. Ed. 2d at 694. See Vale v. Louisiana, 399 U.S. 30 (1970).
[46]   494 U.S. 325, 110 S. Ct. 1093 (1990).
[47]   445 U.S. 573 (1980). Exigent circumstances, *see* State v. Gregory, 331 N.W.2d 140 (Iowa 1983).
[48]   *See* New York v. Belton, 453 U.S. 454 (1981).

glove compartment. Such areas are deemed to be under the control of the occupant of the car and may contain weapons or other instrumentalities that might be used to make an escape. The "grabbing distance" rule of *Chimel* has been broadly interpreted in some cases. In one, a search was upheld even though the defendant was under arrest by several officers, and the search included checking under a blanket on the backseat of the defendant's car. Although the area searched was spatially removed from the defendant, the search was deemed incident to arrest because the defendant was "within leaping range of the guns in the back seat."[49]

The United States Supreme Court confirmed this approach in 2004. An officer arrested a motorist just after the motorist exited his vehicle. At the scene the officer searched the vehicle and found a nine-millimeter handgun under the driver's seat. Among other charges, the defendant was indicted for possession of a firearm by a convicted felon. Was the search of the vehicle that revealed the firearm lawful? Yes, said the Supreme Court. As long as the arrestee was a recent occupant of the vehicle, police could search it incident to arrest. An arrestee is no less likely to lunge for a weapon or destroy evidence if he is outside the vehicle, as opposed to being in it.[50]

Even under such liberal extensions of the scope-of-search rules, however, locked car trunks are probably outside the perimeter of searches incident to arrest, absent special circumstances. Especially when the arrest is for a traffic violation, it is doubtful that authority to search extends to the trunk. Two safer courses for the officer wishing to make such a search arise at this point: (1) obtain a warrant to make the search, or (2) make a consent search by asking the driver, "Could we take a look in the trunk?" If the latter approach fails, the warrant remains a viable possibility.[51]

Another limitation on the officer's right to search an automobile turns on the nature of the traffic charge. It has been established that a person arrested in his or her car may have the open portion of the automobile searched, incident to arrest. What if the officer does not make a custody arrest, but merely issues a traffic citation? The Supreme Court ruled against search in these circumstances. The Court decided that the search of the car was prohibited in this situation.[52] A police officer had stopped a motorist for moving at 18 mph over the speed limit. The officer gave him a speeding ticket, then searched the car. Under the driver's seat, the officer found a bag of marijuana. The United States Supreme Court ruled against the search on the ground that the threat to officer safety from issuing a traffic citation is a good deal less than in the case of an arrest. The Court observed that prior Supreme Court cases had given police

[49] Application of Kiser, 419 F.2d 1134 (8th Cir. 1969).
[50] Thornton v. United States, 124 S. Ct. 2127 (2004).
[51] Lawful stop of vehicle, limited search permitted, *see* Michigan v. Long, 103 S. Ct. 3469 (1983) (stop and frisk principles applied to car, "limited to those areas in which a weapon may be placed or hidden"); Texas v. Brown, 103 S. Ct. 1535 (1983) (car stopped at driver's license checkpoint, contraband in plain view); New York v. Belton, 453 U.S. 454 (1981) (arrest for speeding; passenger compartment of car searched, cocaine found in jacket pocket on back seat).
[52] Knowles v. Iowa, 119 S. Ct. 484 (1998).

authority to protect themselves from danger in similar situations by ordering drivers and passengers out of a car and conducting a "pat-down" of anyone they reasonably suspect may be armed. The considerably greater intrusion that occurs when the officer goes further and conducts an intensive search of the driver as well as the passenger compartment of the car is unjustified. The traffic stop in the Supreme Court case was for speeding. Further evidence of excessive speed was not going to be found in the passenger compartment of the car.

## Vehicles

Searching portions of a vehicle incident to the arrest of the driver has been reviewed, but what about stops and searches of vehicles generally? One other rationale sometimes serves to authorize inspection of a car, including its trunk. When a vehicle is used to transport illegal liquor, drugs, guns, or other contraband, special rules apply. The general rule requiring a search warrant gives way to an exception when vehicles are used for the transportation of contraband goods. The doctrine evolved in the 1920s beginning with the case of *Carroll v. United States*,[53] and has been refined in subsequent decisions. In *United States v. Ross*,[54] police had information from an informant that Ross had just made a narcotics sale and had drugs in the trunk of his car. Police stopped the vehicle and, after opening the trunk, spotted a closed paper bag. It was found to contain heroin. The search was upheld under the exception to the warrant requirement for certain automobile searches (when the automobile is reasonably believed to contain contraband), based on the "mobility" rationale. The inherent mobility of the automobile often creates situations in which securing a warrant is impractical, and the officer's best alternative is an immediate search.

Warrantless searches of vehicles upon probable cause due to the "readily mobile" nature of an automobile was confirmed again in a 1996 decision,[55] following a case in which drugs were found in a vehicle's trunk. The Court reviewed the rationales for allowing the search of a vehicle when probable cause exists to believe it contains contraband:

> Our first cases establishing the automobile exception to the Fourth Amendment's warrant requirement were based on the automobile's "ready mobility," an exigency sufficient to excuse failure to obtain a search warrant once probable cause to conduct the search is clear. *California v. Carney*, 471 U.S. 386, 390-391, 105 S. Ct. 2066, 2068-2069, 85 L. Ed. 2d 406 (1985) (tracing the history of the exception); *Carroll v. United States*, 267 U.S. 132, 45 S. Ct. 280, 69 L. Ed. 543 (1925).

---

[53] 267 U.S. 132, 45 S. Ct. 280, 69 L. Ed. 543 (1925).
[54] 456 U.S. 798 (1982). The *Ross* case is studied in *Note*, 27 ST. L. U.L.J. 745 (1983).
[55] Pennsylvania v. Labron, 116 S. Ct. 2485 (1996).

More recent cases provide a further justification: the individual's reduced expectation of privacy in an automobile, owing to its pervasive regulation. *Carney*, supra at 391-392, 105 S. Ct., at 2069-2070. If a car is readily mobile and probable cause exists to believe it contains contraband, the Fourth Amendment thus permits police to search the vehicle without more.

How pervasively may the officers search pursuant to the *Carroll* doctrine? What about boxes, bags, or containers inside the car? Search of containers located within automobiles was the subject of *California v. Acevedo*.[56] In deciding the case, the Court provided a description of the law allowing search of mobile vehicles on probable cause:

> In *United States v. Ross*, 456 U.S. 798, 102 S. Ct. 2157, 72 L. Ed. 2d 572, decided in 1982, we held that a warrantless search of an automobile under the *Carroll* doctrine could include a search of a container or package found inside the car when such a search was supported by probable cause. The warrantless search of Ross' car occurred after an informant told the police that he had seen Ross complete a drug transaction using drugs stored in the trunk of his car. The police stopped the car, searched it, and discovered in the trunk a brown paper bag containing drugs. We decided that the search of Ross' car was not unreasonable under the Fourth Amendment: "The scope of a warrantless search based on probable cause is no narrower—and no broader—than the scope of a search authorized by a warrant supported by probable cause." Id., at 823, 102 S. Ct. at 2172. Thus, "[i]f probable cause justifies the search of a lawfully stopped vehicle, it justifies the search of every part of the vehicle and its contents that may conceal the object of the search." Id., at 825, 102 S. Ct. at 2173. In *Ross*, therefore, we clarified the scope of the *Carroll* doctrine as properly including a "probing search" of compartments and containers within the automobile so long as the search is supported by probable cause. Id. at 800, S. Ct. at 2160.

The Court adopted one rule to govern both automobile searches and containers found within the car, and eliminated the warrant requirement when probable cause to search exists and the mobility of the vehicle dictates an immediate search.

When an officer makes a simple traffic stop, issues arise as to whether he can order the occupants out of the car. A police officer may, as a matter of course, order the driver of a lawfully stopped car to exit his vehicle. If the cause of the stop is a traffic violation such as running a red light or speeding, can a passenger be directed to leave the car as well? Extension to passengers of a police officer's right to order drivers to exit stopped vehicles was decided in *Maryland v. Wilson*.[57] The car was traveling at 64 miles per hour in a 55 mile-per-hour zone. Wilson, a passenger, was ordered out of the car. At that point there was no reasonable suspicion that the passenger was engaged in criminal activity. When Wilson exited the car, cocaine fell to the ground. The

[56] 500 U.S. 565, 111 S. Ct. 1982 (1991).
[57] 117 S. Ct. 882 (1997).

Supreme Court held that the passenger could be ordered out of the car in these circumstances. "[T]he same weighty interest in officer safety is present regardless of whether the occupant of the stopped car is a driver or passenger." Passengers might be a potential source of danger to the officer. Therefore "an officer making a traffic stop may order passengers to get out of the car pending completion of the stop."

What if an arrest results from a mistaken police report? After a traffic stop a defendant was arrested and his car searched because the computer indicated there was an arrest warrant out against him. The search revealed drugs; however, it turned out that the computer report of an arrest warrant was incorrect. It was held that the clerical error did not save the defendant in *Arizona v. Evans*.[58]

Finally, in traffic violation situations, is it legitimate for officers making a routine traffic stop to walk a drug-sniffing dog around the suspect's car? If the dog alerts, is it proper for officers to search, and to arrest the driver or passengers for drugs found in the vehicle? Some state decisions have cast doubt on this procedure, but the United States Supreme Court approved it, as long as the motorist is not unduly delayed in order to bring the dog into the picture.[59]

### Roadblocks and Checkpoints

Supreme Court application of stop-and-search principles relating to automobiles occurred in *Michigan Dept. of State Police v. Sitz*.[60] At issue was the validity of a highway sobriety checkpoint, which was designed to detect and curb drunk driving. In the view of the Court, sobriety checkpoints in which the police stop every vehicle do not violate the Fourth and Fourteenth Amendment protections against unreasonable searches and seizures and are therefore constitutional. "We reached a similar conclusion as to the intrusion on motorists subjected to a brief stop at a highway checkpoint for detecting illegal aliens."

However, sobriety and border patrol checkpoints may be different from the practice of stopping vehicles to look for evidence of drug crimes committed by occupants of those vehicles. In one case, because police had set up such a checkpoint primarily for general crime control purposes, the Supreme Court ruled that the United States Constitution's Fourth Amendment forbids such auto stops. As a result, stops to simply investigate cars for undefined evidence of criminal activity are barred.

What about stops for information-gathering that result in the officer seeing an incriminating item in a car? If the purpose of the stop was to obtain information on a specific crime, it is permitted. The distinction between this and the general vehicle stops described in the prior paragraph is that a more individualized police purpose is at hand. In a 2004 decision, police in Illinois set up a highway checkpoint to gather information from motorists about a hit-and-run accident a week earlier in the same location. Special law enforcement

---

[58]   115 S. Ct. 1185 (1995).
[59]   Illinois v. Caballes, 125 S. Ct. 834 (2005).
[60]   110 S. Ct. 2481 (1990).

concerns will sometimes justify highway stops without individualized suspicion against a car's driver or passenger, observed the Court. Driver's license or sobriety and border patrol checkpoints illustrate the principle. Exactly so here. Information-seeking highway stops in which police act in a reasonable and nondiscriminatory manner are constitutional. The Court observes that "[t]he Fourth Amendment does not treat a motorist's car as his castle."[61]

### Border Searches

Border searches of automobiles fall into a special category. Searches not based upon probable cause or reasonable suspicion are constitutional even when agents conduct an extensive car search. In one case border agents—without reasonable suspicion—searched the defendant's gas tank and discovered a quantity of marijuana. The Supreme Court upheld the search because it occurred at an international border, "a place where the government's interest in barring terrorists and importations of weapons, explosives, or other illegal items is at its peak."[62]

### Standing

Standing to object to a police search is established when a defendant shows that his personal privacy was invaded by the search. The standing requirement is satisfied when a defendant shows that his dwelling or automobile was searched by police, as distinguished from one who claims prejudice only through a search and seizure directed at someone else. Standing to contest a search requires that a privacy interest of the movant be implicated. In *Rakas v. Illinois*, the Court determined that the exclusionary rule cannot be claimed by a person who does not own the place being searched. Thus, the passengers of a car, not being owners, cannot challenge the legality of a search of that car.[63] *Rakas* was construed in *United States v. Padilla*.[64] The driver and sole occupant of a car gave permission to search a vehicle, and police found 560 pounds of cocaine in the trunk. Other people were charged with conspiracy to distribute cocaine. Could they—not present at the driver's arrest and not owners of the car—assert a privacy interest that was violated by the car's search? The United States Supreme Court refused to embrace a co-conspirator rule wherein a conspirator has standing to challenge a search when he simply puts objects in the place or thing searched.

---

[61]　Illinois v. Lidster, 124 S. Ct. 885 (2004).
[62]　United States v. Flores-Montano, 124 S. Ct. 1582 (2004).
[63]　439 U.S. 128 (1978).
[64]　123 L. Ed.2d 635 (1993).

## Timeliness of Search

As important as the spatial scope of the search is its timing. A valid search incident to arrest must be substantially contemporaneous with the arrest. Because the validity of a warrantless search of this kind depends upon a valid arrest being first accomplished, the search must not precede the arrest. The question then arises, how promptly after the arrest must the search be made? The rule is that the search must follow the arrest as soon as reasonably possible under the circumstances, and the more immediate the better. The courts will allow a short interval to elapse between the arrest and the search, as illustrated by a case in which the seizure of a defendant's clothing took place at the jail following his incarceration. However, where no reasons of public decency dictate such a delay, the best policy is to keep the time between the arrest and the search as short as possible.

A Supreme Court decision demonstrates the danger in bypassing immediate search in favor of a more convenient but less contemporaneous one. The police of Newport, Kentucky, received a telephone complaint at about three o'clock one morning that three men acting suspiciously had been seated in a car for five hours. The police officers went to the location, found three men in a parked car and questioned them. The men admitted that they were unemployed and without funds, and they were arrested for vagrancy. Their car was driven to police headquarters, then towed to a garage. After the men had been booked, the officers promptly went to the garage to search the car. They found two loaded revolvers in the glove compartment, and in the trunk discovered women's stockings, including one with mouth and eye holes, rope, and an illegally manufactured license plate equipped to be snapped over another plate. The use of these articles of evidence in a subsequent trial for conspiracy to rob a federally insured bank (a purpose admitted to by one of the occupants of the car) gave rise to the question of admissibility, which ultimately reached the Supreme Court of the United States:

> The rule allowing contemporaneous searches is justified, for example, by the need to seize weapons and other things which might be used to assault an officer or effect an escape, as well as by the need to prevent the destruction of evidence of the crime—things which might easily happen where the weapon or evidence is on the accused's person or under his immediate control. But these justifications are absent where a search is remote in time or place from the arrest. Once an accused is under arrest and in custody, then a search made at another place, without a warrant, is simply not incident to the arrest.[65]

---

[65] Preston v. United States, 376 U.S. 364, 367, 84 S. Ct. 881, 883, 11 L. Ed. 2d 777, 780 (1964) (citations omitted). *See* New York v. Belton, 453 U.S. 454 (1981); Vale v. Louisiana, 399 U.S. 30 (1970) (Vale arrested on front steps, narcotics found in search of bedroom, search ruled improper).

The *Preston* case states the general rule. An exception may exist where search is partially accomplished at the scene, and special circumstances dictate a brief delay in completing the search. For rationales other than the "incident to arrest" cases which might assist in evaluating vehicle searches, including search of impounded vehicles, consult South Dakota v. Opperman, 428 U.S. 364 (1976) and Florida v. Wells, 495 U.S. 7, 110 S. Ct. 1632 (1990) (inventory of auto, suppression of marijuana).

Under *Preston*, the requirement that a search incident to arrest must be substantially contemporaneous is not met when a person is arrested in an automobile and the automobile is moved to the police impoundment lot and later searched without a warrant. This requirement is also violated when a person is arrested downtown and the police proceed to his outlying apartment, home, or office and conduct a search without a warrant.[66] When probable cause exists to arrest a suspect in his automobile, the warrantless search should be made promptly. If a person is arrested while walking along the street, the defendant and things in his possession should be searched. For a search of a person's home or office, a warrant should be obtained.

## What May Be Seized?

A decision of major import in the area of what may be seized is *Warden v. Hayden*.[67] The case dealt with the proper objects of an otherwise valid search, and the Supreme Court discussed at length the old "mere evidence" rule. Under the "mere evidence" rule, either contraband or the fruits and instrumentalities of a crime could be seized as the result of a valid search, but not objects of evidentiary value only. Thus, if police were investigating a fatal stabbing and the murder suspect was spotted going into his home which was under police surveillance, the police officers who entered and arrested the suspect could then seize a knife which their search discovered. However, under the old rule the same police could not seize a shirt covered with the victim's blood, this latter item constituting "mere evidence."

This rule was founded in 1921 in *Gouled v. United States*,[68] when the court ruled that objects of only evidentiary value can never be seized, even under a search warrant.

Then came the *Hayden* decision in 1967. In *Hayden*, the police entered a house in hot pursuit of an armed robber.[69] The police made a search of the home, and seized a cap hidden under a mattress and a jacket and trousers

---

[66] James v. Louisiana, 382 U.S. 36, 86 S. Ct. 151, 15 L. Ed. 2d 30 (1965); Agnello v. United States, 269 U.S. 20, 30-32, 46 S. Ct. 4, 5-6, 70 L. Ed. 145, 148-149 (1925).

[67] 387 U.S. 294, 87 S. Ct. 1642, 18 L. Ed. 2d 782 (1967).

[68] 255 U.S. 298, 41 S. Ct. 261, 65 L. Ed. 647 (1921) (warrant authorized for seizure of bills for services and contracts allegedly used to defraud the United States; held, that these objects were of purely "evidential value" and immune from seizure under the Fourth Amendment, the Court's opinion validating only searches for stolen property, contraband or instruments of crime).

[69] On the right of hot pursuit, see United States v. Santana, 427 U.S. 38, 96 S. Ct. 2406, 49 L. Ed. 2d 300 (1976). The *Hayden* "hot pursuit" rule does not appear to be affected by subsequent cases declaring that an officer should only enter a private residence to make an arrest under the authority of an arrest warrant, since those recent cases refer to "routine" felony arrests. *See* Payton v. New York, 445 U.S. 573 (1980), discussed at note 47 *supra* and accompanying text.

found in a washing machine.[70] They ultimately found the suspect undressed in bed, and arrested him. The items of evidence previously noted were introduced against Hayden at trial. Hayden was convicted, but appealed. The Supreme Court then reviewed the case; the "mere evidence" rule was reconsidered, rejected, and the Supreme Court proclaimed that nothing in the language of the Fourth Amendment supported the distinction between "mere evidence" and the instrumentalities or fruits of crime. Searches for evidentiary matter should be deemed reasonable as long as there is probable cause to believe the seized item was connected to a crime and the search is not merely exploratory. These rules hold that the other requirements of a valid search be met. Mr. Justice Brennan did not lament the destruction of the old rule: "The 'mere evidence' limitation has spawned exceptions so numerous and confusion so great, in fact, that it is questionable whether it affords meaningful protection. . . . [T]here is no viable reason to distinguish intrusions to secure 'mere evidence' from intrusions to secure fruits, instrumentalities, or contraband."

What are the ramifications of the above analysis for state practice? First, a search incident to arrest permits seizure of evidentiary matter as well as stolen property, contraband, or the instruments of crime. This proposition covers searches of the person as well as searches beyond the physical body of the suspect and within the ambit of reasonable search previously explored in *Chimel*. Thus, the clothing worn by a person at the time of arrest may be taken from him and it may be put to laboratory examination.[71] Officers may seize contraband or evidence of a crime different from the offense for which the arrest is made.[72] The authority to seize is somewhat distinct from the authority to search. Authority to search emanates from the various bases explicated previously, i.e., search for weapons that could be used to injure the officer or effect the suspect's escape, and to avoid destruction of the evidence of the crime for which the accused is arrested. But once a valid search is undertaken for these purposes following a lawful arrest, there is authority that contraband or evidence of other crimes that is discovered along the way may be lawfully seized.

---

[70] What are the ramifications if the police make a search and seizure which precedes the arrest? It is basic law that a warrantless search of a premises incident to arrest must follow lawful arrest and not precede same. Occasionally, however, exceptions are made and there is authority that under special circumstances a premises search may sometimes precede arrest. In Warden v. Hayden a portion of the search did occur before the arrest. The search spread through the first and second floors of the house and the basement while the police were in pursuit of the suspect, thus reversing the usual pattern of arrest followed by search. Items were seized. The Court summarized the propriety of the search: "The Fourth Amendment does not require police officers to delay in the course of an investigation if to do so would gravely endanger their lives or the lives of others. Speed here was essential, and only a thorough search of the house for persons and weapons could have insured that Hayden was the only man present and the police had control of all weapons which could be used against them or to effect an escape."

In *Maryland v. Buie*, 494 U.S. 325, 110 S. Ct. 1093 (1990), the Court approved a "protective sweep" as a "quick and limited search of the premises, incident to an arrest and conducted to protect the safety of police officers and others."

[71] In addition, the officer has a right as an incident of his custodial duties to take possession of an arrested person's money or property for safe-keeping.

[72] Abel v. United States, 362 U.S. 217, 80 S. Ct. 683, 4 L. Ed. 2d 668 (1960).

## Seizure of Material within the Body

Search and seizure aspects are important when considering the testing of bodily substances extracted after arrest. The opinion that set the pattern for modern law in this area is the Supreme Court's decision in *Schmerber v. California*.[73] There, the petitioner was convicted in Los Angeles Municipal Court of the criminal offense of driving an automobile while under the influence of intoxicating liquor. He had been arrested at a hospital while receiving treatment for injuries suffered in an accident involving the automobile that he had been driving. At the direction of a police officer, a blood sample was withdrawn from petitioner's body by a physician at the hospital. The chemical analysis of this sample revealed a percent by weight of alcohol in his blood at the time of the offense that indicated intoxication, and the report of this analysis was admitted in evidence at the trial. Petitioner objected to admission of this evidence on the ground that the blood had been withdrawn despite his refusal, under advice of counsel, to consent to the test. He contended that in the circumstances, the withdrawal of the blood and the admission of the analysis in evidence violated his privilege against self-incrimination under the Fifth Amendment and the search and seizure guarantee in the Fourth Amendment. The appellate department of the California Superior Court rejected the petitioner's contentions and affirmed the conviction.

The Supreme Court of the United States approved the introduction of the blood analysis, holding that the means and procedures employed in taking the petitioner's blood respected relevant Fourth Amendment standards of reasonableness. On the Fifth Amendment question, the court ruled that the privilege against self-incrimination offered no protection against compulsion to submit to fingerprinting, photographing, measurements, or to walk or make a particular gesture for identification. Similarly, the taking of blood did not coerce the defendant to speak against himself, and because it did not constitute a "communicative act or writing by the petitioner, it was not inadmissible on privilege grounds."

States employ the *Schmerber* rationale to approve test results of breath, urine or blood samples taken from a motorist. Where alcohol or drugs impair driving, the presence in a body specimen will often form strong evidence of guilt.

The United States Supreme Court added another dimension in drunk driving cases. The high court approved measures designed to force provision of breath or other samples in the case of *South Dakota v. Neville*.[74] A South Dakota statute, similar to laws operative in other jurisdictions, authorizes revocation of a drunk driving arrestee's license to drive when the driver refuses to take a blood-alcohol test (such as a breath test). The implied consent law in the *Neville* case allowed a suspect to refuse to take such a test, but the refusal was not without a price: evidence of the defendant's refusal could be used in evidence to help convict him of drunk driving. "The simple blood-alcohol test is

---

[73]   384 U.S. 757, 86 S. Ct. 1826, 16 L. Ed. 2d 908 (1966).
[74]   459 U.S. 553, 103 S. Ct. 916 (1983).

so safe, painless, and commonplace that respondent concedes, as he must, that the state could legitimately compel the suspect, against his will, to accede to the test."

What if slurred responses to police inquiries as to whether an alleged drunk driver will submit to tests tend to incriminate the driver by showing him to be drunk? Can the videotape later be shown to the jury, or will the procedure violate the defendant's privilege against self-incrimination? Holding such evidence as a proper part of the government's case is *Pennsylvania v. Muniz*:[75]

> We conclude that *Miranda* does not require suppression of the statements [defendant] Muniz made when asked to submit to a Breathalyzer examination. Officer Deyo read Muniz a prepared script explaining how the test worked, the nature of Pennsylvania's Implied Consent Law, and the legal consequences that would ensue should he refuse. Officer Deyo then asked Muniz whether he understood the nature of the test and the law and whether he would like to submit to the test. Muniz asked Officer Deyo several questions concerning the legal consequences of refusal, which Deyo answered directly, and Muniz then commented upon his state of inebriation. 377 Pa. Super., at 387, 547 A.2d, at 422. After offering to take the test only after waiting a couple of hours or drinking some water, Muniz ultimately refused.

> We believe that Muniz's statements were not prompted by an interrogation within the meaning of *Miranda*, and therefore the absence of *Miranda* warnings does not require suppression of these statements at trial.

*Schmerber* establishes that the Fifth Amendment privilege does not bar minimal intrusions on a suspect's bodily integrity. It was followed by the United States Supreme Court in *Cupp v. Murphy*.[76] The Court held that a scraping of Murphy's fingernails, which produced incriminating material, was a reasonable and limited search. Murphy had voluntarily appeared at the police station for questioning concerning the strangulation of his wife.

However, not all material taken from a suspect's body will be admitted. Some evidence gathering violates the Fourth Amendment. The Supreme Court views some searches that involve bodily intrusions to be violative of the Constitution's protection against unreasonable searches and seizures. The court prohibited the forced removal of a bullet from the chest of an armed robbery suspect in Richmond, Virginia. "A compelled surgical intrusion into an individual's body for evidence," Justice William Brennan stated, "implicates expectations of privacy and security of such magnitude that the intrusion may be 'unreasonable,' even if likely to produce evidence of a crime."[77]

[75]  496 U.S. 582, 110 S. Ct. 2683 (1990).

[76]  412 U.S. 291, 93 S. Ct. 2000, 36 L. Ed. 2d 900 (1973).

[77]  Winston v. Lee, 470 U.S. 753 (1985). The Court dealt with bodily invasions in the same year in a drug context. It ruled that border officials could detain a person suspected of smuggling drugs internally until the suspect had a bowel movement to produce the evidence. The Court, however, did not base the decision on a Fourth Amendment search and seizure analysis, but rather cited precedents holding that people searched at the border do not have the same constitutional rights as U.S. citizens. United States v. Montoya de Hernandez, 473 U.S. 531 (1985).

The *Schmerber* case arose in California, as did *Rochin v. California*.[78] *Rochin* involved the taking of two capsules containing narcotics from the accused by forced pumping of his stomach. This induced vomiting, which resulted in the recovery of narcotics the accused had swallowed. The United States Supreme Court ruled that such evidence was inadmissible because it was obtained by means that violated the due process clause of the federal Constitution. Violent or brutal extraction of evidence, conduct that "shocks the conscience," offends the concept of due process. The concurring opinions of Justices Black and Douglas went further and considered the coerced seizure of "real evidence" to be in violation of the accused's privilege against self-incrimination.

A lingering question in view of the *Rochin* decision is this: Would a different case have been made out in *Schmerber* if the defendant, instead of merely expressing objection to the blood test, resisted physically and then had to be restrained by force in order for the test to proceed? Probably not, as the decision indicates that the police may overcome physical resistance, and only the use of undue force will vitiate the process. As stated in this note to the majority opinion: "We 'cannot see that it should make any difference whether one states unequivocally that he objects or resorts to physical violence in protest or is in such condition that he is unable to protest.' It would be a different case if the police initiated the violence, refused to respect a reasonable request to undergo a different form of testing, or responded to resistance with inappropriate force."[79] The *Rochin* case has been the subject of consideration in subsequent opinions dealing with chemical tests to determine intoxication, and these cases have generally adopted the rule of the majority opinion rather than the broader exclusion indicated in the concurring opinions of Justices Douglas and Black.[80]

## Foreign Searches

When a search crosses the American border, will the exclusionary rule operate? What is the status of evidence seized in a foreign country and used in an American trial? How far beyond our shores does the Fourth Amendment extend? According to the Supreme Court, not to searches and seizures by United States agents when property owned by nonresident aliens is located in a foreign country.[81] Arrested by Mexican police based on a warrant issued in the United States, Verdugo-Urquidez, a Mexican citizen, was tried and convicted in California. American agents working with Mexican officials had obtained evidence after warrantless searches of the suspect's homes in Mexico. The Supreme Court found the evidence admissible because the Fourth Amendment has "no application" in a foreign country.

---

[78]   342 U.S. 165, 72 S. Ct. 205, 96 L. Ed. 2d 183 (1952).

[79]   384 U.S. at 760, 86 S. Ct. at 1825, 16 L. Ed. 2d at 914-915 (citation omitted).

[80]   The *Rochin* problem arose again in California. In *California v. Bracamonte*, 540 P.2d 624 (Cal. 1975), the California Supreme Court invalidated the forced regurgitation of balloons filled with narcotics which had been swallowed by the suspect.

[81]   United States v. Verdugo-Urquidez, 494 U.S. 259, 110 S. Ct. 1056, 108 L. Ed. 2d 222 (1990).

## 2. Consent Searches

A defendant may consent to a warrantless search, and a seizure of incriminating items by an officer will be upheld if the consent was given by the accused without government intimidation or duress. As stated in *Florida v. Royer*: "[W]here the validity of a search rests on consent, the State has the burden of proving that the necessary consent was obtained and that it was freely and voluntarily given . . ."[82]

Sometimes officers board a bus or approach individuals at random in airport lobbies and other public places to ask them questions and to request consent to search their luggage. In *Florida v Bostick*[83] two Florida police officers requested the defendant's consent to search his luggage on a bus. Cocaine was found. The defendant complained about the search, but the courts approved the law enforcement practice of "working the buses." Not every police-citizen encounter is a search, and Bostick was not "compelled" to agree with the officer's request because he could have declined to allow the search.

The rule of *Bostick* was confirmed in *United States v. Drayton*.[84] Again officers were "working the buses." Officer Lang noticed that two bus passengers who were sitting next to each other were wearing heavy clothing, even though it was warm weather. He advised the men that he was with the police department and was "conducting a bus interdiction, attempting to deter drugs and illegal weapons being transported on the bus." Lang asked Drayton and his companion if he could check them, and after they signaled their cooperation he proceeded. Both men had duct-taped plastic bundles of powder cocaine to their thighs.

Drayton claimed he was entitled to suppression of the cocaine. Even though the officer asked politely in a quiet voice for the right to search, he failed to advise that a citizen has the right to decline to consent. The Supreme Court addressed the issue, and rejected the suggestion that police must always inform citizens of their right to refuse a warrantless consent search. While offering such advice may be a good idea, failure to do so does not vitiate a search. The same rule has been applied when police conduct a consent search of an automobile, as explained in the next section of the text. In the bus cases a similar doctrine controlled. Because officer Lang at no time told Drayton that he was required to consent to the search, the Court upheld the seizure of the cocaine.

The Supreme Court also held that a criminal suspect's right to be free from unreasonable searches was not violated when, after he gave a police officer permission to search his automobile, the officer opened a closed container found within the car, which held cocaine.[85]

---

[82]     460 U.S. 491, 103 S. Ct. 1319 (1983).

[83]     501 U.S. 429, 111 S. Ct. 2382, 115 L. Ed.2d 389 (1991) (random bus searches conducted pursuant to a passenger's consent are not per se unconstitutional).

[84]     536 U.S. 194 (2002).

[85]     Florida v. Jimeno, 499 U.S. 934, 111 S. Ct. 1801, 114 L. Ed.2d 297 (1991).

Third-party consent presents special problems. If the police are investigating a husband, may they go to his home and obtain a valid consent to search it from his wife? What about the husband giving consent to search his home for evidence against the wife? A spouse can authorize entry even when the spouse who is under investigation is not there. For example, a husband can allow police to come in to investigate his wife, and what they find can be used against her.

Moreover, the rule is broader than simply husbands and wives. The same approach was used in *United States v. Matlock*,[86] when a person who gave police entry was not married to a bank robbery suspect. Police obtained consent to search the suspect's premises from a woman who occupied the same bedroom with the suspect. The Court found the search valid because permission was obtained from a third party who possessed common authority over the premises or effects sought to be searched: "The authority which justifies the third-party consent does not rest upon the law of property, with its attendant historical and legal refinements . . . but rests rather on mutual use of the property by persons generally having joint access or control for most purposes, so that it is reasonable to recognize that any of the co-inhabitants has the right to permit the inspection in his own right and that the others have assumed the risk that one of their number might permit the common area to be searched."

In 1990, the Court extended the rule to third parties who had apparent but not actual authority over the premises.[87] The defendant was arrested on a drug charge after a woman friend of the defendant reported that she had been assaulted by him. She traveled to the apartment with the police, unlocked the door, and gave police permission to enter. Drugs were in plain view. Justice Scalia concluded that if officers could reasonably believe that the defendant's friend had actual authority to consent to a search of the apartment, the search was reasonable, even though unknown to the police the woman may have moved out and retained a key without his permission.

The right of a husband or wife to consent to a search is distinct from the situation of the motel owner or landlord. Valid consent to search rooms of tenants cannot be obtained from these latter individuals, as a general rule.[88] In such situations, a warrant to search appears essential.

---

[86]   415 U.S. 164, 94 S. Ct. 988, 39 L. Ed. 2d 242 (1974). *See also* Frazier v. Cupp, 394 U.S. 731, 89 S. Ct. 1420, 22 L. Ed. 2d 684 (1969).

[87]   Illinois v. Rodriguez, 497 U.S. 177, 110 S. Ct. 1793 (1990). However, a 10-year-old did not have authority to give police permission to search parent's home in *Davis v. State*, 422 S.E.2d 546 (Ga. 1992) (consent from 10-year-old to search parents' home for evidence against them was not valid). Ability of person who permits police to come in to authorize a search, *see* KLOTTER, KANOVITZ AND KANOVITZ, CONSTITUTIONAL LAW § 4.3(2) (10th ed. 2005).

[88]   Stoner v. California, 376 U.S. 483, 84 S. Ct. 889, 11 L. Ed. 2d 856 (1964); United States v. Jeffers, 342 U.S. 48, 72 S. Ct. 93, 96 L. Ed. 59 (1951) (hotel room entry); Chapman v. United States, 365 U.S. 610, 81 S. Ct. 776, 5 L. Ed. 2d 828 (1961) (landlord consent held ineffective); Pasterchik v. United States, 400 F.2d 696 (9th Cir. 1968) (landlord consent). *Contra*, United States v. Stone, 401 F.2d 32 (7th Cir. 1968) (mother allowed search of son's part of basement); Grant v. State, 589 S.W.2d 11 (Ark. 1979) (stepfather allowed search).

### Warnings Necessary for Valid Consent

Must *Miranda* warnings be given before a valid legal consent is achieved? Further, must police officers tell the defendant that he has a right to refuse permission to make a search? A number of state courts held that *Miranda* requirements did not apply when the officer was obtaining consent to search. In *Schneckloth v. Bustamonte*,[89] the United States Supreme Court adopted a similar rule.

In 1996 the Supreme Court added a further refinement in *Ohio v. Robinette*.[90] An Ohio deputy sheriff stopped Robinette for speeding. Asked whether he was carrying drugs in his car, he said "no." He consented to a search of his car, and controlled substances were found. He was found guilty, after his pre-trial suppression motion was denied. The issue was whether the officer had to tell the motorist he was "legally free to go" in order to secure a valid consent to search the car. The Supreme Court said no:

> In *Schneckloth v. Bustamonte*, 412 U.S. 218, 93 S. Ct. 2041, 36 L. Ed. 2d 854 (1973), it was argued that such a consent could not be valid unless the defendant knew that he had a right to refuse the request. We rejected this argument: "While knowledge of the right to refuse consent is one factor to be taken into account, the government need not establish such knowledge as the sine qua non of an effective consent." Id., at 227, 93 S. Ct., at 2048. And just as it "would be thoroughly impractical to impose on the normal consent search the detailed requirements of an effective warning," id., at 231, 93 S. Ct., at 2050, so too would it be unrealistic to require police officers to always inform detainees that they are free to go before a consent to search may be deemed voluntary.
>
> The Fourth Amendment test for a valid consent to search is that the consent be voluntary, and "[v]oluntariness is a question of fact to be determined from all the circumstances," id., at 248-249, 93 S. Ct. at 2059.

### Form of Consent

Notwithstanding the above point of law, the safest form of oral consent, from the police officer's point of view, is one obtained after the suspect has been informed that he need not give the officer permission to search. At the very least, a consent must be achieved after the officer has asked for the consent in inquiry form, and without telling the person that the officer is going to search whether he obtains consent or not. When properly requested, a citizen may waive his constitutional protection of privacy and the waiver will protect the validity of the search. The person from whom the consent is obtained must be of sufficient intelligence and understanding to appreciate what is going on.[91]

---

[89]    412 U.S. 218, 93 S. Ct. 2041, 36 L. Ed. 2d 854 (1973).

[90]    117 S. Ct. 417 (1996).

[91]    Ten-year-old did not have authority to give police permission to search parent's home in Davis v. State, 422 S.E.2d 546 (Ga. 1992).

In addition, the consent must be voluntary. Things that destroy the validity of a consent search include threats or brandishing of weapons.[92] Consent, once given, may be withdrawn. However, the officer may have located enough evidence when this occurs to place the person who revoked consent under arrest and continue the search incident to lawful arrest.

Is a written consent necessary? The answer is no, but several authorities recommend a written consent when it is possible to obtain one. A sample form was suggested by the United States Department of Justice:[93]

> I, John Doe, know of my constitutional rights to refuse to allow a police search of any part of my house at 711 Royalty Road, Alexandria, Va. However, I have decided to allow Tom Smith and Bill Jones, members of the Metropolitan Police, to search every part of my house. They have my permission to take any letters, papers, materials, or other property they want. I have decided to make this consent carefully, of my own free will, and without being subject to threats or promises. I know that anything discovered may be used against me in a criminal proceeding . . .
>
> January 22, 1967

> Witness. 1. Bob Janitor          (Signed)          John Doe

*Procedural Aspects: Burden of Proof and Trial Testimony*

While the burden of demonstrating that evidence has been illegally procured normally devolves upon the accused, when the government relies upon consent to an otherwise illegal search and seizure, it has the burden of proving by clear and convincing evidence that the consent was voluntary and free from duress and coercion.[94]

An example of trial testimony developing such consent appears in *State v. Gates*.[95] A county sheriff asked the defendant, who was confined in the county jail, if the sheriff could search the trunk of the defendant's car. The sheriff suspected that the trunk contained stolen items. The car was parked in the county jail parking lot. Testimony of the sheriff in response to the prosecuting attorney's questions developed as follows during trial of the case:

Q. Please state what those conversations were as you best recall.
A. I asked him about searching his trunk of his car if we got a key that would open it. He had no objections.

---

[92] United States v. Watson, 423 U.S. 411 (1976); Bumper v. North Carolina, 391 U.S. 543, 88 S. Ct. 1788, 20 L. Ed. 2d 797 (1968). An example of a good consent search appears in Washington v. Chrisman, 455 U.S. 1 (1982) wherein a university student agreed orally and in writing to a search of his dormitory room. The search yielded marijuana and LSD.

[93] Department of Justice, HANDBOOK ON THE LAW OF SEARCH AND SEIZURE, 52 (1967). A general consent to search one's premises may be viewed as a consent to search the premises in its entirety. However, courts require officers to honor any limitations placed on the extensiveness of the search by the consenting party.

[94] Florida v. Royer, 460 U.S. 491, 103 S. Ct. 1319 (1983).

[95] 260 Iowa 772, 150 N.W.2d 617 (1967).

Q. In other words, he said you could search the vehicle?
A. That's right.

Q. Was this before you obtained the can of meat and the two quarts of antifreeze? (stolen items)
A. Yes, it was.

Q. Did you advise the defendant at that time that he need not permit you to make a search of his vehicle?
A. I did.

Q. Yet he consented if you could find a key, is that right?
A. He consented. He was out there when we searched it.

Q. He was present when the search was made?
A. He was present when it was searched.

Q. At the time you were opening the trunk of the vehicle, did the defendant make any statements or objections to your actions at that time?
A. No, he didn't.

The court held that because the defendant had consented to the search, the protection of the Fourth Amendment was lost to him.

## Drug Testing and Other Regulatory Efforts

Sometimes employees and prospective employees agree to drug testing in order to obtain employment or to advance in a job position. Does the requirement of a drug test constitute improper coercion? In *National Treasury Employees Union v. Von Raab*,[96] the Supreme Court upheld mandatory urinalysis testing for customs employees seeking promotion to positions that involve narcotics law enforcement or the carrying of firearms. While the urinalysis test results could not be used in a criminal prosecution against an employee who tested positive, the test requirement was a reasonable effort to help ensure the unimpeachable integrity of officers involved in drug enforcement. The Supreme Court also upheld blood and urine tests of railroad employees who are involved in certain train accidents.[97] Employees who violated specified safety rules could be required to undergo breath or urine tests as a condition of continued employment. The Court ruled that the government, through the Federal Railroad Administration, had a compelling interest in testing certain employees and did not have to show an individualized suspicion.

In the mid-1990s the Supreme Court extended its jurisprudence in this area to schools as well as political elections. In *Vernonia School District 47 J. v. Acton*,[98] the student-athlete drug policy authorized random urinalysis drug testing. Athletes were among the leaders of the drug culture in the Vernonia, Oregon, schools, according to the District Court. The urinalysis policy applied

---

[96]    489 U.S. 656, 109 S. Ct. 1384 (1989).
[97]    Skinner v. Railway Labor Executives Ass'n, 489 U.S. 602, 109 S. Ct. 1402 (1989).
[98]    115 S. Ct. 2386 (1995).

to all students participating in interscholastic athletics. Students signed a consent form. Names of athletes to be tested were blindly drawn from a pool. Acton's parents sued because his refusal to sign the testing consent forms meant that he was denied participation in football. The Supreme Court concluded that Vernonia's policy was reasonable and thus constitutional, based upon the responsibilities imposed on the school system.

The Court distinguished student athletes from politicians in a 1997 drug-testing case. Urinalysis drug testing of candidates for designated state offices, when mandated by statute, effected a search within the meaning of the Fourth and Fourteenth Amendments. In *Chandler v. Miller*[99] the Supreme Court limited the scope of *Vernonia* by announcing that candidates for public office did not fall into the category of persons subject to mandatory drug testing, absent evidence of a drug problem among the state's elected officials. Only Chief Justice Rehnquist dissented, urging that the *Von Raab* case controlled, in which the Supreme Court upheld a Treasury Department regulation requiring mandatory drug testing for drug or other enforcement agents.

Another school decision extended the limits of drug testing in educational environments in 2002. A drug-testing program in an Oklahoma school district applied to any student participating in extracurricular activities. The consequence of a student failing or refusing to take a drug test was to limit or bar the student's participation in activities such as the marching band, Future Farmers of America, choir, academic team or the Future Homemakers of America. The serious problem of drug abuse by teenagers prompted the United States Supreme Court to uphold the constitutionality of the Oklahoma program.[100]

### 3. Emergency Searches and Exigent Circumstances

Sometimes emergency circumstances unfold, making resort to the warrant process difficult or impossible. Under state and federal law, police can enter a home or property without a warrant if they are in hot pursuit of a suspect, believe vital evidence will be destroyed by delay, or when people are in immediate danger within the premises.[101] Some courts restrict the doctrine to situations in which a grave offense is involved, a suspect who is believed to be on the premises is armed, and there is a likelihood that he will escape if not swiftly apprehended. In the O.J. Simpson case in California, detectives entered the Simpson premises under a claim of emergency. The deputy district attorney argued that a warrantless entry by detectives, which produced a bloody glove, was based on an apparent emergency, stating: "What if someone had been injured and lay bleeding while the officers went to get a search warrant?"

---

[99] 117 S. Ct. 1295 (1997).
[100] Board of Education v. Earls, 122 S. Ct. 2559 (2002).
[101] See supra note 69. Exigent circumstances justify warrantless entry into a location based upon an officer's reasonable belief that an emergency exists. Roberts v State, 482 S.E.2d 245 (Ga. 1997). *See* Kirk v. Louisiana, 536 U.S. 635 (2002); United States v. Gori, 230 F.3d 44 (2d Cir. 2000).

One added limitation on the doctrine restricts the amount of searching that police may do. Several courts narrow the scope of the search. If police enter to apprehend a violent suspect or to protect those on the premises from a dangerous felon, they can look for him or her in appropriate places (like a closet) and may gather evidence in plain view along the way, but cannot intensively search in hidden little places for evidence. That requires a search warrant.

## 4. Searches Under Warrant

The Fourth Amendment to the United States Constitution does not bar investigative searches conducted by government agents, only unreasonable searches. In applying this standard, the courts look with greater favor on searches conducted with a warrant. Under the prevailing view, a magistrate must pass upon the adequacy of grounds for the search, and the warrant may be issued only if the magistrate is satisfied that there is probable cause to believe that a basis exists for issuance; thus, the independent judgment of a judicial officer is interposed between the police officer wishing to make a search and the intrusion into the suspect's "castle." Further, the warrant is limited in that it must particularly specify the person or place to be searched and the property sought. Because of these judicial controls, the possibilities of utilizing the search as a "fishing expedition" are restricted, and larger protection against unjustified searches is provided than is the case with searches without a warrant. Of course, the theory outlined here requires that the issuing magistrate exercise an independent review when presented with an application for a warrant. The underlying assumptions are nullified if a magistrate merely rubber-stamps the police request. In an effort to ensure compliance with the constitutional mandate requiring independent review of warrant applications, the United States Congress overhauled the federal magistrate system in 1968. Under the Federal Magistrates Act, magistrates empowered to issue search warrants in federal criminal cases are required to be legally trained. This Act accomplished revision of the prior United States Commissioner system, under which some commissioners were not lawyers.

The search warrant procedure that controls the way in which federal law enforcement officers apply for search warrants has several features that are not dissimilar from most state provisions. Federal Rule of Criminal Procedure 41 provides, in part:

### Rule 41. Search and Seizure

. . .

(b) **Authority to Issue a Warrant.** At the request of a federal law enforcement officer or an attorney for the government:

   (1) a magistrate judge with authority in the district—or if none is reasonably available, a judge of a state court of record in the district —has authority to issue a warrant to search for and seize a person or property located within the district; and

**(2)** a magistrate judge with authority in the district has authority to issue a warrant for a person or property outside the district if the person or property is located within the district when the warrant is issued but might move or be moved outside the district before the warrant is executed; and

**(3)** a magistrate judge—in an investigation of domestic terrorism or international terrorism (as defined in 18 U.S.C. § 2331)—having authority in any district in which activities related to the terrorism may have occurred, may issue a warrant for a person or property within or outside that district.

**(c) Persons or Property Subject to Search and Seizure.** A warrant may be issued for any of the following:

**(1)** evidence of a crime;

**(2)** contraband, fruits of crime, or other items illegally possessed;

**(3)** property designed for use, intended for use, or used in committing a crime; or

**(4)** a person to be arrested or a person who is unlawfully restrained.

**(d) Obtaining a Warrant.**

**(1) Probable Cause.** After receiving an affidavit or other information, a magistrate judge or a judge of a state court of record must issue the warrant if there is probable cause to search for and seize a person or property under Rule 41(c).

**(2) Requesting a Warrant in the Presence of a Judge.**

**(A) Warrant on an Affidavit.** When a federal law enforcement officer or an attorney for the government presents an affidavit in support of a warrant, the judge may require the affiant to appear personally and may examine under oath the affiant and any witness the affiant produces.

**(B) Warrant on Sworn Testimony.** The judge may wholly or partially dispense with a written affidavit and base a warrant on sworn testimony if doing so is reasonable under the circumstances.

**(C) Recording Testimony.** Testimony taken in support of a warrant must be recorded by a court reporter or by a suitable recording device, and the judge must file the transcript or recording with the clerk, along with any affidavit.

**(3) Requesting a Warrant by Telephonic or Other Means.**

**(A) In General.** A magistrate judge may issue a warrant based on information communicated by telephone or other appropriate means, including facsimile transmission.

**(B) Recording Testimony.** Upon learning that an applicant is requesting a warrant, a magistrate judge must:

(i) place under oath the applicant and any person on whose testimony the application is based; and

>(ii) make a verbatim record of the conversation with a suitable recording device, if available, or by a court reporter, or in writing.
>
>**(C) Certifying Testimony.** The magistrate judge must have any recording or court reporter's notes transcribed, certify the transcription's accuracy, and file a copy of the record and the transcription with the clerk. Any written verbatim record must be signed by the magistrate judge and filed with the clerk.
>
>**(D) Suppression Limited.** Absent a finding of bad faith, evidence obtained from a warrant issued under Rule 41(d)(3)(A) is not subject to suppression on the ground that issuing the warrant in that manner was unreasonable under the circumstances.

**(e) Issuing the Warrant.**

>**(1) In General.** The magistrate judge or a judge of a state court of record must issue the warrant to an officer authorized to execute it.
>
>**(2) Contents of the Warrant.** The warrant must identify the person or property to be searched, identify any person or property to be seized, and designate the magistrate judge to whom it must be returned. The warrant must command the officer to:
>**(A)** execute the warrant within a specified time no longer than 10 days;
>**(B)** execute the warrant during the daytime, unless the judge for good cause expressly authorizes execution at another time; and
>**(C)** return the warrant to the magistrate judge designated in the warrant.

It should be noted that subdivision (c) of Rule 41 was expanded to allow search for items of solely evidentiary value, following the guidelines provided in *Warden v. Hayden*.[102] The term "daytime" (see Rule 41(e)) is defined in the Rules to mean the hours from 6:00 A.M. to 10:00 P.M. according to local time. Numerous states follow the federal pattern of requiring daytime searches, absent special conditions. Others authorize the execution of search warrants at any time.

It is to be noted that the life of a warrant is 10 days. Time considerations are also important at the front end of the process. When applying for a warrant, the officer must present fresh evidence of probable cause. While not often stated in a precise formula of the number of days prior to application in which the probable cause must develop, it is clear that the magistrate cannot base a warrant on stale information. In the portion of a search warrant containing a description of the person or property to be seized, the description must be specific. This was lacking when federal agents secured a search warrant that, under the part reserved for a description of things to be seized, simply recited as follows: "[There is, now concealed on the premises] a certain person or property,

---

[102] See note 67 *supra*. Allowing seizure of listed items as well as fruits, instrumentalities, and evidence of crime, see note 110 *infra* and accompanying text.

namely a single dwelling residence two story in height which is blue in color and has two additions attached to the east." The failure to specify items to be seized was held to be fatal to the warrant in a 2004 case.[103]

While appellate courts favor warrant searches, attacks on searches nonetheless occur even when the searching officer makes the effort to prepare a warrant application and secures a search warrant. One frequent attack is whether there was probable cause to support the warrant, or only unsupported suspicion.

The 1983 decision of the United States Supreme Court in *Illinois v. Gates*[104] involved an attack on a search warrant. In *Gates*, an anonymous letter was received by the Bloomingdale, Illinois, police department. The letter stated that Sue and Lance Gates sell drugs, that "most of their buys are done in Florida," and that on May 3 Sue is "driving down there again and Lance will be flying down in a few days to drive it back." The writer also stated that Lance's car trunk would be loaded with drugs worth more than $100,000. The police verified much of the information, including the fact that Lance Gates flew from Chicago to West Palm Beach and took a cab to a hotel, entering a room registered to his wife. Agents reported that he left the area in a Mercury automobile with Illinois license plates. Bloomingdale police secured a search warrant for the Gates's Illinois residence, as well as for the Mercury. The warrant was executed when they returned home, and approximately 350 pounds of marijuana were found in the trunk of the Mercury; drugs, drug paraphernalia, and weapons were discovered in the home.

Even though much of the information contained in the "tips" supplied by the letter writer had been corroborated, the Illinois appellate courts nonetheless held the police action insufficient. Something more was required. The decision to suppress the evidence was based on United States Supreme Court decisions in *Aguilar v. Texas* and *Spinelli v. United States*. These cases had established a "two-pronged test" for deciding whether there was probable cause for issuing a search warrant: the magistrate must be satisfied that the informant received his information in a reliable way and that enough facts have been developed in the case to establish the informant's truthfulness. The Illinois courts indicated that the anonymous letter did not contain sufficiently adequate details to establish that the writer had secured his information in a reliable way.

The United States Supreme Court disagreed, reversed the Illinois courts, and held the search to be a proper one. Although the anonymous letter alone did not provide probable cause, the police had corroborated "major portions of the letter's predictions." The high court overruled an earlier "two-pronged test" and substituted a new "totality of the circumstances" test. "It is enough that there was a fair probability that the writer of the anonymous letter was

---

[103]   Groh v. Ramirez, 1284 S. Ct. 1284 (2004).

[104]   462 U.S. 213, 103 S. Ct. 2317 (1983). Principles for evaluating an informant's tip, *Gates* followed, *see* Alabama v. White, 496 U.S. 325, 110 S. Ct. 2412 (1990).

accurate," said the Court, and a magistrate may issue a search warrant when the totality of the circumstances indicate that evidence of a crime will be found in a certain place.

The Court declined to decide in *Gates* whether the exclusionary rule should be generally modified along "good faith" lines. Some authorities had urged that where police attempt to follow Fourth Amendment guidelines but fall short, perhaps for technical reasons, such searches should nonetheless be upheld in cases in which the police had proceeded in the reasonable belief that the search was proper. "Under this proposal, application of the exclusionary rule would be limited to cases in which police officers intentionally or recklessly violated constitutional rights."[105] The Court did not resolve the constitutionality of the "good faith" exception in *Gates*, as the Court observed, "with apologies to all."

The Court left it to the 1984 case of *United States v. Leon*[106] to engraft a good faith exception on the exclusionary rule. The Court emphasized that its ruling applied when police reasonably relied on a search warrant that is later shown to be defective. When a warrant issued by a neutral magistrate appears to be proper, an officer may rely upon it, even though a lack of probable cause may be established in a subsequent proceeding.

While the good faith of the officer may excuse and justify an otherwise bad warrant search under federal constitutional law, a number of states will not allow this to happen. The courts of these states reject the "good faith" rationale as a matter of state law. In those states, the warrant papers will be scanned for their statement of probable cause, unaided by the officer's proclamation of good faith.[107]

## 5. Execution of Warrants

Various rules govern state and federal officers in the execution of warrants. Illustrative are the principles controlling the execution of federal search warrants contained in Rule 41(f) of the Federal Rules of Criminal Procedure:

**(f)  Executing and Returning the Warrant.**

**(1)  Noting the Time.** The officer executing the warrant must enter on its face the exact date and time it is executed.

**(2)  Inventory.** An officer present during the execution of the warrant must prepare and verify an inventory of any property seized. The officer must do so in the presence of another officer and the person from whom, or from whose premises, the property was taken. If

---

[105] Gerald Ashdown, *Good Faith, The Exclusion Remedy, and Rule-Oriented Adjudication in the Criminal Process*, 24 WM. & MARY L. REV. 335, 338 (1983).

[106] 468 U.S. 897, 104 S. Ct. 3405 (1984).

[107] Georgia is among the group of states that do not excuse an otherwise defective warrant because of good faith. Gary v. State, 262 Ga. 573, 422 S.E.2d 426 (1992).

either one is not present, the officer must prepare and verify the inventory in the presence of at least one other credible person.

**(3) Receipt.** The officer executing the warrant must:

    **(A)** give a copy of the warrant and a receipt for the property taken to the person from whom, or from whose premises, the property was taken; or

    **(B)** leave a copy of the warrant and receipt at the place where the officer took the property.

**(4) Return**. The officer executing the warrant must promptly return it—together with a copy of the inventory—to the magistrate judge designated on the warrant. The judge must, on request, give a copy of the inventory to the person from whom, or from whose premises, the property was taken and to the applicant for the warrant.

The norm in criminal cases contemplates that the defendant who may have been absent when police arrived will be alerted to the fact that his residence was searched. The requirement that a document be left at the residence—a receipt—guarantees the defendant's knowledge that his residence was inspected and seizures were made.

An exception to this rule exists in terrorism investigations. Under the **USA PATRIOT Act**, passed in the wake of the September 11, 2001, attacks in New York and Washington, D.C., covert searches were authorized. When federal agents are investigating terrorism suspects, there may be physical entry into private premises without the owner's permission or knowledge. Often the occupant of the residence is absent when entry occurs, and the process is conducted in secret. Notations in diaries or data in other documents may be inspected and photographed by the authorities. To ensure the stealth of the enterprise, no copy of the warrant or receipt is left behind.

There are other provisions of the USA PATRIOT Act. Enhanced wiretap and electronic surveillance are permitted. But it is the sneak-and-peek search warrant provision that has generated the most explosive debate between federal law enforcement officials and civil libertarians. The United States Attorney General has described the USA PATRIOT Act as al-Qaeda's worst nightmare. It provides the tools to expose and obstruct terrorism, officials say.

Civil libertarians respond that the United States government must not violate standards of decency in the name of preserving a decent society. "The Framers [of the Constitution] would have abhorred sneak and peek searches."[108] Another commentator observed that allowing warrants to be stealthily executed marks a radical departure from accepted search warrant procedure. He warns that this practice poses a dangerous threat to the security of American homes.[109] The debate about whether national security justifies

---

[108]   N. Seltzer, *When History Matters Not: The Fourth Amendment in the Age of Secret Search*, 40 Crim. L. Bull. 105, 144 (2004).

[109]   E. Wilkes, *Sneak and Peek Search Warrants*, The Georgia Defender 1 (Sept. 2002).

this sort of deviation from accepted, conventional search warrant norms will likely continue for years.

Suppose a state or federal law enforcement officer, acting under a search warrant, finds evidence of a felony while executing the warrant; however, the located evidence is not listed in his warrant. Is the officer required to blind himself to what is in plain sight simply because it is disconnected from the purpose for which he entered? There is significant case authority supporting the seizure of unlisted contraband or other illegal items during a proper search for items specified in the warrant.[110]

The need of drug enforcement officers for quick entry when executing warrants led to enactment of a large number of "no-knock" statutes. Traditionally a law enforcement officer executing a search (or an arrest) warrant was required to announce his authority and purpose to the occupants of the premises to be searched prior to execution of the warrant. For example, when Officer Smith of the Ames Police Department has a warrant authorizing the search of a particular apartment for heroin, he might knock on the door and when an occupant opens the door the officer might state that he is a police officer at the premises to execute a search warrant. Under several state laws, only when the officer is denied admittance (e.g., the door is slammed in the officer's face or the occupants are present but refuse to open the door) is the officer empowered to break and enter to execute the warrant.

Laws restricting forcible entry to circumstances in which the officer gives notice of his authority and is denied admittance are historically grounded on several considerations. Included among these is the proposition that the announcement rule serves as "a safeguard for the police themselves who might be mistaken for prowlers and be shot down by a fearful householder."[111] While some jurisdictions have wavered on the question of whether the officer's violation of the notice requirement would result in exclusion of the seized evidence or merely subject the officer to misdemeanor or civil sanctions, under the federal view it has been held that the failure to give notice vitiated the search.

In recent years law enforcement authorities argued that compliance with the notice requirement by police resulted in the destruction of valuable evidence. In searches for marijuana or heroin, for example, upon hearing of the police officer's presence at the door, occupants of the premises might scoop up the contraband and flush it down a toilet. In a gambling investigation where the officer is searching for evidence, lottery tickets and numbers might be printed on flashpaper that could be touched off by a match as soon as the police presence was known. To overcome these difficulties in securing evidence, certain jurisdictions enacted **"no-knock"** or quick-entry **statutes**. These laws dispensed with the notice requirement in specified searches.

---

[110] Horton v. California, 110 S. Ct. 2301 (1990); Abel v. United States, 362 U.S. 217, 238, 80 S. Ct. 683, 697, 4 L. Ed. 2d 668 (1960); State v. Wesson, 260 Iowa 781, 150 N.W.2d 284 (1967).

[111] Miller v. United States, 357 U.S. 301, 313, 78 S. Ct. 1190, 2 L. Ed. 2d 1332 (1958).

In addition to preservation of evidence, the "no-knock" enactments reflected a concern for the safety of police officers in situations in which the officer was investigating a suspect or gang known to be dangerous, and the officer's announcement of his purpose might result in a fusillade of bullets through the door.

It should be noted that unannounced forcible entry may be made under the "judicial authorization" pattern if the magistrate inserts a direction to this effect in the search warrant; thus, an officer must present to the court his or her reasons for requesting the "no-knock" procedure, and prior judicial authorization must be obtained before the customary announcement rule may be dispensed with. In some parts of the country, a competing and broader approach to "no-knock" appeared in certain legislation. Under this approach, "no-knock" authority was significantly widened, allowing unannounced forcible entry if the officer discovered the need for using the procedure upon his arrival at the scene of the arrest or search and not requiring return to the judge or magistrate to obtain a warrant sanctioning an unannounced entry.

The Supreme Court has accorded significant attention to police "no-knock" practices. In *Wilson v. Arkansas*[112] the Supreme Court held that the common law doctrine that requires a law enforcement officer to knock and announce his or her presence and authority prior to search "forms part of the reasonableness inquiry under the Fourth Amendment," in the general run of cases. In other words, unless there are exceptional circumstances, the officer who comes to a place to search must knock and announce his or her presence. What about drug cases? Under *Wilson*, how long must police wait after knocking before they break in? No bright line has been promulgated by the United States Supreme Court, which suggested that the time needed for the person inside to open the door would vary with the size of the residence. While it would take only five seconds or so to open a motel room door, it might take the occupant a couple of minutes to move through a townhouse. In a 2003 case, a wait of 20 seconds by police was deemed to be plenty. Police arrived at the defendant's two-bedroom apartment armed with a search warrant for cocaine. They knocked, announced why they were there, and waited 15 to 20 seconds. When there was no response, they broke open the door with a battering ram. As it turned out, the defendant was in the shower and did not hear the officers. Nonetheless, the quick entry was permitted because a longer lapse of time in drug cases would permit a drug dealer to "flush away the easily disposable cocaine."[113]

However, the Court leaves room for the proposition that all drug cases will not be treated the same, that some drug cases might demand quick entry while others do not require forcible entry. This occurred when the procedure used in executing a search warrant against felony drug activity was explored in *Richards v. Wisconsin*.[114] The Court held that it is unconstitutional for a state to create a

---

[112] 115 S. Ct. 1914 (1995).
[113] United States v. Banks, 124 S. Ct. 521 (2003).
[114] 117 S. Ct. 1416 (1997).

blanket exception to the "knock-and-announce" rule for felony drug cases, finding the force of *Wilson*, which mandates the knock-and-announce rule in the general run of cases, to be controlling. While the requirement can give way when danger to officers or destruction of evidence is present, a rule that officers are never required to knock and announce when executing a drug warrant is unconstitutional.

The Supreme Court looked at the forcible execution question again in *United States v. Ramirez*.[115] At issue was SWAT team conduct at Ramirez's residence after a loudspeaker announcement by police about a search warrant. They broke a window and pointed a gun through the opening. Ramirez and his family had been asleep. Awakened by the noise, Ramirez thought he was being burglarized and grabbed a pistol. Shots were exchanged with police. Asked whether the Fourth Amendment had been violated, the Supreme Court said no. Police were searching for an escaped prisoner named Shelby, thought to be in the Ramirez home. Although he was not there, the emergency nature of the situation supported the police action.

## § 2.3 Booking

Booking is an administrative step that is taken after arrest and involves entry on the police "blotter" at police headquarters of the person's name, the crime for which the arrest was made, and other relevant facts.[116] Fingerprinting and photographing may also occur.

Most courts have upheld the inventorying of items found on the arrestee's person as a part of the booking process. This rule has been held to cover vehicles in police custody in cases in which the inventory "was not a subterfuge to conduct an exploratory search but instead was a bona fide attempt" to secure the inventoried property. In 1996, in *Whren v. United States*[117] the Supreme Court defined "inventory search" to properly include search of property that has been lawfully seized and detained in order to ensure that it is harmless, to secure valuable items, and to protect against false claims of loss or damage. The Court warned that an inventory must not be used as a ruse for a general rummaging in order to discover incriminating evidence.

In *United States v. Edwards*,[118] paint had been chipped from a post office window when entry was attempted with a pry bar. The defendant was arrested for attempted breaking and entering. About 10 hours after his arrest his clothing was taken from him in order to inspect it for the paint chips. There was testimony that clothing was taken from prisoners and kept in official custody as

---

[115]  118 S. Ct. 29 (1997).

[116]  LAFAVE, ISRAEL, AND KING, CRIMINAL PROCEDURE § 1.4 (4th ed. 2004).

[117]  Whren v. United States, 116 S. Ct. 1769 (1996). Other cases emphasize the point. *See* Plitko v. State, 272 A.2d 669 (Md. App. 1971). Vehicle inventories, search of glove compartment of impounded car, see South Dakota v. Opperman, 428 U.S. 364 (1976).

[118]  415 U.S. 800, 94 S. Ct. 1234, 39 L. Ed. 2d 711 (1974), overruled on other grounds in United States v. Chadwick, 433 U.S. 1 (1977).

a routine custom. Paint chips on Edwards' clothing matched samples from the post office window. Edwards objected to the introduction of evidence derived from this process. The United States Supreme Court denied his claim. The Court pointed out that where a prisoner's clothing is taken shortly after his or her arrival at the jail as part of the administrative processing and held under the defendant's name in the "property room," it may be inspected without a warrant. It is also allowed when the property is not taken until sometime after incarceration:

> [O]nce the accused is lawfully arrested and is in custody, the effects in his possession at the place of detention that were subject to search at the time and place of his arrest may lawfully be searched and seized without a warrant even though a substantial period of time has elapsed between the arrest and subsequent administrative processing, on the one hand, and the taking of the property for use as evidence, on the other.

Ten years later, the Supreme Court again confirmed the propriety of removing and inventorying property found on the person of an arrestee. Further, it is not unreasonable for police, "as part of the routine procedure incident to incarcerating an arrested person, to search any container or article in his possession, in accordance with established inventory procedures."[119] However, locked suitcases found in impounded vehicles apparently fall outside this rule of ready inspection, at least where no uniform policy is in place governing this aspect of vehicle inventories. In *Florida v. Wells*,[120] all members of the Court agreed that the inventory of a locked suitcase found in an impounded vehicle was unlawful because "the Florida Highway Patrol had no policy whatever with respect to the opening of closed containers encountered during an inventory search." A search warrant would be needed, or uniform policies regulating such search adopted, in order to legitimate such entries. The ruling leaves undisturbed those cases authorizing impoundment of vehicles and general inventory of the contents. As a customary rule, inventory of automobiles should be conducted promptly after impoundment.

## § 2.4   Initial Appearance

Federal and state statutes require that an arrested person be promptly taken before a judicial officer. Undue delay can result in loss of evidence. These prompt appearance laws prohibit extended custodial retention of the accused, and usually the suspect should be presented to the magistrate in a matter of hours after arrest. However, permissible delay includes time for booking the suspect and the making of a report on the case to a member of the prosecutor's

---

[119]   Illinois v. Lafayette, 462 U.S. 640, 103 S. Ct. 2605 (1983) (warrantless search of defendant's shoulder bag).

[120]   495 U.S. 7, 110 S. Ct. 1632 (1990).

staff.[121] Permissible delay may also mean an overnight delay in areas where a magistrate is not readily available.

In the more serious cases, the prosecutor will prepare a **complaint** or preliminary information if the case is an appropriate one for prosecution, identifying the defendant and stating the charge against him. The complaint will be signed by the arresting officer or other complaining witness. When the defendant is presented before the magistrate, he or she must be informed of this charge. The defendant should also be informed of his or her right to a preliminary hearing and his or her right to counsel by the magistrate. Under some statutes the magistrate is required to advise the defendant of his or her right to remain silent.

Release on bail is a possibility for the defendant as a result of the magistrate's decision upon presentment of the accused. The magistrate sets bail at the initial appearance—evaluating relevant factors, including the nature and severity of the offense. In an appropriate case the defendant can be released on his or her own recognizance. However, the magistrate may require cash bail or a surety bond. The latter is frequently posted by a professional bondsman. Generally the bondsman who acts as a surety will require the defendant to pay the bondsman a bond premium equal to a certain percentage of the bond that is posted, often a cash amount equal to 10 percent of the bond. For example, if the judge sets bail at $5,000, the defendant may have to pay $500 for a surety bond in order to secure release. Bail is not automatic, however. It may be denied in capital cases, and even where set by the magistrate, the defendant may be unable to obtain release because of lack of funds.

The procedure described above, the initial appearance before the magistrate, is sometimes loosely referred to as an arraignment before the magistrate. The misnomer is unfortunate because no plea is entered in a felony or serious misdemeanor case at this proceeding, plea entry being reserved for the arraignment subsequently held before the trial judge. However, uncertainty continues to be spawned by judicial decisions and texts that refer to initial appearance before the magistrate as an arraignment. To avoid confusion, when arraignment in felony cases is referred to in this text, such reference is to the trial court proceeding and not the initial appearance of the defendant before the magistrate.

The variation on this theme is the petty misdemeanor, in which pleas are authorized at the first appearance. In these cases such appearance functions as an arraignment, and if the defendant pleads not guilty, he or she may be tried immediately. No preliminary hearing is held, that step being reserved for serious offenses (felony and high misdemeanor). The special aspects of misdemeanor prosecution are discussed in Chapter 10 of this text.

---

[121] *See* Mallory v. United States, 354 U.S. 449, 454-455, 77 S. Ct. 1356, 1 L. Ed. 2d 1479 (1957):

    The arrested person may, of course, be "booked" by police. . . . The duty enjoined upon arresting officers to arraign "without unnecessary delay" indicates that the command does not call for mechanical or automatic obedience. Circumstances may justify a brief delay between arrest and arraignment, as for instance, where the story volunteered by the accused is susceptible to quick verification through third parties.

## § 2.5    Preliminary Hearing: Basic Purpose

The basic purpose of the **preliminary examination or hearing**, which may be held at the time of the initial appearance but frequently occurs a few days later, is to test the following question: Is there probable cause to believe that a crime has been committed and that the defendant committed it? Put differently, would a reasonable person think that the defendant committed the crime charged in the complaint, based on the evidence presented by the government at the hearing? These are the questions the magistrate must ask himself or herself after the government completes presentation of its proof. A number of options can result at the preliminary hearing:

1.  If a reasonable belief of guilt is not generated in the magistrate's mind, the complaint against the defendant should be dismissed and the accused released.

2.  If the government's proof demonstrates probable cause, however, the magistrate should bind the defendant over for subsequent proceedings in the trial court.

3.  When the evidence presented at the preliminary hearing supports a lesser charge than that originally presented, the magistrate generally has authority to reduce the seriousness of the offense and bind the defendant over on the lesser crime.

Note that the government's evidence need not prove the case against the defendant beyond a reasonable doubt; the standard is somewhat lower, requiring instead that a reasonable belief of guilt be generated.

In the event that the magistrate finds insufficient probable cause and releases the accused, it is important to point out that the defendant generally remains subject to reprosecution. The double jeopardy protections have been construed to permit filing of charges following preliminary dismissal of the case against the accused.[122]

In addition to the basic purpose of the preliminary hearing noted in this section, it is frequently utilized by defense counsel for two other functions: discovery and fixing the testimony of government witnesses. These terms require amplification.

## § 2.6    Discovery

Statistics indicate that instances of dismissal of the government's case are infrequent at preliminary hearings. Why, then, do defense attorneys sometimes insist upon a hearing even though the prospects for winning dismissal of the

---

[122]  Double jeopardy is discussed in Chapter 9 *infra*.

case are slim at this stage? The answer is that the hearing provides the defense with an excellent chance to find out what evidence the government has against the defendant. In states where little other **pretrial discovery** of the government's case is allowed, the preliminary hearing affords the defendant a cardinal opportunity to cross-examine government witnesses in advance of trial.

In this connection, the burden of proof on the government at the hearing should be remembered. It is not proof beyond a reasonable doubt but rather proof of probable cause, a lesser standard. Accordingly, all the witnesses that the government intends to produce at trial need not testify at the hearing, only a sufficient number to develop probable cause. The prosecutor will frequently limit the witnesses with this in mind. In this way, wholesale fishing expeditions by the defense into the entirety of the government's evidence may be avoided. In addition, many states relax the rules of evidence at the preliminary hearing. In these states, an investigating officer can cover testimony of witnesses favorable to the government by reporting what they told him. This hearsay evidence is prohibited once the government's case finally goes to trial before a jury, but its allowance to some degree at the preliminary hearing serves to further restrict discovery of the details of the government's case by the interrogating defense lawyer.

In federal practice, a 1997 rule change opens fresh discovery opportunities. After a witness testifies on direct examination, the opposing party may request any written or recorded statement made by the witness prior to the hearing. For example, a witness to a bank robbery may have provided police with a statement outlining his observations of the robbery. After the witness testifies for the prosecution at the hearing, the defense may obtain the witness's statement. This is pursuant to Federal Rule of Criminal Procedure 26.2(g)(5).

## § 2.7 Detailing Government Testimony

Another use to which the defendant may put the preliminary hearing is that of freezing the testimony of prosecution witnesses. As will be developed later in the criminal trial chapter of this text, Chapter 6, a witness who makes statements at a preliminary hearing or elsewhere in advance of trial of a case may, when testifying later at the trial, be confronted with and contradicted by these statements, if they are inconsistent with his or her trial testimony. For this reason, defense counsel frequently examines the officer in detail at preliminary hearing to nail down his or her testimony, hoping that the officer will deviate from this account at trial. Because most hearings are recorded by a court reporter, a permanent record of the officer's testimony generally will be available. This record should be reviewed with care by the testifying officer prior to trial; in addition, opportunity should be afforded the officer prior to the preliminary hearing to confer with the government attorney handling the case, in order to avoid committing errors or creating misimpressions in the officer's testimony.

## § 2.8   Waiver of Hearing

The defendant may waive preliminary examination if the waiver is knowingly and intelligently made. The decision to do so is usually called for at first appearance. Waiver requires meaningful communication by the magistrate to the defendant of his or her right to a hearing, and an affirmative indication on the defendant's part of a desire to waive his or her right. Under the modern rule, waiver of the right to a hearing does not occur merely because the defendant is passive and fails to demand it;[123] he or she must freely elect to waive after being given a choice in the matter. When a waiver of the hearing occurs, there is no contest on the issue of probable cause and the defendant is automatically bound over to the trial court. On a national basis, statistics indicate that preliminary hearings are waived in about one-half of the cases brought before committing magistrates.

## § 2.9   Does the Defendant Have a Constitutional Right to a Hearing?

As outlined in § 2.8, a defendant can waive his or her right to a preliminary hearing, but can the defendant be foreclosed from his hearing opportunity in any other manner? In jurisdictions using the grand jury, the hearing is sometimes eliminated when the grand jury indicts the defendant prior to the scheduled hearing. Under numerous authorities, such a grand jury indictment establishes probable cause and thus eliminates the need for a magistrate's hearing to investigate the probable cause question.[124] The practice of some prosecutors to delay the preliminary hearing, meanwhile submitting their case to the grand jury and obtaining an indictment in the interim, has triggered a major legal debate over whether the defendant has a constitutional right to a preliminary hearing. Although good arguments may be made urging that there should be a general constitutional right to a preliminary hearing, this position has been undercut by case authority and by the Federal Magistrates Act.[125] However, some states have special constitutional or statutory provisions requiring preliminary hearings in their jurisdiction.[126] In addition, a decision of the United States Supreme Court requires a probable cause hearing (although per-

---

[123]   *See* Brookhart v. Janis, 384 U.S. 1, 86 S. Ct. 1245, 16 L. Ed. 2d 314 (1965).

[124]   *See* 18 U.S.C. § 3060(e) (1976) (no preliminary examination required in federal courts if, subsequent to initial appearance of the defendant before a magistrate, an indictment is returned). See also Dubose v. State, 369 S.E.2d 924 (Ga. App. 1988) (failure of court to hold a probable cause hearing provides no ground for appellate review once there has been an indictment and conviction). Indictment is defined and discussed in Chapter 4 of this text.

[125]   18 U.S.C. § 3060 (1976); Sciortino v. Zampano, 385 F.2d 132 (2d Cir. 1967), cert. denied, 390 U.S. 906 (1968); Bowman v. Bordenkircher, 522 F.2d 209 (4th Cir. 1975); Commonwealth v. Crowe, 488 N.E.2d 780 (Mass. App. 1986).

[126]   Several states make preliminary hearing mandatory when prosecution is allowed on information rather than indictment.

haps not a full-blown preliminary hearing) under the federal constitution in specified situations. In the case of *Gerstein v. Pugh*,[127] the Court was concerned about prisoners who were arrested without a warrant, held in custody, and ultimately tried under a prosecutor's **information** (as opposed to an indictment). The case involved Florida prisoners, and in Florida a prosecutor could charge non-capital crimes by information, without prior preliminary hearing and without obtaining **leave of court**. The United States Supreme Court ruled that this prosecutorial judgment standing alone did not provide a sufficient safeguard against potentially unfounded (and perhaps extended) detention of defendants jailed before trial. After arrest, such defendants are entitled to a probable cause determination by someone like a magistrate, who is independent of police and prosecution. This may come at the suspect's first appearance before the magistrate; it may be an adjunct of the bail-setting procedure; or it could be handled through a traditional preliminary hearing. But for suspects who are held in jail before trial, as opposed to those out on bail, "the Fourth Amendment requires a timely judicial determination of probable cause as a prerequisite to detention."[128]

Impact to this point was added by the Supreme Court's opinion in a subsequent holding.[129] For defendants arrested without warrants and regarding whom no probable cause determination had thus been made by a neutral magistrate, a 48-hour rule was invoked—a jurisdiction complies with the promptness requirement when a judicial inquiry into probable cause occurs within 48 hours of arrest. The U.S. Supreme Court observed that such a determination should occur "as soon as is reasonably feasible, but in no event later than 48 hours after arrest." Another case provided further support for the 48-hour rule. A defendant was held for four days prior to a finding of probable cause to hold him for a preliminary hearing. Because detaining an individual for more than 48 hours prior to judicial confirmation of probable cause violates the defendant's rights, evidence taken from a defendant at the fourth day of such a hold must be excluded.[130]

The magistrate's preliminary inquiry into probable cause under the 48-hour rule is often less formal than a full-blown preliminary hearing. It may be accomplished by the judge reviewing an officer's sworn affidavit setting out the facts. The court may then note its conclusion on the court's docket or in the case file, ordering that the accused be held for further processing or perhaps taking other appropriate action.

---

[127] 420 U.S. 103, 95 S. Ct. 854, 43 L. Ed. 2d 54 (1975). Discussing the effect of *Gerstein* violations, *see* Thomas, *The Poisoned Fruit of Pretrial Detention*, 61 N.Y.U. L. REV. 413 (1986).

[128] 420 U.S. at 126, 95 S. Ct. at 869, 43 L. Ed. 2d at 72. The Supreme Court makes clear that while a review of probable cause is indicated, a full adversary hearing is not required. Also, the probable cause procedures are not required when the arrest of the prisoner is made under a warrant because "a person arrested under a warrant would have received a prior judicial determination of probable cause." Finally, the Gerstein rule applies only to suspects who suffer "significant restraints on liberty" before trial.

[129] County of Riverside v. McLaughlin, 500 U.S. 413, 111 S. Ct. 1661 (1991).

[130] Powell v. Nevada, 114 S. Ct. 1280 (1994).

## § 2.10   Does the Prosecution Have a Right to a Hearing?

Before advancing to resolution of the question of the prosecutor's right to insist upon a preliminary hearing, we will consider the instances in which a prosecutor might want a hearing to be held. It has been previously noted that hearings are valued by the defense but are rarely welcomed by the prosecutor. In certain circumstances, however, the hearing may be advantageous to the government. For example, there may be cases in which prosecution witnesses are aged or likely to leave the jurisdiction. The hearing will preserve the testimony of these witnesses, and if a witness is unable to be at the trial or cannot be found, the transcript of the preliminary hearing testimony may be read to the jury.[131]

What if the defendant waives preliminary hearing, but the prosecutor would like to proceed with it? Is there a right on the part of the state to insist upon a preliminary examination in these circumstances? Notwithstanding strong arguments that (1) the hearing is for the sole benefit of the accused, and (2) techniques other than preliminary hearing are available to the state to perpetuate government testimony for trial, a few court decisions give the government a right to demand preliminary examination.[132] This right is justified on reciprocal grounds, under the theory that the prosecutor should be entitled to explore the sufficiency of his or her evidence just as the defense is entitled to do. In certain cases a further advantage to the government may be the opportunity to demonstrate the strength of its evidence, thereby convincing the defendant of the futility of going to trial, inducing a guilty plea.

## § 2.11   Time of Hearing

Usually statutes or judicial interpretations of statutes require that the preliminary examination take place within a reasonable time. In certain jurisdictions this has been construed to mean having a hearing within a specified number of days from the time the accused was initially presented to the magistrate. Because the hearing is basically designed to guard against extended detention of persons improperly incarcerated without probable cause, numerous adjournments at the government's request are not favored.

Federal prosecutors are controlled by the Federal Magistrates Act, which requires preliminary hearing within 10 days after initial appearance before the magistrate. If a jailed person is not indicted or given a preliminary hearing within that period, he or she is entitled to be discharged from custody. This provision is designed to assure that the probable cause question will be

---

[131]   On the hearsay use of prior recorded testimony, see § 6.14(3) of this text.

[132]   22 C.J.S. CRIMINAL LAW, § 333 (1961). In some states the same result is reached by requiring the prosecutor's consent before a hearing may be waived. Other courts deny any prosecutor participation in the hearing decision.

inquired into, either by hearing or through the grand jury, within a reasonable time after the initial appearance of a prisoner. "No citizen's liberty ought to be restrained for any considerable period of time without a determination by either a judicial officer or a grand jury that probable cause exists for that restraint."[133]

## § 2.12   Public or Private Hearing

As in a trial, the defendant may ask the magistrate to separate and exclude from the courtroom prospective witnesses until they testify at the preliminary examination. This prevents a witness from hearing in advance the testimony of other witnesses, and the prosecutor may request similar exclusion of defense witnesses.

A separate question from whether witnesses may be excluded until they testify is the question of closing a hearing, and excluding the public. The United States Supreme Court has spoken on the point, and is hostile to the notion that hearings generally should be "held privately."[134] A preliminary hearing is sufficiently like a trial to require public access, said the Court. "The established and widespread tradition of open preliminary hearings among the states . . . is controlling here."[135]

In the face of concerns that open hearings and press coverage will in some drastic cases prejudice a defendant's fair trial rights, the Court has framed a test for occasionally closing such hearings: "[T]he preliminary hearing shall be closed only if specific findings are made demonstrating that, first, there is a substantial probability that the defendant's right to a fair trial will be prejudiced by publicity that closure would prevent and, second, reasonable alternatives to closure cannot adequately protect the defendant's fair trial rights."

A final question, distinct from the issue of whether the press or public may attend a hearing, is electronic coverage of the proceeding. Will the court allow televising of a preliminary hearing? In prominent or sensational cases, such as the O.J. Simpson case in California, there was great public interest in and national television coverage of the hearing. A number of states are less permissive in allowing cameras in preliminary proceedings.

Although numerous states have recently relaxed restrictions on filming of trials in the courtroom, other jurisdictions and courts are concerned with unduly publicizing cases and bar photography or television filming of proceedings. In the latter group of states, restrictions on filming apply when the

---

[133] Report No. 371, Senate Judiciary Committee Report on 18 U.S.C. § 3060 (1968), 90th Cong. 1st Sess. Some states provide that a defendant in custody shall have his or her case dismissed if he or she is not given a hearing within a certain period, as within 10 days after first appearance. The defendant may waive this right. On the need for an informal probable cause review, as well as discussion of whether a prosecutor's information cuts off hearing rights, *see* Gerstein v. Pugh, § 2.9 of this text.
[134] El Vocero v. Puerto Rico, 113 S. Ct. 2004 (1993).
[135] 113 S. Ct. at 2006.

litigation is in the preliminary hearing phase as well as at the trial of the case to a jury. Federal magistrate courts also follow this rule and prohibit filming of federal preliminary hearings.

## § 2.13  Evidence and Objections

**Hearsay evidence** is frequently introduced on behalf of the prosecution at preliminary hearings. While some jurisdictions exclude hearsay during these preliminary examinations, the general rule renders admissible this form of proof. Thus, hearsay may come into evidence to support probable cause in the majority of American jurisdictions.

Physical evidence seized from the accused or his or her environs at the time of arrest, or evidence of a suspect's admissions or confessions, are normally admissible at preliminary hearings. Most magistrates take the position that at a preliminary hearing they will not throw out evidence based on constitutional challenges. Defense objections to evidence allegedly seized by police in violation of the suspect's Fourth or Fifth Amendment rights will be entertained at a special **suppression hearing** in the trial court, and are reserved for that proceeding.[136]

The approach in federal courts is revealed in Rule 5.1 of the Federal Rules of Criminal Procedure (2004):

> (e)  **Hearing and Finding.** At the preliminary hearing, the defendant may cross-examine adverse witnesses and may introduce evidence *but may not object to evidence on the ground that it was unlawfully acquired.* If the magistrate judge finds probable cause to believe an offense has been committed and the defendant committed it, the magistrate judge must promptly require the defendant to appear for further proceedings. (emphasis added)

The approach of the police officer in providing testimony at the preliminary hearing is important. The officer has the right to go over the case with the prosecutor prior to the hearing, and he or she should review it with the prosecutor when this is possible. The officer should never hesitate to admit, if asked by defense counsel, that he or she has conferred with the prosecutor concerning the facts of the case. In terms of demeanor as a witness at the preliminary hearing, the officer should strive to develop, maintain, and convey a fair and impartial attitude toward the case. General rules for being an effective witness in court, covered in § 6.36 of this book, should guide the officer during preliminary hearing. One of the guidelines suggested there, which appears especially recommended in view of the discovery purpose to which defense counsel may put the hearing, is the emphasis on short and concise answers. The prosecutor can ask the questions necessary to bring the essential and rel-

---

[136]  See FED. R. CRIM. P. 5.1(a). On suppression hearings, see § 6.3(2), *infra*.

evant information to the attention of the magistrate. Volunteering information not required by either a prosecutor's question or a cross-examination inquiry can be damaging.

## § 2.14  Witnesses for the Defense

The government's burden of presenting probable cause proof at preliminary hearing has been discussed. Is the defendant required to present evidence at preliminary hearing? The answer is no, but in many jurisdictions the defendant is entitled to do so if he or she wishes. Thus, for example, defense counsel may call witnesses to show that the defendant was elsewhere than at the scene of the crime charged when it was committed. Occasionally, defense counsel will **subpoena** witnesses hostile to the defense (witnesses whom the prosecutor expects to use at trial but who are not scheduled to testify at the preliminary hearing) to discover what they have to say. This tactic is closely scrutinized by the courts, and several court decisions that have considered this approach prevented defense counsel from employing it. As stated in one of these, while the defense lawyer may call witnesses to help the defendant's cause, there is no constitutional or statutory right to call witnesses at a preliminary hearing simply for the purpose of discovery.[137]

A final consideration is whether the defendant will testify. Although the accused has this right in many jurisdictions, the defendant will ordinarily not avail himself or herself of this opportunity because such action would expose the defendant to sweeping government cross-examination. And the government is prohibited from simply calling the accused as a witness. The defendant has a privilege to refuse to testify, and this protects the accused at preliminary hearings as well as at trial of the case.

In summary, the prosecution will present its key witnesses at the hearing and the defense will limit its response to cross-examination of those witnesses. No defense witnesses are usually called. Traditional defense strategy advises against subjecting defense witnesses to cross-examination in pretrial proceedings.[138]

## § 2.15  Effect of Dismissal of Complaint

If a magistrate finds that the government has not established probable cause and dismisses the complaint, does this necessarily end the case? Generally no, for even after such discharge the defendant remains subject to reprosecution. The double jeopardy clause is not violated should the government file another complaint against the defendant or submit the dismissed case to a grand jury. The law on this point was aptly summarized in *Collins v. Loisel*:[139]

---

[137]  Williams v. Commonwealth, 160 S.E.2d 781, 784 (Va. 1968).
[138]  LAFAVE, ISRAEL, AND KING, CRIMINAL PROCEDURE § 1.3 (4th ed. 2004).
[139]  262 U.S. 426, 429, 43 S. Ct. 618, 67 L. Ed. 1062 (1923).

"The constitutional provision against double jeopardy can have no application unless a prisoner has, theretofore, been placed on trial. . . . The preliminary examination of one arrested on suspicion of a crime is not a trial; and his discharge by the magistrate upon such examination is not an acquittal."

Modern rules of criminal procedure apply this principle in today's prosecutions. The controlling guidelines for federal courts are spelled out in Rule 5.1 of the Federal Rules of Criminal Procedure:

> **(f)  Discharging the Defendant.** If the magistrate judge finds no probable cause to believe an offense has been committed or that the defendant committed it, the magistrate judge must dismiss the complaint and discharge the defendant. A discharge does not preclude the government from later prosecuting the defendant for the same offense.

In practical terms, it may be necessary and desirable to develop new evidence between the time of dismissal of the case and the swearing out of a second complaint, where renewed presentation of the cause to a magistrate is contemplated. The magistrate may believe that because the original evidence was not sufficiently meritorious to establish probable cause, unless something new is added to the mix, the case continues to be a defective one.[140]

## § 2.16   Defendant's Right to Appointed Counsel

It is unquestioned that the defendant has a right to be represented by a lawyer when he or she has retained one to assist him or her at the preliminary hearing. Numerous state statutes require that magistrates inform defendants of their right to appear before the magistrate assisted by such attorneys. A more difficult question arises when the defendant has no funds to hire a lawyer: Must the magistrate appoint a defense lawyer to serve without financial charge to the accused?[141] While many courts make such appointments mandatory, an important question relates to whether the federal constitution requires states that do not presently appoint lawyers to do so.

The defendant has a right to assigned counsel at his or her preliminary hearing when the preliminary hearing is a "critical stage" of the prosecution.[142] Precisely when the preliminary hearing constitutes a critical stage for these purposes was clarified in a series of decisions. If the magistrate can accept a guilty plea to a felony charge and dispose of the cause, the hearing stage is crucial. But what about the many states where the magistrate has no such power? Are preliminary hearings in these jurisdictions sufficiently critical to require assigned counsel for the defendant?

---

[140]  On refilings, *see* People v. Uhlemann, 511 P.2d 609 (Cal. 1973). Some states may require any refiling to be before a different magistrate. *See*, e.g., In re Riggins, 254 A.2d 616 (Pa. 1969).

[141]  *See* Rule 5(c), FED. R. CRIM. P.

[142]  KLOTTER, KANOVITZ AND KANOVITZ, CONSTITUTIONAL LAW § 8.3 (10th ed. 2005), citing White v. Maryland, 373 U.S. 59, 83 S. Ct. 1050, 10 L. Ed. 2d 193 (1963).

In a case from Iowa, the United States Supreme Court decided *Long v. District Court*.[143] This opinion pointed up one approach to the "critical stage" question. Under the state practice involved, magistrates were not permitted to dispose of felony cases at the magistrate level. However, the fact that prisoner Long had attempted to plead guilty when he appeared before the magistrate shortly after his arrest for larceny (he claimed he was intoxicated at the time) was brought up by the prosecution at his later larceny trial, shown to the jury, and used against him to help obtain his conviction. Because his attempts to plead guilty could be used as an admission of guilt upon trial of the case, the preliminary hearing was conceded to be a critical stage by the prosecution. As such, it required the presence of counsel on behalf of the defendant.

*Coleman v. Alabama*[144] significantly expanded the "critical stage" concept by holding that a preliminary hearing is critical if evidence is developed that the defendant may use to impeach witnesses later called at trial of the case. As a critical stage in the proceeding where probable cause is determined and bail is fixed, a defendant who cannot afford a lawyer is entitled to appointed counsel.

There may be practical reasons for *prosecutors* to insist that penniless defendants receive a free lawyer. No evidence drawn from a preliminary hearing may be used against the accused unless the defendant had a right to counsel at the hearing. What if a key government witness, one whom the prosecutor is counting on to win a verdict, is ill, feeble, or elderly? If this witness is not around for subsequent trial of the case, her preliminary hearing transcript may be read to the jury only if the defendant had a lawyer. A 2004 decision from the United States Supreme Court so holds.[145]

[143] 385 U.S. 192 n.1, 87 S. Ct. 362 n.1, 17 L. Ed. 2d 290 n.1 (1966).
[144] 399 U.S. 1, 90 S. Ct. 1999, 26 L. Ed. 2d 387 (1970). *Coleman* was held nonretroactive in *Adams v. Illinois*, 406 U.S. 278, 92 S. Ct. 916, 31 L. Ed. 2d 202 (1972).
[145] Crawford v. Washington, 124 S. Ct. 1354 (2004).

# Bail

# 3

## Chapter Outline

## § 3.1  Why a Bail System?

### 1.  History of Bail

The practice of releasing a defendant after his or her arrest and permitting him or her to remain free until trial is an ancient one. Under the English common law, which established the pattern for American courts, defendants were released subject only to conditions designed to ensure that a defendant would appear at his or her trial. Specific reasons supported this pretrial freedom for accused persons: (1) fairness to the accused who, responsible for preparing his or her defense at his or her trial, was prevented from doing so if held in jail; (2) avoidance of inordinate imprisonment suffered by defendants eventually found not guilty in an era when some accused persons had to wait months for the judge to arrive and trial to begin.

Similar considerations support American bail practice. The historical basis underlying bail, as well as the evolution of the modern bail system, was aptly traced by one commentator.[1]

> The precursor of the American system of bail originated in England during the thirteenth century. The release of an accused before trial was imperative under the procedures of the English law of that period. The incarcerated defendant was unable to prepare adequately for trial. Trial for minor offenses was in a court of record which met only twice a year, and more serious offenses were not tried until the arrival of justices, which often meant a delay of years. A defendant could, therefore, be imprisoned before trial for a period in excess of the sentence that he would receive if found guilty of the offense with which he was charged. Nevertheless, release of an accused before trial

---

[1]   Note, 53 Iowa L. Rev. 170 (1967) (footnotes omitted).

was not mandatory, but subject to the discretion of the sheriff. The sheriff, in exercising this discretion, was to consider the gravity of the charge, the weight of the evidence, and the character of the defendant. Release in all situations was conditioned upon a promise that the accused would appear for trial, given either by the accused or a third party.

The appearance of defects in this system of bail prompted its alteration. Restrictions were placed upon the discretion of the sheriff. In addition, bail was made available only if a friend or relative of the accused promised to forfeit a specified sum of money to the court if the accused failed to appear for trial. This latter development gave rise to the keystone of the American system of bail—the bail bond. Initially, the English practice of requiring a personal relationship between the accused and his surety was adopted in the United States. However, because the private surety often did not have the financial resources to conduct widespread searches for fugitive bailees, this practice was soon abandoned. In its stead appeared the commercial bail bondsman. The bailment or delivery of an accused to the bailbondsman was brought about by the execution of a bond conditioned upon the re-delivery of the accused to custody at the time and place stated in the bond. In return for this service, the accused was charged a premium, generally proportioned to the amount of the bond. If the bailbondsman was unable to return his charge, the bond was forfeited. This method of shifting the responsibility and expense of assuring the presence of an accused at trial from society to the accused and his surety remains an integral part of the present American system of bail.

As the above passage suggests, **bail** is designed to assure the presence of a defendant at trial. This is the core philosophy of requiring bail. If the defendant has roots in the community—a home, family, and job in the place where the trial is to be held—the Bill of Rights of the United States Constitution directs that bail should not be set at a high figure simply to keep the defendant in jail. The **Eighth Amendment** to the Constitution provides that "Excessive bail shall not be required . . ."

The United States Supreme Court defined excessive bail in *Stack v. Boyle*.[2] The Court first spoke of the principles behind pretrial release of the defendant: "This traditional right to freedom before conviction permits the unhampered preparation of a defense, and serves to prevent the infliction of punishment prior to conviction. . . . Unless this right to bail before trial is preserved, the presumption of innocence, secured only after centuries of struggle, would lose its meaning." The Court pointed out that bail should be set in an amount sufficient to secure the defendant's presence at trial. "Bail set at a figure higher than an amount reasonably calculated to fulfill this purpose is 'excessive' under the Eighth Amendment."

---

[2]    342 U.S. 1, 72 S. Ct. 1, 96 L. Ed. 3 (1951).

## 2. Amount of Bail

What constitutes excessive bail is subject to varying interpretations in specific cases around the country. Probably much depends upon local conditions, diverse views as to the severity of particular crimes, the record and history of the individual defendant and other related factors. Dramatic differences in treatment sometimes mark the process. Decisions in state and federal courts illustrate the point. For example, bail was deemed reasonable and appropriate when it was set at:

- $1,500,000 in Texas when the defendant was charged with three counts of capital murder in the armed robbery of a restaurant.[3]

- $25,000 in Florida in a case involving battery on a law enforcement officer.[4]

- $600,000 when the accused was charged with possession of a controlled substance with intent to illegally deliver it.[5]

- $90,000 for three counts of theft by taking in Georgia ($30,000 for each theft offense). A police lieutenant testified that a high bond was necessary because police suspected the defendant of shooting his mother, police were concerned for the safety of the defendant's father if the defendant returned home, and there was a chance the accused might leave town to escape punishment for the thefts. The state supreme court ruled that the judge who sets bail "is to consider chiefly the probability that the accused, if freed, will appear at trial; other factors to be considered include the accused's ability to pay, the seriousness of the offense, and the accused's character and reputation."[6]

- $750,000 in a case of conspiracy to possess marijuana with intent to distribute it. Before trial bail was originally set at $1,000,000, but was reduced to $750,000 upon defendant's application. The United States Supreme Court adjudicated the propriety of continuing this amount after defendant's trial and conviction pending appeal of his case. Bail was continued in the stated amount by the Supreme Court.[7]

- $350,000 and $1,000,000 in connection with two indictments charging the defendant with 13 firearms violations. The defendant had close ties to Mexico, there was no extradition treaty in force at the time providing for the return to the United States of citizens of Mexico who were wanted for crimes here, and the place of trial was Brownsville, Texas, a city close to Mexico. Defendant had claims upon substantial financial resources. A United States magistrate fixed bail in the amounts stated in

---

[3]   Ex parte Henson, 131 S.W.3d 645 (Tex. Ct. App. 2004).

[4]   Henley v. Jenne, 796 So. 2d 1273 (Fla. Dist. Ct. App. 2001).

[5]   Ex parte Rodriguez, 148 S.W.3d 496, 2004 Tex. Ct. App. Lexis 5018 (2004).

[6]   Spence v. State, 313 S.E.2d 475, 478 (Ga. 1984).

[7]   Mecom v. United States, 434 U.S. 1340 (1977).

this paragraph. The defendant sought to reduce bail by filing motions in the district court. The district court found the amount of bail set by the federal magistrate not to be excessive, and the Court of Appeals affirmed.[8]

- $1 million in a case in which the accused was arrested in a domestic violence incident. There was concern that if the accused got out of jail he might cause harm to the victim or her children.[9]

- $450,000 for charges of jumping bail, failing to appear in court when required, and tampering with evidence. This defendant had been previously charged with murder, and failed to appear even though he had posted $300,000 bail. He was ultimately located, tried, and acquitted of the murder, but was subsequently charged for bail jumping. The high amount of bail was justified, in part, on the ground that the defendant's family possessed "tremendous wealth."[10]

However, bail was ruled too high and deemed excessive when it was set at:

- $5,000 in Vermont when the defendant was charged with alleged sale of marijuana.[11]

- $1,000,000 in a case involving unlawful delivery of a controlled substance. Bond in such a large amount was excessive for a defendant who stated he had $1,000 available to make bail and that his only assets consisted of a Camaro valued at $750, and who had never been convicted of an offense in the United States. The Court of Appeals reduced bail to $250,000.[12]

- $100,000 imposed by a Mississippi judge on a defendant charged with aggravated assault. The Mississippi Supreme Court found the defendant to be indigent and without funds, and that the trial judge erred in the bail decision by setting it too high.[13]

- $150,000 in a murder case was excessive with respect to an indigent defendant who was a lifelong resident of the state and had numerous friends in the city, had no criminal record, and owned a house prior to incarceration.[14]

The foregoing list of rulings illustrates the tremendous variation in bail amounts depending on the nature of the charge, the financial circumstances of

---

[8]   United States v. Montemayor, 666 F.2d 235 (5th Cir. 1982).
[9]   Galen v. County of Los Angeles, 322 F. Supp. 2d 1045 (C.D. Cal. 2004).
[10]  Ex parte Durst, 148 S.W.2d 496, 2004 Texas App. Lexis 7560 (Tex. Ct. App. 2004).
[11]  State v. Lake, 325 A.2d 1 (Vt. 1974). This was the ruling notwithstanding testimony that the accused would, if given the chance, "kill the SOB who turned him in."
[12]  Ex parte Bonilla, 742 S.W.2d 743 (Tex. Ct. App. 1987).
[13]  Clay v. State, 757 So. 2d 236 (Miss. 2000).
[14]  State v. Duff, 563 A.2d 258 (Vt. 1989).

the defendant, and the part of the country where bail is set. $1.5 million was deemed a proper bail in a Texas murder case, but $150,000 was excessive for a murder in Vermont. In California a domestic violence incident resulted in $1 million bail, while a Mississippi assault defendant's bail set at $100,000 was too high. In addition to geographical variations, some judges setting bail have individual propensities for setting high bail in certain cases. There are judges who see drug cases as especially heinous, for example, while for others it is domestic assaults. Perhaps the most dominant factor is the character and history of the accused person.

As these rulings demonstrate, in major cases the amount of bail is a particular decision which must be shaped in each prosecution to the circumstances of the alleged offender.

### 3. Dangerousness of the Accused

What about the case of a person with community roots, one likely to show up for his trial, but who is also potentially dangerous and poses a threat to public safety if released after arrest? While some courts use this factor to set a high bail and confine a defendant before trial, the decisions of the United States Supreme Court suggest that a different method must be found to restrain a combative defendant. As stated in *Stack v. Boyle*, the function of bail is limited, its narrow aim being simply to assure the defendant's appearance when the case comes up in court. Preventive detention is quite a different concept and is treated in § 3.8. A federal law enacted in 1984 brings this issue before the courts. The Comprehensive Crime Control Act permits federal judges to consider the danger posed to the community by the accused in setting bail conditions. There is power to deny bail altogether where the government proves by clear and convincing evidence that no conditions of release will reasonably assure the safety of the community and the appearance of the defendant at trial. However, when judges are inclined to deny liberty before trial based primarily or exclusively on a defendant's dangerousness, the defendant is accorded a special hearing on this issue. At the hearing, the arrestee is entitled to dispute the government's characterization of the defendant as a danger to society.

### 4. Application to States

As indicated earlier in this section of the text, a major provision of the United States Constitution referring to bail is the Eighth Amendment, which provides: "Excessive bail shall not be required, nor excessive fines imposed, nor cruel and unusual punishments inflicted." Does this provision limit and control the size of bail in state cases as well as in federal tribunals? In *Schilb v. Kuebel*,[15] Justice Blackmun observed: "Bail, of course, is basic to our system of law . . . and the Eighth Amendment's proscription of excessive bail has

---

[15] 404 U.S. 357 (1971).

been assumed to have application to the states through the Fourteenth Amendment." Urging that the Amendment, including the fines clause, applies in its entirety to the states, see Justice O'Connor's concurring opinion in *Browning-Ferris Industries v. Kelco Disposal, Inc.*[16]

What this means is that both local as well as federal judges must be mindful of the need to avoid setting bail in excessive amounts. Bail should be appropriately adjusted to the needs of the justice system as well as the circumstances of the offense and the offender.

## § 3.2   Cases Subject to Bail

Most states consider felonies to be **bailable offenses**. However, in states where selected felonies are potentially punishable by death or life imprisonment, these felonies present situations in which the courts can deny bail altogether under some state court rules. In such cases the magistrate or judge has the power to refuse to set bail. This action is frequently authorized where the defendant is charged with murder and the likelihood of a first degree murder conviction seems great. The theory behind denying bail in such cases is that the severity of the punishment is so monumental that there is great likelihood that the defendant will flee the jurisdiction once released on bail before trial.[15] Several authorities emphasize that even in this situation bail is not denied because the defendant may be a dangerous person, but rather because of the possibility that he will not appear when scheduled at his trial.

Beyond capital cases, how far may states go in denying bail to accused persons? Can serious noncapital felonies be placed in the category of crimes not subject to bail? The question has special impact for jurisdictions that do not allow capital punishment. There is authority for denying bail rights in important noncapital crimes—serious felonies that are not punishable by death.[17] A prime example exists in states without capital punishment. Judges in these states may order defendants held without bail in homicide cases, and in aggravated murders, judges in such jurisdictions are often required by law to deny bail.

To summarize, when a defendant is charged with a crime, he or she has the right to have bail set, and set in a reasonable amount. The exception to this rule occurs when the defendant is charged with a very serious felony, like a murder. In many states the judge has discretion in such cases to deny bail altogether. The comments previously made in connection with the defendant's right to bail control bail practice before the defendant is tried. Once the defendant has pled guilty or has been tried and convicted, the right to bail terminates in felony cases. Thus, while a defendant has a constitutional right to a reasonable bail before trial in most cases, after conviction the situation changes.[18] Post-trial bail is a matter of privilege and must be specially requested by the defendant.

---

[16] 109 S. Ct. 2909, 2925 (1989).
[17] Sistrunk v. Lyons, 646 F.2d 64 (3d Cir. 1981).
[18] United States v. Bynum, 344 F. Supp. 647 (S.D.N.Y. 1972).

Federal statutory law provides a mechanism by which a defendant may obtain release from custody pending sentencing or appeal in the general run of cases. In misdemeanors, the accused may still insist that bail be set where an appeal is taken, as a general rule.[19]

Respecting felony appeals, the fact that a defendant is appealing his or her conviction does not necessarily save him or her from incarceration in the state penitentiary while the appeal is pending. Many prisoners serve the early portion of their sentence while awaiting argument and decision on the appeal. The way for a prisoner to avoid pre-decision imprisonment is to obtain admission to bail pending appeal, which stays the execution of the sentence. As indicated, the defendant has no absolute right to such bail; however, many states permit the trial judge to admit the defendant to bail on appeal, in the sound discretion of the judge. During such freedom, restrictions on the travel of the defendant will often be imposed. However, wrestling with travel restrictions is frequently avoided by the judge's decision to simply deny bail on appeal. Denial of bail is the norm, save for exceptional cases, for a number of reasons. Factors that militate against allowing a defendant his freedom include the potential risk that the defendant will flee, that the appeal appears devoid of merit and is only taken for delay; or that the appellant, if released, would pose a danger to the community.[20]

Where the defendant is not likely to flee and is considered nondangerous, he or she may be continued on trial bail after conviction, although the usual practice is to increase bail from the pretrial figure when it is allowed pending an appellate court decision. The federal pattern specifies the measure of proof on the flight issue. Federal law provides that if a person has been found guilty and sentenced to a term of imprisonment, bail shall be discontinued and the person imprisoned unless the sentencing judge finds the person unlikely to flee and nondangerous. The first element of 18 U.S.C. § 3143(b) places on the defendant the burden of showing "by clear and convincing evidence that he is not likely to flee or pose a danger to the safety of any other person or the community. . . ." The judicial officer must also find, in order to allow the defendant to remain free pending appeal, that "the appeal is not for the purpose of delay and raises a substantial question of law or fact that is likely to result in [a successful appeal for the accused]."[21]

The issue of the availability of bail for defendants convicted of serious crimes can command wide attention. The eyes of the world focused on the case of two Los Angeles police officers, Sergeant Stacey C. Koon and Officer Laurence M. Powell, who were convicted of violating the civil rights of Rodney King. The earlier acquittal of Koon, Powell, and two fellow officers on all criminal charges in a 1992 California state proceeding led to several days of deadly rioting in Los Angeles. In the federal action, Koon and Powell were

---

[19]   E.g., PA. R. CRIM. P. 521 B.

[20]   *See* Chambers v. Mississippi, 405 U.S. 1205, 92 S. Ct. 754, 30 L. Ed. 2d 773 (1972) (Powell, J.); Harris v. United States, 404 U.S. 1232, 92 S. Ct. 10, 30 L. Ed. 2d 25 (1971) (Douglas, J.).

[21]   In United States v. Buchbinder, 614 F. Supp. 1561 (D.C. Ill. 1985), the court ruled that the defendant bears the burden of proving these conditions before a court may grant bail pending appeal. Rule 46(c), FED. R. CRIM. P. contained such a provision.

convicted of criminal civil rights violations for assaulting King and they moved for bail pending appeal of their sentences.[22]

The federal statute mandates detention pending the sentencing or appeal of defendants convicted of certain serious crimes, specifically drug traffickers or violent criminals. Release of defendants convicted of these serious crimes is only allowed if certain conditions are met and there are "exceptional reasons" why such person's detention would not be appropriate.

Koon and Powell had been previously released on bail pending sentencing. Following the judge's decision sentencing them to 30 months' imprisonment, both defendants moved for bail pending appeal of their convictions. Federal courts in California found that there were no "exceptional reasons" justifying the release of Koon and Powell.

Koon and Powell both filed appeals with the United States Supreme Court. The Court rejected both motions. The Court had never before addressed the "exceptional reasons" exception to mandatory detention, which had gone into effect in 1990.

On the other hand, bail has been allowed on appeal in some high-profile cases. Martha Stewart, the television expert on gardening and homemaking, was convicted in 2004 of charges arising from her sale of Imclone stock.[23] She was free on bail pending her appeal of a sentence amounting to 10 months, including five months in prison and five months of home confinement wearing an electronic bracelet.[24] During the appeal process she abruptly decided to serve her sentence while the appeal was pending, entering the federal prison in Alderson, West Virginia. Alderson was the first federal prison camp for women in the United States. The reason she gave for going to jail early was to put the "nightmare" behind her. The appeal continued while she served her time.

## § 3.3   When Bail Is Set

Practices vary, but in some states after the police officer files a complaint with a magistrate and applies for issuance of an arrest warrant for an at-large suspect, the magistrate will endorse upon the warrant the amount of bail required. When the warrant is executed by the making of an arrest, bail in the designated amount can be taken from the suspect even though the magistrate may be unavailable. And if the bail that is endorsed on the warrant is too high, the defendant can point this out and obtain reduction of the amount when he or she comes before the magistrate at first appearance.

**Station-house bail** is another way bail can be set and secured from a defendant prior to this initial appearance before the magistrate. Under this system, defendants in custody at police headquarters may post bail in an amount

---

[22] Jonathan S. Rosen, *An Examination of the "Exceptional Reasons" Jurisprudence of the Mandatory Detention Act, Title 18 U.S.C. §§ 3143, 3145(c)*, 19 VT. L. REV. 19 (1994).

[23] The case was tried in federal court in New York City.

[24] Codefendant Peter Bacanovic, Martha Stewart's stock broker, was convicted of conspiring with Stewart to lie to investigators. He was also allowed to stay out of prison while he appealed.

set by a police officer in accordance with a schedule for the particular offense charged. The bail schedule is generally one that has been reviewed and approved by the judges in the county or district, the amount of required bail increasing with the accelerating seriousness of the listed offenses. When the charge in a particular case is especially serious or the offense appears to be an aggravated one, the police officer taking bail should advance cautiously and should consult with the prosecuting attorney before proceeding with any release.[25] In borderline cases, release decisions should await presentation of the defendant to the magistrate.

Station-house bail is particularly important in misdemeanor cases. Bail for a misdemeanor is frequently established in the amount of the standard fine for the offense charged, and many defendants dispose of their cases by forfeiting bail rather than appearing in court. While the defendant may be pursued if the misdemeanor is a serious one, the practice in many states (especially if the offense is a traffic charge) is to consider the matter closed upon forfeiture of the collateral posted by the accused. Further, some codes now provide that a forfeiture of collateral security in lieu of appearance by the accused constitutes a proper and complete disposition of the case.

Thus far the discussion has touched on pre-appearance bail, including station-house bail, and that endorsed on the warrant of arrest. Bail also may be originally set by the magistrate at first appearance, and in most jurisdictions this is where initial bail-setting takes place in the felony case. When urging at first appearance that bail be set in a low amount, the defendant presents detailed information supporting his or her position. The prosecutor may also present arguments respecting the proper amount of bail, and it is customary for both prosecution and defense to make liberal use of hearsay evidence in presenting the relevant facts. While many magistrates make an individualized assessment of the bail figure, others follow a prearranged bail schedule. Under such schedules, one formula is to set bail in a total amount equal to $2,000 for each year of the maximum sentence provided under the state code for the involved crime.

Serious cases, such as kidnapping or murder charges, will often prompt the magistrate to set a **special hearing on bail**. Prearranged formulas regarding the amount of bond are not employed because of the seriousness of the case and the need for an individualized determination. In such situations, the magistrate may set a date and time shortly after first appearance to investigate the pretrial release issue. As noted earlier, hearsay may be received at such hearings. The formal rules of evidence usually do not apply.[26] However, rules with respect to the law of privileges must be respected, and when the state calls witnesses, numerous courts give the accused "a full opportunity to examine State's witnesses" as to relevant issues.[27] The defendant may wish to present testimony from a witness or two of his own. The magistrate will consider the totality of the evidence in light of the applicable criteria and will decide whether, and in what amount, bail is appropriate.

---

[25] Station house bail is restricted to misdemeanors in some states.

[26] United States v. Montemayor, 666 F.2d 235 (5th Cir. 1982).

[27] Stansel v. State, 297 So. 2d 63 (Fla. Dist. Ct. App. 1974). Preventive detention hearings, *see* § 3.8 infra.

Unrestricted by technical evidentiary doctrines, the court may make a wide-ranging inquiry when determining bail issues. A defendant objected when a federal judge took judicial notice at a bail hearing of the fugitive rate experienced in the court's criminal docket. Defendant's bail in a federal firearms case was established at $1,350,000. He complained that the "default rate" evidence should not have been considered, and he cited the Federal Rules of Evidence. The United States Court of Appeals found that the formal rules of evidence did not apply to proceedings for release on bail.[28]

However, while all of the rules of evidence may not be strictly applied—for example, hearsay evidence will usually be received and considered at bail hearings—not all procedural safeguards are dispensed with. Admittedly a bail proceeding, whether one to originally establish bail or a court hearing to consider reduction of bail, does not have the formalities of a trial. Bail adjudication is, however, clearly an adversary hearing.[29] When witness testimony is presented by the government in support of high bail, the defendant's usual right to cross-examine and impeach witnesses exists. Case law warns against the state submitting evidence to the judge *in camera*—in private—over a defendant's objection. The court should state its reasons for fixing bail, particularly where a high bond is set.[30]

Where the question is not simply the amount of bail but preventive detention, a full panoply of rights inure to the defendant. Procedural aspects of preventive detention are outlined in § 3.8 of this chapter.

Bail questions in the trial court (as opposed to the magistrate's setting of bail) are generally dealt with at arraignment. Usually the arguments that the trial court judge hears at arraignment are those by defense counsel asking the court to reduce bail. Bail reduction (or the release of defendant without bail) is the primary focus at arraignment, as opposed to the setting of bail as an original matter, because in most cases an initial bail figure has already been established by the magistrate.[31] Suppose a defendant complains about the amount of pretrial bail, claiming he or she cannot post bond in so large a sum. How many steps are available to test or challenge the amount of pretrial bail? Where the magistrate adjudicated the bail question initially, a federal case wherein virtually all of the available review stages are utilized by a defendant would include:

1.  Magistrate sets bail.

2.  Application to same magistrate to review the order fixing bail. Acting upon the application, a magistrate's bail review hearing may follow.

---

[28]  United States v. Montemayor, 666 F.2d 235 (5th Cir. 1982).

[29]  Stansel v. State, 297 So. 2d 63 (Fla. Dist. Ct. App. 1974) ($500,000 bail in conspiracy to possess marijuana case).

[30]  Mecom v. United States, 434 U.S. 1340 (1977) (bail in amount of $750,000 was established before trial and continued on appeal; charge and conviction of conspiracy to possess marijuana with intent to distribute).

[31]  The trial judge has several choices in this situation. If a defendant has been released by the magistrate, the arraignment judge can continue bail on the same terms. Where a defendant is in custody, the judge can release him on his own recognizance or on a reduced amount of bail. The judge has broad powers to ensure expeditious progress of a trial, and incident thereto may revoke bail and remit the defendant to custody. Bitter v. United States, 389 U.S. 15, 88 S. Ct. 6, 19 L. Ed. 2d 15 (1967).

3.  After the magistrate finalizes conditions of pretrial release, motion for reduction of bail may be filed in the United States District Court. See 18 U.S.C. § 3145.

4.  After hearing on motion, if the district court declines to disturb the magistrate's decision, appeal of the bail decision may be pursued in the United States Court of Appeals.[32]

5.  Following a Court of Appeals decision, further relief can conceivably be sought by application for review by the United States Supreme Court.

Of course, rare is the accused person who pursues all of these steps. Customarily, bail decisions are fought out at the magistrate's level, with perhaps a single review of that decision in the district court.

However, there are cases in which the district court acts initially. In one situation the trial court arraignment contemplates an original bail hearing. When a grand jury indictment is returned before arrest, the defendant may be arrested and taken directly to the district court (or other general trial court, depending on the descriptive name applied to it in the state) to be advised of his or her rights and to decide bail, bypassing the magistrate's procedure entirely.[33]

Whether a defendant can be admitted to bail on appeal has been discussed in § 3.2. The judge who presided over trial of the case makes this determination initially. If he or she denies bail pending appeal, or sets it in an unattainable amount, the imprisoned defendant may make application to the appellate court to review the trial court's bail determination.

## § 3.4   Types of Bail

Release of an accused person in our legal system takes place in two major ways—bail or nonmonetary release, based upon specified conditions. Use of the latter method has been increasing, sparked by recent movement toward bail reform in America.

Monetary bail requires the defendant to post a money bond. The theory is that the possible loss of a substantial amount of money will deter the defendant from fleeing the jurisdiction or otherwise failing to appear when required at his or her trial. In cases in which the defendant does fail to appear, a forfeiture of bail is declared by the trial judge.

The defendant may post monetary bail by depositing with the clerk of court cash, securities, or other liquid assets in the full amount of the bond. Real property may be given as security by a person who holds title to sufficient unencumbered property and who is financially solvent. This may be pledged by another person as security for the accused's subsequent appearance or by the defendant himself or herself. The defendant may also meet the bail

---

[32]   United States v. Montemayor, *supra* note 28.

[33]   See the discussion of circumvention of magistrate's procedures contained in § 2.9.

requirement by posting a surety bond written by a professional bondsman. Generally, the bondsman must be certified or must "justify" in the court in which he proposes to give bail, a procedure whereby the bondsman proves to the court his or her ability to make good on the bond in the event of a forfeiture.[34] In exchange for posting the bail necessary to procure the prisoner's freedom, the bondsman collects a premium from defendant. In many areas of the country this is cash in the amount of 10 percent of the face amount of the bond. Such bond premium is retained by the bondsman as a charge for writing the bond. The bondsman may also require collateral security from the defendant, a deposit of stocks or bonds where available or perhaps a mortgage on the defendant's home, in addition to the cash premium. These will be sacrificed to the bondsman if the defendant fails to appear at his hearing and the bondsman is required to pay the face amount of the bail into the court.

A sample surety bond might read as follows:

---

Know all persons by these presents:

That we, John Jones, as principal, and Acme Bonding Company, as surety are held and firmly bound jointly and severally to the state of _____, plaintiff, in the sum of $25,000.00

Whereas, the said John Jones was arrested by the sheriff of the County of Scott, state of _____, for alleged violation of Section 102 of the Penal Code, _____ [grand larceny], and

Whereas, an order of the District Court of the state of _____ was made and delivered to the sheriff requiring him to hold the defendant John Jones to bail in the amount of $25,000.00, and the defendant is in custody by virtue of said order, and is desirous of securing his discharge;

Now John Jones and Acme Bonding Company are bound to the plaintiff in the sum stated in the above mentioned order of court as sufficient for procuring the discharge of the defendant from custody. The condition of this obligation is that the defendant will at all times render himself amenable to the process of the District Court of _____ during the pendency of the criminal action against him; that he will personally appear as required by the court; and that he will not depart from this state without permission of this court during the pendency of said action.

Dated this ___ day of _____, 20__.

                                          [Signatures]
                                          /s/ Defendant
                                          /s/ Surety

---

[34] FED. R. CRIM. P. 46(e), provides that one justifying by affidavit may be required to describe his property, encumbrances thereon, and the amount of other bonds entered into by him.

---

AFFIDAVIT OF JUSTIFICATION OF CORPORATE SURETY

William Green, being first duly sworn, states as follows:
That he is an officer of the Acme Bonding Company, the surety in the annexed bond, and is authorized to execute this bond on behalf of said company.

That this surety is a corporation licensed to engage in the business of underwriting appearance bonds in the state of _____and maintains its principal offices in _____ County, [state].

That the said company is worth the sum of $550,000.00 over and above all debts and liabilities, in property within the state of _____, which property is not by law exempt from execution. [Alternate form] That Acme Bonding Company, having been given due notice to appear for examination for justification, duly attended before the District Court of the state of _____, _____-___ County, for said examination under oath, and on _____, _____, 20__, said company was certified by the district court as sufficient to serve as surety upon appearance bonds posted with said court in amounts exceeding that secured by the annexed bond.[35]

[Date]
[Signature]

---

Nonmonetary release is based upon the defendant living up to special conditions imposed by the court. Under this approach, the defendant is released on his or her own recognizance (a written promise to appear signed by the defendant under oath) or released on an unsecured bail bond (defendant enters into a written undertaking promising to pay into the court a specified sum if he or she fails to appear, but no professional bondsman is required to act as surety). In addition to these written undertakings, the court may impose one or more of the following restrictions when the accused is released on nonmonetary conditions:

- Placing the defendant under the supervision of a designated person or agency (frequently a probation officer) until the defendant is tried and requiring him or her to make regular reports to this officer or other supervising person;

- Placing restrictions on the travel, association, or place of abode of the defendant during the period of release;[36]

---

[35] The forms presented here are for illustrative purposes. In many states the exact form of the bond is prescribed by a statute which must be followed. For this reason, state requirements as to the contents of the bond vary. For other bail forms generally, see 4 AM. JUR. *Pleading and Practice Forms, Bail and Recognizance* §§ 4-9 (2004). Affidavits of justification of the surety, especially applicable when the surety is an individual, are treated in 19 AM. JUR. *Pleading and Practice Forms, Suretyship* §§ 79-80 (2004).

[36] *See* the Federal Bail Reform Act of 1984, 18 U.S.C. § 3142(c)(1)(B)(iv)(2000).

- Imposing partial detention on the defendant by allowing him or her to go to his or her job or school during the day and requiring his or her return to custody (jail) on a daily basis after specified hours;

- Other restrictions adjusted to the individual case, such as requiring a defendant accused of child molestation who met his victim online to refrain from using a computer. In exceptional situations, the defendant may be released but required to wear an electronic monitoring device to track his or her whereabouts. The wristwatch-like transmitter may be locked around a defendant's ankle. In these cases the defendant will be released from jail after guaranteeing that he or she will not flee, and after agreeing to wear the monitoring device.

The preceding discussion concerning release with sureties or pursuant to supervision has primary application to felonies and other serious offenses. In the situation of traffic cases and nonviolent misdemeanors, it is frequently recommended that police officers employ alternatives to arrest, which result in pretrial freedom of the defendant without resort to the bail system. These alternatives include the summons and the citation. Under the **citation**, a police officer prepares an order directing the suspect to appear in a designated court at a future time. A **summons** is issued by a judicial officer directing the defendant to do the same thing. Advantages of these devices are readily apparent. Because every minor lawbreaker need not be physically restrained, the citation fulfills the goals of law enforcement without the expense and inconvenience of a custodial arrest.[37]

## § 3.5  Factors in Setting Bail

Several elements are generally considered in determining whether a felony defendant should be entitled to a low bail or release on nonmonetary conditions.

### 1. Nature of the Charge

A serious offense carrying a heavy penalty is one justification for substantial bail. The idea is that the lengthy sentence that can attend conviction in a serious case may inspire the accused to flee after pretrial release, and that flight is probable unless the accused is anchored by the prospect of significant property loss.

---

[37]  *See* § 2.1(3) for discussion, and § 10.8, for sample forms.

## 2. Employment History and Family Ties

The defendant's roots in the community is a relevant factor, and where he or she has a favorable employment record with a local company and dependents in the locale, the prospect of flight is diminished. Accordingly, these factors weigh in the direction of low bail or nonmonetary release when they appear in a given case. Still, if the offense is an aggravated one and there is a good possibility of protracted imprisonment, the "roots" consideration may be outweighed.

## 3. Prior Criminal Record

If the defendant has a criminal record that includes bail jumping, escape from prison, or violation of probation or parole, the risk of flight is enhanced. Also relative are consecutive convictions of specified felonies that may potentially subject the defendant to increased punishment under habitual offender laws if convicted again.[38] But prior convictions are a two-edged sword. If the record shows that the defendant was freed before trial several times in prior years in connection with other arrests or offenses, and the record further shows that he or she dutifully appeared as required in each instance, this could work to the defendant's advantage.

## 4. Mental Condition

Active narcotics addicts, except those making an effort to break the habit, may be untrustworthy and high-risk cases if released before trial. Prior escapes of the defendant from a mental institution, present mental illness, or the fact that the offense with which the defendant is presently charged was the product of a mental disorder may be indicators in a given case that the defendant has a diminished understanding of his or her obligation to appear in court pursuant to judicial order or an inability to comply.

These are some of the significant considerations that may be relevant in any bail decision. Others may be important depending upon the particular facts of each case. In reviewing all the criteria, however, one guiding principle controls. Bail should be fixed in an amount or with conditions adequate to deter flight and ensure a defendant's appearance in court. Bail set at a higher figure simply to ensure defendant's incarceration before trial may be open to attack as "excessive" under the United States Constitution.[39]

---

[38] These laws are briefly reviewed in § 6.23.

[39] *See* § 3.1 of this chapter. In making the bail decision, the court generally need not apply the formal rules of evidence. See United States v. Montemayor, 666 F.2d 235 (5th Cir. 1982); Kinson v. Carson, 409 So. 2d 1212 (Fla. Dist. Ct. App. 1982).

## § 3.6 Penalties for Non-Appearance: Revoking Bail

As previously suggested, the trial judge has broad power to revoke the pretrial release of a defendant for willful violation of release conditions. Release conditions are violated when the defendant fails to appear at a court hearing or trial when scheduled, or when he or she engages in criminal activity while free on bail.

Unless the defendant was ill, improperly notified of his appearance date, or presents some other bona fide excuse for nonappearance, several sanctions follow when the accused who is free on bond violates release conditions by failing to appear. Where monetary bail has been posted by the defendant or a professional bondsman, this bond will be declared forfeited by the court. "If the defendant fails to appear at the time and place when the defendant's personal appearance is lawfully required . . . the undertaking of the defendant's bail, or the money deposited, is thereupon forfeited."[40] Relief from this loss of funds, where such is sought, must take place in a specified way. In most jurisdictions a defendant who has failed to appear must voluntarily surrender himself within a specified period following his default (e.g., within 60 days thereafter) in order for the forfeiture to be vacated or set aside and the amount of the bond returned to the defendant or his bondsman.

In addition to revocation of freedom or bail forfeiture, criminal sanctions may flow from violation of release conditions. An arrest warrant may be issued for the apprehension of the accused. Contempt of court may be imposed against a defendant, and bail-jumping is a crime in most states. In addition, it is a federal crime to flee a jurisdiction to avoid prosecution.[41]

## § 3.7 Reform of the Bail System

Several approaches have been adopted in recent years that are designed to streamline the American bail system. In the case of a defendant whose intent is to dutifully appear in court when scheduled, it has long been considered unfair to penalize him by causing the irretrievable loss of cash in the amount of 10 percent of the bail figure for a bond premium. Accordingly, reform provisions in the federal courts and in Illinois incorporated a new bail concept. The 10 percent cash amount normally paid to a bondsman was to be paid to the court by the defendant. However, there was one important difference. If the defendant appeared as ordered, the major portion of this cash amount was to be returned to the defendant.

---

[40] Iowa Code § 811.6 (1994). For an example of forfeiture for violation of travel restrictions (as opposed to failure to appear) see Brown v. United States, 410 F.2d 212 (5th Cir. 1969).

[41] 18 U.S.C. § 1073.

In *Schilb v. Kuebel*[42] the United States Supreme Court reviewed the Illinois law and upheld the right of the state to retain one percent of the specified bail for administrative costs:

> John Schilb was arrested and charged (a) with leaving the scene of an automobile accident and (b) with obstructing traffic. In order to gain his liberty pending trial, and in accord with the Illinois bail statutes hereinafter described, Schilb deposited $75 in cash with the clerk of the court. This amount was 10% of the aggregate bail fixed on the two charges ($500 on the first and $250 on the second). At his ensuing trial Schilb was acquitted on the charge of leaving the scene, but was convicted of traffic obstruction. When he paid his fine, the amount Schilb had deposited was returned to him decreased, however, by $7.50 retained as "bail bond costs" by the court clerk pursuant to the statute. The amount so retained was 1% of the specified bail and 10% of the amount actually deposited.
>
> Schilb, by this purported state class action against the court clerk, the county, and the county treasurer, attacks the statutory 1% charge on Fourteenth Amendment due process and equal protection grounds. . . .
>
> Prior to 1964 the professional bail bondsman system with all its abuses was in full and odorous bloom in Illinois. Under that system the bail bondsman customarily collected the maximum fee (10% of the amount of the bond) permitted by statute, and retained that entire amount even though the accused fully satisfied the conditions of the bond. Payment of this substantial "premium" was required of the good risk as well as of the bad. The results were that a heavy and irretrievable burden fell upon the accused, to the excellent profit of the bondsman, and that professional bondsmen, and not the courts, exercised significant control over the actual workings of the bail system.
>
> One of the stated purposes of the new bail provisions in the 1963 Code was to rectify this offensive situation. The purpose appears to have been accomplished.

Where release on personal recognizance, unsecured bond, or other non-monetary condition would assure the defendant's appearance at trial, these methods were to be preferred to surety bonds under the revised provisions.[43] Other alternatives to cash bail have been suggested. Wider use of the summons and citation has been recommended by certain authorities.[44]

In addition to streamlining and liberalizing access to pretrial freedom for apt candidates, there has also been a contemporary trend in bail practice that seeks to safeguard the security of witnesses and the community. One manifestation of this has been the preventive detention approach discussed in the next section. Another was the amendment of the Federal Bail Reform Act in

---

[42]   404 U.S. 357 (1971).

[43]   *See* the Federal Bail Reform of 1984, 18 U.S.C. §§ 3141-3150 (2000).

[44]   AMERICAN BAR ASSOCIATION, STANDARDS RELATING TO PRE-TRIAL RELEASE. In this text, § 2.1(3) discusses the summons and citation.

1982 by the "Victim and Witness Protection Act." In every case in which an accused person is released before trial, a condition of release is that the defendant will not retaliate against a witness or an informant.

## § 3.8   Preventive Detention

Controversy and considerable publicity have attended efforts to enact preventive detention laws applicable to prisoners. What is preventive detention? In its simplest form, preventive detention is a procedure that allows a judicial officer (such as a magistrate at the preliminary hearing) to refuse bail for a defendant when the judicial officer finds that the safety of the community will be threatened by the defendant's release. It applies in non-capital as well as capital cases, markedly expanding the offenses for which bail might be denied. Such denial would come only after a judicial hearing and determination that the defendant, if released, will likely commit further crimes or interfere with prospective witnesses or evidence.

The need for preventive detention has been cited by a number of authorities who argue that the commission of crimes by defendants free on bail is "one of the major problems in the war against crime.[45] Although many European countries have accepted preventive detention, the American legal system prior to the 1980s generally did not authorize detention of offenders on the ground that they might, if free on bail, commit additional crimes. Impacting the freedom of an accused person prior to trial was legitimate if the person was likely to flee, but not for other reasons.[46] Our system has operated on the premise that the purpose of bail is to "secure assurance of the presence of the accused" at his or her trial.[47] One of the chief criticisms of the American bail system has been that it fails to provide adequate protection from vicious defendants who may prey upon society while free on bond. To meet this criticism, the concept of preventive detention developed.

Congress put a federal law in place that subjected certain federal offenders to pretrial detention if their release would "endanger the safety of any other person or the community." When a defendant is arrested for a serious offense, such as a capital offense or a crime of violence, his or her release before trial may be denied.

For federal courts, the element of danger has been included as a permissible element of consideration in bail decisions. The Comprehensive Crime Control Act of 1984 allows federal judges to consider danger to the community when setting bail conditions. Bail may be denied where the government proves by clear and convincing evidence that no conditions of release will rea-

---

[45]   III Congressional Record 27, 109 (daily edition Oct. 15, 1965) (remarks of Senator Tydings).
[46]   The pretrial detention laws of the 1980s thus represented a break from this tradition.
[47]   Stack v. Boyle, 342 U.S. 1, 72 S. Ct. 1, 96 L. Ed. 3 (1951); U.S. CONST. AMEND. VIII.

sonably assure the safety of the community and the appearance of the defendant for court proceedings.

The issue is a controversial one, with numerous commentators opposed to such statutes. Other authorities consider this an appropriate way of grappling with the problem of potentially dangerous persons, rather than perverting the bail concept by resorting to excessively high bail to detain dangerous suspects under the guise of preventing flight.

The federal act received scrutiny by the United States Supreme Court in 1987 and was found to be constitutional. In *United States v. Salerno*,[48] defendants Anthony Salerno and Vincent Cafaro were arrested on charges of racketeering, mail fraud, and extortion. The government moved to have Salerno and Cafaro detained pursuant to the federal preventive detention law. At a hearing before a federal judge, the government's case showed that Salerno was the boss of a crime family. The government also offered the testimony of two witnesses who asserted that Salerno participated in two murder conspiracies.

The judge ordered the defendants detained in custody until trial, concluding that the government had established by clear and convincing evidence that pretrial release of the individuals would pose a danger to the community. The defendants appealed, claiming that the 1984 Federal Bail Reform Act was unconstitutional. A key issue was raised. Could bail be denied and a defendant locked up before trial on the ground of future dangerousness when a judge finds it likely that the arrestee will commit additional crimes if released? The United States Supreme Court supplied an affirmative answer to this question. "The [Bail Reform] Act operates only on individuals who have been arrested for a specific category of extremely serious offenses. . . . Nor is the Act by any means a scattershot attempt to incapacitate those who are merely suspected of these serious crimes. The government must first of all demonstrate probable cause to believe that the charged crime has been committed by the arrestee, but that is not enough. In a full-blown adversary hearing, the government must convince a neutral decisionmaker by clear and convincing evidence that no conditions of release can reasonably assure the safety of the community or any person."

The Supreme Court placed emphasis upon the fact that detainees have several rights under the Bail Reform Act. These include a right to counsel at the court hearing that must be held before bail is denied and a defendant is held in jail as a potentially dangerous person. Other rights of the accused include a right to present evidence and to cross-examine the government's witnesses, and the requirement that the government sustain its position by clear and convincing evidence. The magistrate must supply written findings justifying his or her decision to hold the defendant. The Court held that such protections render the pretrial detention process a constitutional one. "We think these extensive safeguards suffice to repel a facial challenge [to the constitutionality of the Bail Reform Act]."[49]

---

[48]    107 S. Ct. 2095 (1987).
[49]    107 S. Ct. at 2104.

The provisions of the federal law were applied to preventively detain arrestees in a 2003 case. It illustrates how the law works. The government produced credible evidence that the defendants attended a terrorist training camp, and demonstrated by clear and convincing evidence that they posed a danger to the community. Moreover, the government demonstrated by a preponderance of the evidence that each defendant posed a risk of flight if released. At their initial appearances following arrests for providing support to a foreign terrorist, the government moved for the pretrial detention of each defendant. After a comprehensive detention hearing that lasted four days, the federal judge agreed.[50] Later, each of the men pled guilty to one count of providing resources to a foreign terrorist organization.

Some states have embraced the basic concept contained in the Bail Reform Act. They permit pretrial detention based upon the suspect's assaultive character, and have added considerations of dangerousness to the statutorily enumerated factors under which the judicial officer may deny bail. Along with the nature and circumstances of the charge as well as the history of the suspect and his risk of flight, state statutes sometimes empower the magistrate to factor into the release decision the magistrate's conclusions as to whether the person poses a significant threat or danger to any person or to the community. However, such state bail codes frequently do not incorporate the procedural protections that the Supreme Court considered so important in *Salerno*. The Court seems to suggest that the procedural guarantees touched upon above stand as virtually essential companion features to a dangerousness clause in order to uphold the constitutionality of "future dangerousness" detention provisions. One commentator concludes that local statutes that are devoid of "*Salerno* requirements" would not "survive the . . . *Salerno* constitutionality test."[51]

In 1997 the Supreme Court upheld preventive detention of sexual predators by way of civil commitment after they completed a criminal sentence.[52] A Kansas law established procedures for commitment of persons likely to engage in acts of sexual violence. The Court approved such statutes "provided the confinement takes place pursuant to proper procedures and evidentiary standards." In this latter emphasis, the Court's language is consistent with the demand for procedural protections contained in *Salerno*.

## § 3.9   Detention Hearings

Section 3.3 of this text made reference to the fact that when preventive pretrial detention of an allegedly dangerous suspect is at issue, as opposed to an issue of simple bail, special considerations apply. Under the 1984 Federal Bail Reform Act, the magistrate must provide a full-blown hearing when the federal prosecutor requests confinement of a defendant before trial on account

---

[50]   United States v. Goba, 240 F. Supp. 2d 242 (W.D.N.Y. 2003).
[51]   Note, 22 GA. L. REV. 805, 827, 829 (1988) (citing GA. STAT. § 17-6-1(e)(2)).
[52]   Kansas v. Hendricks, 117 S. Ct. 2071 (1997).

of the dangerous propensities of the arrestee. The prosecutor's motion is to be made at the defendant's first appearance in court. **Preventive detention laws** allow the court to deny bail when the accused is charged with an extremely serious crime and his or her release before trial of the crime would place the public in significant peril. Some of the crimes enumerated in the federal law that trigger preventive detention are crimes of violence, offenses for which the maximum sentence is life imprisonment or death, narcotics offenses carrying a maximum term of imprisonment of 10 years or more, or a felony committed by a repeat offender. At the hearing, the arrestee must be shown to be charged with one of these crimes. In addition, probable cause must be shown that he or she committed the charged offense, and there must be proof by clear and convincing evidence that the defendant poses a danger to other persons or to the community.

The hearing to make these determinations shall be held immediately upon the arrestee's first appearance unless a continuance is granted. Often a brief delay occurs, and the detention hearing frequently takes place a few days after first appearance. "At the hearing, the [arrested] person has the right to be represented by counsel, and, if financially unable to obtain adequate representation, to have counsel appointed. The person shall be afforded an opportunity to testify, to present witnesses, to cross-examine witnesses who appear at the hearing, and to present information by proffer or otherwise. The rules concerning admissibility of evidence in criminal trials do not apply to the presentation and consideration of information at the hearing."[53]

If the magistrate finds clear and convincing evidence to support the conclusion that the community's safety will be endangered by the release of the arrested person, he or she will prepare a detention order. It will include the magistrate's written findings and a statement of reasons for ordering or continuing the detention of the accused until the completion of the trial and sentencing.

The time frames established under the pretrial detention law have been the object of litigation. In *United States v. Holloway*,[54] a defendant's bond was set at $250,000 at his first appearance before the magistrate. Later, the prosecution learned that the defendant's wealth was approximately $700,000. Concerned that the defendant would post bond and flee, the government moved for and was granted a pretrial detention order two days after the first appearance. The defendant appealed his detention, and the United States Court of Appeals set aside the detention order. The court ruled that the prosecutor's initial attempt to use bail as a means of detaining the defendant was contrary to the intention and spirit of the Bail Reform Act of 1984. Further, the pretrial detention law requires that a hearing be held on the issue of whether the defendant should be detained under that statute at first appearance. This is so unless a continuance is granted. Because the government did not move for the hearing

---

[53] 18 U.S.C. § 3142(f) (2000).
[54] 781 F.2d 124 (8th Cir. 1986).

until two days after first appearance, the motion was untimely and the detention order was not valid.

A watered-down approach to time constraints was adopted by the United States Supreme Court in a case decided after *Holloway*. While there may be sanctions for governmental noncompliance with the timing provisions, release of a fugitive is not required. The Court's 1990 decision held that once the government discovers that time limits have expired, it could ask for a prompt hearing and make its case.[55] All other procedural requirements must be observed when so doing. Dissenting justices insisted that all procedural incidents, including the timing provisions, were critical elements of preventive detention. In his dissent Justice Stevens concluded that "Congress has written detailed legislation in a sensitive area that requires the Government to turn square corners. The Court today, however, permits federal prosecutors to violate the law with impunity."

Procedural correctness in another area was required by the appellate court in *United States v. Hurtado*.[56] The United States District Court refused to disturb a bail decision made by a United States magistrate. The record revealed no independent fact-finding and no statement as to why the District Court upheld the amount of defendant's bail. By so doing, the District Court committed reversible error. The United States Court of Appeals ruled that under the Bail Reform Act, the District Court must make a factual determination on the merits of the defendant's bail claim, and provide its own findings of fact and a statement of the reasons supporting its decision.

Although the bail clause of the Eighth Amendment of the United States Constitution applies to the states,[57] nothing in the Constitution requires states to embrace the concept of preventive detention. States may reject the notion. On the other hand, jurisdictions that already have or wish to emulate the federal pattern may do so with confidence. One commentator summarizes the law: In *Salerno*, the Supreme Court finally rejected the primary argument against the use of such legislation, namely, that preventive detention legislation is unconstitutional. As noted previously, the Court found that statutes that contain the requisite procedural protections and that carefully limit the circumstances under which detention may be used do not violate an arrestee's due process rights. Moreover, by painstakingly listing the necessary provisions that allow a statute to meet minimum requirements of substantive and procedural due process, the *Salerno* Court provided these states with a framework for drafting constitutionally acceptable preventive detention legislation. Thus, states with no detention legislation need only draft their provisions in accordance with *Salerno*'s instructions."[58]

---

[55]   United States v. Montalvo-Murillo, 110 S. Ct. 2072 (1990).

[56]   779 F.2d 1467 (11th Cir. 1985).

[57]   The major provision of the United States Constitution referring to bail is the Eighth Amendment, which provides: "Excessive bail shall not be required, nor excessive fines imposed, nor cruel and unusual punishments inflicted." In *Schilb v. Kuebel*, *supra* note 42, Justice Blackmun observed: "Bail, of course, is basic to our system of law. . . and the Eighth Amendment's proscription of excessive bail has been assumed to have application to the states through the Fourteenth Amendment."

[58]   Note, *supra* note 51 at 830.

The importance of an adversary hearing on the issue of a defendant's dangerousness was underlined in a 1992 Supreme Court opinion. In *Foucha v. Louisiana*,[59] the state sought to keep the defendant in jail on grounds of dangerousness. He had been committed to a psychiatric hospital after he was acquitted of a serious crime by reason of insanity. Although not a bail case, it caused the Supreme Court to reinforce notions relevant to confining criminal case defendants on the ground of dangerousness. The state relied on *Salerno* in an effort to uphold the Louisiana law that said an inmate would remain in confinement until he could prove he was not dangerous to himself or others. Hospital officials were of the opinion that the defendant was not insane. The state's approach was found to be constitutionally defective. The Supreme Court ruled: "Unlike the sharply focused scheme at issue in *Salerno*, the Louisiana scheme of confinement is not carefully limited." The absence of a special hearing on the dangerousness issue was specifically targeted for castigation by the Court: "Under the state statute, Foucha is not now entitled to an adversary hearing at which the State must prove by clear and convincing evidence that he is demonstrably dangerous to the community." The Court saw a sharp difference between this procedure versus bail decision making, in which a hearing is required before a defendant is deemed dangerous and preventively detained. That is the feature that makes bail practice constitutional. As the Court stated: "[In *Salerno*] the government was required, in a 'full-blown adversary hearing,' to convince a neutral decision maker by clear and convincing evidence that no conditions of release can reasonably assure the safety of the community. . . ." Unlike the narrowly focused pretrial detention of arrestees permitted by the Bail Reform Act, the Louisiana law that allowed for the indefinite detention of those acquitted by reason of insanity lacked *Salerno*-type due process steps.

## § 3.10   Bail for Witnesses

Under the law in most states, a material witness to a crime a may be required by the magistrate or trial court judge to give bail to ensure that the witness will appear and testify when needed. When these statutes are employed, the bail requirement is sometimes imposed on the witness at the time the suspect who is accused of the crime is bound over by the magistrate.

The Georgia statutes illustrate the potential use of bail in the case of witnesses:

> 17-7-26. Binding over witnesses. In the event of a commitment of the accused person, the court, in its discretion, may require the witnesses, on behalf of the State or others, to give suitable bonds to secure their appearance at court, with or without sureties, as the circumstances seem to demand.

---

[59]   112 S. Ct. 1780 (1992).

17-7-27. Amount of bonds for appearance of witnesses, sureties. The sheriffs and constables shall accept bond in such reasonable amount as may be just and fair to secure the appearance of any witness to attend the courts, provided the sureties tendered and offered on the bond are approved by a sheriff of any county.

Upon failure to post bail, the witness can be held in custody.

The Wisconsin provision in this area of law reflects further upon state authority to incarcerate material witnesses:

969.01(3) Bail for witness. If it appears by affidavit that the testimony of a person is material in any felony criminal proceeding and that it may become impracticable to secure the person's presence by subpoena, the judge may require such person to give bail for the person's appearance as a witness. If the witness is not in court, a warrant for the person's arrest may be issued and upon return thereof the court may require the person to give bail as provided in § 969.03 for the person's appearance as a witness. If the person fails to give bail, the person may be committed to the custody of the sheriff for a period not to exceed 15 days within which time the person's deposition shall be taken. . . .

Such laws are brought into operation in cases where there is a strong likelihood that the witness will flee, and they should not be employed to incarcerate local citizens with community roots. Of special interest to the police officer in this field is the authority of a law enforcement officer to take a material witness into custody. While most witnesses will cooperate upon appropriate request by the officer, the legal basis becomes significant when an important witness to a crime appears recalcitrant and resort to the arrest power is deemed necessary by the officer. When resorting to arrest in this situation, general arrest principles still apply. A leading case on the subject takes the view that a peace officer may arrest without a warrant when he or she has probable cause to believe a person is a necessary and material witness to a crime punishable by imprisonment for more than one year and that the person might be unavailable for service of subpoena.[60] People today travel widely and move their residences frequently. "In the face of this swift movement from one area to another, if a police officer cannot immediately hold the man who has seen a crime but is reluctant to cooperate, he is faced with the possible loss of the witness or a possible delay in obtaining information. . . ."[61] Arrest warrants for witnesses are authorized in federal courts.[62]

Under most state laws, arrest and detention of witnesses typically cannot occur unless criminal charges are already pending against another person, a defendant.[63] Under many codes, misdemeanor cases are outside the scope of

---

[60]  See State v. Hand, 242 A.2d 888, 893 (N.J. 1968).
[61]  Id. at 894 (N.J. 1968).
[62]  United States v. Oliver, 683 F.2d 224 (7th Cir. 1982).
[63]  State v. Misik, 569 A.2d 894, 904 (N.J. Super. 1989) (issuance of warrant was illegal because of lack of pending criminal action).

material witness laws. A serious crime must be under investigation in order to trigger the court's authority to detain witnesses. Modern statutes providing this power generally restrict it to witnesses in cases in which the defendant who committed the offense was charged with a felony. It is to be remembered that when witnesses are imprisoned, the extraordinary situation of innocent persons being held in custody occurs, and the unusual power to do this should be utilized cautiously and sparingly.

Many of the material witness statutes are based upon century-old laws. Some have no procedural safeguards at all for dealing with a potential witness who may have important testimony to give but who may not be amenable or responsive to a subpoena or court order requiring him or her to appear in court when the defendant's case comes up.[64] The question of the extent to which constitutional due process of law rights safeguard against peremptory detention of a material witness has yet to be decided by the United States Supreme Court.

Unfortunately, abuses have occasionally crept into the system. In one state, migrant farm workers who observed a homicide were arrested as material witnesses. They were placed in an adult correctional institution, confined with convicted offenders, and required to wear prison garb during 158 days of incarceration. Denied access to persons outside the penitentiary for three months, the workers filed petitions for habeas corpus when they were ultimately accorded such access. The petitions were successful, and the "prisoners" were ordered to be discharged. In summarizing the affair, the Supreme Court of Rhode Island made this pointed observation in the case of one of the workers: "To the innocent even a momentary deprivation of liberty is intolerable: 158 days is an outrage. Confinement of the plaintiff for so long a period among criminals and forcing him to wear prison garb added the grossest insult to injury."[65]

Compensation for incarcerated witnesses can be minimal. In one state, it is three dollars per day for every day the witness is held in confinement. Some cases in other states have held that the witness is entitled to nothing.[66]

Because witnesses may at times be held in jail for weeks while the person accused of the crime is free on bail, there has been recent movement to reform in the field of witness-confinement laws. Holding of the witnesses for only a short period and obtaining their deposition has been suggested, and operates in some jurisdictions.[67] Some codes have begun to address the lack of counsel and compensation problems.[68] Others have enacted reforms in other areas. For example, New Jersey's revised material witness statute provides for a hearing to inquire into the matter before a person is deemed to be a material witness.

---

[64] State v. Misik, 569 A.2d at 900.

[65] Quince v. State, 179 A.2d 485, 487 (R.I. 1962). See Carlson & Voelpel, *Material Witness and Material Injustice*, 58 WASH. U.L.Q. 1 (1980), collecting state and federal cases and statutes.

[66] Cochran v. County of Lincoln, 280 N.W.2d 897 (1979). *See also* Hurtado v. United States, 410 U.S. 578, 93 S. Ct. 1157, 35 L. Ed. 2d 508 (1973).

[67] 18 U.S.C. § 3144; FED. R. CRIM. P. 15; CAL. PENAL CODE § 882.

[68] Kling, *A Mandatory Right to Counsel for the Material Witness*, 19 U. MICH. J. L. REFORM 473, 477 n. 24 (1986).

A judge may issue an arrest warrant for a witness, but only upon clear and convincing evidence that the person will not be available unless immediately arrested. The statute also increased the fees paid to detained witnesses.[69]

## § 3.11  Terrorism Cases

As indicated in § 3.10 of the text, if a witness observes a crime and there is a strong possibility that the person will not be around to testify against the wrongdoer, the witness may be arrested. For example, section 804.11 of the Iowa Code provides that "[w]hen a law enforcement officer has probable cause to believe that a person is a necessary and material witness to a felony and that such person might be unavailable [to testify]," the officer may arrest the witness.[70] As noted, many states require that in order for the arrest of a witness to be lawful, the main wrongdoer (the defendant whom the witness observed commit the crime) must have been arrested and be in custody. In other words, witness W may be held and confined as a witness only if defendant D has been apprehended and is charged with a crime.

In federal cases, federal authorities have sometimes employed the material witness laws in an unusual pattern, different from the foregoing description. Instead of arresting W as a witness to a murder or an assault committed by D, in 2004 there were numerous examples of W being arrested *as a witness to the possible crime of W*. Under this new interpretation, a witness may be arrested *as a witness* and held pending the investigation of whether he or she did something wrong. Of course, a witness has fewer rights when placed under confinement than an arrestee who is charged with a crime. Accordingly, this methodology has become a convenient way to warehouse detainees while investigating them.

Brandon Mayfield, a Portland, Oregon, lawyer was taken into custody under a material witness warrant. A fingerprint supposedly belonging to Mayfield had allegedly been found on a bag of detonators connected to a catastrophic terrorist bombing in Madrid, Spain. But there was an error, as later investigation showed. Apparently the print was not Mayfield's, after all. Spanish police reportedly tied the fingerprint on the bag to an Algerian citizen. After two weeks of confinement, Mayfield walked out of jail a free man.

Not all witnesses have been so fortunate. Since September 11, 2001, material witness arrests have become more common. Rather than being used merely to guarantee that a witness will be available to testify after an indictment against someone else is issued, "it has been employed to hold suspects who are themselves under investigation. The result is that dozens of people across the country have been detained for varying periods of time while the government seeks to compile evidence against them. The circumstances of

---

[69]  N.J. STAT. ANN. §§ 2C:104-1-9 (West 1995). The history of the New Jersey law is traced in Burke, *New Jersey's New Material Witness Statute*, 19 SETON H. LEG. J. 475, 482 (1995).

[70]  State v. Hernandez-Lopez, 639 N.W.2d 226 (Iowa 2002).

these detentions are shrouded in secrecy, as are the names of the detainees and even the raw number of them."[71]

Putting the witness laws to this sort of use has drawn fire from legal commentators. Critics say federal prosecutors should not be using the material witness law for a purpose that was never intended. "An arrest or detention solely for investigative purposes, other than a momentary stop of a citizen, would violate a number of the detainee's rights [including] the right to be free from 'unreasonable' government searches and seizures."[72] Nor should the laws be used as a shortcut to preventive detention, others say. "Detention for preventive reasons raises a host of civil liberty concerns, and has only been approved in very limited circumstances with many procedural safeguards."[73]

Clearly, balancing civil liberties with national security in the war on terrorism is a challenge to the justice system. Everyone wants a secure nation. However, misapplication of the material witness laws may not be the best method for confronting anti-terrorism cases. If more preventive detention is needed in the post-9/11 world, the most direct solution would be for legislators to address the question. Better to vigorously debate a new terrorism detention statute in Congress than to continue to emasculate the material witness laws by bending them to this purpose, experts urge.[74]

---

[71]  WASHINGTON Post, *Arresting Witnesses*, May 22, 2004:A26.

[72]  Studnicki and Apol, *Witness Detention and Intimidation: The History and Future of Material Witness Law*, 76 ST. JOHN'S L. REV. 483, 522-523 (2002).

[73]  *The Costs of Post-9/11 National Security Strategy*, 22 YALE L. & POL'Y REV. 197, 215 n. 125 (2004).

[74]  A. Liptak, *For Post-9/11 Material Witness, It Is a Terror of a Different Kind*, N.Y. TIMES August 19, 2004:1A.

# The Charging Instrument:
## Indictment or Information

# 4

## Chapter Outline

## § 4.1   Constitutional Considerations

An information, like an indictment, is a legal instrument formally setting forth the specific violation with which the defendant is charged. "The indictment or the information shall be a plain, concise and definite written statement of the essential facts constituting the offense charged."[1] In many states these accusatory documents are signed by different people—the indictment by the foreperson of the grand jury, the information by the prosecutor. They go through very different screening processes. The indictment may be found only upon a majority vote of the grand jurors after hearing the government's evidence in a secret proceeding. An information may be filed against a defendant in the discretion of the prosecutor without going through this process.[2]

Federal law and the United States Constitution require that offenses carrying a term in excess of one year (felonies) go through the indictment process.[3] An opening question thus presents itself in this chapter: Must defendants accused of state crimes have their cases screened by a grand jury before they can be put to trial for felony violations of state law?

An early case on this problem dealt with a California law of the 1880s, which permitted prosecution on information. A defendant named Hurtado was charged with murder under a prosecutor's information rather than an indict-

---

[1]   FED. R. CRIM. P. 7.

[2]   The information alluded to here is the formal charge filed in the district court or other court of general felony trial jurisdiction. It is to be distinguished from the magistrate's complaint, which is sometimes termed a preliminary information. See § 2.4.

[3]   U.S. CONST. amend. V: "No person shall be held to answer for a capital or otherwise infamous crime, unless on a presentment or indictment of a Grand Jury." FED. R. CRIM. P. 7 (offense punishable by term exceeding one year shall be prosecuted by indictment).

ment. He was convicted, sentenced to death, and the conviction was affirmed by the California Supreme Court. Thereafter Hurtado carried his case to the United States Supreme Court, arguing that the federal Constitution's provision concerning grand juries guaranteed him a right to be prosecuted by indictment. The Supreme Court responded that while the federal government must prosecute felonies on indictment, states were free to proceed on either indictment or information.[4] The point of law has not been overturned to this day. Accordingly, state felony charges may be prosecuted by indictment or formal information, and a majority of states authorize both methods of prosecution. The option is in the hands of the prosecutor in these jurisdictions. The balance of the states are called "indictment states" as opposed to "information states." About 40 percent of the states follow the federal pattern and require felony prosecution by indictment. Several states also prescribe indictments for serious misdemeanors.

In states that permit prosecution under either method, practices vary as to which accusatory vehicle will be used. Surveys reveal that in the states that provide both alternatives to the prosecutor, the indictment is used in urban counties where there is a steady flow of criminal cases, but that the prosecuting attorney's information is the chief charging instrument in less populous counties where criminal cases are more sporadic. In the latter counties, the prosecutor may put the grand jury to work in two major situations, however. First, where prosecution of the accused is being "pushed" by a vexed citizen, but the prosecutor has doubts or reservations about the government's evidence in the case, the grand jury can run a preliminary test of the proof. If the evidence is defective (as the prosecutor suspects) and a subsequent petit jury would likely acquit, the grand jury can refuse to indict and return "no true bill." Another situation in which a grand jury may be invoked in less populous counties is the capital case, or other offense of a very serious nature. The prosecuting attorney frequently desires the strength of an indictment to fortify his or her case.

In screening cases generally, the prosecutor's decision to prosecute must not be motivated by malice or other improper motive. Nor can arrests be made by a selection process that is driven by a discriminatory motivation. While the authorities retain a significant amount of discretion in deciding whom to prosecute, there are limits. Demands are sometimes heard from defendants that the case against them be dismissed because they were improperly targeted for punishment. Claims by defendants of selective enforcement of law or discriminatory **selective prosecution** will be successful if a defendant can show one of two conditions: (1) that the authorities had an unconstitutional motive to discriminate, or (2) that the prosecutor's decision to prosecute was completely arbitrary. The first condition is shown when a defendant establishes that he or she was chosen for prosecution from among several who committed an offense because of his race, religion, or other similar improper reason.

---

4     Hurtado v. California, 110 U.S. 516, 4 S. Ct. 111, 28 L. Ed. 232 (1884).

An improper reason was not found in a 1996 Supreme Court decision, *United States v. Armstrong*.[5] The defendants were charged with conspiring to distribute crack cocaine. The defendants alleged they "were selected for federal prosecution because they are black. . . . Our cases delineating the necessary elements to prove a claim of selective prosecution have taken great pains to explain that the standard [for winning a case on this ground] is a demanding one." In the ordinary case the decision whether to prosecute and what charge to bring before a grand jury generally rests entirely within the prosecutor's discretion. There is a presumption that in bringing charges the prosecutor has not violated a defendant's equal protection rights, and under Supreme Court law, the presumption must be dispelled by "clear evidence to the contrary." Statistics were produced in *Armstrong* and they were included in the Court's opinion: "More than 90 percent of the persons sentenced in 1994 for crack cocaine trafficking were black; 93.4 percent of convicted LSD dealers were white; and 91 percent of those convicted for pornography or prostitution were white." The Supreme Court concluded that people of other races were not being treated differently from the defendants, and relief was denied.

In today's America there are aggressive governmental efforts to confront threats to national security. Defendants are sometimes charged with conspiring to provide support to a foreign terrorist organization. One way for a defendant to defeat such a charge is to successfully claim that the prosecution was based on the unjustifiable standards of religion or ethnicity. Motions to dismiss indictments sometimes allege that the defendant is a Muslim of Middle Eastern descent and that alone made him the target of prosecutors. In such cases the judge must determine whether the prosecutor's decision to prosecute was motivated by a discriminatory purpose, or was, on the other hand, a legitimate effort to stop terrorist activity. For the defense to prevail, the defendant must demonstrate "clear evidence" that the prosecutor's decision was prejudiced.

In addition to the charging decision, prosecutorial discretion plays a role at the other end of the process as well, during sentencing. The next chapter deals with plea bargaining and illustrates the manner in which a prosecutor may affect the sentence by his or her recommendations. Even in courts in which strict sentencing guidelines control, the prosecutor's actions may dramatically influence the outcome. Under Section 3553(e) of Title 18 of the United States Code, and § 5K.1 of the Sentencing Guidelines, a defendant may receive a reduction in sentence for substantial assistance in the prosecution of other cases. However, the reduction is contingent upon a motion by the government. This motion is in the discretion of the prosecutor. In *Wade v. United States*,[6] Wade complained that the government did not move for a reduction on his behalf, even though he had provided substantial assistance in the prosecution of several cases. Without the motion, his sentence would not be reduced. Wade contended that a prosecutor's discretion in exercising the power to move for a sentence reduction is subject to constitutional restrictions.

[5]   116 S. Ct. 1480 (1996). In *Whren v. United States*, 116 S. Ct. 1769 (1996) the Court makes clear that selective prosecution claims—objecting to intentionally discriminatory application of law based upon considerations such as race—rely upon the equal protection clause, not the Fourth Amendment.
[6]   112 S. Ct. 1840 (1992).

The Court, in a unanimous opinion written by Justice Souter, concluded that a prosecutor's refusal to file a substantial-assistance motion should be regulated to the same extent as a prosecutor's other decisions. Generally, there is little court interference with these decisions. Accordingly, the Court concluded that a defendant would be entitled to relief from a prosecutor's refusal to file a substantial-assistance motion only if he could show one of two conditions: (1) that the prosecutor had an unconstitutional motive in refusing to file the motion, such as to discriminate against a defendant on the basis of race or religion; or (2) that the prosecutor's refusal was completely arbitrary.

On the facts, Justice Souter rejected Wade's contention that the prosecutor had acted unconstitutionally in this case. According to Justice Souter, the mere fact that Wade had provided substantial assistance could not be grounds for relief, because the government has "a power, not a duty, to file a motion when the defendant has substantially assisted." Additional details respecting these motions appear at the end of § 5.4 of this text.

## § 4.2   Information

A prosecutor has several choices once the magistrate binds the defendant over. He or she can choose not to prosecute and dismiss the case completely, dismiss the felony and charge the defendant with a misdemeanor, or proceed with a felony prosecution. A factor that may influence the prosecutor to exercise one of the first two options is some weakness in the government's evidence, a weakness that reduces the chance of a felony conviction. Occasionally even with adequate proof the prosecutor may entertain a reasoned expectation that the jury will refuse to convict on sympathy grounds in a particular case. Policy statements prepared for prosecutors by a state's office of the attorney general, or other executive agency, will sometimes guide an individual prosecutor's discretion. Considerations frequently listed as reasons for declining prosecution, to be looked at in combination, include:

1.  No deterrent effect will be served by this prosecution; others in the community will not be substantially dissuaded from repeating similar criminal conduct by forging ahead with this prosecution.

2.  The offense, and its manner of commission, were not of serious character.

3.  The defendant has no history of other criminal activity.

4.  The person who is charged is willing to cooperate in the investigation or prosecution of others more seriously involved.[7]

Notwithstanding occasional close cases and problems of proof, the prosecutor will determine to proceed with prosecution in the majority of cases that have gone through felony preliminaries in the magistrate's court (prosecution is carried out in about 70 to 80 percent of such cases). The next decision is choice of charge. Proceeding by way of information, two or more offenses may be charged in the same information, where the offenses arise out of the

---

[7]   *See,* e.g., U.S. Department of Justice, *Principles of Federal Prosecution* (July 28, 1980).

same transaction. For example, suppose Smith enters a jewelry store, pulls a gun on the proprietor and takes jewels. Upon making escape from the premises he exchanges gunfire with a pursuing officer. Under these facts he may be charged with both robbery and assault upon a peace officer in the same information, and perhaps other offenses as well, depending on the substantive criminal law of the jurisdiction. When joined in an information, separate violations must be contained in distinct counts of the information, each **count** specifying the individual statutory provision violated by the defendant's conduct on the occasion in question. Similarly, two or more defendants may be charged in the same information if they jointly participated in illegal conduct.

States that permit prosecution upon information sometimes specify the specific form of this charging vehicle in the state code. An example appears in Rule 30, Iowa Rules of Criminal Procedure (1998):

---

TRIAL INFORMATION
IN THE IOWA DISTRICT COURT FOR _____ COUNTY

THE STATE OF IOWA                    TRIAL INFORMATION
          vs.
_____, Defendant          No. _____

---

COMES NOW _____ as Prosecuting Attorney of _____ County, Iowa, and in the name and by the Authority of the State of Iowa accuses _____ of the crime of _____ committed as follows: The said _____ on or about the __ day of _____, 20__, in the County of _____ and State of Iowa did unlawfully and willfully

---

in violation of _____ of The Iowa Criminal Code.

A TRUE INFORMATION

---

Prosecuting Attorney

On _____ I find that the evidence contained in the within Trial Information and minutes of evidence, if unexplained, would _____ warrant a conviction by the trial jury and being satisfied from the showing made herein that this case should _____ be prosecuted by Trial Information the same is _____ approved.

Defendant is released on:
1.   personal recognizance _____
2.   appearance bond $_____
     a. unsecured _____
     b. secured _____
3.   other (specify) _____

---

Judge of the _____ Judicial
District of the State of Iowa

(Court file stamp)

---

Form 8 (back side)

This Trial Information, together with the minutes of evidence relating thereto, is duly filed in the District Court of Iowa for _____ County this _____ day of _____, 20____.

_____

Clerk of the District Court
of Iowa for _____ County
By: _____
District Clerk

Names of Witnesses

_____

_____

_____

_____

---

## § 4.3  Grand Jury Procedure

As noted in § 4.2, a prosecutor is not bound by the magistrate's decision to bind over the accused. Under the law of most jurisdictions the case may be pursued or, if deemed nonmeritorious, abandoned. As a general proposition the district attorney has the power to dismiss a case prior to indictment. "Whether to prosecute and what charge to bring before a grand jury are decisions that generally rest in the prosecutor's discretion."[8] In taking a case to the grand jury, the prosecutor's exercise of discretion to prosecute should not harmfully discriminate against any person.[9] The magistrate's decision does not bind the grand jury. If there has been a preliminary hearing and the magistrate dismissed the case, the prosecution can be reinstituted. On the other hand, a magistrate's decision at preliminary hearing that is adverse to the accused does not control the grand jury. "It [the grand jury] may refuse to indict even though the magistrate found probable cause."[10]

Justice Harlan, in his dissenting opinion in *Hurtado v. California*,[11] stressed the value of the grand jury as a mechanism for weeding out false or spiteful claims:

> In the secrecy of the investigations by grand juries, the weak and helpless—proscribed, perhaps, because of their race, or pursued by an unreasoning public clamor—have found, and will continue to find, security against official oppression, the cruelty of mobs, the machinations of falsehood, and the malevolence of private persons who would use the machinery of the law to bring ruin upon their personal enemies.

---

[8]   Slater v. State, 185 Ga. App. 889, 366 S.E.2d 240 (1988).

[9]   Selective prosecution claims, *see* Wayte v. United States, 470 U.S. 598 (1985).

[10]  KAMISAR, LAFAVE, ISRAEL, AND KING, MODERN CRIMINAL PROCEDURE ch. 1, § 3 (10th ed. 2002).

[11]  110 U.S. 516, 554-555, 4 S. Ct. 111, 28 L. Ed. 232 (1884).

Grand jury proceedings are cloaked with secrecy, as a general rule, to protect the accused if the bill of indictment is not found to be a **"true bill."**[12] The grand jury is conducting a screening of the evidence in a case, not a trial. Generally those present are attorneys for the government (prosecutors), witnesses under examination, a court reporter and the jurors. The accused does not have a right to present evidence or a right to counsel at this proceeding. Statutes or court rules prevent the disclosure of evidence taken before the grand jury. As in the preliminary hearing, hearsay evidence is admissible, and police officers who investigated the case may be the major witnesses.[13]

In federal court a grand jury may consist of 16 to 23 jurors, a pattern not dissimilar from that found in several states. A specified majority is generally required to indict a defendant—in federal procedure, 12 jurors. Usually no people other than the jurors may be present while the grand jury is deliberating or voting. If the evidence convinces the jurors that a crime has been committed and there is probable cause to believe the defendant committed it, an indictment (also called a true bill) is found and returned against the defendant, constituting the formal accusation. If no probable cause is found, a "no-bill" results.

In drawing names for and constructing the grand jury, court officials must take care that various population segments are not discriminated against. Proper selection of the grand jury panel requires that no large and identifiable segment of the community be excluded from jury service. Defense attorneys regularly make motions to dismiss an indictment if an indictment approved by a grand jury was not drawn from a fair cross section of the community.

Finding racial discrimination in the makeup of a grand jury that indicted the defendant more than 24 years earlier, the Supreme Court unsettled the defendant's conviction in *Vasquez v. Hillery*.[14] "[E]ven if a grand jury's determination of probable cause is confirmed in hindsight of a conviction on the indicted offense, that confirmation in no way suggests that the discrimination did not impermissibly infect the framing of the indictment and, consequently, the nature or very existence of the proceedings to come."

The indictment in *Vasquez* was defective because of discrimination on the basis of race in the selection of members of a grand jury. When a defendant is indicted, other pretrial attacks may be made by the defense in an effort to have the indictment dismissed. The following kinds of questions may be raised. When the grand jury considered probable cause, were any unauthorized people present in the grand jury room?[15] While hearsay may be used, did the pros-

---

[12]  FED. R. CRIM. P. 6. On the right of the defendant to discover anything about grand jury testimony, see § 6.3.

[13]  Costello v. United States, 350 U.S. 359, 76 S. Ct. 406, 100 L. Ed. 397 (1956). A few states reject Costello's hearsay holding.

[14]  474 U.S. 254 (1986). On the issue of whether a nonminority defendant can complain about racial exclusion of blacks as grand jury foremen, see Campbell v. Louisiana, 118 S. Ct. 1419 (1998) (white defendant has standing to raise equal protection objection to discrimination against black persons).

[15]  United States v. Mechanik, 106 S. Ct. 938 (1986).

ecutor misrepresent its character to the grand jurors by failing to inform them that the evidence was hearsay? Were there other instances of prosecutorial misconduct, such as failing to safeguard grand jury secrecy?

A Supreme Court opinion addressed the last of these questions. May a judge dismiss an indictment for prosecutorial misconduct in a grand jury investigation? The issue was raised when a defendant complained that a prosecutor improperly argued with an expert witness in a tax fraud investigation after the witness gave testimony adverse to the government. This occurred in the presence of some grand jurors. In addition, it was claimed that the prosecutor violated the secrecy provisions of grand jury rules—provisions that cloak the investigations and deliberations of grand juries with privacy—by publicly identifying the targets and the subject matter of the grand jury investigation. The key question, in the view of the Supreme Court, was whether any misconduct by the prosecutor substantially influenced the grand jury's decision to indict. Here, the conclusion was that the totality of the circumstances did not lead to a conclusion that the grand jury's independence was infringed. There was no justification for dismissing the indictment against the defendant on the basis of prosecutorial misconduct, absent a finding that the defendant was prejudiced by such misconduct.[16]

Must the prosecutor present to the grand jury any significant evidence known to the prosecution that is helpful to the defendant, along with the customary presentation of prosecution proof and witnesses? Is it misconduct to fail to do so? Will the charge be dismissed if the prosecutor refuses to tell the grand jury about proof that favors a defendant, and the prosecutor's conduct is later found out? A court rule in one federal circuit required prosecutors to present "substantial **exculpatory evidence**" to the grand jury. The United States Supreme Court struck down this rule. Justice Scalia wrote for the court: "Imposing upon the prosecutor a legal obligation to present exculpatory evidence in his possession would be incompatible with the [grand jury] system." The Court's holding came in the face of a passage in the Manual for United States Attorneys, which provided that when a prosecutor is personally aware of substantial evidence that directly negates the guilt of a subject under investigation, the prosecutor must "disclose such evidence to the grand jury before seeking an indictment against such person."[17]

While the rule of grand jury secrecy extends to attorneys, clerks, and grand jurors, witnesses are not included. Can a judge enter a special "gag" order on witnesses? What if a state passes a law prohibiting disclosure of testimony to the press or otherwise by a grand jury witness? Such an effort by one state was unsuccessful in *Butterworth v. Smith*,[18] at least after the grand jury's term had ended. The case established a new First Amendment principle.

---

[16] Bank of Nova Scotia v. United States, 108 S. Ct. 2369 (1988). A similar result obtained when defendant complained of public disclosure by the government of grand jury matters in another case, Midland Asphalt Corp. v. United States, 109 S. Ct. 1494 (1989).
[17] United States v. Williams, 112 S. Ct. 1735, 118 L. Ed. 2d 352 (1992).
[18] 110 S. Ct. 1376 (1990).

Although state and federal grand juries have traditionally been carried on in secret in order to encourage witnesses to come forward and to permit thorough investigations, Florida's law was overbroad. The state's interest in secrecy was not sufficiently compelling to warrant punishing witnesses with criminal sanctions when they reveal the contents of their own grand jury testimony. The Court stated:

> We also take note of the fact that neither the drafters of the Federal Rules of Criminal Procedure, nor the drafters of similar rules in the majority of the States, found it necessary to impose an obligation of secrecy on grand jury witnesses with respect to their own testimony to protect reputational interests or any of the other interests asserted by Florida. Federal Rule of Criminal Procedure 6(e)(2), governing grand jury secrecy, expressly prohibits certain individuals other than witnesses from disclosing "matters occurring before the grand jury," and provides that "[n]o obligation of secrecy may be imposed on any person except in accordance with this rule." The pertinent Advisory Committee Notes on Rule 6(e)(2), 18 U.S.C.App., p. 726, expressly exempt witnesses from the obligation of secrecy, stating that "[t]he seal of secrecy on witnesses seems an unnecessary hardship and may lead to injustice if a witness is not permitted to make a disclosure to counsel or to an associate."

Florida's law took a different direction from the above and prohibited a witness from ever disclosing testimony given before a grand jury, even after the grand jury's term had ended. By so doing it unconstitutionally violated First Amendment rights.

In the grand jury inquiry of President Clinton involving Monica Lewinsky, a number of witnesses went before microphones in front of the federal courthouse in Washington D.C. immediately following their grand jury appearance. They summarized what they had just told the grand jury.

In addition to the screening function of the grand jury in ordinary criminal cases, it sometimes operates as an investigative agency. Especially prominent in cases of civic corruption or misconduct by public officers, the grand jury may independently subpoena witnesses to advance its investigative aims. The general discussion of the indictment process to this point has assumed the usual situation of the suspect's arrest, followed by eventual presentation of the case to a grand jury. But the grand jury can also look into criminal conduct prior to the arrest of any suspect, and frequently this pattern is followed in illegal drug cases.[19] The inquisitorial power of the grand jury may operate to develop evidence against civic corruption, organized crime, or a broad array of criminal activity.

In recent years there has been substantial litigation over the rights of witnesses to withhold evidence from grand juries. Newsgatherers have fought court battles to protect their sources of information. Where the source's information exposes criminal activity in the community, the newspaper reporter has no federal constitutional privilege to withhold the information and may be

---

[19]   *Id.* at 466, citing United States v. Thompson, 251 U.S. 407, 40 S. Ct. 289, 64 L. Ed. 333 (1920).

required to identify the source.[20] However, in many jurisdictions there are state "shield" laws that supply a privilege for news sources, allowing reporters to keep confidential the names of those who supply information.

The witness who is called before a grand jury may be a member of a criminal gang that is under investigation. Thus, the witness may be suspected of participation in criminal activity. Is such a witness entitled to refuse to answer grand jury questions? The self-incrimination privilege is available to witnesses before the grand jury, and if a witness is asked a question that would show that the witness himself was engaged in criminal activity, the witness could refuse to answer on Fifth Amendment grounds. One way for the grand jury to cut off the witness's right to withhold evidence is to grant him or her immunity.[21] With the approval of a judge, the prosecutor may secure an order protecting the witness from having his or her words used against him or her by granting the witness **immunity from prosecution**. Once this is granted, the witness must answer or be held in contempt. This immunity device is sometimes employed when a lesser member of a criminal gang appears as a witness and evidence against one of the higher-ups is sought by the grand jury.

While the Fifth Amendment may be asserted by a grand jury witness to block questions, at least before immunity is granted, objections by the witness based on the Fourth Amendment are treated differently.

Sometimes a witness declines to answer grand jury questions because the information that gave rise to the question was gained from an illegal entry and search of the witness's home or business. In a loan-sharking case from Ohio, a witness raised just such an objection to grand jury questions. The United States Supreme Court denied any right of the witness to refuse to cooperate. The Court reasoned that to allow a witness to invoke the exclusionary rule in cases like this would "unduly interfere with the effective . . . discharge of the grand jury's duties."[22]

The grand jury witness appears before the jury unaccompanied by counsel. However, sometimes a lawyer is retained to advise the witness and comes to the courthouse. For example, the federal grand jury investigating the Iran-Contra matter in June 1990 called Oliver North as a witness. "North repeatedly left the secret proceedings during nearly three hours of testimony to confer with his attorneys in a courthouse hallway."[23]

---

[20]    Branzburg v. Hayes, 408 U.S. 665, 92 S. Ct. 2646, 33 L. Ed. 2d 626 (1972). The above text refers to the absence of a federally-guaranteed news privilege; a number of states do provide such privileges to reporters as a matter of state policy.

[21]    What a witness says may not be later used to prosecute that witness, under an immunity grant, nor may leads from the immunized testimony be used to supply evidence against the accused. Kastigar v. United States, 406 U.S. 441, 92 S. Ct. 1653, 32 L. Ed. 2d 212 (1972).

[22]    United States v. Calandra, 414 U.S. 338, 94 S. Ct. 613, 38 L. Ed. 2d 561 (1974) (exclusionary rule does not operate in grand jury proceedings). But see Gelbard v. United States, 408 U.S. 41, 92 S. Ct. 2357, 33 L. Ed. 2d 179 (1972), where the government intrusion was not a physical one but consisted of electronic surveillance.

[23]    ATLANTA CONST., June 3, 1990. Oliver North was convicted of some of the charges brought against him, but ultimately defeated them on appeal. United States v. North, 920 F.2d 940 (D.C. Cir. 1990).

Subpoenas for information and records are frequently issued by grand juries as they investigate and seek evidence necessary to resolve the question of whether to indict.[24] A **subpoena** is an order directing the recipient to supply documents or to appear and testify. If a corporation is under investigation, a bookkeeper or company officer may be ordered to bring forward corporate books and records reflecting financial dealings. While purely personal records may be withheld by the individual under the Fifth Amendment privilege against self-incrimination, the cloak of privilege does not extend to company documents. In *Braswell v. United States*,[25] a federal grand jury issued a subpoena to Braswell requiring him to produce the books and records of a company of which he was the sole shareholder. Braswell moved to quash the subpoena, arguing that the act of producing the records would violate his constitutional rights. The Supreme Court responded: "[P]etitioner has operated his business through the corporate form, and we have long recognized that for purposes of the Fifth Amendment, corporations and other collective entities are treated differently from individuals. . . . [T]he Court developed the **collective entity rule**, which declares simply that corporate records are not private and therefore are not protected by the Fifth Amendment."

Information gathering by grand juries formed the focus of another Supreme Court decision. In *Doe v. United States*,[26] the target of a grand jury investigation was ordered to produce records of transactions in accounts at three named banks in the Cayman Islands and Bermuda. The District Court found the defendant in contempt of court when he refused to comply with demands for cooperation, and the judge ordered him to be confined until he did so. The grand jury's investigation of suspected fraudulent manipulation of oil cargoes and receipt of unreported income awaited Supreme Court resolution of the constitutional question. The Court decided that a court order compelling disclosure of foreign bank records did not violate the individual's Fifth Amendment privilege against self-incrimination. The decision concluded that there was "no question that the foreign banks cannot invoke the Fifth Amendment in declining to produce the documents; the privilege does not extend to such artificial entities. . . . [As to the target of the grand jury's investigation, constitutional rights are involved when the Government's demand for information is a request for testimonial information; it is only] the attempt to force him 'to disclose the contents of his own mind' that implicates the self-incrimination clause."[27] Because the request here did not involve forced production of a communication—written or oral words disclosing guilty knowledge or

---

24    In United States v. Dionisio, 410 U.S. 1, 93 S. Ct. 764, 35 L. Ed. 2d 67 (1973), the Supreme Court upheld grand jury subpoenas directing 20 persons to submit to voice recordings in order to match them with recordings of unknown voices obtained by court-approved wiretaps. 108 S. Ct. 64 (1988).

25    108 S. Ct. 64 (1988).

26    108 S. Ct. 2341 (1988).

27    108 S. Ct. at 2348. Cases cited by the Court involved forced production of physical evidence, including handwriting exemplars, blood samples, voice exemplars, as well as requiring an accused to wear particular clothing for identification. These examples were condoned by the Court; none involved intrusions upon the contents of the mind of the accused.

admissions of criminality by the accused—the self-incrimination clause was not violated by the District Court, and the contempt order against the defendant was affirmed.

These cases affirm and advance the evidence-gathering capability of grand juries as they pursue investigations.

## § 4.4   Indictment

Once probable cause is established the grand jury may vote to indict. The indictment must clearly and specifically state the offense that the defendant has allegedly committed. Thus, the indictment should adequately inform the defendant as to the charges he must defend himself against. Rule 7(c) of the Federal Rules of Criminal Procedure requires that the indictment contain a plain, concise, and definite written statement of the essential facts constituting the offense charged. The indictment shall refer to the statute or other provision of law that the defendant is alleged to have violated. Where an indictment fails to satisfy these requirements or there are other defects in the grand jury's work, complaints against an indictment are raised in a defendant's motion to dismiss.

How does an indictment read? Sample grand jury indictments used in federal courts are instructive as to the form of this charging vehicle:

---

INDICTMENT FOR MURDER IN THE FIRST DEGREE
OF FEDERAL OFFICER

In the United States District Court for the _____ District of
_____, _____ Division.

UNITED STATES OF AMERICA
v.
JOHN DOE

No. _____

(18 U.S.C. §§ 1111, 1114)

The grand jury charges:

On or about the _____ day of _____, 20___, in the _____ _____ District of _____, John Doe with premeditation and by means of shooting murdered John Roe, who was then an officer of the Federal Bureau of Investigation of the Department of Justice engaged in the performance of his official duties.

A True Bill.

_____,
*Foreperson.*

_____,
*United States Attorney.*

(As amended Dec. 27, 1948, eff. Oct. 20, 1949.)

---

INDICTMENT FOR MAIL FRAUD

In the United States District Court for the _____ District of _____, _____ Division.

UNITED STATES OF AMERICA

v.

JOHN DOE ET AL.

No._____

(18 U.S.C. § 1341)

The grand jury charges:

1. Prior to the _____ day of _____, 20___, and continuing to the _____ day of _____, 20___,[1] the defendants John Doe, Richard Roe, John Stiles and Richard Miles devised and intended to devise a scheme and artifice to defraud purchasers of stock of XY Company, a California corporation, and to obtain money and property by means of the following false and fraudulent pretenses, representations and promises, well knowing at the time that the pretenses, representations and promises would be false when made: That the XY Company owned a mine at or near San Bernardino, California; that the mine was in actual operation; that gold ore was being obtained at the mine and sold at a profit; that the current earnings of the company would be sufficient to pay dividends on its stock at the rate of six percent per annum.

2. On the _____ day of _____, 20___, in the _____ District of _____, the defendants for the purpose of executing the aforesaid scheme and artifice and attempting to do so, caused to be placed in an authorized depository for mail matter a letter addressed to Mrs. Mary Brown, 110 Main Street, Stockton, California, to be sent or delivered by the Post Office Establishment of the United States.

Second Count

1. The Grand Jury realleges all of the allegations of the first count of this indictment, except those contained in the last paragraph thereof.

2. On the _____ day of _____, 20___, in the _____ District of _____, the defendants, for the purpose of executing the aforesaid scheme and artifice and attempting to do so, caused to be placed in an authorized depository for mail matter a letter addressed to Mr. John J. Jones, 220 First Street, Batavia, New York, to be sent or delivered by the Post Office Establishment of the United States.

A True Bill.

_____,
*Foreperson.*

_____,
*United States Attorney.*

---

[1] Insert last mailing date alleged.

(As amended Dec. 27, 1948, eff. Oct. 20, 1949. Forms are made available to United States Attorneys by the Department of Justice. Official forms are no longer appended to the Federal Rules of Criminal Procedure, Rule 58 abrogated.)

## § 4.5 Joinder and Severance

**Joinder** of offenses arising out of the same transaction, as well as joinder of defendants, is permitted in a single indictment as in the case of a prosecuting attorney's information.[28] The point is illustrated in the federal mail fraud indictment that appeared at the end of § 4.4.

In the illustrative indictments set forth in § 4.4, defendants John Doe, Richard Roe, John Stiles, and Richard Miles were charged in a **joint indictment**. As previously noted, two or more defendants may be joined for trial or charged in the same indictment if they participated in the same transaction constituting the alleged offense.[29] **Joint trials** of more than one defendant lend themselves to judicial economy, leading one Supreme Court Justice to remark: "Joint trials play a vital role in the criminal justice system, accounting for almost one third of federal criminal trials in the past five years. Many joint trials—for example, those involving large conspiracies to import and distribute illegal drugs—involve a dozen or more codefendants."[30]

Although a joint indictment is permissible, continuing that joinder into trial is not always possible. **Severance** of defendants and separate, individual trials will be held where one defendant asks that his case be separated from that of other defendants and proves the need for a separate trial. In the federal murder prosecution of Timothy McVeigh and Terry Nichols for bombing the federal building in Oklahoma City, Nichols successfully won the right to a separate trial. His 1997 conviction resulted in a life sentence, unlike the death sentence handed down in the trial of McVeigh.

There are a number of ways for defendants who are indicted together to seek separate trials. One situation involves a defendant who makes claims that are totally at odds and inconsistent with the defense asserted by the other defendants. Another complicating factor occurs when one defendant has confessed and the government seeks to use that confession to convict not only the confessing defendant, but his or her codefendant as well. Separate proceedings may be required, with the confession being used in one trial but excluded from the trial of the nonconfessing defendant. The United States Supreme Court has held that a defendant is deprived of his or her rights under the Constitution's confrontation clause when a nontestifying codefendant's confession naming the defendant as a participant in the crime is introduced at their joint trial.[31]

---

[28] FED. R. CRIM. P. 8 authorizes two or more offenses to be charged in the same indictment if they are of similar character or are based on acts constituting parts of a common scheme. *See* Albernaz v. United States, 450 U.S. 333 (1981).

[29] FED. R. CRIM. P. 8(b). This rule is construed in Lee v. Illinois, 476 U.S. 530 (1986).

[30] Richardson v. Marsh, 107 S. Ct. 1702 (1987) (name of nonconfessing codefendant redacted (edited) from confession; joint trial served the interests of justice, and use of confessions is essential to convict and punish those who violate the law).

[31] Bruton v. United States, 391 U.S. 123 (1968). Where a codefendant's name is deleted from a confession, the redaction must be effective and must not point to the nonconfessing defendant. Gray v. Maryland, 118 S. Ct. 1151 (1998).

The government can ask that defendants who are charged separately be tried together, as long as the charges arise out of the same transaction. Defendants, on the other hand, frequently ask for individual trials. They must demonstrate that trial together would be unfair, unless state law provides for separate trials generally or for separate proceedings when defendants are charged with specified serious offenses.[32]

When the court addresses a government motion for **consolidation**, or joinder, of defendants who are separately indicted for trial, or when defendants who are jointly indicted ask for a severance, a hearing will frequently follow. The issue in both sorts of proceedings, consolidation or severance, will be basically the same: Is a joint trial fair, or will it prejudice the rights of a defendant? The Supreme Court has spoken on this situation, cases in which defendants make general claims of prejudice.[33] In the view of the Court, the cases should usually be tried together and the trial court should order separate trial of defendants only if: (1) there is a serious risk that a joint trial would compromise a specific trial right of one of the defendants, or (2) joint trials would prevent the jury from making a reliable judgment about guilt or innocence as "might occur when evidence that the jury should not consider against a defendant . . . is admitted against a codefendant."

The foregoing comments refer to joinder of defendants. What about the rules relating to joinder of offenses (as opposed to joinder of defendants)? When dealing with a defendant's motion to sever and separately try offenses that have been joined in an indictment, certain questions confront the judge. Suppose an indictment is returned against a single defendant, but it contains allegations of several different crimes. In determining whether to try all the charges together or whether to try one or more of the crimes separately, important criminal procedure issues will be addressed. Are the offenses related? If not, the judge may order the crimes to be adjudicated in separate trials. Do the interests of justice demand separate proceedings as to various charges because of the complexity of the case? Where charges are separate and distinct, will the jury's potential ability to distinguish the evidence that relates to only one count of the indictment be compromised? Is it prejudicial to the accused to try separate and different crimes together? While no single one of these questions will usually be totally controlling, collectively they are factors the judge will consider in exercising his or her discretion to determine whether the government's claims will be tried together or apart.

The issue of joint or separate trials has generated extensive litigation. Joinder is probable when the government's proof ties two crimes together. Where it would be almost impossible to present to a jury the evidence of one of the crimes without also permitting evidence of the other, joint trial of the alleged crimes is proper.[34] Sometimes the motive for one offense is supplied

---

[32]   E.g., Ga. Stat. § 17-8-4 (capital offenses; separate trial if defendant files motion to sever).
[33]   Zafiro v. United States, 113 S. Ct. 933 (1993).
[34]   Stewart v. State, 239 Ga. 588, 238 S.E.2d 540 (1977).

by another crime.[35] In other cases, the court may find the needed nexus to permit joint trial of two or more offenses when a defendant has committed separate crimes in a similar and distinctive manner. In *Commonwealth v. Morris*,[36] the defendant was charged with two separate robberies. Both occurred on elevators in a housing project. The victim in each case was a woman, and during each of the robberies the assailant opened the clothing of the victim and searched their brassieres for any possible hidden money. Both of the victims later identified the defendant as the perpetrator. The court concluded that trial of both crimes in a single proceeding was proper:

> The similarity in the timing, implementation and even the plan of escape of each robbery provides the distinctive and unusual modus operandi which would justify the conclusion that the perpetrator of one was the perpetrator of the other. It is difficult to conceive of any situation where the propriety of joinder could be clearer. We, therefore, affirm the learned trial court's ruling which permitted these robberies to be tried in a single trial.

So much, for the moment, on the issue of separate trials. Our concern returns to the charging instrument, the information or indictment. The next step in the typical case is arraignment.

## § 4.6   Bypassing the Indictment Stage

As indicated earlier in this chapter, typical charging instruments are indictments or informations. In grand jury jurisdictions, the defendant may be tried upon an information (or an accusation in some states) when the defendant waives indictment by a grand jury. In federal court, Rule 7(b) of the Federal Rules of Criminal Procedure provides:

> **(b) Waiving Indictment.** An offense punishable by imprisonment for more than one year may be prosecuted by information if the defendant—in open court and after being advised of the nature of the charge and of the defendant's rights—waives prosecution by indictment.

Sometimes defendants in serious crimes waive the indictment stage because they want to rapidly move the case to trial, avoiding extended publicity in a case in which they want a speedy trial in an effort to clear their name. Most cases will go through formal processes, however, and the reading of the felony charge to a defendant at arraignment will be from a grand jury indictment.

---

[35]   United States v. Gorecki, 813 F.2d 40 (3d Cir. 1987) (interrelated offenses; separate but related offense was deemed vital part of plan to possess and distribute drugs).
[36]   425 A.2d 715 (Pa. 1981).

## § 4.7   Presentation to the Accused: Arraignment

An arraignment is conducted by the trial judge and consists of reading the indictment or information to the defendant, unless he or she waives same. In most states, a copy of the charging instrument must also be delivered to the defendant at the arraignment or before. The defendant must answer the charge by pleading to it at this time, and various pleas may be entered. In federal court, the defendants may plead *guilty*, *not guilty*, or *nolo contendere* ("no contest"). A defendant who pleads not guilty denies the averments of the charge and will have his or her case set for trial. Some state statutes permit other pleas to be entered, and in at least one the defendant may plead double jeopardy at arraignment.

# Guilty Pleas

# 5

## Chapter Outline

## § 5.1   Federal Cases

Rule 11 of the Federal Rules of Criminal Procedure provides that a defendant may plead guilty, not guilty, or (with the consent of the court) nolo contendere. **Nolo contendere** literally means "I do not desire to contest the action," and in many respects is the equivalent of a plea of guilty, with one major exception: unlike a plea of guilty, a plea of nolo contendere may not be used against a defendant in any later civil action arising out of the acts that gave birth to the criminal case. The court raises questions to make certain the nolo plea is knowingly and voluntarily entered by the defendant. The trial judge may inquire whether the defendant has committed the act charged. Sentencing can proceed after acceptance of a plea of nolo contendere as with guilty pleas.

A **guilty plea** is an admission of every material allegation in the accusatory pleading (indictment or information). There is no triable issue after a plea of guilty and it is a waiver of most matters of defense, including the question of illegally obtained evidence.

A large number of cases are disposed of by means of guilty pleas. One survey extending over a 10-year period showed guilty pleas running between 81 percent to 90 percent of criminal cases, with modest year-by-year variation.[1] The Commission writing federal sentencing guidelines observed that nearly 90 percent of all federal criminal cases involve guilty pleas.

Because of the pervasive effect of a guilty plea, Federal Rule 11 requires the trial judge before whom the plea is entered to address the defendant personally and determine that the plea is made voluntarily and with understanding of the nature of the charge and the consequence of the plea.[2] "The court

---

[1]   People v. Allen, 420 N.W.2d 499, 566 (Mich. 1988). In 1996, 91.4% of federal criminal cases were resolved by pleas. Saris, *Below the Radar Screens: Have the Sentencing Guidelines Eliminated Disparity? One Judge's Perspective*, 30 SUFFOLK L. REV. 1027, 1052 n.122 (1997).

[2]   FED. R. CRIM. P. 11.

shall not enter a judgment upon a plea without making such inquiry as shall satisfy it, that there is a factual basis for the plea."[3] In determining whether the plea is made voluntarily, the court might ask the defendant in open court whether any agent of the government has made any promises or threats to induce the defendant to plead guilty. The accused must also receive real notice of the true charge against him or her, the first requirement of due process of law. In determining whether the defendant understands the nature of the charge, the court will inquire whether the defendant is aware of the maximum sentence permissible for the offense involved. The court may also bring out the point that the defendant has a right to trial on the charge, including a right to trial by jury. Finally, the court will ask the defendant if he or she in fact committed the offense or offenses alleged in the indictment. Only after the court is satisfied in the particulars mentioned will it accept the plea of guilty.

A leading federal case on the judge's duties in accepting pleas is *McCarthy v. United States*.[4] In this case, the trial judge failed to address the defendant personally when the defendant entered his plea, and the defendant later claimed that he did not understand what he was giving up when his lawyer announced that he wished to plead guilty. The United States Supreme Court announced that "prejudice inheres in a failure to comply with Rule 11" of the Federal Rules. The guilty plea was set aside and the defendant was given the opportunity to plead anew.

Criminal indictments increase in volume annually and the workload on our nation's courts and prosecutors continues to grow. Guilty pleas facilitate efficient disposition of criminal cases. As noted, pleas of nolo contendere and guilty represented an average of 80 to 90 percent of the **dispositions** in criminal cases. To achieve such dispositions, prosecutors frequently engage in plea bargaining, and a broad range of plea alternatives are open. The prosecutor may agree to recommend a particular sentence in exchange for the plea (in jurisdictions where such recommendations are received and considered by the court), allow the defendant to plead guilty to a lesser offense than that contained in the original indictment, or dismiss some counts in an indictment in exchange for the defendant's guilty plea to others. The mere fact that the defense has negotiated with the government, and that the negotiations resulted in a plea of guilty, does not under prevailing law render the plea involuntary and subject it to successful attack on appeal by the defendant.[5]

While sentencing of the defendant can take place immediately after entry of his or her guilty plea, it normally occurs a short time later. This allows the probation service of the court to make a **presentence investigation** of the

---

3   Marshall v. Lonberger, 103 S. Ct. 843 (1983) (transcript of exchange between court and defendant at time of plea and sentencing appears in opinion).

4   394 U.S. 459, 89 S. Ct. 1166, 22 L. Ed. 2d 418 (1969).

5   Santobello v. New York, 404 U.S. 257, 92 S. Ct. 495, 30 L. Ed. 2d 427 (1971); ABA Report, *Standards Relating to Pleas of Guilty*, § 3.1 (1967). Plea bargaining is discussed in § 5.4. *See also*, United States v. Rodriguez-DeMaya, 674 F.2d 1122 (5th Cir. 1982) (defense attorney "in the best of tradition and in the interest of his client, had previously been in touch with United States attorney"; plea bargain resulted).

defendant's background and character for the sentencing judge, in order that the court will be intelligently informed when it passes sentence. A guilty plea that has been entered by the defendant may be withdrawn at any time until the time sentence is imposed for "any fair and just reason." In 1997, the United States Supreme Court characterized the entry of a plea of guilty as a serious act, and pointed out that the defendant does not have an absolute right to withdraw the plea prior to sentence. He or she may not change his or her mind "simply on a lark," but can only back out for a compelling, fair, and just reason, as set forth in the rules.[6] After sentencing, pleas are much more difficult to withdraw, and a plea will be set aside only by appeal or special motion.[7]

## § 5.2   State Cases

The Supreme Court opinion in *Boykin v. Alabama*[8] is the state counterpart to the *McCarthy* case, which set the tone for federal practice as outlined above. *Boykin* involved an Alabama defendant charged in state court with armed robbery. He pled guilty to five armed robbery indictments and was sentenced to death. The record in the case did not disclose whether the sentencing judge inquired of Boykin if he knew the possible consequences of the guilty pleas. In the Supreme Court's view, the record was defective in failing to demonstrate that the judge personally questioned the defendant in any way. The Court pointed out that the government has a responsibility to record the personal colloquy between court and defendant that ensures the validity of the guilty plea:

> The requirement that the prosecution spread on the record the prerequisites of a valid waiver is no constitutional innovation. In *Carnley v. Cochran*, 369 U.S. 506, 82 S. Ct. 884, 8 L. Ed. 2d 70 (1962), we dealt with a problem of waiver of the right to counsel, a Sixth Amendment right. We held: "Presuming waiver from a silent record is impermissible. The record must show, or there must be an allegation and evidence which show, that an accused was offered counsel but intelligently and understandingly rejected the offer. Anything less is not waiver."

> We think that the same standard must be applied to determining whether a guilty plea is voluntarily made. For, as we have said, a plea of guilty is more than an admission of conduct; it is a conviction. Ignorance, incomprehension, coercion, terror, inducements, [or] subtle or blatant threats might be a perfect coverup of unconstitutionality.

The Court overturned Boykin's conviction. Justice Harlan, in objecting to this result, made an observation that appears highly instructive in terms of the effect wrought by the *Boykin* case. "So far as one can make out from the

---

[6]    United States v. Hyde, 117 S. Ct. 1630 (1997).
[7]    FED. R. CRIM. P. 32(e).
[8]    395 U.S. 238, 89 S. Ct. 1709, 23 L. Ed. 2d 274 (1969).

Court's opinion, what is now in effect being held is that the prophylactic procedures of [Federal] Criminal Rule 11 are substantially applicable to the States
as a matter of federal constitutional due process."

In complying with federal standards, points typically covered in a sentencing hearing were mentioned in § 5.1 above. When explaining the effect of
the plea to the accused, the court should describe the possible range of punishment. The court should also explain that when a plea of guilty or nolo contendere is accepted, trial rights are extinguished. And failure of a court to
inquire whether fear or promises induced the plea will invalidate that plea.
However, under some decisions the court need not warn the defendant of "collateral consequences" of the plea, such as the fact that the felony conviction
could be used in a habitual criminal prosecution if the defendant is later convicted of another felony.

One thing the court must determine is whether there is a factual basis for
the plea; that is, did the accused commit the offense? Before 1970 it was frequently assumed that a factual basis did not exist if the defendant told the
court he was innocent, and in this situation the offered plea could not be
received. The Supreme Court's decision in *North Carolina v. Alford* cast doubt
on the validity of that conclusion. A defendant indicted for murder in North
Carolina pled guilty, but before the plea was accepted the judge heard evidence in the form of sworn testimony from state and defense witnesses. The
witnesses made out a strong case of murder against the accused. Although the
defendant desired to plead guilty, he insisted at the same time he was innocent.
The judge sentenced him to 30 years' imprisonment. Later, the defendant
attacked the sentence by filing a petition for writ of habeas corpus, claiming
that an admission of guilt by the defendant is a necessary prerequisite to a
valid and binding guilty plea. The United States Supreme Court stated in
*North Carolina v. Alford*:

> Ordinarily, a judgment of conviction resting on a plea of guilty is justified by
> the defendant's admission that he committed the crime charged against him
> and his consent that judgment be entered without a trial of any kind. The plea
> usually subsumes both elements, and justifiably so, even though there is no
> separate, express admission by the defendant that he committed the particu-
> lar acts claimed to constitute the crime charged in the indictment. . . . Here
> Alford entered his plea but accompanied it with the statement that he had not
> shot the victim.

> If Alford's statements were to be credited as sincere assertions of his innocence,
> there obviously existed a factual and legal dispute between him and the State.
> Without more, it might be argued that the conviction entered on his guilty plea
> was invalid, since his assertion of innocence negatived any admission of guilt,
> which, as we observed last Term in *Brady*, is normally "[c]entral to the plea and
> the foundation for entering judgment against the defendant. . . ."

> State and lower federal courts are divided upon whether a guilty plea can be
> accepted when it is accompanied by protestations of innocence and hence con-
> tains only a waiver of trial but no admission of guilt. . . . Thus, while most pleas

of guilty consist of both a waiver of trial and an express admission of guilt, the latter element is not a constitutional requisite to the imposition of criminal penalty. An individual accused of crime may voluntarily, knowingly, and understandingly consent to the imposition of a prison sentence even if he is unwilling or unable to admit his participation in the acts constituting the crime.[9]

The *Alford* decision notes that states may apply a more restrictive rule than that suggested there. Several states do, requiring a personal admission of guilt before acceptance of a plea.

In both state and federal courts, a defendant is entitled to the help of a lawyer when he or she pleads guilty to a serious crime. However, a defendant who wants to represent himself and "go it alone" is constitutionally permitted to do so. Just as an accused is privileged under the constitution to try his own case (see text § 6.34), so also can he plead guilty without the assistance of counsel. The judge who accepts the guilty plea must be certain the defendant knows what he is doing. The defendant's waiver of counsel must be made knowingly and intelligently.[10]

While the Supreme Court appears to be aligning state and federal criminal procedure on the question of what constitutes a valid plea of guilty, certain differences in other areas appear. Federal provisions restricting the withdrawal of guilty pleas after sentence have been briefly sketched. While several states follow this approach, some make it easier to withdraw a plea after sentence in state court prosecutions. In addition, while most states follow the rule that a plea of guilty waives defense objections that evidence against the defendant was illegally seized, a distinct contrary rule has appeared in some states.[11]

The drafters of the Federal Rules of Criminal Procedure endeavored to address the waiver problem by creating a conditional plea. Interlocutory appeal of a pretrial motion to suppress evidence is not generally allowed, causing many defendants who lost the pretrial motion to go through an entire trial simply to preserve the pretrial issues for later appellate review. The Federal Advisory Committee noted: "This results in a waste of prosecutorial and judicial resources, and causes delay in the trial of other cases . . ." To remedy the problem, a 1983 amendment of the rules allows appeals from suppression motions notwithstanding a guilty plea. In order to do so, however, the defendant must obtain the approval of the court and the prosecutor. After pleading guilty and appealing her evidence point, Federal Rule of Criminal Procedure

---

[9] 400 U.S. 25, 91 S. Ct. 160, 27 L. Ed. 2d 162 (1970). In note 11 to the opinion the Supreme Court noted that states are free to follow a different rule than that suggested by *Alford*:
"[T]he States may bar their courts from accepting guilty pleas from any defendants who assert their innocence."

[10] Iowa v. Tovar, 124 S. Ct. 1379 (2004).

[11] In McMann v. Richardson, 397 U.S. 759, 90 S. Ct. 1441, 25 L. Ed. 2d 763 (1970), the Supreme Court ruled that a guilty plea waives the right to contest the admissibility of any evidence the state might have offered, unless the state law provides otherwise. However, in 1983 the Supreme Court held that a plaintiff's guilty plea did not constitute a waiver of illegal search claims for purposes of a damage suit against police in a civil rights action. Haring v. Prosise, 103 S. Ct. 2368 (1983). Further details on *Haring* are contained in § 10.15 of this text.

11(a)(2) endorses the following procedure on behalf of a successful defendant: "A defendant who prevails on appeal shall be allowed to withdraw the plea."

A further distinction between state and federal practice lies in the narrow range of pleas to the indictment allowed in federal court. In addition to customary pleas of guilty, not guilty or nolo contendere, state codes have expanded plea procedure to allow pleas of not guilty by reason of insanity or guilty but mentally ill at the time of the crime.[12] See § 6.15 for more detail on insanity pleas.

## § 5.3    Underlying Principles

Unfortunately, legal history in the guilty plea field occasionally has been marked with the occurrence of defendants losing their right to trial by jury and other rights without understanding these consequences when they pled guilty. Cases like *McCarthy* and *Boykin* attempt to avert this problem. One factor that should assist in meeting the legal requirement that a defendant be fully informed when he or she pleads guilty is the provision of counsel at this stage of the prosecution. Constitutional decisions make clear that the right to counsel applies in both state and federal court when the accused pleads guilty to a felony charge.[13] This includes a right to appointed counsel when the defendant is without funds to hire a lawyer. Of course, the aim of the judicial system is that such assistance by counsel will be competent and effective. Where this is not the case, there have been decisions that allow defendants who are in the penitentiary to attack and set aside their pleas and sentences. Thus, in one case in which the court found that the defense attorney failed to fully advise the defendant of the consequences of his guilty plea, failed to initiate plea bargaining, and failed to interview possible defense witnesses to the alleged crime, the defendant successfully argued that his guilty plea was invalid.[14]

Sometimes the state seeks to enhance the sentence of a defendant based on other guilty pleas entered earlier in the defendant's life. Habitual offender laws, often carrying very severe sentences, are triggered by a current criminal conviction when it is preceded by two or three prior convictions. Occasionally a defendant resists imposition of severe punishment on the ground that his or her old convictions were based on guilty pleas entered in violation of his or her rights. Kentucky applies a presumption of regularity to such prior convictions, deeming them to be properly entered until contrary evidence is shown. It was up to an accused recidivist to come up with evidence that his or her

---

[12]    E.g., GA. STAT. §§ 17-7-94, 95, 131.

[13]    *See* § 7.8. A Supreme Court case supporting the point is Kitchens v. Smith, 401 U.S. 847, 91 S. Ct. 1089, 28 L. Ed. 2d 519 (1971) (indigent state prisoner's right to be furnished counsel when he entered plea of guilty did not depend on a request for assistance of counsel).

[14]    Hawkman v. Parratt, 661 F.2d 1161 (8th Cir.), reh'g denied, 1981. *See* Lamb v. Estelle, 667 F.2d 492, 494 (5th Cir. 1982) (counsel has the duty of assuring that the guilty plea is knowingly and voluntarily made). A defendant may attack his or her guilty plea on the ground of ineffective assistance of counsel. Bradbury v. Wainwright, 658 F.2d 1083 (5th Cir. 1981).

rights were infringed upon in the prior proceeding if he or she wanted to attack the impact of a prior conviction. If the defendant could show some evidence of irregularity in an old conviction, the burden shifted to the state to prove the actual validity of the prior conviction by a preponderance of the evidence. The Court held that the Kentucky procedure was fair.[15]

What if a defendant is mentally incompetent to understand the charges against him or her when the judge explains them? The validity of a guilty plea depends on the defendant's competence to make a plea. The test for competency to plead guilty is similar to the standard for a defendant's ability to stand trial. Is the defendant able to consult with his or her lawyer with a reasonable degree of rational understanding? Does the accused have a rational as well as a factual understanding of the proceedings against him or her? If the answers to these questions are "yes," the defendant is deemed to be competent.[16]

A final question in this section involves a controversial criminal procedure question. The issue is whether a defendant who pleads guilty should, by reason of that plea, be given any special consideration as to the length of sentence in a criminal case. Recognizing that trials are costly in terms of time and money, many state and federal judges take the view that a defendant who pleads guilty is entitled to a "break." The American Bar Association studied the question, and in the ABA Standards [for Criminal Justice] Relating to Pleas of Guilty, the study concluded that it is proper to grant sentence concessions to defendants who plead guilty. Among other factors, leniency may be called for when a plea of guilty is entered and substantial evidence establishes that:

1.  The defendant is genuinely contrite;

2.  A reduced sentence or other concession will prevent undue harm to the defendant from the form of the conviction;

3.  The defendant is seeking to avoid trial so he can make restitution to the victim or avoid public attention and embarrassment to the victims; or

4.  The defendant is cooperating with the authorities in the apprehension or prosecution of serious offenders.[17]

A correlative principle has also been adopted. Where the defendant does not plead guilty, insists upon a trial, and then lies to the judge or jury, enhanced punishment may be the result. The Supreme Court has held that a defendant who testifies falsely at trial may have his or her sentence increased upon a sentencing judge's finding that perjury was committed.[18]

---

[15]　Parke v. Raley, 113 S. Ct. 517 (1992).

[16]　Godinez v. Moran, 113 S. Ct. 2680 (1993).

[17]　A.B.A. STANDARDS, *Pleas of Guilty* § 14-1.8 (2d ed. 1979).

[18]　United States v. Dunnigan, 113 S. Ct. 1111 (1993).

## § 5.4   Plea Bargaining

**Plea bargaining** is a controversial feature of the American justice system. It is appropriate, having reviewed in this chapter the plea procedures in state and federal courts, to look at what has been called the "invisible process" behind guilty pleas. Under one view, plea bargaining is essential and (if properly implemented) even desirable. A competing view demands the end to this "dangerous and unwholesome feature of American justice." Because of the import of this debate, selections supporting each view are presented for review.

First, drawing together ideas that favor plea bargaining is the Federal Advisory Committee Note to Rule 11, Federal Rules of Criminal Procedure:

> In *Santobello v. New York*, 404 U.S. 257, 260, 92 S. Ct. 495, 498, 30 L. Ed. 2d 427 (1971), the court said:
>
> "The disposition of criminal charges by agreement between the prosecutor and the accused, sometimes loosely called 'plea bargaining,' is an essential component of the administration of justice. Properly administered, it is to be encouraged."
>
> Administratively, the criminal justice system has come to depend upon pleas of guilty and, hence, upon plea discussions. See, e.g., President's Commission on Law Enforcement and Administration of Justice, Task Report: The Courts 9 (1967); Note, Guilty Plea Bargaining: Compromises By Prosecutors To Secure Guilty Pleas, 112 U. Pa. L. Rev. 865 (1964).
>
> . . .
>
> Where the defendant by his plea aids in insuring prompt and certain application of correctional measures, the proper ends of the criminal justice system are furthered because swift and certain punishment serves the ends of both general deterrence and the rehabilitation of the individual defendant. Cf. Note, The Influence of the Defendant's Plea on Judicial Determination of Sentence, 66 Yale L.J. 204, 211 (1956). Where the defendant has acknowledged his guilt and shown a willingness to assume responsibility for his conduct, it has been thought proper to recognize this in sentencing. . . . A plea of guilty avoids the necessity of a public trial and may protect the innocent victim of a crime against the trauma of direct and cross-examination.

The Federal Advisory Committee discussed some of the primary methods of plea bargaining, describing the concessions that may be given to induce a defendant to plead guilty. "First, the charge may be reduced to a lesser or related offense. Second, the attorney for the government may promise to move for dismissal of other charges. Third, the attorney for the government may agree to recommend or not oppose the imposition of a particular sentence. Fourth, the attorneys for the government and the defense may agree that a given sentence is an appropriate disposition of the case."[19]

---

[19]   In the federal system, the flexibility to make a specific sentence recommendation has been affected by federal sentencing guidelines. State prosecutors remain generally able to plea bargain in this fashion, however.

To provide for adequate judicial policing of plea agreements, the Federal Advisory Committee cited the need to bring plea agreements into the open.

> Because the process has been abused, there needs to be judicial oversight of plea agreements. The only way to accomplish this is to require their disclosure.

Under federal law, where an agreement is struck between the prosecutor and the defense attorney, it must be disclosed in open court, in most cases. Subdivision (e) referred to in the foregoing passage is a section of the Federal Rules of Criminal Procedure applicable to guilty pleas in federal cases. In order to bring plea agreements out into the open, the Federal Rules of Criminal Procedure were amended by adding the following provision to the guilty plea rule, Rule 11:

> **Disclosing a Plea Agreement.** The parties must disclose the plea agreement in open court when the plea is offered, unless the court for good cause allows the parties to disclose the plea agreement *in camera*.

*In camera* is defined as "in private" and often involves a proceeding in the judge's chambers, away from the public courtroom.

The United States Supreme Court has upheld the practice of plea bargaining as necessary and proper. The *Santobello* case has already been mentioned. In *Bordenkircher v. Hayes*,[20] the Court observed that plea bargaining is an important component of this country's criminal justice system. A plea may be induced by the prosecutor's promise that he or she will recommend a lenient sentence or drop charges; the fact that a defendant who asks for a trial risks more severe punishment does not render the process unconstitutional. A prosecutor should not be prohibited from persuading a defendant to plead guilty, in the opinion of the Court.

A different view of plea bargaining was taken by the National Advisory Commission on Criminal Justice Standards and Goals. While this commission favored opening plea agreements and making them matters of record as the Federal Rules of Criminal Procedure have done, the Commission urged the abolition of plea bargaining as an ultimate goal. In its report,[21] the Commission argued as follows:

---

[20]    434 U.S. 357 (1978).
[21]    REPORT ON COURTS, NATIONAL ADVISORY COMMISSION ON CRIMINAL JUSTICE STANDARDS AND GOALS, 43-44 (1973).

Danger to Society's Need for Protection

Critics of plea bargaining have asserted that since the prosecutor must give up something in return for the defendant's agreement to plead guilty, the frequent result of plea bargaining is that defendants are not dealt with as severely as might otherwise be the case. Thus plea bargaining results in leniency that reduces the deterrent impact of the law.

These opinions resulted in a recommendation by the National Commission on Criminal Justice Standards quite at odds with views previously advanced in this section. The comments of the Federal Rules Advisory Committee, as well as the view of former Chief Justice Warren Burger who wrote the *Santobello* opinion cited in that selection, reveal a different appraisal of plea bargaining. The opposing National Commission report recommended the abolition of this process. Views similar to those contained in the Commission's recommendations prompted Alaska to abandon plea bargaining. In 1975, the Attorney General of Alaska forbade all prosecutors in that state to engage in plea negotiations, including abolition of the practice of reducing or dropping charges in exchange for a guilty plea. Three years later, an empirical study on the effects of the Alaska experiment concluded that although the rate of trials did increase substantially, the unmanageable onslaught that had been forecast did not materialize.[22]

The Alaska experience was evaluated again 15 years after the attorney general had originally banned plea bargaining.[23] It was concluded that during that time, the ban had caused a substantial decrease in sentence bargaining. The Alaska Judicial Council's Report found that over the 15-year period, the percentage of convicted offenders sentenced to jail time increased, as did the length of sentence. On the other hand, while the Alaska approach seems to have virtually ended bargaining over sentences, it was apparently not effective in stanching bargaining over charges. The Alaska rules were modestly revised a few years after their inception to allow prosecutors some leeway to reduce and dismiss the charges they had originally filed, in order to resolve cases.

In the federal system today, post-indictment plea bargaining seems to have been sharply reduced by the advent of the Federal Sentencing Guidelines. The history of these guidelines is traced in §§ 7.2(2) and 7.6(2) of this text. Under them, the prosecutor's discretion to drop charges has been limited by Justice Department standards. Charges are not to be bargained away or dismissed unless the prosecutor has a good-faith doubt about the prosecution's ability to readily prove a charge. One area of bargaining that remains is the ability of the prosecutor to recommend reduction of the sentence when the defendant substantially assists the government in the investigation or prosecution of another person. The court may make a downward adjustment in the sentence on motion by the government; the adjustment requires court approval and the request should be clearly presented to the court as part of the plea agreement so the judge can accept or reject it.

---

[22]　Rubenstein and White, *Plea Bargaining: Can Alaska Live Without It?* 62 JUDICATURE 266 (1978).

[23]　Carns and Kruse, *A Re-Evaluation of Alaska's Plea Bargaining Ban,* 8 ALASKA L. REV. 27 (1991).

While the Federal Sentencing Guidelines had as an objective the elimination of significant, unwarranted disparity in sentences imposed by judges on similarly situated defendants, the rate of downward departures has been difficult to police. Without a government motion, a court cannot reduce a sentence. Accordingly, whether a defendant gets a "break" depends on the prosecutor. The process is largely secret, and the rate of downward departures based on substantial assistance varies dramatically from place to place. The goal of uniformity in sentencing across the country has not been completely achieved.[24]

Recently, however, Congress has imposed restrictions on judicial reduction of sentences. This effort to even out sentences around the country will be detailed in the next paragraphs of this section, as well as in § 7.6(2).

The legislative effort to equalize sentencing concessions resulted in a national enactment in 2003. Reductions in federal sentences that depart from stated guidelines became a target for Congressional critics of lenient sentencing. Some members of Congress were harshly critical of judges who too readily departed downward from established sentencing norms. In addition to reductions because a defendant helped to convict other parties, judges have adjusted sentences downward for a host of additional reasons. These included factors such as whether a defendant made monetary restitution to the victim or because the accused had local community ties and family responsibilities. While these are valuable things to do, they do not warrant a dramatically lowered sentence, in the view of many lawmakers. Accordingly, Congress passed legislation in 2003 to prevent these latter considerations from being used to reduce sentences.

In addition, the Justice Department decided to gather data on federal judges who regularly sentence defendants to prison terms that are less than those called for by law. The United States Attorney General distributed a directive to federal prosecutors to report federal judges to the Department of Justice when a judge issues a sentence that falls below sentencing guidelines.

As is apparent, the foregoing steps make it more difficult for a prosecutor to offer a light sentence to a defendant in order to get him to plead guilty. Plea bargaining is restricted. In addition, to further impede generous plea deals, the Justice Department took direct action to cut down on the number of plea concessions by prosecutors. Plea bargaining in the federal system was discouraged in a directive from Attorney General John Ashcroft to all federal prosecutors. It provided: "It is the policy of the Department of Justice that, in all federal criminal cases, federal prosecutors *must charge and pursue* the most serious, readily provable offense or offenses that are supported by the facts of the case . . ." (emphasis added). United States Department of Justice, *Departmental Policy Concerning Criminal Offenses, Disposition of Charges and Sentencing* (2003).

---

[24]   Saris, *Below the Radar Screens: Have the Sentencing Guidelines Eliminated Disparity? One Judge's Perspective*, 30 SUFFOLK L. REV. 1027 (1997).

## § 5.5    Unsuccessful Pleas and Bargains

Assume a defendant is charged in a multiple count indictment. What if the prosecution and the defense reach tentative agreement on a specific sentence for one offense as well as dismissal of the remaining charges, then one side refuses to carry out its part of the deal? Suppose, for example, the prosecutor agrees to recommend a suspended sentence for X if X will testify against Y. X does so and Y is convicted. However, when X later comes to court for his sentencing, the prosecutor backs out. Can an agreed-upon bargain be enforced?

While courts may refuse to support some plea bargains, an unambiguous promise by the prosecutor that the defendant has acted upon must be fulfilled by the state. Such a condition is described in the prior paragraph. Similarly, where a plea agreement is reached between the prosecution and the defendant and the prosecutor fulfills his or her part of the covenant, the agreement can often be enforced against the defendant. "[A] court properly may enforce an agreement in which a criminal defendant releases his right to file a § 1983 action (suit for federal civil rights violation) in return for a prosecutor's dismissal of pending criminal charges."[25]

On the other hand, sometimes the parties are simply put back in their original positions. In the event of a refusal by one side to comply with a clear agreement, the other side is relieved of its obligation. The parties may be returned to status quo. For example, if a prosecutor promises to reduce a charge against X in return for X testifying against Y, and X subsequently refuses to so testify, the prosecution may reinstate the original charge against X and prosecute him on it.[26]

Sometimes plea discussions between the prosecutor and the defendant's agent, the defense counsel, are open and freewheeling as they work toward settlement of the case. The defendant himself or herself may sometimes be a participant. However, a plea deal may not necessarily be achieved. Should the defendant be free to initiate and participate in plea negotiations without having his or her comments subsequently quoted by the prosecutor in a later trial? Can the defendant talk freely in the presence of prosecutors when compromise is sought before trial?

Sometimes the issue arises because of declarations made by the defendant in a courtroom. As noted earlier, guilty plea proceedings take place in open court, and the court must address the defendant personally. Suppose the following occurs:

---

[25]    Town of Newton v. Rumery, 107 S. Ct. 1187 (1987) (criminal defendant's civil rights action alleged town and its officers had violated his constitutional rights by arresting him, defaming him, and imprisoning him falsely).

[26]    Ricketts v. Adamson, 107 S. Ct. 2680 (1987).

Judge: "You are charged with auto theft and your lawyer says you wish to plead guilty. Did you steal a car?"

Defendant: "Yes. It was about 3 a.m. I saw this Cadillac sitting in a dark spot in the middle of Oak Street. I hot-wired it and got it cooking and took off."

Judge: "Do you understand the consequences of your plea?"

Defendant: "Yes."

Judge: "Do you understand that parole has been abolished for auto theft in this state, and that if you are sentenced in accordance with the statute you will not be released on parole?

Defendant: "Oops. Nobody told me that."

Judge: "With that knowledge, do you wish to go ahead with your plea of guilty?"

Defendant: "No, your honor."

Judge: "The offered plea of guilty is not accepted. Defendant stands on his former plea of not guilty. Trial is set for two weeks from Monday."

At the subsequent trial for auto theft, can the damaging admissions made by the defendant about the Cadillac be read into the trial record in front of the jury? Based on what is presented in this case, the answer is no. The rules relating to this problem are geared toward encouraging disposition without trial. The rules are so responsive toward defendants who endeavor to plead guilty that statements made in that effort are privileged. Similarly, careless remarks made during plea bargaining are, subject to limited exceptions, insulated from use against a defendant in a later trial. If the bargaining breaks down and is unsuccessful, the defendant's remarks are inadmissible. In pertinent part, Federal Rule of Evidence 410 provides:

Inadmissibility of Pleas, Plea Discussions, and Related Statements. Except as otherwise provided in this paragraph, evidence of the following is not, in any civil or criminal proceeding, admissible against the defendant who made the plea or was a participant in the plea discussions:
(1) a plea of guilty which was later withdrawn;
(2) a plea of nolo contendere;
(3) any statement made in the course of any proceedings under Rule 11 of the Federal Rules of Criminal Procedure or comparable state procedure regarding either of the foregoing pleas; or
(4) any statement made in the course of plea discussions with an attorney for the prosecuting authority which do not result in a plea of guilty or which result in a plea of guilty later withdrawn. However, such a statement is admissible (i) in any proceeding wherein another statement made in the course of the same plea or plea discussions has been introduced and the statement ought in fairness be considered contemporaneously with it, or (ii) in a criminal proceeding for perjury or false statement if the statement was made by the defendant under oath, on the record and in the presence of counsel.

However, such a statement is admissible (i) in any proceeding in which another statement made in the course of the same plea or plea discussions has been introduced and the statement ought in fairness to be considered contemporaneously with it, or (ii) in a criminal proceeding for perjury or false statement if the statement was made by the defendant under oath, on the record, and in the presence of counsel.

Can a defendant bargain away his or her protection under the part of Rule 410 that makes confidential plea discussions or the defendant's attempts to plea bargain? Yes, said the United States Supreme Court in a case in which the United States Attorney conditioned his agreement to plea bargain with the defendant on the defendant's waiver of confidentiality. Before any discussions, the defendant had to agree that any statements he made could be used to impeach him if the case went to trial. No plea agreement was reached, the case went to trial, and the defendant was impeached. Statements he made during negotiations were used to cross-examine him. He later claimed that the protection of Rule 410 could not be waived and that it was unfair to use his plea bargain discussions against him. The Supreme Court disagreed.[27]

---

[27]    United States v. Mezzanato, 115 S. Ct. 797 (1995). *Mezzanato* was tried under Federal Rule of Criminal Procedure 11 (e)(6). The provisions of that rule have now been moved to Rule 410, Federal Rules of Evidence.

# Criminal Trial

# 6

## Chapter Outline

## Key Terms and Concepts

adjudication
American Law Institute test
burden of proof
challenge for cause
change of venue
closing argument (final argument
    or summation)
cross-examination
depositions
direct examination (examination
    in chief)
dismissal with prejudice
dismissal without prejudice
*Durham* test
exclusionary rule
exculpatory evidence
expert witness
Fifth Amendment
habitual offender laws
hearsay
hung jury
impeachment of witness
*in camera*
"irresistible impulse" test
*Jackson v. Denno* hearing
Jencks Act
jury instructions
jury nullification
lineup
*M'Naghten* Rule
motion for judgment
    notwithstanding the verdict
    (judgment N.O.V., also known
    as a directed verdict)

motion for a new trial
motion in limine
motion to suppress
omnibus hearing
opening statement
ordinary witness
peremptory challenge
preclusion sanction
predicate acts
preponderance of evidence
pretrial conference
pretrial discovery
prima facie evidence
probative value
proof beyond a reasonable doubt
real evidence
re-direct
res gestae statements
RICO
rules of evidence
sequestration
severance
showup
Sixth Amendment
spoliation
subpoena duces tecum
venire
verdict
voir dire

## § 6.1  Significance

It is frequently stated that guilty pleas dispose of the great bulk of criminal cases, with trials being held in a small percentage of the total volume. Statistics show that on an annual basis only about 10 to 15 percent of all criminal
cases are tried.[1] The figures are deceptive, however. On the surface they

---

[1]   See ch. 5 n. 1 *supra*.

143

appear to denigrate the role of the trial process by emphasizing the multitude of cases concluded under guilty pleas. For this reason, a deeper look is important, and it becomes apparent that guilty pleas are achieved precisely because of the trial process.

The government's success in litigated criminal cases has a direct bearing on the ability of the prosecutor to negotiate a guilty plea and thus avoid litigation in other cases. People learn by example. With the government prevailing in 70 to 80 percent of the cases that actually go to trial, the odds of conviction are great for the defendant whose case is tried. Doubtless the high conviction rate in tried cases inspires many defendants to think very seriously before insisting on litigation of the charge against them. The point is illustrated by the experience in many rural counties around the country. A small prosecutor's office is often in charge of criminal matters, with perhaps two or three county attorneys handling the area's criminal trials. Where this office suffers a series of reverses in criminal trials, the incidence of defendants thereafter insisting upon the right to trial rises sharply, and the cases in which a guilty plea can be negotiated by the government swiftly decline.

From these comments it can be seen that the criminal trial sets the tone for the entire dispositional process. The law enforcement officer occupies a prominent role when case disposition is by way of trial. As an active assistant to the prosecutor in the investigation, and as a trial witness for the government, his or her importance should not be underestimated. For these reasons, the officer needs to understand the trial process and know the rules of evidence.

## § 6.2   The Litigation Process

Where the defendant pleads not guilty at arraignment, he or she has by this plea controverted the elements of the charge, and it is incumbent upon the government to prove these by trial of the case. Before the case reaches the courtroom, however, there may be one or several advance-of-trial hearings or conferences to deal with preliminary matters. Once these are disposed of and the trial begins, the following steps characteristically mark the trial process:

1.   Voir dire examination and selection of the jury

2.   Opening statement by the prosecutor

3.   Opening statement by the defense[2]

4.   Presentation of government evidence: witnesses and exhibits

5.   Presentation and argument of defense motions

---

[2]   In most cases, this will be presented at the point indicated in the text; in some states the defendant's opening statement can be reserved and presented just before the defendant begins presentation of his or her evidence. Another variation may mark the other end of the trial process; in some states, jury instructions precede the final argument.

6.  Presentation of defense evidence

7.  Presentation of rebuttal evidence by the government

8.  Prosecutor's closing argument to the jury

9.  Defendant's argument

10. Prosecutor's reply argument

11. Judge's instructions to the jury on the applicable law

12. Jury deliberation and verdict

Each of the above steps will be explored and analyzed, with particular emphasis on the portions of the process in which the officer participates as a trial witness.

## § 6.3  Pretrial Motions and Hearings

Pretrial hearings commonly deal with one of four areas of criminal law and procedure: (1) discovery of evidence; (2) suppression of seized evidence; (3) suppression of a defendant's confession; or (4) suppression of lineup and eyewitness testimony.

### 1.  Discovery of Evidence

Defense lawyers frequently make a motion asking the trial judge to require the prosecutor to turn over certain records or documents to help the defendant prepare for trial of the case. Examples of items that might be requested by the defense include statements given to the police or the prosecutor by government witnesses; reports of scientific tests made by the government (ballistics, fingerprints, etc.); or copies of photographs taken by the police photographer in a homicide case showing the position of the victim's body at the crime scene. On many occasions the prosecutor may not want the defendant to see and inspect certain of these items before the trial. When controversy exists about whether or not a defendant is entitled to see a specific item, the court must hold a hearing in advance of the trial to determine whether the government is correct in resisting the defendant's desire to inspect a particular item or document. At the hearing the defendant is the moving or requesting party. As such, he or she has the burden of proving that the item he wants to inspect is material to the preparation of the defendant's case and that his request is reasonable.

Why do prosecutors resist requests to see several items in the government's possession? Certain arguments have been advanced: (1) fabrication of evidence to meet the government's proof might result if the defendant knows the details of the prosecutor's evidence in advance of trial; (2) witness intimidation could increase if the defendant learns the identity of a witness and the substance of his or her testimony.

When the defendant is successful in securing information from the prosecutor in advance of the trial, this process is referred to as **pretrial discovery** of the government's case. In several respects, discovery by a criminal defendant is more limited than is the discovery process available to parties in personal injury or products liability cases. For example, under most state codes a criminal defendant cannot freely notice the government's witnesses for discovery **depositions**. On the other hand, at such depositions in civil cases, opposing witnesses are regularly required to name all other persons who might have observed the incident or occurrence under investigation. As noted, this sort of discovery is disallowed under numerous state codes in criminal cases. The contrast with civil practice is apparent.

Whether the defendant should be entitled to more liberal discovery than is allowed under current law in most states is a source of legal debate. Arguments on both sides of this issue are drawn from the writings of two prominent jurists. In the first, Chief Justice Vanderbilt of the New Jersey Supreme Court lodged several objections to pretrial discovery:[3]

> In criminal proceedings long experience has taught the courts that often discovery will lead not to honest fact-finding, but on the contrary to perjury and the suppression of evidence. Thus the criminal who is aware of the whole case against him will often procure perjured testimony in order to set up a false defense.

> Another result of full discovery would be that the criminal defendant who is informed of the names of all of the State's witnesses may take steps to bribe or frighten them into giving perjured testimony or into absenting themselves so that they are unavailable to testify. Moreover, many witnesses, if they know that the defendant will have knowledge of their names prior to trial, will be reluctant to come forward with information during the investigation of the crime.

A different view is provided by Justice William Brennan Jr. of the United States Supreme Court:[4]

> The argument that disclosure may lead to witness intimidation has proved a major obstacle to discovery of witness lists which would enable the defense to interview and investigate prosecution witnesses and which are a prerequisite to the taking of depositions by the defense. It has also stood in the way of pretrial disclosure of witness statements. I do not deny that discovery may lead to the intimidation—or worse—of some witnesses in some cases, or that it may dissuade some witnesses from coming forward in the first place. We have all read of instances in which informants who have agreed to testify, in

[3]   State v. Tune, 98 A.2d 881, 884 (N.J. 1953).
[4]   Brennan, *The Criminal Prosecution: Sporting Event or Quest for Truth? A Progress Report*, 68 WASH. U.L.Q. 1, 14 (1990).

particular against organized crime, have been threatened or murdered, and the federal witness protection program is clearly a very costly and disruptive method of protecting witnesses who may be in danger. But the proper response to the intimidation problem cannot be to prevent discovery altogether; it is rather to regulate discovery in those cases in which it is thought that witness intimidation is a real possibility. It is idle to suggest that we cannot tailor discovery of witness lists and the like to particular cases. As one scholar has put it, "there is a considerable difference between a tax evasion or antitrust case and a case involving murder or organized crime, and between the ordinary indigent accused and the hardened professional criminal."

The discovery debate continues. Assistant Attorney General Edward S.G. Dennis Jr. responded to Justice Brennan's 1989 lecture and 1990 article: "Justice Brennan's arguments are, in our judgment, based on flawed assumptions. First, the assumption that reform is needed is incorrect. Federal criminal trials are fair now, a fact not disputed directly by advocates of broader discovery. . . . As long as human nature drives defendants to take desperate measures to escape criminal liability, broader discovery will only promote and facilitate defendants' attempts to subvert justice. This is what the majority in *Tune* so clearly understood in 1953, and human nature has not changed drastically in thirty-six years."[5]

### a. *Discovery Under Federal Practice*

Under Rule 16 of the Federal Rules of Criminal Procedure the defendant may obtain a copy of any confession that he or she previously gave the authorities, or any recorded testimony of the defendant if he or she appeared as a witness before the grand jury. However, the defendant will face great difficulty in attempts to obtain a copy of statements given by other witnesses to the police (as opposed to statements previously made by the defendant himself or herself). Federal Rule 16(a)(2) provides that statements made by "prospective government witnesses" are exempt from discovery in the months and weeks prior to trial. While these documents will be turned over to the accused once the case is under way, there will be no *pretrial* disclosure. In this respect the discovery rules reflect the influence of Chief Justice Vanderbilt's arguments, in particular his argument that early disclosure of witness statements will lead to carefully crafted perjury by the defendant.

The prosecutor is not required to divulge the manner in which she plans to argue the case, nor reveal her own memos to her case file respecting her reaction to witnesses she has interviewed. Also exempt are so-called "internal documents," confidential investigation reports or notes made by the prosecutor to assist his or her trial preparation or strategy.

---

[5]   Dennis, *The Discovery Process in Criminal Prosecutions: Toward Fair Trials and Just Verdicts*, 68 WASH. U.L.Q. 63, 64-65 (1990).

Federal Rule 16 embraces a policy of giving the defense an opportunity to copy any recorded grand jury testimony given by the defendant in the event that he previously appeared as a grand jury witness in his own case. In the view of the Federal Criminal Rules Advisory Committee, "The traditional rationale behind grand jury secrecy—protection of witnesses—does not apply when the accused seeks discovery of his own testimony." In another provision, upon request of the defendant the government is required to furnish to the defendant a copy of his or her prior criminal record. "A defendant may be uncertain of the precise nature of his prior record and it seems therefore in the interest of efficient and fair administration to make it possible to resolve prior to trial any disputes as to the correctness of the relevant criminal record of the defendant." The government is not required to automatically furnish a list of the names and addresses of most trial witnesses upon the defendant's request, although such a procedure had been advocated by several authorities. Congress disagreed, and the idea did not become a part of the federal rules.

Expert witness testimony is an exception to the foregoing rule. An important advance occurred on December 1, 1993. Effective as of that date, at the defendant's request the government is required to disclose to the defendant a written summary of the expected trial testimony of government *expert* witnesses. The document must describe the qualifications of each named expert witness and must contain a summary of his or her opinions. Importantly, the information is supplied to the defense prior to trial, as opposed to during the hectic events of the trial itself.

The Federal Rules provide an interesting reciprocal device whereby discovery becomes a two-way street in federal practice. After the defendant has received permission to require disclosure of experts or inspect government proof, Rule 16 allows discovery by the government of medical reports or documents held by the defendant that the defendant intends to produce at trial. Once the defendant has availed himself or herself of the opportunity to require disclosure of experts or inspect government, scientific, or other expert reports, the government has the right to ask for discovery from the defendant.[6]

One procedural reform in the discovery field that is presently in operation in numerous federal courts is the so-called **omnibus hearing**. This hearing takes place after arraignment and before trial. It provides an opportunity for pretrial motions and other requests to be considered by the court at one proceeding with a minimum of formality.[7] At such a hearing the trial court ascertains whether the parties have completed discovery and, if not, makes orders appropriate to expedite its completion.

---

[6]    FED. R. CRIM. P. 16.

[7]    Tom C. Clark, *The Omnibus Hearing in State and Federal Court*, 59 CORNELL L. REV. 761 (1974). *See* A.B.A. STANDARDS 5.3, cited at note 14 *infra*.

## b. State Cases

The trend is clearly in the direction of more liberalized discovery, with several states having moved in the direction of broader discovery. Notwithstanding this general trend, however, some states still sharply limit a defendant's right to discovery. The scope of pretrial discovery varies from jurisdiction to jurisdiction. In many states, certain items (e.g., witness statements) are not subject to discovery under any circumstances. Other items may be discoverable in the discretion of the trial court.[8] Under virtually every state formulation, however, certain matters are not subject to disclosure: work product (notes on strategy and similar memoranda) of the government attorney, identities of informants, and matters of national security.

States that have broadened discovery in recent years emphasize the need to allow defense counsel to explore the truth of assertions contained in a defendant's confession, to see the report of state psychiatrists where the defendant was examined as to mental condition while in custody, to utilize the discovery deposition as a fact-finding device, or to know in advance of trial in certain cases who the government's material witnesses will be. In addition to specific demands, the defendant often makes the further broad request for production of "any **exculpatory evidence**," a frequently-included item in defense discovery requests.

The Supreme Court has **adjudicated** a number of discovery disputes arising from state court litigation.

One matter the Court has carefully protected is the defendant's right to learn about information that is helpful to him, information that police or prosecutors have turned up in the course of their investigation.

Suppose that a prosecutor has exculpatory evidence in his or her files and no revelations of this fact are made to the defense. What if this situation is disclosed only after the defendant is convicted? In these circumstances, a *Brady* violation may have occurred, a legal problem that takes its name from the case of *Brady v. Maryland*.[9] A conviction can be set aside if it is demonstrated that relevant and material evidence was hidden from the defense. In order for the court to grant a new trial, the defendant must demonstrate by a preponderance of the evidence that because of the government's conduct, he or she was denied a fair trial. If a defendant proves it likely that a fair trial was denied because of exclusion of the nondisclosed evidence, the attack on the original conviction will be successful.

Under *Brady* and *United States v. Bagley*,[10] the evidence that the government suppressed must be important in order for the foregoing result to occur. In *Wood v. Bartholomew*,[11] the defendant failed to meet the *Bagley* standard.

---

[8]  Although several states deny discovery of witness statements, many of these require the prosecutor to make pretrial disclosure of the names of state witnesses.

[9]  373 U.S. 83 (1963).

[10]  473 U.S. 667 (1985).

[11]  116 S. Ct. 7 (1995).

Although the defendant established the prosecution's failure to disclose the results of polygraph tests it had administered to two of its witnesses, the defendant's conviction was affirmed. Damage to the defendant's case was minimal because the results of such tests were inadmissible under state law, even to impeach.

On the other hand, a *Brady* violation was made out in *Banks v. Dretke*.[12] While testifying, a prosecution witness denied that he had talked to anyone about his testimony. In fact, he had rehearsed his testimony with the prosecutor. Because the prosecution did not correct the witness's testimony or disclose the coaching it had done, the United States Supreme Court found the state's suppression of this information entitled the defendant to relief.

Defense motions for discovery sometimes request "all *Brady* material." This refers to exculpatory information gathered or otherwise in the hands of the government that is material to the guilt or punishment of the accused. The defendant is entitled to any evidence of a scientific test when an expert witness testifies for the state and bases his or her testimony on scientific testing. Results of tests of the defendant's blood and urine for the presence of controlled substances must be submitted to the defendant upon his or her request. Failure to do so in *Durden v. State*[13] should have resulted in exclusion of the testimony of a forensic expert. The expert was erroneously permitted to testify at length as to test results not stated in the crime lab report. The error was fatal to the state's case. The defendant's conviction of driving under the influence was reversed by the appellate court.

The defendant is also entitled to know whether a trial witness for the government was a paid informer. A prosecution witness whose testimony was crucial in a case took the stand and denied any connection to the state. In fact, he was a paid informer. The prosecutor did not correct the witness's perjury. Because the defendant had asked for all *Brady* material prior to the trial, the nondisclosure of the informer's status made the defendant's subsequent conviction subject to reversal.[14]

### c. Destruction of Evidence Samples

What if the government cannot produce an object in order to allow the defendant to make pretrial inspection of it because the item, once in the hands of the police, has been lost, stolen, discarded, or destroyed? There is precedent in such situations for giving a jury instruction permitting the jury to infer from the party's failure to preserve evidence that the evidence would have been adverse to the nonpreserving party. For example, if fingerprints found at a murder scene are later smudged or discarded by police and rendered useless or unavailable for examination by the defense, the defense might ask for a jury charge that tells the jury that a print was found at the crime scene and the jurors can infer it was not the print of the defendant. This is a **"spoliation"** instruc-

---

[12]   124 S. Ct. 1256 (2004).
[13]   369 S.E.2d 764 (Ga. App. 1988), followed in Box v. State, 370 S.E.2d 28 (Ga. 1988).
[14]   Banks v. Dretke, 124 S. Ct. 1256 (2004).

tion; because a party in possession of evidence spoiled it, adverse inferences may be drawn against that party. The good faith of the party who originally held the evidence, as well as the expected admissibility of the evidence at trial, are factors that will play roles in determining whether a spoliation instruction is appropriate.[15]

Defense requests for more pervasive relief have not met with success, as the *Trombetta* case suggests. In *California v. Trombetta*,[16] the state failed to preserve breath samples in a drunk driving case, and the defendant wanted to suppress the test results, which showed intoxication. The Court rejected the defense argument. Consistent with *Trombetta*, another United States Supreme Court case holds that failure of police to preserve potential defense evidence may not be a denial of due process of law unless the defendant proves bad faith on the part of the police. A showing of bad faith appears to be necessary under this decision in order for the defense to request relief by way of exclusion of prosecution evidence before trial or, after conviction, to successfully request a new trial based on suppression/destruction of evidence. In *Arizona v. Youngblood*,[17] the defendant complained of the failure of police to test semen samples with a newer device than was actually used, as well as failure of police to refrigerate the clothing of the sexual assault victim for tests on semen samples. The Court stated:

> In this case, the police collected the rectal swab and clothing on the night of the crime; respondent was not taken into custody until six weeks later. The failure of the police to refrigerate the clothing and to perform tests on the semen samples can at worst be described as negligent. None of this information was concealed from respondent at trial, and the evidence—such as it was—was made available to respondent's expert who declined to perform any tests on the samples.

A 2004 decision by the United States Supreme Court again emphasized the point that no sanctions will be taken against the prosecution unless the prosecution destroys evidence in bad faith. To be punishable, the destruction must be malicious, designed to hurt the defendant's case. There was no allegation of bad faith in the 2004 decision. Accordingly, the failure of police to preserve evidence that the defendant might have tested—cocaine contained in a plastic bag seized from the defendant—did not entitle the defendant to an acquittal.[18]

### d. Discovery by the Prosecution

Florida's notice-of-alibi rule is in essence a requirement that a defendant submit to a limited form of pretrial discovery by the state whenever the defen-

[15] State v. Vincik, 398 N.W.2d 788 (Iowa 1987), citing II J. Wigmore, EVIDENCE § 291 (Chadbourn rev. 1972). *See Altered or Absent Evidence: The Tort of Spoliation*, 43 ARK L. REV. 453 (1990).
[16] 467 U.S. 479 (1984).
[17] 109 S. Ct. 333 (1988).
[18] Illinois v. Fisher, 124 S. Ct. 1200 (2004).

dant intends to rely at trial on the defense of alibi.[19] The Florida rule requires a defendant, on written demand of the prosecuting attorney, to give notice in advance of trial if the defendant intends to claim an alibi, along with the names and addresses of the alibi witnesses he or she intends to use. The Supreme Court approved the validity of this Florida rule in *Williams v. Florida*,[20] emphasizing that while Florida law gave the prosecutor alibi discovery rights, it also contained liberal discovery in favor of a defendant in criminal cases. Under the Court's view, in order for a state to maintain a notice-of-alibi requirement the prosecution must similarly be open to substantial discovery obligations.[21]

The Federal Rules of Criminal Procedure provide as follows in three subdivisions of Rule 12.1:

### Rule 12.1 Notice of Alibi

**(a) Government's Request for Notice and Defendant's Response.**
   **(1) Government's Request.** An attorney for the government may request in writing that the defendant notify an attorney for the government of any intended alibi defense. The request must state the time, date, and place of the alleged offense.
   **(2) Defendant's Response.** Within 10 days after the request, or at some other time the court sets, the defendant must serve written notice on an attorney for the government of any intended alibi defense. The defendant's notice must state:
     **(A)** each specific place where the defendant claims to have been at the time of the alleged offense; and
     **(B)** the name, address, and telephone number of each alibi witness on whom the defendant intends to rely.

**(b) Disclosing Government Witnesses.**
   **(1) Disclosure.** If the defendant serves a Rule 12.1(a)(2) notice, an attorney for the government must disclose in writing to the defendant or the defendant's attorney:
     **(A)** the name, address, and telephone number of each witness the government intends to rely on to establish the defendant's presence at the scene of the alleged offense; and
     **(B)** each government rebuttal witness to the defendant's alibi defense.

. . .

**(e) Failure to Comply.** If a party fails to comply with this rule, the court may exclude the testimony of any undisclosed witness regarding the defendant's alibi. This rule does not limit the defendant's right to testify.

Although federal statutory provisions do not mandate that federal prosecutors supply a full list of government trial witnesses, a list of all the witnesses whom the prosecutor will call to support the charge, many states now

[19] Williams v. Florida, 399 U.S. 78, 90 S. Ct. 1893, 26 L. Ed. 2d 446 (1970). *See also* FED. R. CRIM. P. 12.1.
[20] 399 U.S. 78, 90 S. Ct. 1893, 26 L. Ed. 2d 446 (1970).
[21] The burden of proof on the defenses of alibi and insanity is discussed in § 6.25 of this chapter.

require that the defendant be furnished with a list of the state's witnesses along with the indictment.[22] Upon written motion of the prosecutor, some courts also require the defense counsel to inform the state of the names and addresses of persons whom counsel intends to call as trial witnesses. In *Taylor v. Illinois*,[23] the prosecutor filed a pretrial discovery motion requesting a list of defense witnesses. A witness named Wormley was not included on the defense counsel's list of expected trial witnesses. Later, on the second day of trial after the prosecution had proceeded with witnesses of its own, defense counsel asked to be allowed to call Wormley. The trial judge excluded Wormley's testimony. The United States Supreme Court agreed that when discovery rules are violated, the trial judge may exclude the evidence that the violating party wishes to introduce. "A trial judge may certainly insist on an explanation for a party's failure to comply with a request to identify his or her witnesses in advance of trial. If that explanation reveals that the omission was willful and motivated by a desire to obtain a tactical advantage that would minimize the effectiveness of cross-examination and the ability to adduce rebuttal evidence, it would be entirely consistent with the purposes of the compulsory process clause simply to exclude the witness's testimony."

While *Taylor* authorizes a strong sanction for nondisclosure by the defense, not all courts follow this rule. Other courts have refused to exclude defense witnesses even though the defendant missed the deadline for providing notice of such witnesses or notice of a special defense. The **preclusion sanction**, say these courts, is not to be imposed lightly.

Sometimes when prosecutors use subpoenas and other discovery rules to require disclosure of information from the defendant, there is objection. Prosecutor requests for information will occasionally be resisted on privilege grounds. Suppose a prosecutor attempts to subpoena copies of letters written by a defendant, and the defendant's correspondence includes letters to an attorney in connection with legal advice. The attorney-client privilege will block disclosure of confidential lawyer and client communications unless the client sought advice to commit a crime.[24]

An amendment to the Federal Rules of Criminal Procedure gave prosecutors additional discovery rights. Rule 26.2 directs the defense, on motion of the government, to produce the pretrial written statements of any witness who testifies for the defense, other than the defendant.[25] Rendition is to be made after the witness completes his or her direct testimony and prior to cross-examination. A 1997 addition to the Federal Rules of Criminal Procedure extends this rule to preliminary hearings as well as trials. The defendant has the same right to request statements of government witnesses after the witness

---

[22]　E.g., GA. UNIF. SUP. CT. R. 30.3.
[23]　108 S. Ct. 646 (1988). *See* Heiderscheit, *Taylor v. Illinois: The New and Not-So-New Approach to Defense Witness Preclusion Sanctions For Criminal Discovery Rule Violations*, 23 GA. L. REV. 479 (1989).
[24]　The crime-fraud exception to the privilege was raised in United States v. Zolin, 109 S. Ct. 2619 (1989).
[25]　United States v. Nobles, 422 U.S. 225 (1975). The right becomes operative after a witness other than the defendant testifies on direct.

completes his direct testimony at the trial or hearing. It is to be remembered that such written statements are not produced *prior* to trial, but only after the trial or hearing is under way.

## 2. Suppression of Evidence

In addition to discovery requests made by the accused, pretrial hearings may be concerned with suppression of evidence. When the authorities have obtained a confession from the defendant or have in their possession incriminating items seized from his person (narcotics, concealed weapons, etc.), the defendant may ask the trial judge to prohibit the prosecutor from showing these items to the jury or introducing them into evidence upon trial of the case. If the judge agrees with this request, the evidence will be suppressed. Such a decision is crucial. Once a confession is suppressed, for example, no government witness may refer to it in his or her testimony before the jury or even intimate that a confession was obtained from the accused. The same rule applies in connection with suppressed physical evidence.

**Motions to suppress** government evidence are usually made before trial, and a pretrial hearing without the trial jury being present is the normal mode of litigation. In federal practice, Rule 12 provides that a motion to suppress must be made prior to trial. Frequently this motion is coupled with one for return of property. There is also a rule covering return of property:

Rule 41

. . .

**(g) Motion to Return Property.** A person aggrieved by an unlawful search and seizure of property or by the deprivation of property may move for the property's return. The motion must be filed in the district where the property was seized. The court must receive evidence on any factual issue necessary to decide the motion. If it grants the motion, the court must return the property to the movant, but may impose reasonable conditions to protect access to the property and its use in later proceedings.

Similar practice exists in numerous states as a result of court rule or judicial decision.

At the suppression hearing, it is essential that the defendant establish "standing" to object to the seizure of evidence, i.e., to show that his personal privacy was somehow invaded and his Fourth Amendment rights thereby violated. This is established when the defendant demonstrates that he was the "victim of a search and seizure, one against whom the search was directed, as distinguished from one who claims prejudice only through the use of evidence gathered as a consequence of a search and seizure directed at someone else." Only a defendant whose rights were violated when police obtained the evidence can demand suppression.[26]

To carry this burden, the defendant sometimes takes the stand at the suppression hearing. By so doing, he or she does not waive the right to refuse to testify at later trial on the merits, nor can a transcript of his or her hearing testimony be used against him or her at a subsequent trial.[27] In addition, where the defendant has taken the stand to testify to a narrow point, such as denying possession of a contraband item, the prosecutor cannot expand the suppression hearing to explore every avenue in the case. As stated in the Federal Rules of Evidence, "The accused does not, by testifying upon a preliminary matter, subject himself to cross-examination as to other issues in the case." (Rule 104).

When the defendant objects that evidence was illegally seized, the burden of showing that the challenged evidence was the product of an illegal search and seizure normally devolves upon the challenging party (the defendant) at the suppression hearing. However, there is one major exception to this rule, that being where the government searched without a warrant but claims the search was validated by a consent. "[I]t has the burden of proving by clear and convincing evidence that the consent was voluntary and free from duress and coercion."[28] Where the challenged evidence is not a seized physical item but a confession, upon whom does the responsibility of carrying the burden of proof fall? Most jurisdictions place the burden on the prosecution in responding to a motion to suppress a confession. While some states hold that the government must carry this burden of proof beyond a reasonable doubt, the Supreme Court has authorized a less stringent standard. Thus, the prosecution must prove at least by a preponderance of the evidence that the confession was voluntary.[29] In lineup cases, once it is shown that the lineup was held during a critical stage in the proceedings, the prosecution is generally assumed to carry the burden of establishing that the defendant intelligently waived his right to counsel at lineup.

### a. Form of Motion to Suppress

Today, countless texts address exclusionary rules in the criminal law field. While their coverage of constitutional rules may be adequate, very little attention is given to providing the reader with a glimpse of the courtroom motion used to

---

[26] KLOTTER, KANOVITZ AND KANOVITZ, CONSTITUTIONAL LAW § 4.17 (10th ed. 2005). In a premises search, anyone legitimately on the premises where a search occurs may challenge its legality by way of a motion to suppress, when the person has a reasonable expectation of privacy and the fruits are proposed to be used against him or her. Automobile searches, see Rakas v. Illinois, 439 U.S. 128 (1978). Business office searches, see Mancusi v. DeForte, 392 U.S. 364, 88 S. Ct. 2120, 20 L. Ed. 2d 1154 (1968). Other cases on standing, see Minnesota v. Olson, 495 U.S. 91, 110 S. Ct. 1684, 109 L. Ed. 2d 85 (1990) (overnight guest).

[27] Simmons v. United States, 390 U.S. 377, 88 S. Ct. 967, 19 L. Ed. 2d 1247 (1968).

[28] State v. Shephard, 124 N.W.2d 712 (Iowa 1963). See also Bumper v. North Carolina, 391 U.S. 543, 88 S. Ct. 1788, 20 L. Ed. 2d 797 (1968); Florida v. Royer, 460 U.S. 491, 103 S. Ct. 1319 (1983).

[29] Lego v. Twomey, 404 U.S. 477 (1972). Preponderance of the evidence has been variously defined as 51 percent of the evidence, or 50.1 percent of the persuasiveness of the proof, or by the greater weight of the evidence but not so great as proof beyond a reasonable doubt.

invoke the **exclusionary rule**. This text will visually treat the subject of the method of raising objections to government evidence, and will show the motion by which attorneys move the court to exclude constitutionally tainted proof.

The constitutional cases and rules governing exclusion of physical evidence illegally seized from an accused have been discussed in § 2.2. As indicated previously in this chapter, a motion to suppress is the procedural vehicle to object to such evidence. When the property sought to be suppressed is not a physical item, such as a weapon seized from the accused, but rather consists of an oral admission made to police, what method of challenge may be employed? Again the motion to suppress evidence is a popular vehicle for raising objection to confessions or admissions.[30] In some criminal cases a **motion in limine**[31] has been employed, and this may be another procedural method that is used to block the government from using a confession at trial.

It is helpful for the reader to see a motion to suppress at this point, and an illustrative motion to suppress physical evidence in federal court is reproduced here:

---

**Motion to Suppress Evidence**[32]

Attorneys for _____
In the United States District Court in and for the Southern District
of California Southern Division

United States of America,
    Plaintiff,
      v.

_____      No. _____
_____      Motion to Suppress Evidence
_____

  Defendants.

Come now defendants _____ and _____, jointly and severally, by and through their counsel, and, pursuant to the provisions of Rule 12 of the Federal Rules of Criminal Procedure, hereby moves the Court for an Order to suppress for use in evidence the contraband upon which the indictment in the above-entitled cause is predicated, to-wit, approximately 20 pounds of marijuana, together with all other items of physical evidence obtained by persons who investigated the offenses charged against the moving defendants.

This Motion is based on the instant Motion, the Notice of Motion attached hereto, the affidavit attached hereto, the records and files in the above-entitled cause, and any and all other matters which may be presented prior to or at the time of the hearing of said Motion.

---

[30] Much of the remainder of this section of the text is adapted from LADD & CARLSON, CASES AND MATERIALS ON EVIDENCE 425 (1972), as is § 6.9.

[31] "A 'motion in limine' is a term used to describe a written motion that is usually made before or after the beginning of a jury trial for a protective order against prejudicial questions and statements." Burrus v. Silhavy, 155 Ind. App. 558, 293 N.E.2d 794, at 796 (1973).

[32] HANDBOOK ON CRIMINAL PROCEDURE IN THE UNITED STATES DISTRICT COURT §§ 6.32, 6.34 (1967). Reprinted by permission of copyright owner. New cases and rule numbers added to original by author of this text.

By _____
Attorney for Defendant

_____
Attorney for Defendant

### Points and Authorities in Support of Motion to Suppress

Attorney for defendants _____

In the United States District Court in and for the Southern
District of California Southern Division

United States of America,
    Plaintiff,
        v.

_____

_____

_____

_____

Defendants.

No. _____
Points and Authorities in Support
of Motion to Suppress

#### I.

". . . Those lawfully within the country, entitled to use public highways, have a right to free passage without interruption or search unless there is known to a competent official authorized to search, probable cause for believing that their vehicles are carrying contraband or illegal merchandise."

Carroll v. United States, 267 US 132, 154, 45 S Ct 280, 285, 69 L Ed 543, 39 ALR 790 (1925), certiorari denied 282 US 873, 51 S Ct 78, 75 L Ed 771 (1930).

"But after entry has been completed, a search and seizure can be made only on a showing of probable cause."

Cervantes v. United States, 263 F2d 800, 830 (9th Cir, 1959).

See also: Plazola v. United States, 291 F2d 56 (9th Cir, 1961), and Jones v. United States, 326 F2d 124, (9th Cir, 1964), certiorari denied 377 US 956, 84 S Ct 1635, 12 L Ed2d 499 (1964).

#### II.

"The word automobile is not a talisman in whose presence the Fourth Amendment fades away and disappears."

Coolidge v. New Hampshire, 403 U.S. 433 (1971).

The defendant has standing to raise this motion in that he was the owner and operator of the vehicle which was searched in the instant case. In order to complain that a search and seizure was illegal and resulted in contraband, marijuana or narcotics being seized, the moving party need not be placed in the dilemma of asserting an interest in the contraband in order to complain of the search and seizure.

Jones v. United States, 362 US 257, 80 S Ct 725, 4 L Ed2d 697, 78 ALR2d 233 (1960).

Respectfully submitted:

By _____
Attorney for defendant _____
By _____
Attorney for defendant _____

Why is it frequently required that motions objecting to evidence on constitutional grounds be filed prior to trial of the case on the merits? State and
federal rules of criminal procedure require that these motions be made early,
often within a specified period after arraignment and at the latest seven days
before trial. A primary reason supporting this approach is that constitutional
objections, which must be decided by the court, frequently involve complex
factual and legal issues. The jury must be excused during the presentation and
argument of the motion. Thus, when counsel makes the motion during trial, it
causes considerable delay and jury "dead time," sometimes lasting a matter of
days. For this reason many appellate courts have indicated a decided preference for resolution of these motions at pretrial hearings. Some have gone so
far as to assert a doctrine of waiver against defendants who failed to timely
assert their constitutional claims.

### b. Particular Problems: Confessions and Lineups

In addition to defense efforts to suppress items of physical evidence that
were seized from the accused or his or her environs, attempted suppression of
confessions also occurs with frequency in felony trials. The potential success
of defense efforts to suppress government evidence will depend in large measure on whether police employed necessary legal rules during the evidence-
gathering phase of the case. In confession practice, police interrogators must
follow the dictates of the *Miranda* decision.[33] When police have not accurately done so in the past, court review of their actions followed.[34] In recent years,
such review by the Supreme Court has resulted in some softening of *Miranda's* application. A Supreme Court ruling that undercut *Miranda* allowed
investigators to explore leads obtained from *Miranda*-violated confessions,
the Court also permitted police to interrogate a suspect about one crime (crime
B) when he had previously asserted his right to remain silent as to another
crime (crime A).[35] Admissions that were made to a polygraph examiner after
a lie detector test were deemed voluntary in *Wyrick v. Fields*.[36]

An inevitable discovery exception was added to the rules. If the police
would have found incriminating evidence anyway, the fact that they discovered
it as a product of constitutionally questionable interrogation did not make the
evidence unreliable.[37] And a public safety exception amended the *Miranda*
doctrine. Where a hidden weapon poses a threat to public safety, a defendant
who has been apprehended near the suspected location of the weapon may be
questioned there without *Miranda* warnings.[38]

---

[33]    The case that established the interrogation rules is *Miranda v. Arizona*, 384 U.S. 436, 86 S. Ct. 1602,
16 L. Ed. 2d 694 (1966). It is discussed in § 2.1 of this book.
[34]    Missouri v. Seibert, 124 S. Ct. 2601 (2004).
[35]    Michigan v. Mosley, 423 U.S. 96, 96 S. Ct. 321, 46 L. Ed. 2d 313 (1975). *See also* Oregon v. Hass, 420
U.S. 714 (1975) (*Miranda*-tainted confession usable to impeach).
[36]    103 S. Ct. 394 (1982).
[37]    Nix v. Williams, 104 S. Ct. 2501 (1984).
[38]    New York v. Quarles, 104 S. Ct. 2626 (1984).

In *Rhode Island v. Innis*,[39] the Court allowed the statements of a defendant, who made admissions while riding in the back of a squad car, to come into evidence. The defendant had asserted his right to silence, then spoke as the two police officers who were taking him to the station talked with each other. The police were not interrogating him, in the view of the Court.

Other cases have turned away from the *Miranda* decision. In *Moran v. Burbine*,[40] the Supreme Court addressed the question of whether a defendant could validly waive *Miranda* rights during the period when an attorney, secured by the defendant's sister, was trying to contact him. When the attorney called and was connected with the detective branch, she was informed that the police would not be questioning the defendant and that they were through with him for the night. Meanwhile, officers questioned the accused, administered *Miranda* warnings, and took a four-page statement that the defendant signed. He waived his constitutional rights and acknowledged responsibility for the crime. Later that night, another incriminating statement was secured from the defendant. Justice Stevens' dissent quoted from Macaulay, who observed: "the guilty are almost always the first to suffer those hardships which are afterwards used as precedents against the innocent." Notwithstanding, the majority held that the trial judge properly denied the defendant's pretrial motion to suppress the statements. The Court observed:

> We granted certiorari to decide whether a pre-arraignment confession preceded by an otherwise valid waiver must be suppressed either because the police misinformed an inquiring attorney about their plans concerning the suspect or because they failed to inform the suspect of the attorney's efforts to reach him. [The purpose of the *Miranda* warnings] is to dissipate the compulsion inherent in custodial interrogation and, in so doing, guard against abridgment of the suspect's Fifth Amendment rights. Clearly, a rule that focuses on how the police treat an attorney—conduct that has no relevance at all to the degree of compulsion experienced by the defendant during interrogation—would ignore *Miranda's* mission and its only source of legitimacy.
>
> Nor are we prepared to adopt a rule requiring that the police inform a suspect of an attorney's efforts to reach him.

The waiver form and *Miranda* advisements need not be given in the exact pattern described in the *Miranda* decision. Prior to interrogation in one criminal case the suspect was advised, in addition to other constitutional admonitions, that an attorney would be appointed "if and when he went to court." This was not found to be constitutionally defective as falsely suggesting that indigents have no right to an attorney unless they go to court. In *Duckworth v. Eagan*,[41] the Supreme Court observed: "We have never insisted that *Miranda* warnings be given in the exact form described in that decision."

---

[39]     446 U.S. 291 (1980).
[40]     106 S. Ct. 1135 (1986).
[41]     109 S. Ct. 2875 (1989).

A 1990 decision continued the trend to soften *Miranda*. In *Illinois v. Perkins*,[42] the Supreme Court upheld the lack of *Miranda* warnings in an undercover jail interrogation. A police officer posing as a jail inmate was not required to give warnings to an incarcerated suspect before the officer asked questions likely to elicit an incriminating response. The conversation took place before the defendant was formally charged, however, and statements made by a suspect in this situation may be admitted at trial.

When a witness takes the stand, completes her direct testimony, and then is confronted on cross-examination with a prior writing that contradicts his or her direct testimony, the process is termed "impeachment." If the defendant takes the stand in her own defense, she may be contradicted by her prior confession. What if the confession was taken from a defendant who did not receive correct *Miranda* warnings?

Concerning impeachment use of *Miranda*-tainted confessions, see § 6.22 of this text. Unless a confession was beaten from a defendant, it can be used to contradict him at trial if he gets on the stand to testify. This is so even if the interrogating officers gave a defective or only partial list of warnings, or perhaps no *Miranda* warnings at all.

In a 2004 case, officers began the warnings with "you have a right to remain silent" when the defendant interrupted. He knew his rights, he said, and neither of the two police officers attempted to complete the warnings. The defendant talked to the police. When he later complained that his Glock pistol was located by these same police because of a bad interrogation, the United States Supreme Court denied him any relief. The *Miranda* rule, and the requirement that a suspect receive full *Miranda* warnings, are provisions designed to prevent a defendant's coerced statements *from being used against him at trial*. It does not prevent police from using unwarned statements to locate incriminating physical items, like a gun.[43] It also does not bar a prosecutor from using statements taken without *Miranda* warnings to attack a defendant's own testimony at trial, as explained later in this text.

*Miranda* requires that constitutional advice be given to the arrested person. If the suspect waives his or her right to counsel after receiving *Miranda* warnings, police are free to question him or her. If the suspect requests counsel at any time during the interview, he or she is not to be questioned until a lawyer has been made available or the suspect himself or herself reinitiates conversation with the police. But what if, instead of directly asking for a lawyer, the arrestee simply says "I don't know if I should say any more until I talk to somebody." In such a situation, a 1994 Supreme Court opinion says that the accused has not invoked the right to counsel in the absence of a clear request for counsel. Officers are not required to cease questioning.[44]

---

[42]    110 S. Ct. 2394 (1990).

[43]    United States v. Patane, 124 S. Ct. 2620 (2004).

[44]    Davis v. United States, 114 S. Ct. 2350 (1994) ("maybe I should talk to a lawyer" deemed not to be an unambiguous request for counsel; questioning can continue in the absence of counsel in the face of such an observation by the defendant).

Historically, the *Miranda* rule does not apply to street encounters, nor to general on-the-scene questioning in the home if it is the site of a disturbance. Questions that are merely investigatory and that are asked at the threshold of a criminal investigation, as opposed to custodial interrogation, do not invoke *Miranda*. For example, when officers arrived at the scene of a domestic dispute, they asked which spouse was the aggressor. The victim told police his wife had thrown a stereo speaker at him. The wife made statements that implicated herself. She was charged and taken to jail. She argued that she was entitled to *Miranda* warnings as soon as police entered the residence. The court disagreed. The questioning was held to have occurred during the investigatory stage of the arrest.[45]

While a number of cases have undercut *Miranda*, the Supreme Court's fallback from stringent police interrogation rules has been an uneven one. Some decisions have attacked *Miranda*, while others have reasserted it. A decision in the latter category is *Arizona v. Roberson*.[46] The United States Supreme Court considered the propriety of resuming the questioning of a subject about unrelated crime B, after the suspect has asserted his right to counsel regarding original crime A. In *Roberson* the defendant was arrested at the scene of a burglary. When advised of his rights, he asserted that he wanted a lawyer before answering any questions. Three days later, while this defendant was still in custody, the police initiated interrogation about a different burglary. Instead of asserting his rights as he had done previously, when informed of his rights the defendant decided to talk and made an incriminating statement. The United States Supreme Court saw the process as a violation of *Miranda* as well as *Edwards v. Arizona*, another case excluding a defendant's post-arrest statements: "Finally, we attach no significance to the fact that the officer who conducted the second interrogation did not know that respondent had made a *request for counsel*. In addition to the fact that *Edwards* focuses on the state of mind of the suspect and not of the police, custodial interrogation must be conducted pursuant to established procedures, and those procedures in turn must enable an officer who proposes to initiate an interrogation to determine whether the suspect has previously requested counsel. In this case the [defendant's] request had been properly memorialized in a written report but the officer who conducted the interrogation simply failed to examine that report. Whether a contemplated reinterrogation concerns the same or a different offense, or whether the same or different law enforcement authorities are involved in the second investigation, the same need to determine whether the suspect has requested counsel exists. The police department's failure to honor that request cannot be justified by the lack of diligence of a particular officer." (emphasis added)

---

[45]   State v. Leprich, 465 N.W.2d 844 (Wis. App. 1991).
[46]   108 S. Ct. 2093 (1988).

To summarize, if at any time during interrogation an accused invokes his or her constitutional rights, all custodial interrogation must cease. Furthermore, after a request for counsel, *Edwards* makes clear that police may not reapproach the accused. However, federal law demands that the request for counsel to be clear and unequivocal.

*Edwards* and *Roberson* apply when the police interrogate. On the other hand, if the prisoner initiates conversation with the police or a government informant, the prisoner's admissions are usable against him, and this is so even if the conversation takes place after formal charges are filed.[47]

Intelligent and knowing waiver of *Miranda* is sometimes an issue. A showing that a person who confessed to a crime may have suffered from a mental disability is not routinely a basis on which to exclude the confession.[48] Coupling this factor with offensive interrogation techniques, however, may result in exclusion of incriminating statements. In *Miller v. Fenton*,[49] state police made a tape recording of an interrogation. Defendant Frank Miller was being questioned about the death of a young female, and a detective appealed to Miller's conscience:

> "Okay, listen Frank, if I promise to, you know, do all I can with the psychiatrist and everything, and we get the proper help for you, will you talk to me about it?"

> Later, the following took place after Miller denied killing the girl.

> "Honest, Frank? It's got to come out. You can't leave it in. It's hard for you, I realize that, how hard it is, how difficult it is, I realize that, but you've got to help yourself before anybody else can help you. And we're going to see to it that you get the proper help. This is our job, Frank. This is our job. This is what I want to do."

The lower court held that the defendant's confession was voluntary; however, a dissenting opinion condemned what another court had termed "Svengalian" police efforts. At issue was whether the ultimate determination of "voluntariness" is a legal question. The Supreme Court decided in accord with the result urged by the dissenting opinion and reversed. The Court observed that certain interrogation techniques may be offensive, as *Miller* illustrates.

When a defendant is held in custody and interrogated, his arrest in the first instance must have been lawful. See *Taylor v. Alabama*.[50] The Supreme Court invalidated the petitioner's confession because it was the fruit of an illegal arrest. The Court observed that the mere giving of *Miranda* warnings will not "cleanse" a confession that is the fruit of an illegal arrest.

---

[47]  Patterson v. Illinois, 108 S. Ct. 2389 (1988); Kuhlmann v. Wilson, 477 U.S. 436 (1986).
[48]  Marlowe v. State, 370 S.E.2d 20 (Ga. App. 1988).
[49]  106 S. Ct. 445 (1985).
[50]  457 U.S. 687 (1982).

Other confession cases have provided relief to defendants on right-to-counsel grounds. In *Brewer v. Williams*[51] the defendant could not be interrogated in the absence of counsel after police knew he was represented by an attorney. In *Massiah v. United States*[52] the defendant could not be covertly questioned by a government informant after the defendant had been indicted, had retained a lawyer, and was free on bail.

Recent *Miranda* decisions have cut in both directions, with some cases limiting *Miranda* rights. Decisions in the latter category led some to speculate that the warning rule would be discarded. However, *Miranda* survived the storm in 2000. As noted, some legal commentators had expected the United States Supreme Court to repudiate the "required warnings" doctrine. Instead, the Court refused to overrule *Miranda* and affirmed its continued application during custodial interrogation in both state and federal courts. "*Miranda* has become embedded in routine police practice to the point where the warnings have become part of our national culture."[53]

In 2004 the Supreme Court addressed problems created when police delay giving *Miranda* warnings. Can officers thoroughly interrogate a subject, secure damaging admissions or a confession from him, then communicate to him his *Miranda* rights and have him repeat the confession? Will the "second" confession hold up? Will police be able to claim the second one is constitutional because it came after *Miranda* warnings? The answer to these questions is no. Where a police strategy is adopted to interrogate, then warn, the confession will be thrown out by the courts. Custodial interrogation *prior* to warnings is barred. Because the "question-first" tactic effectively threatens to thwart *Miranda*'s purpose, the confession of a defendant exposed to this police strategy will be suppressed.[54] No such "end run" around *Miranda* will be permitted.

Finally, when attacking the validity of a defendant's confession and moving its exclusion, the defense may claim (1) a *Miranda* violation, and/or (2) that the confession was involuntary. There are occasional cases in which the latter doctrine is more protective of a defendant's rights than the *Miranda* rule.[55]

### c. Jackson v. Denno *Hearings*

When a defendant makes *Miranda* or voluntariness objections to the validity of his or her confession, this triggers a pretrial hearing in which the court hears evidence from both parties—deciding whether the trial jury will subsequently hear and see the confession. Often this is called a **Jackson v. Denno hearing**. Most states follow the "orthodox" procedure of having voluntariness finally determined by the judge. But even where the judge admits

---

[51]     430 U.S. 387 (1977).
[52]     377 U.S. 201 (1964).
[53]     Dickerson v. United States, 530 U.S. 428 (2000).
[54]     Missouri v. Seibert, 124 S. Ct. 2601 (2004).
[55]     *See* United States v. Murphy, 763 F.2d 202 (1985), disapproved on other grounds in United States v. Coleman, 1991 U.S. App. 5070 (6th Cir. 1991).

the confession into evidence, the defendant is entitled upon trial to introduce evidence attacking it. This evidence by the defense often seeks to cast doubt on the voluntariness of the confession, and thus diminishes the weight to be given the statement. The fact that the trial court has made a pretrial voluntariness determination does not undercut the defendant's traditional prerogative to challenge the confession's reliability during the trial.

### d. Eyewitness Testimony

Eyewitness identification of the accused as the perpetrator of the crime is frequently challenged on constitutional grounds. Where the eyewitness picked the defendant out of a **lineup**, sometimes days or weeks after the criminal act, the lineup may constitute a critical stage in the prosecution requiring either counsel for the accused or knowing waiver of counsel. This is the rule if the lineup is held after defendant has been indicted.[56] In such situations the accused may seek to suppress an eyewitness's trial testimony as tainted by an illegal lineup if there was no counsel present. Pre-indictment lineups, on the other hand, may be conducted in the absence of counsel if they are not unduly suggestive.[57]

### 3. The Exclusionary Rule

The practice of suppressing illegally seized evidence occupied the discussion in the preceding section of this text. The suppression process is dependent upon the exclusionary rule in American trials.[58] Today, many authorities question the exclusionary principle. They urge other sanctions to deter illegal police seizure and they ask why "[t]he criminal is to go free because the constable blundered."[59] Strong arguments have been made for and against the rule. Its future has been studied and is discussed in § 10.18 of this book. A Canadian study provides insight on the debate:

> It is particularly interesting to note that the development of the American exclusionary rule is directly tied to judicial interpretation of the Constitution of the United States and the problem of guaranteeing individual liberties and fundamental human rights. American courts have held that the exclusion of illegally obtained evidence and all evidence derived from it constitutes a reasonable protection of fundamental liberties at two levels. First of all, it has an exemplary value for police officers. By excluding all evidence they may obtain illegally, it is hoped that the police will be discouraged in the future

---

[56]   Gilbert v. California, 388 U.S. 263, 87 S. Ct. 1951, 18 L. Ed. 2d 1178 (1967) (post-indictment pretrial lineup at which the accused is exhibited to identifying witnesses is a critical stage, and when the police hold such a lineup without notice to and in absence of counsel, this denies the accused his or her Sixth Amendment rights).

[57]   Kirby v. Illinois, 406 U.S. 682, 92 S. Ct. 1877, 32 L. Ed. 2d 411 (1972). Of course, some states go beyond *Kirby* and extend counsel to pre-indictment lineups.

[58]   The exclusionary rule is defined in Chapter 2.

[59]   Quote is from People v. Defore, 242 N.Y. 13, 150 N.E. 585 (1926) (Cardozo, J.).

from using such tactics and that in the long term, the entire criminal investigation system will be improved. Secondly, excluding evidence indicates that American law truly respects the need for "due process," ranking it above all other considerations including law enforcement. In essence, the American position rests on the belief that fundamental liberties guaranteed by the United States Constitution are undermined if the rule of law is not respected.[60]

The United States Supreme Court has engrafted a "good faith" exception on the exclusionary rule in search warrant cases. The two cases that accomplished this change in the law were *United States v. Leon* and *Massachusetts v. Sheppard*.[61] Justice White authored these opinions, which held that when the officer who conducted the search acted in "objectively reasonable reliance" on a warrant issued by a detached and neutral magistrate, the search will be upheld even though the warrant is subsequently determined to be invalid. In *Sheppard*, a detective applied for a search warrant with an affidavit listing items the police were seeking in a murder case, including clothing of the victim and a blunt instrument that might have been used to commit the crime. The detective used a search warrant application form customarily used for search for controlled substances. The detective presented the form to a magistrate, who changed the form to fit the instant situation, and the resulting search warrant failed to incorporate the affidavit that specified the items to be seized. The warrant was executed, and the defendant moved to suppress evidence because the warrant failed to specify the things to be seized. The Supreme Court ruled that because the police had acted in good faith in executing what they reasonably believed was a valid warrant, the search and seizure would be upheld. The Court ruled that there was "an objectively reasonable basis" for the officers' mistaken belief that they were proceeding appropriately in carrying out the search.

### 4. Other Pretrial Proceedings

In addition to evidentiary questions, defense requests for separate trials of defendants may trigger a pretrial hearing. In cases in which multiple defendants are joined for trial in a single indictment, the defendants frequently argue that each should be tried separately. If this occurs, a hearing over the question of whether defendants should be tried collectively will result. Where one defendant has made a confession implicating accomplices who are on trial but who did not confess, the confession is admissible only against the confessor. To avoid confusing the jury, a **severance** may be ordered in this situation.[62] Other facts could also show that a defendant (or the government) would be prejudiced by a joint trial of offenses or defendants.[63]

---

[60] Evidence Project of the Law Reform Commission of Canada (1974).
[61] 104 S. Ct. 3424 (1984).
[62] *See* Bruton v. United States, 391 U.S. 123 (1968). Sections 4.3 and 4.5 of this text deal with joint indictment of defendants.
[63] FED. R. CRIM. P. 14 deals with relief from prejudicial joinder. Other motions that may be dealt with in a pretrial hearing include motions for change of venue, consolidation of defendants or offenses, continuance, or for a mental examination of the defendant.

A final type of hearing that may be held in advance of trial is the **pretrial conference**.[64] At this meeting, generally held in the judge's chambers, attorneys for the state and defense explore the possibility of stipulating to the admission of certain evidence, such as photographs, without formal proof. Another topic for discussion may be the scheduling of certain witnesses, especially medical doctors. This type of pretrial conference is also frequently used in civil cases, often serving as a catalyst for settlement of the civil case prior to trial.

## § 6.4    Jury Selection and Trial

Under controlling United States Supreme Court cases, defendants have a right to trial by jury, but this right does not extend to offenses carrying a punishment of six months or less.[65] Occasionally defendants will waive a jury trial, in which case the jury selection process discussed in this section will be dispensed with. Some estimates of the number of felony prosecutions tried to the court without a jury range to 40 percent.[66] When the trial is before the judge alone, however, the other aspects of criminal trial outlined previously in § 6.2, including opening statements, production of evidence and closing arguments, still occur, although introduction of the evidence may be somewhat less formal and stringent than in a jury trial.

The traditional mode of felony trial is to the jury, and selection of the jurors who will decide the case is the first phase of the process. Attorneys for both the government and the defense interrogate jurors during **voir dire** examination. Counsel will typically ask each potential juror whether he or she knows the defendant or any of the attorneys or witnesses in the case, whether he or she has read about the case in the newspapers, and will glean the juror's views on capital punishment if the offense charged carries the death penalty.

There are two types of challenges in the jury selection process. A challenge for cause leads to dismissal for causes specified by law, and these causes vary from state to state. A peremptory challenge is a dismissal by either party, with no reason required to be given. The number of peremptory challenges is set at the start, with the number varying by state and type of case.

On the basis of information gained through the voir dire, the lawyers exercise peremptory challenges, each side striking from the prospective jury panel those it deems least receptive to its position. This is a difficult commodity for

---

[64]   *See* FED. R. CRIM. P. 17.1.

[65]   Duncan v. Louisiana, 391 U.S. 145, 88 S. Ct. 1444, 20 L. Ed. 2d 491 (1968); Frank v. United States, 395 U.S. 147 (1969). Duncan v. Louisiana extended the federal Constitution's guarantee of trial by jury to the states.

     When a defendant is charged with two misdemeanors arising out of a transaction, each of which carries six months, there is authority that the right to jury trial does not arise because the gravity of each crime still simply amounts to a petty offense. Lewis v. United States, 116 S. Ct. 2163, 135 L. Ed 2d 590 (1996).

[66]   Duncan v. Louisiana, 391 U.S. 145, 190, 88 S. Ct. 1444, 20 L. Ed. 2d 491 (1968) (Harlan dissent). On the question of waiver of a jury in a criminal case, *see* Singer v. United States, 380 U.S. 24, 85 S. Ct. 783, 13 L. Ed. 2d 630 (1965); People v. Carroll, 148 N.E.2d 875 (N.Y. 1958).

the trial attorney to gauge, and a few defense attorneys even enlist a psychiatrist to assist them in exercising challenges.

In federal courts, the number of challenges allowed is:

| | | |
|---|---|---|
| Capital cases | U.S.: 20 | Defendant: 20 |
| Felonies | U.S.:  6 | Defendant: 10 |
| Misdemeanors | U.S.:  3 | Defendant:  3 |

In most jurisdictions, the jury box is filled with a specified number of people, typically 12. If a juror is challenged, a new juror is called to fill the vacant seat until all of the challenges are exhausted and a jury of 12 remains.[67] After the jury is sworn, the judge admonishes the jurors to discuss the case with no one until it deliberates to decide the case after hearing all the evidence. In most trials the jurors are permitted to go home after each trial day, being **sequestered** (kept together by the bailiff and lodged collectively overnight as necessary in a hotel or elsewhere) only during deliberations. However, in a very important case, one attended with massive publicity and great public attention, nightly sequestration of the jury may begin earlier.

When a juror has formed a fixed opinion as to guilt or innocence as a result of pretrial publicity, the juror will be excused for cause. In capital punishment cases, a juror who announces that he or she could never vote for the death penalty even though it is authorized by state law will also be so excused. However, the prosecutor is not entitled to challenge for cause those jurors who, while not enthusiastic about capital punishment, could approve it in a compelling case.

In a capital murder case in Mississippi, a juror expressed conscientious scruples against the death penalty. Although the juror equivocated, she ultimately stated that she could consider the death penalty in an appropriate case. By the time this juror was called to the jury box, the prosecutor had exercised all 12 of the state's peremptory challenges. The defense counsel objected to granting the state a 13th peremptory challenge. The prosecutor urged that the juror be removed for cause. Over objection by the defense, the court excused the juror for cause. This was held to be reversible constitutional error. The United States Supreme Court noted: "[T]his Court held that a capital defendant's right, under the Sixth and Fourteenth Amendments, to an impartial jury prohibited the exclusion of **venire** members 'simply because they voiced general objections to the death penalty or expressed conscientious or religious scruples against its infliction.'" Although the Mississippi defendant had been convicted by the trial jury, his death sentence was reversed by the United

---

[67] Juries of less than 12 may be used in certain states. *See* Williams v. Florida, 397 U.S. 902, 90 S. Ct. 914, 25 L. Ed. 2d 84 (1970).

    In longer trials, most jurisdictions provide by statute or court rule for selection of extra jurors. One or more persons specifically identified as alternates are chosen in advance of trial. The alternates sit in court with the jury and hear all the evidence up until the time the jury retires to deliberate. If a juror becomes sick during the trial, one of the alternates is designated to take his or her place.

States Supreme Court. Thus, if a single venire member is erroneously excluded for cause because of his or her views on the death penalty, it has been found that a subsequently imposed capital sentence is invalid.[68]

The prior paragraph addresses jurors who oppose capital punishment. What about those who enthusiastically embrace it? In death penalty cases, a juror who states that he or she would automatically vote for the death penalty may be stricken. In *Morgan v. Illinois*,[69] the Supreme Court held that a trial court's general questions to venire members about their ability to be fair and impartial and to follow the law were not sufficient to detect those in the venire who automatically would vote for the death penalty. The defendant was entitled, upon his request, to an inquiry concerning those jurors who, even prior to the state's case-in-chief, had predetermined the issue of whether to impose the death penalty.

What other questions will be allowed on voir dire? Along with inquiries about possible racial bias when an interracial crime is at issue,[70] courts have approved defense counsel's voir dire questions inquiring as to whether any panel members have close relatives who work for law enforcement agencies or have ever been the victim of any crime.

While very wide latitude is normally allowed in such questions, the United States Supreme Court has indicated that the trial court might impose certain limitations. The Supreme Court did not find any fault in a trial judge's action in an obscenity case in which the trial court disallowed questions probing the jurors' sexual and religious preferences as they might affect their views on obscenity.[71]

The group of citizens from which trial juries are selected has formed a subject for United States Supreme Court scrutiny. In *Taylor v. Louisiana*, the defendant was convicted of rape in Louisiana. On appeal to the Supreme Court, he challenged the makeup of the jury. There were no women jurors. Under Louisiana law a woman could not be selected for jury service unless she had previously filed a written declaration of her desire to be subject to jury duty. In the *Taylor* case there was not a single woman to choose from in the venire from which the petit (trial) jury was selected. The Supreme Court ruled that the Louisiana law was unconstitutional.[72] On its face it did not disqualify women from jury service, but in its effect operated to exclude them systematically. Further, this system violated the defendant's right to have a jury selected from a representative cross section of the community (although there were no women on the venire, 53 percent of citizens living in the judicial district were women).

In *Duren v. Missouri*,[73] the defendant established that, under Missouri law and practice, any woman could decline jury service by claiming an exemption or by simply not reporting for jury duty. The defendant's conviction was overturned because, in selecting the trial jury, insufficient women were available.

[68]  Gray v. Mississippi, 107 S. Ct. 2045 (1987). The *Witherspoon* case is clarified in note 94 *supra*.
[69]  112 S. Ct. 2222 (1992).
[70]  Turner v. Murray, 106 S. Ct. 1683 (1986).
[71]  Hamling v. United States, 418 U.S. 87, 94 S. Ct. 2887, 41 L. Ed. 2d 590 (1974).
[72]  419 U.S. 522, 95 S. Ct. 692, 42 L. Ed. 2d 690 (1975).
[73]  439 U.S. 357 (1979).

Racial and gender discrimination in the makeup of the jury pool is prohibited. Nor may a prosecutor use peremptory challenges at trial in a racially discriminatory manner. The Supreme Court has ruled: "[T]he Equal Protection Clause forbids the prosecutor to challenge potential jurors solely on account of their race or on the assumption that black jurors as a group will be unable impartially to consider the State's case against a black defendant."[74]

Some lower courts extended this rule to assist defendants who were not a part of the challenged group. The United States Supreme Court followed suit in 1990, holding in *Holland v. Illinois*[75] that a white defendant had standing to object, on "fair cross section" grounds, to a prosecutor's use of peremptory challenges that excluded blacks from a jury.

In *Trevino v. Texas*,[76] the United States Supreme Court held that a Hispanic defendant's objection when blacks were excluded from the venire made out the elements of an equal protection claim. The Court noted that the defendant's pretrial motion to prohibit the prosecution from excusing black jurors on the basis of race sufficiently set forth a long-term pattern of racially motivated peremptory challenges.

What about defense attorneys? Does the rule of *Batson v. Kentucky*, which bars jury strikes based on racial grounds, control only prosecutors? Under *Batson*, a defense attorney is also barred from striking jurors on racial grounds, just as the prosecutor is barred.[77]

The principles of *Batson v. Kentucky* have also been extended to gender-based peremptory challenges. The Supreme Court determined the issue in a case from Alabama.[78] Intentional discrimination occurs when one lawyer or the other systematically strikes men or women from the jury solely on the basis of their sex. This practice violates the Equal Protection Clause of the United States Constitution. In the case from Alabama, the defendant objected to the state's use of nine of its 10 peremptory challenges to remove male jurors in a paternity trial.

## § 6.5　Opening Statement

The **opening statement** of the prosecutor is generally presented right after the empaneling of the jury. In this statement, he or she gives a factual outline of what he or she intends to prove by his or her evidence. Following the prosecutor, defense counsel is permitted to make an opening statement to the jury. Some defense attorneys do so at this point; others wait and deliver the opening statement after the prosecutor has put in his or her evidence. By reserving the opening statement in this fashion, the defendant may conceal the course of his or her defense until the government's proof is disclosed.

---

[74]　Batson v. Kentucky, 106 S. Ct. 1712 (1986). *Batson* was construed in Purkett v. Elem, 115 S. Ct. 1769 (1995) (race-neutral explanations for jury strikes).

[75]　110 S. Ct. 803 (1990).

[76]　112 S. Ct. 1547, 118 L. Ed. 2d 193 (1992).

[77]　Georgia v. McCollum, 112 S. Ct. 2348 (1992).

[78]　J.E.B. v. Alabama, 114 S. Ct. 1419 (1994).

## § 6.6   Government Proof and Witnesses

After the opening statement, the government begins introduction of its proof. It is entitled to go first in this respect because it is the plaintiff in the case. As such, it has the **burden of proof**. The party with this burden is entitled to both the first and the last word during the evidence presentation phase of the case, as well as in the closing arguments.

## § 6.7   Government Case-in-Chief: Rules of Evidence

The **rules of evidence** are basically a system of protective devices. Their aim is to exclude from the trial of the case testimony that is untrustworthy or incompetent for the trier of fact, usually a jury, to hear. As such, the rules accomplish a worthwhile purpose and occupy a central place in the American system of criminal trials. Their existence lends order and uniform treatment to the introduction of testimony, and guards against incompetent proof finding its way into a trial. The basic rules that make up the law of evidence, those that regulate admission of proof in the trial of a case, will be detailed in §§ 6.8-6.23.

## § 6.8   Relevancy

Evidence will be rejected if it is incompetent, irrelevant, and immaterial. All evidence must bear a rational relationship to the issues in the case, and must have a tendency to prove a fact that is material to the dispute. To illustrate this point, suppose a police officer saw Smith fleeing the scene of a robbery with a heavily filled sack. Smith was arrested on the robbery charge and while free on bail exposed himself to two schoolchildren, whereupon bail was revoked. Appearing as witness in the robbery case, the officer could testify to his observation of Smith fleeing the robbery scene. However, a question by the prosecutor probing the officer's knowledge of the incident with the children would ask for matter that is irrelevant. The information sought has no relationship to the disputed issues in the robbery case.

## § 6.9   Competency

Criminal trials frequently involve the question of whether children or others may take the stand and testify. Defense attorneys sometimes object that a child is too young to understand the seriousness of the situation and thus is incompetent to be a witness. This can be a critical point, as for example in a child molestation case in which the child is the government's major witness.

As will be seen in the subsequent passage,[79] children of quite young years have been qualified as witnesses. This is accomplished by showing through preliminary questions that the child understands the nature of the witness's oath. In addition to the problem of the child witness, a prosecutor may sometimes need to present witnesses who have a history of mental illness. The point is potentially crucial where assaults have been committed on such people, and they (the victims) are the only eyewitnesses:

> The trial court's authority to conduct a preliminary hearing on the mental qualifications of a prospective witness where the witness has been in a mental institution, as well as the inherent power of a court to order a psychiatric examination of a challenged witness was affirmed in *State v. Butler*, 27 NJ 560, 143 A2d 530 (1958).

> In the case of children, those of quite young years have been permitted to testify, including children of five years of age. The cases are catalogued in *State v. Meyer*, 135 Iowa 507, 113 NW 332 (1907), wherein a child six years old testified in a case involving an assault upon her person: "It is apparent from what we have set out that the judge did not abuse his discretion in holding that the child, though of tender years, had 'sufficient capacity to understand the obligation of an oath.' She may have been unable to define the words 'oath' and 'testimony,' but this was not determinative of her capacity. If, without being familiar with the use of such words, she had an adequate sense of the impropriety of falsehood, she understood the nature of an oath, even though not able to state what those words meant.

> The modern rule is, briefly, the witness will be deemed competent if he has the ability to observe, recollect and communicate the essentials about which he is called to testify with accuracy sufficient to make the narration correspond to the knowledge and the recollection. In addition he must appreciate the nature and obligation of an oath.

## § 6.10  Demonstrative Evidence

**Real evidence** refers to an actual physical object that is relevant to a case. This may be the burglary tools seized from a defendant in a burglary prosecution, the knife used in a homicide, or loot discovered in the defendant's apartment in a robbery case. The physical items involved can be marked as exhibits and introduced into evidence at trial (state's Exhibit A, etc.). The presentation of this proof allows the court or jury to reach a factual conclusion through both sight and touch, and its effectiveness as evidence against the accused underlines the need for police officers to make good searches and seizures.

---

[79] Adapted from LADD & CARLSON, CASES AND MATERIALS ON EVIDENCE 299-302 (1972). *See* also FED. R. EVID. 601.

Even though validly seized, real evidence sometimes presents a special problem. Its emotional appeal may be great, and sometimes its grisly or gory nature is such that the exhibit's emotional impact outweighs its **probative value**. The issue has arisen in murder trials. "In one extreme and apparently erroneous decision, the prosecution was allowed to exhibit the severed head of the victim, preserved in a jar of alcohol, to establish identity."[80] Other methods of proving identity, like the testimony of the next of kin who saw the body, are generally available in such a case. This is a good example of a situation in which the exhibit has some probative value, but such value is outweighed by the danger of prejudice arising from the nature of the exhibit. Sometimes the defense will stipulate to the existence of a wound in order to foreclose display of it.[81]

In situations in which a party to the litigation seeks to present real evidence that has a heavy emotional impact, the trial judge must decide whether the probative value of the exhibit outweighs its prejudicial effect on the jury. If so, the judge permits the jury to see it. Otherwise, it is excluded because of the danger that undue prejudice will be generated by its introduction into evidence. The objection that evidence is "inflammatory and prejudicial" is frequently lodged against proof of this type. As stated in the Federal Rules of Evidence, Rule 403: "Although relevant, evidence may be excluded if its probative value is substantially outweighed by the danger of unfair prejudice, confusion of the issues, or misleading the jury, or by considerations of undue delay, waste of time, or needless presentation of cumulative evidence."

Police officers often serve as authenticating witnesses for physical exhibits. The mechanics of introduction of the exhibit into evidence follow a similar pattern in most courts. An arresting officer, after being sworn and taking the stand, will be asked certain background questions concerning his or her employment, length of time he or she has served as a police officer, and hours of duty on the day of a particular crime. Depending on the case, the officer may next be asked to describe the arrest of the defendant and attendant search of him or her, if this is in the fact picture. Assuming for the moment that the officer had seized a gun from the accused that the prosecutor now seeks to introduce into evidence, the weapon will be marked for identification by the court reporter. Then the officer will be handed the exhibit and asked if he can identify it. When he does so, assuming he states it is the weapon he seized from the accused, the prosecutor will ask further questions concerning how the officer marked or labeled the gun for identification. Custody of the weapon from the time of seizure until its appearance in the courtroom may have to be traced. When these identifying questions are exhausted, the prosecutor will move to have the exhibit received into evidence, doing so with an

---

[80]    Note, 14 BROOKLYN L. REV. 261 (1948), citing State v. Vincent, 24 Iowa 570 (1868). *See also* Rost v. Brooklyn Heights R. R. Co., 41 N.Y.S. 1069, 1072 (1896), which held it error for the plaintiff's physician to produce a plaintiff's amputated foot preserved in a glass jar in a personal injury case. The plaintiff was in court to be seen, and the exhibit added little except to inflame the jury, in the view of the court. In many cases, however, the relevancy of the exhibit overbears its prejudicial nature.

[81]    *See generally* on the topic of stipulations the case of *Old Chief v. United States*, 117 S. Ct. 644 (1997).

offer more or less in these terms: "Your honor, the state offers state's Exhibit A for identification into evidence as state's Exhibit A in evidence." At this point the defendant has an opportunity to object to introduction of the evidence. Only after the item has been offered in this manner and received by the court does it come into evidence and form a part of the body of proof in the case.

A question is sometimes raised about whether and what items may go back with the jury during deliberations. Two commentators summarize variations in practice:

> Some courts treat demonstrative exhibits exactly like they do substantive exhibits, by formally admitting them into evidence and allowing the jury to view the exhibits during deliberations. Other courts admit demonstrative exhibits into a twilight zone reserved for "demonstrative purposes only," apparently indicating that such exhibits can be identified for the record but must be precluded from use by the jury during deliberations. Still other courts admit demonstrative exhibits "for limited purposes," but nevertheless permit the jury to view the exhibits during deliberations. Finally, some courts explicitly refuse to "admit" demonstrative exhibits into evidence at all, but allow witnesses to refer to them during testimony. Even among those courts, . . . there is a difference of opinion—some permitting the jury to view this unadmitted evidence during deliberations, while others do not.[82]

Effective in 1993, Maine Rule of Evidence 616(d) provides that "illustrative aids shall not accompany the jury during deliberations unless by consent of all parties or order of court on good cause shown."

A final form of demonstrative evidence that should be mentioned is photographic proof. Occasionally those unfamiliar with evidence law are of the view that photographs may only be introduced into evidence if the photographer who took a particular picture is in court to verify it. This is incorrect. A photograph may be authenticated by the operator of the camera; however, a police officer or other person with personal knowledge who testifies that the photo accurately depicts the scene or objects portrayed therein may also be the authenticating witness. For example, at trial of a case involving a collision of automobiles, the officer who was called to the scene may be handed a photo taken by another person showing the position of two cars after impact. The officer may identify the cars and testify that they appear in the photo in the position that he remembered them from the time of the accident, and may further state that the picture accurately represents the accident scene. The photo may then be introduced into evidence and handed to the jury to view.

Occasionally it may be helpful for the jury actually to see the scene of a crime. They are not permitted to go there on their own, but the judge can authorize a court officer (usually the bailiff) to take the jurors on a view of the premises. The purpose of the view is to aid the jury's understanding and evaluation of the testimony of the witnesses in the case. The attorneys for both

---

[82]    Robert D. Brain and Daniel J. Broderick, *The Derivative Relevance of Demonstrative Evidence: Charting Its Proper Evidentiary Status*, 25 U.C.D.L. REV. 957, 965-66 (1992).

sides are usually present during the view but no conversation with jurors is permitted by the bailiff or other court-appointed "guide."

In similar fashion, prosecutors sometimes want jurors to see an item that is too bulky to bring into the courtroom. Scott Peterson's fishing boat provides an example. Prosecutors alleged that Peterson killed his pregnant wife, Laci, in their Modesto, California, home and dumped her body into San Francisco Bay. They wanted jurors to see the boat he used to do this, so it was brought on its trailer into the basement garage area of the courthouse. Jurors were taken there to see it during Peterson's 2004 murder trial.

## § 6.11   Police Reports: Refreshing Recollection or Introduction into Evidence

When a police officer has maintained a notebook reflecting his or her observations at the scene of an incident (length of skid marks in an accident case, location of debris, etc.) or has prepared a report, the controlling legal principles are clear. The officer can consult the notes before the trial, and probably should bring them to court when he or she testifies. While on the witness stand, if the officer cannot accurately detail all of the information asked about from memory, he or she may request leave to consult his or her notes. The officer, recollection refreshed by his or her report or notes, can then respond to the questions.

Occasionally the prosecutor will want to go further and introduce the report itself into evidence. Sometimes he or she must do so, such as where the witness states after reviewing it that he or she has no present recollection of the events recorded, but knows his or her records of past events are accurate. In the event the prosecutor proceeds to offer the actual report into evidence, he or she will have the officer identify it, then testify: (1) that at one time the testifying officer had personal knowledge of the facts recorded in the report; (2) that the writing, when made, was an accurate record of the event; and (3) that it was made shortly after the event recorded.

Consider the following scenario. A police officer refers to a report or notes to refresh his recall of skid marks made by a car at an accident scene, then places the notes back in his pocket. After he testifies to the length of the skid marks and other details, the opposing attorney cross-examines the witness. She—the cross-examiner—asks the officer to hand over the notes for inspection. In this situation, where the prosecutor does not wish to introduce the notes into evidence, must the officer nonetheless surrender his notes? In federal court and a large number of states, the answer is yes. Because the officer used the material to aid his direct testimony on the witness stand, the defense has a right to look at what the officer looked at when he testified.[83]

---

[83]   *See* FED. R. EVID. 612.

## § 6.12  Opinion Testimony: Lay or Expert Witnesses

Most witnesses must testify to facts, not opinions. The witness is generally required to testify concerning that which he or she personally saw or heard, rather than provide conclusions on matters supported only by mere conjecture. However, the fact that a witness couches his or her testimony in terms of "I think" or "I believe" does not necessarily mean he or she is giving an opinion; the witness may be basing his or her testimony upon observed fact, but is simply very careful not to overstate his or her recollection of the situation.

### 1.  Ordinary Witnesses

The term **ordinary witness** simply refers to a nonexpert, such as bystander eyewitnesses to events and others who must testify to facts, not opinions. Notwithstanding the general rule against opinions, certain things may be summarized in opinion form, such as the witness's impression of the speed of a moving vehicle. For the witness to detail all the facts that sustained his or her impression that a car was traveling at about 30 m.p.h., for example, would be difficult and time-consuming; hence, a witness can give his or her general estimate or opinion. Also, a witness may express an opinion as to whether someone was intoxicated. However, while witnesses can supply facts and some opinions that support a theory of guilt or innocence of a defendant, no witness in a criminal case can give an opinion on the ultimate fact in issue. This rule bars any testimony by a witness to the effect that he believes a person is guilty or innocent of a crime.

### 2.  Expert Witnesses

#### a.  Introduction

Unlike the ordinary witness, the **expert witness** may freely cast his or her testimony in opinion form when speaking in an area of his or her expertise. To elicit testimony of this kind, the prosecutor or defense attorney must qualify the witness as an expert. This is done through a series of questions that establish the number of years the person has engaged in a particular field and the scope of his or her experience with the problem concerning which an opinion is to be propounded.

As an example, it may be relevant in connection with an auto collision case to show which side of the road the impact between two vehicles occurred upon. Assuming there are no eyewitnesses to the occurrence except the drivers of the two vehicles, each of whom claims that the other was in the wrong lane of travel, the investigating officer's opinion can be crucial. He or she can be qualified as an expert to assert an opinion as to point of impact, but only after the trial court has been shown certain things—for example, that the officer investigated numerous accidents in the past, has attended special in-service training schools for traffic accident investigation, and personally observed the location of the vehicles, debris, and skid marks involved in the case. With such qualification, his or her opinion testimony as to the place of impact should be admitted by the trial court.

### b. Varied Subjects of Expert Proof

In criminal cases, experts in ballistics, blood, handwriting, fingerprints, fiber comparison, narcotics analysis, and other specialty fields may appear as witnesses.[84] Larger local police departments may have laboratories to do some of this work. Experts may also be available at colleges, state criminal investigation bureaus, or from the FBI and other federal agencies. In an emerging expert field, the polygraph or lie detector examiner can be helpful in clearing cases and eliminating suspects. However, these results remain unfavored evidence in American courts, except where the defendant stipulates prior to taking the test that the results will be admissible, whether favorable to him or not.

Fiber evidence played a key role in the trial of Wayne Williams. A series of young black males were killed in Atlanta in the late 1970s, and Williams was tried for the murders of two such victims. Graphs of fiber taken from Williams' car and bedroom were compared with graphs of fiber taken from the victims. The fibers matched, according to the prosecution experts. With expert support, the prosecution advocated the proposition that there was little chance that anyone but Williams could have put the deceased victims in contact with the same type of bedroom and automobile floorboard carpets.[85]

Scientific evidence of various kinds continues to play an ever-increasing role in American criminal trials. DNA typing is one of the most important scientific techniques used to solve crimes. Thrust into the public eye in the O.J. Simpson case, this form of scientific testing enjoys a high level of technical acceptance. How does it work? A body specimen such as blood or semen may be found at a crime scene. The specimen contains chromosomes that identify their source. The first stage of the testing process typically involves chemical extraction of the DNA—deoxyribonucleic acid—from the specimen. Through electrophoresis and related scientific processes the specimen is broken down, rearranged, probed, and matched to a sample from a known defendant. This is DNA "fingerprinting."[86]

In criminal cases involving the technique, expert testimony will be supplied by the prosecution suggesting a match between the crime scene specimen and the known sample. Sometimes the expert testimony will be objected to on the basis that DNA testing has not been correctly conducted. In the face of such an objection, the trial judge will look at the particular case to see if appropriate samples were taken and proper laboratory procedures followed.

---

[84]   FED. R. EVID. 702.
[85]   Williams v. State, 251 Ga. 749, 312 S.E.2d 40 (1983).
[86]   Harvey and Berry, *DNA Typing: Keeping the State Out of Your Client's Genes*, THE CHAMPION 6 (August 1989).

Hypnosis sometimes plays a role in assisting detection of crime. Some states allow hypnotically enhanced evidence to be produced in court through a witness who could remember little at an earlier point but after hypnosis reveals numerous details about the incident. Some states, wary of hypnotic suggestion, reject any testimony taken after hypnosis.

Opinion on the mental state of another is often the subject of expert testimony. For example, a defense psychiatrist may be called as a witness to testify that the defendant was suffering from paranoia or a compulsion at the time of the crime. However, a psychiatrist is not allowed to testify that a defendant is not guilty on account of defendant's mental infirmity. It is the jury's function to provide that conclusion. Federal Rule of Evidence 704(b) prohibits an expert in a criminal case from testifying "as to whether the defendant did or did not have the mental state or condition constituting an element of the crime charged or of a defense thereto. Such ultimate issues are matters for the trier of fact alone."

### c. Legal Tests for Scientific Evidence

Experts often explain the results of traditional scientific examinations like ballistics or fingerprints to juries. They also perform tests of a more novel scientific nature such as lie detector examinations or checking voiceprints. Criminal cases involving voice identification techniques were prominently cited in the Supreme Court's most important decision on scientific evidence, the case of *Daubert v. Merrell Dow Pharmaceuticals, Inc.*[87] Under an older standard called the *Frye* test, a scientist could not testify to a new or novel scientific or chemical technique unless the process at issue had broad scientific approval. The Supreme Court looked at the history of the rule: "The *Frye* test has its origin in a short citation-free 1923 decision concerning the admissibility of evidence derived from a systolic blood pressure deception test, a crude precursor to the polygraph machine. In what has become a famous (perhaps infamous) passage, the then Court of Appeals for the District of Columbia described the device and its operation and declared: 'Just when a scientific principle or discovery crosses the line between the experimental and demonstrable stages is difficult to define. Somewhere in this twilight zone the evidential force of the principle must be recognized, and while courts will go a long way in admitting expert testimony deduced from a well-recognized scientific principle or discovery, the thing from which the deduction is made must be sufficiently established to have gained general acceptance in the particular field in which it belongs.' 54 App. D.C., at 47, 293 F., at 1014. Because the deception test [polygraph] had not yet gained such standing and scientific recognition among physiological and psychological authorities as would justify the courts in admitting expert testimony deduced from the discovery, development, and experiments thus far made, evidence of its results was ruled inadmissible."

---

[87]   113 S. Ct. 2786 (1994).

Observing that "[i]n the 70 years since its formulation, in the *Frye* case, the general acceptance test has been the dominant standard for determining the admissibility of novel scientific evidence at trial," the United States Supreme Court instead adopted a reliability standard. The latter standard now controls federal scientific evidence, and federal courts and numerous states follow the *Daubert* reliability doctrine for admitting scientific testimony, like DNA proof. Other jurisdictions continue to cling to the *Frye* rule.

A 1998 decision by the United States Supreme Court revisited the issue of the admissibility of polygraph evidence. The defendant sought to lay a foundation for the admission of favorable results of a polygraph examination. His request was denied, and he argued to the Supreme Court that his right to present a defense to a criminal charge was impermissibly abridged by the denial of his polygraph evidence. The Supreme Court disagreed, citing doubts about whether polygraph results constitute reliable evidence.[88]

### d. Opinions on Law

Legal opinions by experts sometimes become an issue. The text has already noted the bar relating to psychiatric experts. They are prohibited from testifying in an improper manner, and are not allowed to state: "The defendant is not guilty of this crime due to his dementia." In similar fashion, an expert in criminology is not permitted to conclude his or her testimony by stating something such as: "review of the evidence convinces me that the defendant is guilty of the crime charged under section 716 of the state penal code." This is a prohibited legal opinion. Regarding the barring of experts from testifying as to legal standards and prohibited issues of mixed law and fact, see *United States v. DiDomenico*: "While DiDomenico proclaims that she did not offer Dr. Grove to testify as to the ultimate issue of whether she knew the computer equipment was stolen, this is semantic camouflage. We read Dr. Grove's proffered testimony as stating the bottom line inference and leaving it to the jury merely to murmur, 'Amen.'"[89]

## § 6.13  Hearsay

The classic definition of **hearsay** is a "statement made out of court and offered in court to prove the truth of the facts asserted in the statement." When the prosecutor asks a question that calls for hearsay, the police officer will be barred from answering it if defense counsel makes proper and timely objection. An illustration will help further define the important concept of hearsay. Suppose Jones is a police officer who is investigating an automobile accident. On the day after the accident he talks to W, a witness who personally observed

88  United States v. Scheffer, 118 S. Ct. 1261 (1998). State court rejection of polygraph, *see* State v. Countryman, 573 N.W.2d 265 (Iowa 1998).
89  985 F.2d 1159, 1165 (2d Cir. 1993).

the collision between cars driven by D and X. X was killed in the crash. In the trial of D for vehicular homicide, Jones is on the witness stand. The prosecutor asks him if he interviewed witnesses who were at the accident scene, and Jones replies that he did. The prosecutor then asks Jones to relate any conversations that occurred with such witnesses. Jones is about to answer that he talked to W, that W reported seeing the accident, and that W saw D traveling at a high rate of speed prior to the collision. Jones is interrupted by defense counsel's objection that the question calls for hearsay. If W is in the jurisdiction, he should be subpoenaed into court to testify himself.

> It makes good sense when trying to find out about something to make inquiry of the person who has personally perceived the matter. The courts in establishing the hearsay rule are simply fulfilling a demand that people would generally make in obtaining information about a fact from the person who had actual knowledge. The truth about a matter in dispute can be discovered from those who know about it, rather than have another testify as to what the man who knew had said. In this respect, the hearsay rule is like the best evidence rule, which requires the production of the original, if available.[90]

## § 6.14  Exceptions to the Hearsay Rule

While most hearsay evidence is inadmissible in criminal trials, certain types of hearsay, because of their special reliability, are admissible. The classes of hearsay evidence that are admissible are categorized as exceptions to the hearsay rule. Some of the exceptions most commonly encountered in criminal cases are briefly outlined.

### 1.  Confessions and Admissions

Whether oral or written, this class of hearsay is admissible where constitutional guidelines were observed in taking the statements. Confessions are powerful proof against a defendant, and may be introduced early in the prosecutor's case-in-chief. Often the method of introduction is to have the detective who interrogated the defendant read the defendant's words to the jury. In this manner confessions may be employed to show the defendant's guilt during the prosecutor's case. Also, during the defense presentation of evidence, a confession may be used to impeach the accused if he or she takes the stand to testify, and the live testimony is contradicted by the prior written statement.

### 2.  Dying Declarations

This is another example of an out-of-court statement made by a witness that is introduced in court through testimony of a different person. A man dies, but before he expires, he whispers to a police officer "D killed me." When D

---

[90]  LADD & CARLSON, CASES AND MATERIALS ON EVIDENCE, 803-804 (1972).

is tried for murder, the officer is entitled to take the stand and relate what the man whispered. The reasons are twofold: (a) the deceased is no longer available, and a special necessity to allow hearsay proof as to his pre-death declaration arises; (b) special reliability is provided by the fact that the man realized he was near death when he spoke. The law has long assumed that a deathbed statement will be truthful, in almost all cases, and that a person will not go to his death with a lie on his lips.

In most states, certain matters must coalesce in order to render the dying declaration admissible: (1) the declarant must be conscious of his impending death; (2) the declarant must be shown to have had an opportunity to know the facts, and the statement sought to be admitted must be a declaration of fact, not opinion; and (3) the statement is admissible only in criminal homicide cases dealing with the death of the deceased who made the declaration. Evidence rules for federal trials alter this pattern in federal courts. Under the Federal Rules of Evidence, dying declarations are admissible in prosecutions for homicide or in civil actions.

### 3. Reported Testimony

Suppose Smith is tried for murder. On the testimony of X, an eyewitness to the homicide, he is convicted. However, Smith appeals his case, wins on the appeal, and the case is remanded to the trial court for retrial.[91] Fourteen months elapse between the time of the first trial and the retrial, the delay being attributable to the time-consuming task of preparing, briefing, and arguing the case through the appellate courts. In the interim X, who was an elderly man at the time of the first trial, dies. Several questions now arise. Can X's testimony be presented in some form at the retrial? Would his earlier testimony be hearsay in the second trial? What about the right of the accused to confront the witness against him?

One commentator responds to these questions:[92]

> The admission of former testimony in a subsequent proceeding is conditioned upon (1) an inability to obtain the witness; (2) an opportunity to cross-examine the witness in the former trial; (3) an identity or substantial identity of issues in the two proceedings; and (4) substantial identity of parties. The opportunity for cross-examination is considered to be the most essential element because the credibility of the witness can be tested through direct confrontation.

---

[91]   When a prisoner successfully appeals because improper evidence was used against him, *see* § 9.6 of this text on the state's right to retry him on the same charge.

[92]   Note, *The Use of Prior Recorded Testimony and the Right of Confrontation*, 54 IOWA L. REV. 360 (1968). If there was adequate opportunity for prior cross-examination and the witness is unavailable for trial, the constitutional right to confrontation appears satisfied. A similar question is confronted when the prosecution decides to use a transcript of the preliminary hearing to place in evidence the testimony of a state witness who appeared there but has since become unavailable.

In *Ohio v. Roberts*[93] the trial judge permitted the prosecutor to prove the state's case by reading into the trial record a witness's preliminary hearing testimony. The witness had been called by the defense at the preliminary hearing to testify, in effect, as a hostile witness. After the preliminary hearing, the witness apparently left the area and could not be located by the prosecutor for trial. The Supreme Court ruled that the defendant's confrontation rights were not denied by the prosecutor's use of the earlier testimony; the defense had the opportunity to interrogate the witness at the preliminary hearing.

Preliminary hearing testimony should be sharply distinguished from a grand jury transcript. It is to be remembered that a grand jury is not an adversary proceeding. The defense is not present, and is unable to cross-examine government witnesses. Grand jury testimony may not be substituted for live testimony of a trial witness.

When the trial judge rules that the prior recorded testimony is admissible matter in the second trial, the evidence is usually presented by the official court reporter reading to the jury his notes of the questions put to the witness at the first trial, and the answers given by the witness. If these notes have been put into typed form (transcript) before the second trial, the prosecutor may authenticate the transcript by the testimony of the court reporter, then introduce the typewritten document into evidence.

### 4. Official Statements

Official records that a public official has a duty to maintain are admissible. Thus, reports of the county medical examiner as to the time and cause of death, weather reports maintained by the United States Weather Bureau, and recorded deeds or mortgages come into evidence under this exception to the hearsay rule. So also may the physician's report on blood-alcohol content in a drunk-driving case, although the presence of the physician to authenticate the report and to be cross-examined will probably be required.

### 5. Miscellaneous Exceptions

There are several other hearsay problems that may arise in a criminal case, including the admissibility of statements of co-conspirators in a conspiracy trial,[94] **res gestae statements**,[95] declarations against interest, especially by per-

---

[93] 448 U.S. 56 (1980).

[94] Declarations of one co-conspirator are admissible against another if they were made while the conspiracy was pending and in furtherance of its objectives. LADD & CARLSON, *supra* note 90, at 895-899.

[95] Res gestae is a term decried by evidence commentators but employed by most courts. Courts commonly classify excited utterances of people who saw a crime under the res gestae exception to the hearsay rule and render these statements admissible. An excited utterance, admissible as an exception to the hearsay rule, is defined in Rule 803(2), Federal Rules of Evidence: "A statement relating to a startling event or condition made while the defendant was under the stress of excitement caused by the event or condition."

sons who declare themselves guilty of a crime charged against another,[96] flight by the accused, and business records. Suppose that immediately after a murder the chief suspect flees the jurisdiction and is eventually returned from another state by extradition or an unlawful flight warrant. From an evidentiary standpoint, the known facts that establish his flight can be described to the jury upon his trial for murder. Like a confession, flight is receivable as evidence of guilt.

Business and hospital records of facts that are routinely made and kept and that are relied on in the daily work of the institution are admissible.[97] Statements made to doctors and nurses when a person is being treated medically can be reported in a later court case by that doctor or nurse. This is the medical examination exception to the hearsay rule.

Accomplice confessions or incriminating statements are frequently offered into evidence against a defendant. Suppose A and D are jointly suspected of pulling a robbery, and A is picked up. A tells police he knows all about the robbery. D did it, A says, and A helped to fence the objects that D stole. At the trial of State versus D, the prosecutor may seek to have Officer X read the accomplice's signed statement into the record against D. Will the judge permit this? "No" is the answer supplied by the United States Supreme Court. In *Crawford v. Washington*,[98] decided in 2004, such hearsay statements are inadmissible unless the accomplice is cross-examined at trial. A must testify as a witness, and in his absence his statement is worthless. Testimonial statements such as the one from the accomplice in this illustration, statements that a declarant would reasonably expect to be used against a defendant at trial, must be exposed to the defendant's cross-examination. The right to confront adverse witnesses that is contained in the Sixth Amendment to the United States Constitution demands nothing less.

## 6. Child Abuse Cases

There has been a movement to enact legislation allowing hearsay statements from a child relating to child abuse to be introduced as evidence. Suppose it is suspected that a child has been abused. He or she is interviewed by a doctor or a social worker. Under the new laws, the social worker could testify in a criminal case and repeat the child's accusatory statements against the defendant.

A number of states have also enacted statutes that allow the testimony of child sexual abuse victims to be videotaped. This procedure spares the victim the ordeal of appearing as a live witness in open court. Although the use of

---

[96]   Chambers was charged with murder. McDonald had stated to friends that he, McDonald, had done the killing Chambers was charged with. The Mississippi courts would not allow Chambers to prove this at trial, but the United States Supreme Court disagreed. The Court cited the declaration against interest exception to the hearsay rule, and authorized the admission of McDonald's statements. Declarations against interest constitute "an exception founded on the assumption that a person is unlikely to fabricate a statement against his own interest" unless it be true. Chambers v. Mississippi, 410 U.S. 284, 93 S. Ct. 1038, 35 L. Ed. 2d 297 (1973).

[97]   *See* FED. R. EVID. 803(6) (business records exception to hearsay rule).

[98]   124 S. Ct. 1354 (2004).

videotaped testimony significantly eases the child's burden in testifying, serious questions arise. A videotape of a child's testimony is a form of hearsay.

As such, future court tests of this mode of supplying the jury with the child's story (showing them the videotape) may be hedged with legal restrictions. One of these might be a requirement that the accused be present and his or her lawyer allowed to cross-examine the witness while the witness is videotaped. It seems certain that stiff defense challenges to creative methods for reproducing child testimony will be asserted. In the end, perhaps the only way for the videotaped statement to pass constitutional muster may be for the defendant and the defense attorney to be there, with a right to cross-examine the child.

In addition to videotape, some courts have created special procedures to shield child victims from viewing the defendant when they come to court to testify. Confrontation objections have been made to such procedures. With statutes in the majority of states providing one or more of the foregoing special provisions for child witness testimony, the Supreme Court is in the process of examining the constitutionality of state laws.

One case dealt with the concept of allowing an adult to whom the child spoke to become the chief witness at trial, sparing the child the burden of coming to court.[99] The prosecution was not required to produce the four-year-old victim of a sexual assault at trial. Nor was it required that the court make a finding that the victim was unavailable for direct testimony at trial before the child's statements to others would be received in evidence. These statements included declarations to the child's babysitter and mother, as well as to a police officer, to whom the child made spontaneous statements about the defendant's abuse. The defendant had been seen leaving the child's room. A doctor later examined the child in the emergency room, and the youngster provided an account of events that was essentially identical to the one she gave earlier to her mother and police. Because the statements to the doctor fell within the medical examination exception to the hearsay rule and those made to the other witnesses were spontaneous declarations, neither the hearsay rule nor the confrontation clause was violated by the trial court's ruling allowing testimony by these adults in lieu of direct trial testimony by the child. These witnesses could lawfully come to the trial and testify to what the child said because the child's words to them fell within "firmly rooted" exceptions to the hearsay rule. The defendant's criminal sexual assault conviction was affirmed.

At the outset of this section it was mentioned that laws often provide special provisions for shielding children from the view of the defendant at trial. This concept is separate from that of keeping children out of the courthouse entirely by means of allowing adults to repeat the child's words in court, as explained in the previous paragraph. Different laws allow youthful witnesses to come to the trial but permit them to remain out of the gaze of the defendant.

---

[99] White v. Illinois, 112 S. Ct. 736 (1992). For states that have enacted new statutes to admit child hearsay statements into evidence, see Mosteller, *Remaking Confrontation Clause and Hearsay Doctrine Under the Challenge of Child Sexual Abuse Prosecutions*, 1993 ILL. L. REV. 691.

Sometimes the child is placed in a private room and his or her testimony is beamed into the courtroom by means of a television camera. Whether the courts will approve this procedure may turn somewhat on the age of the minor. Using closed-circuit television with a six-year-old child assault victim was approved in *Maryland v. Craig*.[100] However, when two 15-year-old females testified from behind a screen in Iowa, the Supreme Court ruled that the setup was unconstitutional.

In *Coy v. Iowa,* the Court pointed out that, at trial, the defendant is entitled to cross-examine opposing witnesses. It is a general rule in criminal trials that when the defendant is cross-examining, he or she has the right to directly confront accusing witnesses. The Sixth Amendment to the United States Constitution provides: "In all criminal prosecutions, the accused shall enjoy the right. . . . to be confronted with the witnesses against him." This incorporates the right to a "face-to-face meeting with the witnesses appearing before the trier of fact," often including child witnesses in sexual molestation cases. In *Coy*,[101] two 15-year-old female complainants testified from behind a screen that blocked the defendant from their sight but allowed him to see them dimly and to hear them. Justice Scalia remarked on behalf of the Supreme Court: "It is always more difficult to tell a lie about a person 'to his face' than 'behind his back'. . . . Since [Coy's] right to face-to-face confrontation was violated, we reverse the judgment of the Iowa Supreme Court [against Coy for lascivious acts with a child] and remand the case."

The case of the six-year-old was treated differently. If the trial judge explores the situation and finds the child would be traumatized by looking at the defendant while he gives his testimony, special provisions may be made. Because the trial judge made an individualized finding in *Maryland v. Craig* that the young witness needed special protection, the United States Supreme Court was able to distinguish *Coy v. Iowa*. Where a special showing of need is made on behalf of a child, closed-circuit television will be approved:

> In sum, we conclude that where necessary to protect a child witness from trauma that would be caused by testifying in the physical presence of the defendant, at least where such trauma would impair the child's ability to communicate, the Confrontation Clause does not prohibit use of a procedure that, despite the absence of face-to-face confrontation, ensures the reliability of the evidence by subjecting it to rigorous adversarial testing and thereby preserves the essence of effective confrontation. Because there is no dispute that the child witnesses in this case testified under oath, were subject to full cross-examination, and were able to be observed by the judge, jury, and defendant as they testified, we conclude that, to the extent that a proper finding of necessity has been made, the admission of such testimony would be consonant with the Confrontation Clause.

---

[100] 110 S. Ct. 3157 (1990).
[101] 108 S. Ct. 2798 (1988).

Dissenting Justice Scalia, joined by Justices Brennan, Marshall, and Stevens, complained: "Seldom has this Court failed so conspicuously to sustain a categorical guarantee of the Constitution against the tide of prevailing current opinion. The Sixth Amendment provides, with unmistakable clarity, that '[i]n all criminal prosecutions, the accused shall enjoy the right . . . to be confronted with the witnesses against him.' The purpose of enshrining this protection in the Constitution was to assure that none of the many policy interests from time to time pursued by statutory law could overcome a defendant's right to face his or her accusers in court."

## § 6.15  Defense Evidence

The defendant may present one of several possible defenses, depending on the case. Affirmative defenses, including alibi, insanity, intoxication, self-defense, entrapment,[102] automatism, coercion, and duress may be raised to avoid responsibility. In presenting any of these defenses, the defendant will call a disparate assortment of witnesses. The insanity defense almost always requires the production of expert testimony, usually from a psychiatrist, to explain the defendant's mental condition at the time of the crime.[103] In connection with alibi, if the defendant says he or she was elsewhere than at the scene at the time of a crime, supporting witnesses will usually be called to substantiate the defendant's story. The accused himself or herself is a competent witness to give evidence on his or her own behalf on any of these issues when he or she is being tried.

When a defendant claims insanity, the jury may be charged that every person is presumed to be of sound mind, and (where the governing code places the burden on the accused) that the defendant must prove his or her mental incapacity by a preponderance of the evidence. Several courts treat insanity as an affirmative defense that the defendant must prove. The Supreme Court also allows such burden-shifting to the defense when self-defense is claimed, if local law places the burden on the accused as to such defense.[104]

---

[102]  The defense of entrapment is established when the evidence demonstrates that a person, not otherwise inclined to commit a criminal offense, is enticed by a police officer to commit same. Sherman v. United States, 356 U.S. 369, 78 S. Ct. 819, 2 L. Ed. 2d 848 (1958). However, if government agents set a trap for a criminal otherwise bent on crime, merely affording an opportunity or facilities for the commission of the offense, they have not entrapped.

[103]  This is to be distinguished from defendant's mental condition at the time of the *trial*. A mentally defective defendant cannot be tried for a crime. Drope v. Missouri, 420 U.S. 162, 95 S. Ct. 896, 43 L. Ed. 2d 103 (1975). On recent developments with the insanity defense, including the verdict of "guilty but mentally ill," *see* Chapter 7.

[104]  Martin v. Ohio, 107 S. Ct. 1098 (1987) (Ohio's requirement that defendant prove self-defense by a preponderance of evidence is not unconstitutional). However, many states do not require any special notice of self-defense and allow it to be raised under a plea of not guilty without any shifting of the burden of persuasion.

The language defining insanity in the Federal Crime Control Act of 1984 follows the M'Naghten Rule. This test of insanity also applies in a number of states. When insanity is raised as a defense, under the **M'Naghten Rule** the jury will be instructed to acquit if it finds that the defendant *did not understand the nature and quality of his or her acts or did not know right from wrong.*

Under the **"irresistible impulse" test** the defendant must show that he or she *did not know the nature or quality of the act, did not know the act was wrong, or did not have the ability to control his or her conduct even if he or she knew it was wrong.*

Many psychiatrists advocate a more flexible insanity standard than *M'Naghten*, and some courts follow the *Durham* (or product) **test**, under which the defendant's evidence needs to show that his or her *unlawful act was the product of mental disease or defect* in order to excuse his or her conduct.

Finally, the **American Law Institute** developed a modernized insanity **test**, which excuses criminal responsibility if it is shown that a defendant possessed a *mental defect that deprived him or her of the capacity either to appreciate the criminality of his or her conduct or to conform his or her conduct to the requirements of the law.*

Psychological profile testimony of other types is on the ascendancy. The government frequently offers rape trauma syndrome testimony to prove that the victim was raped, and in child abuse cases may have an expert testify about child abuse syndrome. The defendant may also offer profile testimony. The late 1990s and the years 2000-2005 witnessed increasing application of the battered spouse syndrome defense, which has been asserted in crimes involving assaults and homicides in which the defendant claims she or he was the victim. The defendant argues that she or he acted in self-defense and had to maim or kill her or his attacker.[105]

At least three views are applied to battered spouse syndrome proof: (1) testimony regarding battered spouse syndrome will be excluded; (2) battered spouse syndrome evidence will be admitted as an adjunct of a self-defense claim, and particularly when the jurisdiction otherwise imposes a general requirement of retreat in connection with pleas of self-defense; (3) such proof is admissible in a relatively independent fashion, and meets the standards for admissibility of scientific evidence.

Recent years have witnessed the birth of numerous new defenses for mitigating criminal responsibility. These defenses, much like battered spouse syndrome defense, are psychologically based but depend on the individual defendant's situation. Basically, the accused person says that he or she is really the victim, not the person whom the accused has killed or maimed. Often it takes the form of asserting "he was doing this or that to me, so I struck back." Using such a defense, attorneys attempt to account for their client's behavior by arguing that a defendant's judgment was adversely affected by any number of fac-

[105] Discussion of admissibility of expert testimony on the battered woman syndrome, see 10 GEO. MASON U. L. REV. 171 (1989). One court's view approving admissibility of expert opinion regarding battered woman syndrome is contained in Smith v. State, 247 Ga. 612, 277 S.E.2d 678 (1981).

tors, including past child abuse. Other factors that defense attorneys sometimes claim accounted for the defendant's antisocial conduct include racial discrimination, premenstrual syndrome, post-traumatic stress, and drug-induced psychosis.[106] Victimization defenses have sometimes been used in sensational, high-profile cases.

Can a defendant legally maintain "inconsistent" defenses? Can he or she say "I didn't do it, but if you find I did, I was entrapped into it"? Is a defendant who claims that he or she is not guilty nonetheless entitled to use an entrapment defense? In *Matthews v. United States*,[107] the Supreme Court held that even if a defendant denies one or more elements of the crime, he or she is entitled to an instruction allowing the jury to acquit him or her because of entrapment whenever there is reasonable evidence to support that claim.

## § 6.16   Defendant as a Witness

Under the earlier common law, those with an interest in the outcome of a trial were disqualified from testifying. When this rule controlled, defendants in criminal trials were deemed incompetent to give evidence because of their interest in the case. However, statutory destruction of the rule began in the mid-1800s.

The first American statute according the defendant capacity to give evidence was enacted in 1864. In 1878 Congress passed a statute that provided that a person charged with a federal offense could be a competent witness at his or her own trial. Following these grants of capacity to testify, it became relevant for the courts to explore the application to testifying defendants of the federal privilege against self-incrimination.

## § 6.17   Constitutional Privilege

The **Fifth Amendment** to the United States Constitution provides that no person ". . . shall be compelled in any criminal case to be a witness against himself." The provision has two ramifications for trials.

This protection can be asserted "in any proceeding, civil or criminal, administrative or judicial, investigatory or adjudicatory, in which the witness reasonably believes that the information sought [could be used against the person] in a subsequent state or federal criminal proceeding.[108]

---

[106]   Stephanie B. Goldberg, *Fault Lines*, 80 A.B.A. J. 40 (1994).

[107]   485 U.S. 58 (1988). Entrapment is defined in note 102, *supra*.

[108]   United States v. Balsys, 118 S. Ct. 2218 (1998) (but threat of foreign prosecution does not justify witness in refusing to answer).

## 1. When the Defendant Does Not Testify

The accused may refuse to take the stand at his or her trial. This silence of the accused may not be pointed out to the jury by the prosecutor as evidence of the defendant's guilt. Nor may the judge make unfavorable reference to the defendant's silence in his or her instructions to the jury.[109] The defendant is entitled to an instruction, when he or she requests it, that the members of the jury are to draw no adverse inferences from a defendant's silence.[110]

## 2. When the Defendant Testifies

Statutes in several states limit the prosecutor to cross-examination of the defendant on only those points brought up by the defendant in his direct testimony.[111] If during direct examination the defendant maintained silence on a relevant area of inquiry and did not avail himself or herself of favorable testimony in a particular field, the prosecutor cannot require him or her to talk about that area.[112] This rule of limited cross-examination appears to state the approach required under the Fifth Amendment when it is the defendant in the case who is testifying.[113] It has been maintained as the general mode of cross-examination in federal courts for many years, and was embraced in the Federal Rules of Evidence.[114]

The Fifth Amendment also barred the practice in one state whereby a defendant who testified at his or her own trial was required to testify first in the order of defense witnesses. A Tennessee statute that directed that a criminal defendant "desiring to testify shall do so before any other testimony for the defense is heard" was held unconstitutional in *Brooks v. Tennessee*.[115]

The privilege against self-incrimination has been expanded and it now extends significantly into the pretrial phases of criminal prosecutions.[116] The privilege applies and may be claimed not only at trials, but in other proceedings as well. *Garrity v. New Jersey*[117] is an example in point. New Jersey police officers were being investigated for allegedly fixing parking tickets. They were told that if they refused to answer the investigator's questions, they would be removed from their positions. The officers answered the questions, then were later prosecuted for conspiracy to obstruct administration of the state's

---

[109] Griffin v. California, 380 U.S. 609 (1965). Where the accused attempts to use this silence as a sword, however, the prosecutor has the right to reply. People v. Finney, 232 N.E.2d 247 (Ill. 1967).

[110] Carter v. Kentucky, 450 U.S. 288 (1981).

[111] FED. R. EVID. 611(b) has been embraced in a large number of jurisdictions.

[112] A contrary rule of so-called "wide open" cross-examination prevails in approximately 13 states. The definitional breakdown between direct and cross-examination appears in § 6.20.

[113] Fitzpatrick v. United States, 178 U.S. 304, 20 S. Ct. 944, 44 L. Ed. 1078 (1900); United States v. Barker, 11 F.R.D. 421, 422 (N.D. Cal. 1951). See the cases collected in Carlson, *Cross-Examination of the Accused*, 52 CORNELL L.Q. 705 (1967); MCCORMICK, EVIDENCE § 26 (1984).

[114] FED. R. EVID. 611(b) (2004) was enacted into law in 1975.

[115] 406 U.S. 605, 92 S. Ct. 1891, 32 L. Ed. 2d 358 (1972).

[116] Miranda v. Arizona, 384 U.S. 436, 86 S. Ct. 1602, 16 L. Ed. 2d 694 (1966).

[117] 385 U.S. 493, 87 S. Ct. 616, 17 L. Ed. 2d 562 (1967).

traffic laws. The statements they had given the investigator were used against them at trial, and they were convicted. Relying on the privilege against self-incrimination, the United States Supreme Court overturned the convictions with these words: "We think the confessions were infected by the coercion inherent in this scheme of questioning and cannot be sustained as voluntary. . . ."

## § 6.18   Privileges Generally

Suppose a defendant is accused of obtaining money by false pretenses and his wife knows the details of the fraudulent scheme operated by the defendant. The defendant denies guilt and the case goes to trial. Can the wife be subpoenaed by the government, placed on the witness stand, and required to testify concerning the information in her possession that incriminates her husband? Suppose the marriage has fallen upon difficult days since the arrest and the wife wants to testify, volunteering to the prosecutor information gleaned through the marriage relationship. Can she take the stand and relate the information to the jury? The answer to both questions is no, if the defendant makes a timely objection to the testimony. An accused in a criminal action has a privilege to prevent his or her spouse from testifying in such action with respect to any confidential communication between them while they were husband and wife. However, statements made during the course of a domestic assault are not privileged, and a spouse can testify to the other spouse's words or conduct during the attack. For example, where the husband commits an assault on the wife or a crime against the children of the marriage, this information is not privileged. In 1980, the Supreme Court narrowed the federal husband-wife privilege by allowing a wife to testify against her husband in a narcotics case. While she could not disclose her husband's confidential words, she could testify to the criminal acts that she observed.[118]

The law throws a protective cloak of privilege around other confidential communications, including those between attorney and client,[119] doctor and patient, and the priest, rabbi, or minister and parishioner. The theory behind these privilege rules is that society wishes to protect and foster an important confidentiality between the parties to the conversation. It is important for members of society to be able to make full disclosure to their lawyers or minister, for example, from whom guidance is obtained on legal and spiritual matters. Requiring those who hear the disclosure to come into court and testify about what was said will destroy the confidence of the citizen, and will severely injure the relationship between the parties to the conversation. The relationship

---

[118]   Trammel v. United States, 445 U.S. 40 (1980).
[119]   Attorney-client privilege for corporations, *see* Upjohn Co. v. United States, 449 U.S. 383 (1981). Professional ethics require a lawyer to refrain from disclosing past client crimes. People v. Belge, 376 N.Y.S.2d 771 (N.Y. App. Div. 1975). However, future planned crimes or perjury by a defendant are different. Nix v. Whiteside, 475 U.S. 157 (1986) (client perjury case).

is often enduring. Rules that govern conduct by attorneys, for example, impose a duty of confidentiality, which remains in place even if a client dies.[120]

Of special interest to law enforcement officers is the protection extended to conversations between officers and government informers. Frequently the officers wish to withhold from the defense in a criminal case the identity of an informer. Under the rule announced in *Scher v. United States*,[121] public policy forbids the disclosure of an informer's identity unless essential to the defense, and this rule has been reaffirmed since that case. Sometimes, in order to make a determination of whether the informer's identity is so sensitive that nondisclosure should prevail (as when the informer is still undercover), the judge may conduct an ***in camera*** or private examination of the informer's situation. As a general rule, courts are inclined to shield informer privacy, at least until full trial of the case. A division is often applied by courts between rules applicable to pretrial hearings versus the trial itself. The informer's identity will be protected up to the trial, at which time it may be disclosed. At trial "the need for a truthful verdict outweighs society's need for the informer privilege."[122]

## § 6.19 Character Testimony

The defendant sometimes calls witnesses to the stand to testify that the defendant is a truth-telling individual. This is designed to bolster the impression the jury has of the defendant's character and to support the conclusion that the defendant told the truth when he or she testified. The defendant may also introduce proof of a particular personality or character trait, for example, proof that he or she is a peaceable person to show that it is unlikely that he or she was the aggressor in an assault case. The accepted means of proving character is to show the reputation of the defendant in the community for the character trait in question. The object of the law in making reputation the test of character is to obtain the aggregate judgment of the community. Congress authorized federal courts to receive character evidence in the form of reputation proof, or by way of personal opinion of the witness who is testifying to another's character.[123]

A typical examination-in-chief by defense counsel on the issue of reputation appears in *Michelson v. United States*.[124] The attorney first established that the witness had known defendant Michelson for about 30 years:

---

[120] A 1998 Supreme Court case adjudicated whether the privilege survives the death of the client, and decided that it does. Swidler & Berlin v. United States, 118 S. Ct. 2081 (1998) (disclosures by Deputy White House Counsel Vincent Foster).

[121] 305 U.S. 251, 59 S. Ct. 174, 83 L. Ed. 151 (1938). *See* Comment, 17 TEXAS L. REV. 522 (1939).

[122] McCray v. Illinois, 386 U.S. 300, 87 S. Ct. 1056, 18 L. Ed. 2d 62 (1967) (arresting officers testified fully in open court to what informer told them; disclosure of undercover employee's identity not required unless essential to a fair determination of the case).

The question of whether there is a privilege for reporters and newsgatherers to keep their sources confidential is discussed in § 4.3.

[123] FED. R. EVID. 405.

[124] 335 U.S. 469, 69 S. Ct. 213, 93 L. Ed. 168 (1948).

Q. Do you know other people who know him?

A. Yes.

Q. Have you had occasion to discuss his reputation for honesty and truth-fulness and for being a law-abiding citizen?

A. It is very good.

Q. You have talked to others?

A. Yes.

Q. And what is his reputation?

A. Very good.

Can the government reply with witnesses who swear to the defendant's bad reputation? While the state cannot initiate this line of evidence, once the defendant opens up the subject the state is permitted to respond with counter-ing witnesses.

Sometimes defendants seek to prove the bad character of government witnesses. This happens in rape cases in which the prosecuting witness (in several courts she is called the prosecutrix) alleges that she was raped, while the defendant admits to sexual intercourse with her but claims it was consensual. Under former law the defendant was allowed to call witnesses and put into evidence the prosecutrix's prior acts of sexual intercourse with other men under the theory that this tended to show a greater likelihood of consent on the occasion of the alleged crime. The great majority of states, however, now disallow proof of individual prior occurrences and limit the attack on the prosecutrix. In many states, reform legislation has restricted wide-ranging defense cross-examination.

The arrest on rape charges of basketball star Kobe Bryant raised many of these issues. Hearings were held to determine whether details of the woman's sex life could be introduced into evidence by the defense in Bryant's criminal trial in Colorado. The prosecution fought to limit defense questioning of the alleged victim. Colorado's rape shield law prevents defense attorneys from using unrelated details of a woman's sexual past to destroy her credibility. Although the stage was set for a major test of the rape shield law, a new development intervened. Before the issue was reached at trial, prosecutors dismissed the criminal charges against Bryant. He could have received a sentence of up to life in prison if convicted. The dismissal ended the criminal case and left only the complainant's civil case for monetary damages pending against the defendant.

While the law seeks to limit cross-examination of rape victims in sex offense litigation, evidentiary rules allow a defendant to initiate a reputation attack in another type of case. In fights, physical assaults occasionally result in the death of one of the participants. The government frequently offers evidence that the defendant who is charged with homicide was the aggressor. The defendant may argue self-defense. Courts take the view that a defendant may produce evidence that attacks the reputation of the deceased for peacefulness. As a turbulent and violent person, the theory goes, it is more likely that the deceased provoked the attack. Thus, the reputation of the deceased in an assault/homicide case is subject to attack when self-defense is the question. It is widely held that the government may rebut such homicide case proof by countering with character witnesses who testify to the deceased's good reputation for peacefulness.

## § 6.20   Cross-Examination: Purpose

When a person is examined by the attorney who called the person as a witness, this "friendly" examination is the **direct examination**, or the examination-in-chief. The prosecutor's examination of a police witness in a felony case is such an examination. It is followed by a **cross-examination** by opposing counsel, after which the attorney who conducted the direct examination has the chance to rehabilitate the witness, or **re-direct** examination.[125]

Leading questions, those that suggest the answer and may be answered "yes" or "no," will frequently be employed by defense counsel when the officer is cross-examined. This mode of interrogation is not generally permitted for the prosecutor when the officer is examined in chief, where the officer must (with rare exceptions) relate his or her answers in narrative form.

## § 6.21   Scope of Examination

In addition to constitutional considerations when the defendant takes the stand, many states, as well as the federal courts, limit cross-examination of all witnesses by statute or court rule to matters talked about by the witness during the direct examination.[126] A competing approach applied in some states follows the English or Massachusetts rule, allowing cross-examination on anything relevant to the case, regardless of the areas to which the direct examiner limited his or her examination. The trend has been to allow wider cross-examination of police officers when they appear in court as government witnesses, and to permit defense counsel to probe relevant areas beyond the scope of direct examination.

Unsettling to many officers, especially the first time it occurs in a court case, is the interjection by the trial judge of questions to the officer-witness. A police officer may go through several trials before this occurs, probably

---

[125]   A witness on redirect examination may give his or her reasons for his or her actions in order to refute unfavorable inferences from matters brought out on cross-examination.

[126]   *See* Rule 611(b), Rules of Evidence for the United States District Courts and Magistrates (1988). See also § 6.17 of this chapter respecting constitutional considerations when the defendant is a witness. These are reviewed in Carlson, *Scope of Cross-Examination and the Proposed Federal Rules*, 32 FED. B.J. 244 (1973).

because some judges do not readily interrupt with questions in jury cases. Others do. The judge has inherent power to examine witnesses called to the stand by either party, to bring out needed facts. The judge must be careful not to intimate a belief that a witness is lying or suggest partisanship for either side when this happens.

## § 6.22   Impeachment

Frequently the believability or credibility of a witness is attacked, and this process is described as **impeachment of the witness**. One mode of impeachment of the defendant has already been discussed, that of character proof that reflects adversely on his or her reputation for truth and veracity. There are additional methods for impeaching the defendant, and other witnesses may be impeached as well. A common method is impeachment by prior inconsistent statement. Sometimes a witness at trial makes a point that is inconsistent with an oral or written statement he or she made at another time, for example, in a report that the witness prepared after investigating the case. If counsel for the adverse party has access to the report, the witness may be confronted with it and asked to explain the inconsistency.[127]

In federal cases the impeachment of government witnesses is facilitated by the Jencks Act.[128] This act required the witness to produce any pretrial report made by the witness that relates to the subject matter of his or her testimony, if requested by the defendant. The report must be produced and given to the defendant for inspection between the direct and cross-examination of the government agent.

An effective form of impeachment is to show that an otherwise independent-appearing witness is biased, that he or she favors one side for a personal reason, or has his or her own axe to grind in the trial. Bias examination was the subject of the Supreme Court decision in *Olden v. Kentucky*.[129] The court found it impossible to conclude that the restrictions on the defendant's right to cross-examine as to bias were harmless. The defendant's conviction was reversed. The defendant consistently asserted that Starla Matthews had consented to have sex with him. The defendant explained that Matthews feared this act would jeopardize her relationship with another man, so she claimed rape. The defendant was not allowed by the trial court to pursue the alleged victim's motivation on cross-examination. Apparently the trial judge barred this sort of cross-examination because witness Matthews and the man she was involved in a relationship with were of different races, a point adverted to by the Supreme Court in this passage:

---

[127]   *See* FED. R. EVID. 613.
[128]   18 U.S.C. § 3500.
[129]   109 S. Ct. 480 (1988).

"[T]he [Kentucky] court held that petitioner's right to effective cross-exami-nation was outweighed by the danger that revealing Matthews' interracial relationship would prejudice the jury against her. While a trial court may, of course, impose reasonable limits on defense counsel's inquiry into the poten-tial bias of a prosecution witness . . . the limitation there was beyond reason. Speculation as to the effect of jurors' racial biases cannot justify exclusion of cross-examination with such strong potential to demonstrate the falsity of Matthews' testimony."

Another method of impeachment occurs when an attorney asks a witness on cross-examination if he or she has ever been convicted of a felony. Defen-dants who testify in criminal cases are frequently impeached in this manner. The number of times the witness has been convicted may be explored, and if the witness denies a conviction when one exists, interrogating counsel can offer into evidence a certified copy of the conviction. Especially when the prior conviction is for perjury or false swearing, this can be an effective method of impeachment. It is restricted in the vast majority of jurisdictions to confrontation of the witness with prior felonies, not misdemeanors, and the felony must be reduced to conviction; mere arrests are insufficient.[130]

Sometimes government witnesses or those called by the defense have felony convictions in their background. May the evidence of these prior con-victions be brought out on cross-examination to impeach the witness? The answer is yes, if the cross-examination is not deemed unfairly prejudicial to the witness or the side that called him or her. Rule 609 of the Federal Rules of Evidence was amended in 1990 in a manner that clarified the right of all who give testimony, witnesses as well as defendants, to claim that bringing up an old, prior conviction in open court is prejudicial to them. When this objection is made, the judge will weigh the prejudicial impact against the probative value of the conviction and decide whether to allow the jury to hear about it.

A final form of impeachment applies specifically to impeachment of the criminal defendant, as opposed to witnesses generally. As noted above, prior arrests standing alone are insufficient and may not be brought out to impeach the witness's credibility. *Walder v. United States*[131] provides the exception to this rule. In this case the government was prosecuting Walder for illicit trans-actions in narcotics. When he took the stand, the following testimony occurred during the direct examination of defendant Walder, which was conducted by his own counsel:

Q. Now, first Mr. Walder, before we go further in your testimony, I want to you [sic] tell the Court and jury whether, not referring to these inform-ers in this case, but whether you have ever sold any narcotics to anyone.

A. I have never sold any narcotics to anyone in my life.

---

[130] FED. R. EVID. 609 (impeachment by felonies or crimes involving dishonesty or false statement).
[131] 347 U.S. 62 (1954).

Q. Have you ever had any narcotics in your possession, other than what may have been given to you by a physician for an ailment?

A. No.

Q. Now, I will ask you one more thing. Have you ever handed or given any narcotics to anyone as a gift or in any other manner without the receipt of any money or any other compensation?

A. I have not.

Q. Have you ever even acted as, say, have you acted as a conduit for the purpose of handling what you knew to be a narcotic from one person to another?

A. No, Sir.

Because the defendant had made affirmative remonstrances that he never possessed narcotics, he opened the door to impeachment of his testimony by the government showing that two years earlier the defendant had been indicted for illegal possession of heroin seized from his home. The fact that this former heroin seizure was the product of an illegal search (which eventually resulted in the dismissal of the case) did not prevent the government from putting on the stand one of the officers who participated in the search to show the defendant's prior possession of narcotics.

In similar fashion, a confession that was obtained in violation of *Miranda* rules may not be introduced in the government's case-in-chief, but may be used to impeach if the defendant takes the stand and presents evidence that contradicts it.[132] To illustrate the point, a defendant charged with auto theft who confesses his crime can have his confession read to the jury. The detective who secured the confession from him might do this during the prosecutor's case-in-chief. On the other hand, if the confession was taken without giving the accused any *Miranda* warnings, the confession cannot be employed in the manner described above. It is relegated to a limited role. Confessions obtained in violation of *Miranda* are only usable to attack a defendant if he takes the stand and tells his story differently from the way he told it in the confession. In the case of the auto theft defendant, if he tells the jury that he never stole a car, his confession regarding taking the vehicle will be used by the prosecutor to attack him on cross-examination. But if the defendant refuses to testify, a confession that is defective under the *Miranda* doctrine cannot be used by the prosecutor.

To summarize, when evidence has been illegally seized, either a confession that was obtained in violation of *Miranda* or physical evidence seized in violation of the Fourth Amendment, certain rules apply.

---

[132] Harris v. New York, 401 U.S. 222, 91 S. Ct. 643, 28 L. Ed. 2d 1 (1971).

- Illegally seized evidence may be used for impeachment of a criminal defendant who testifies in his or her own case if the evidence contradicts a particular statement made by a defendant in the course of his or her direct examination.[133]

- A defendant's statements made in response to proper cross-examination reasonably suggested by the defendant's direct examination are subject to impeachment by the government, even by evidence that has been illegally obtained, and this is so, even though the illegally seized evidence is inadmissible on the government's direct case as substantive evidence of guilt.[134]

- The foregoing exceptions to the exclusionary rule—the rule that otherwise would bar mention of the illegal evidence—are limited to the defendant's testimony, and the exceptions will not broadly extend to other defense witnesses.

The last point, protection of defense witnesses from this sort of impeachment, was clarified in a 1990 Supreme Court opinion: "The impeachment exception to the exclusionary rule permits the prosecution in a criminal proceeding to introduce illegally obtained evidence to impeach the defendant's own testimony. The Illinois Supreme Court extended this exception to permit the prosecution to impeach the testimony of all defense witnesses with illegally obtained evidence. Finding this extension inconsistent with the balance of values underlying our previous applications of the exclusionary rule, we reverse."[135]

## § 6.23  Evidence of Other Crimes

It has been pointed out that evidence of crimes committed by a witness that have not been reduced to a felony conviction cannot be shown to the jury for the purpose of impeaching the witness's testimony. However, evidence of crimes not reduced to conviction, and in some instances not even prosecuted, may come before the jury in a different way. Preparation for the principal crime charged may include the commission of other crimes. For instance, it is proper to show that the defendant stole a truck (even though he was not charged or convicted of this larceny) to carry away the loot from a robbery, when the defendant is on trial on the robbery charge. Where other crimes form a part of the same transaction as the offense charged, they may be shown. For instance, when a defendant shoots a police officer or a pedestrian in making a robbery getaway, proof of this fact may be shown at his or her robbery trial.

The Federal Rules of Evidence endorse this approach in Rule 404(b):

[133] Walder v. United States, 347 U.S. 62 (1954); Harris v. New York, 401 U.S. 222 (1971); Oregon v. Hass, 420 U.S. 714 (1975).
[134] United States v. Havens, 446 U.S. 620 (1980).
[135] James v. Illinois, 110 S. Ct. 648 (1990).

**Other crimes, wrongs, or acts**. Evidence of other crimes, wrongs, or acts is not admissible to prove the character of a person in order to show action in conformity therewith. It may, however, be admissible for other purposes, such as proof of motive, opportunity, intent,[136] preparation, plan, knowledge, identity, or absence of mistake or accident, provided that upon request by the accused, the prosecution in a criminal case shall provide reasonable notice in advance of trial, or during trial if the court excuses pretrial notice on good cause shown, of the general nature of any such evidence it intends to introduce at trial.

In *Dowling v. United States*,[137] the Supreme Court held that proof was admissible notwithstanding the fact that the defendant had been found not guilty. Evidence "relating to an alleged crime that the defendant had previously been acquitted of committing" was admissible in a later proceeding under Rule 404(b) of the Federal Rules of Evidence. After the evidence was admitted, the district judge instructed the jury of the acquittal and advised them the evidence could only be considered for a "limited purpose." The Court rejected the defendant's contention that it was "fundamentally unfair" to admit this evidence. The defense had urged that the introduction of such "other crimes" testimony "contravenes a tradition that the government may not force a person acquitted in one trial to defend against the same accusation in [another trial]." Justices Brennan, Marshall, and Stevens believed the evidence should be excluded, and dissented.

Sometimes an issue arises as to whether the prosecutor offered evidence in a case based on a good faith belief in its truthfulness. There is a requirement that when district attorneys are cross-examining defense witnesses, they must do so with questions that are asked in good faith and based on reliable information that can be supported by admissible evidence. A similar requirement underlies the right of the prosecutor to demonstrate other crimes of the defendant as affirmative proof of the defendant's criminal intent, preparation for the main crime, or to show that the defendant acted knowingly and criminally and not as the result of a mistake or accident. Crimes that the prosecutor says demonstrate these things must be offered up by the prosecution in good faith. The prosecutor must have an honest and reasonable belief that the accused committed them.

It is important to distinguish between offering crimes into evidence that prove something substantive about the case, so-called affirmative proof, and impeachment.

In impeachment, whether the prosecutor can present proof of a prior felony conviction of the defendant depends upon the accused taking the stand. If he does not do so, prior felony convictions cannot be shown for impeachment, inasmuch as their purpose is to attack the believability of the testimony of a witness who presents evidence in the case. In a special type of prosecu-

---

[136] On the use of other crimes to prove intent, *see* Whaley v. United States, 324 F.2d 356 (9th Cir.), cert. denied, 376 U.S. 911 (1963). The *Whaley* case involved impersonation of an FBI agent.

[137] 110 S. Ct. 668 (1990).

tion, however, prior felony convictions may be brought into evidence regardless of whether the defendant testifies. This is when the defendant is additionally charged with being a habitual criminal, along with the offense for which he or she was arrested. Many states have statutes that authorize increased punishment of the defendant when he or she is convicted a stipulated number of times for specified offenses.

Under **habitual offender laws**, if a defendant is on trial for robbery and he or she has been previously convicted of robbery on two prior occasions, the trial jury is usually informed through the allegations of the indictment and the introduction of proof of the defendant's previous crimes. Typically, under the various state statutes the jurors may convict the defendant of the principal crime and of being a habitual criminal as well. Habitual offender statutes have been upheld as constitutional by the United States Supreme Court.[138]

Finally, evidence of crimes committed by a defendant may be proved by the government when the defendant has been charged under the RICO statute. There is a federal statute that punishes a variety of criminal activities, including conspiracies to defraud citizens or the government. This is the Racketeer Influenced and Corrupt Organization Act (RICO). After the government proves a defendant committed certain preliminary acts, the defendant becomes eligible for enhanced sentencing under the RICO law. This sort of prosecution necessarily requires the government to provide evidence of the defendant's assorted crimes, and the trial of a RICO case is usually marked by prosecution proof of a number of the defendant's criminal acts.

The essence of a RICO prosecution is a pattern of racketeering activity. To establish the existence of such a pattern, the government adduces proof of a series of acts directed toward a criminal purpose. These are called **predicate acts**, and proof of them is essential to convict a defendant of an extortion conspiracy, a conspiracy to bribe public officials, or other targets of a RICO prosecution.

## § 6.24　Securing Witnesses at Trial

Subpoenas are available to both sides in a criminal case to secure witnesses for trial, as well as documents that are not privileged or confidential, the latter under a **subpoena duces tecum**. The rules for federal courts illustrate the point:

Federal Criminal Procedure Rule 17. Subpoena

    **(a)　Content.** A subpoena must state the court's name and the title of the proceeding, include the seal of the court, and command the witness to attend and testify at the time and place the subpoena specifies. The clerk must issue a blank subpoena—signed and sealed—to the party requesting it, and that party must fill in the blanks before the subpoena is served.

---

[138]　Spencer v. Texas, 385 U.S. 554, 87 S. Ct. 648, 17 L. Ed. 2d 606 (1967).

**(b)  Defendant Unable to Pay.** Upon a defendant's ex parte application, the court must order that a subpoena be issued for a named witness if the defendant shows an inability to pay the witness's fees and the necessity of the witness's presence for an adequate defense. If the court orders a subpoena to be issued, the process costs and witness fees will be paid in the same manner as those paid for witnesses the government subpoenas.

**(c)  Producing Documents and Objects.**

**(1)  In General.** A subpoena may order the witness to produce any books, papers, documents, data, or other objects the subpoena designates. The court may direct the witness to produce the designated items in court before trial or before they are to be offered in evidence. When the items arrive, the court may permit the parties and their attorneys to inspect all or part of them.

**(2)  Quashing or Modifying the Subpoena.** On motion made promptly, the court may quash or modify the subpoena if compliance would be unreasonable or oppressive.

. . .

**(g)  Contempt.** The court (other than a magistrate judge) may hold in contempt a witness who, without adequate excuse, disobeys a subpoena issued by a federal court in that district. A magistrate judge may hold in contempt a witness who, without adequate excuse, disobeys a subpoena issued by that magistrate judge as provided in 28 U.S.C. § 636(e).

# § 6.25  Burden of Proof and Rule of Reasonable Doubt

United States Supreme Court rulings have held that the United States Constitution compelled the **"proof beyond a reasonable doubt"** standard in state and federal criminal trials.[139] The Court set forth the role of this standard in American criminal procedure:

> The requirement of proof beyond a reasonable doubt has this vital role in our criminal procedure for cogent reasons. The accused during a criminal prosecution has at stake interests of immense importance, both because of the possibility that he may lose his liberty upon conviction and because of the certainty that he would be stigmatized by the conviction. Accordingly, a society that values the good name and freedom of every individual should not condemn a man for commission of a crime when there is reasonable doubt about his guilt.

. . .

---

[139]  In re Winship, 397 U.S. 358, 90 S. Ct. 1068, 25 L. Ed. 2d 368 (1970). *Winship* principles were applied to invalidate Maine procedures that put the burden on a homicide case defendant to prove heat of passion in Mullaney v. Wilbur, 421 U.S. 684, 95 S. Ct. 1881, 44 L. Ed. 2d 508 (1975). *See also* Sandstrom v. Montana, 442 U.S. 510 (1979).

Moreover, use of the reasonable-doubt standard is indispensable to command the respect and confidence of the community in applications of the criminal law. It is critical that the moral force of the criminal law not be diluted by a standard of proof which leaves people in doubt whether innocent men are being condemned. It is also important in our free society that every individual going about his ordinary affairs have confidence that his government cannot adjudge him guilty of a criminal offense without convincing a proper fact finder of his guilt with utmost certainty.

Lest there remain any doubt about the constitutional stature of the reasonable-doubt standard, we explicitly hold that the Due Process Clause protects the accused against conviction except upon proof beyond a reasonable doubt of every fact necessary to constitute the crime with which he is charged.

A burden of proof is cast upon prosecutors to convince the trier of fact by this high measure of evidence that the accused is guilty. Occasionally the question of burden of proof arises in connection with special defenses, such as insanity. As indicated by the Supreme Court, the state must shoulder the burden of producing evidence at the trial sufficient to convict the defendant beyond a reasonable doubt. This must be done in connection with every element of the offense charged. Where the defendant introduces the defense of insanity, however, numerous states require the defendant to prove that he or she was legally insane at the time of the crime, because this is not deemed an element of the offense but is an "affirmative defense."[140] However, when the defendant relies on alibi, this has been distinguished from insanity. The state may require the accused to disclose the names of his or her alibi witnesses.[141] However, it may not cast the burden of proof on the defendant. It has been held unconstitutional to require the defendant to prove that he or she was not present at the scene of a crime.[142]

Sometimes a defendant claims he or she is mentally incompetent to stand trial, that he or she cannot understand the proceedings, nor assist his or her attorney. The claim of mental deficiency in this regard is to be distinguished from insanity at the time of the crime, discussed in the foregoing paragraph. When a defendant claims that he or she is too mentally deficient to stand trial or enter a plea, many states require the defendant to prove his or her mental disability. Often, this must be established by a **preponderance of the evidence**.[143]

In carrying the burden of proving the defendant guilty in a criminal case, occasionally statutory law imposes a special corroboration requirement on the

---

[140] For cases requiring the defendant to prove the defense of insanity, *see* Leland v. Oregon, 343 U.S. 790, 72 S. Ct. 1002, 96 L. Ed. 1302 (1952); Patterson v. New York, 432 U.S. 197 (1977).

[141] Holding constitutional statutes in this effect, see Williams v. Florida, 399 U.S. 78, 90 S. Ct. 1893, 26 L. Ed. 2d 446 (1970), discussed in § 6.3.

    A number of states have adopted statutory provisions requiring the defendant to enter a special plea where he or she intends to raise the defense of insanity.

[142] Johnson v. Bennett, 414 F.2d 50 (8th Cir. 1969); Stump v. Bennett, 398 F.2d 111 (8th Cir. 1968). The *Johnson* case discusses the nature of the alibi defense.

[143] Cooper v. Oklahoma, 116 S. Ct. 1373 (1996).

government. For example, a common though not universal requirement dictates that an accused person cannot be convicted solely on the testimony of an accomplice. To sufficiently corroborate the testimony of an accomplice, there should be some fact testified to, entirely independent of the accomplice's evidence, that, taken by itself, leads to the inference not only that a crime has been committed, but also that the defendant is implicated in it.

There are other examples of special corroboration requirements that are sometimes imposed on the state. Such a requirement is applied in many jurisdictions when a confession is offered; many states require it to be corroborated. Other examples appear, including requirements for corroboration of children and mentally deranged witnesses, and corroboration of hound-tracking evidence where the accused is located by bloodhounds or police dogs and a conviction is sought upon this evidence.[144]

## § 6.26    Motion for Judgment of Acquittal

Sometimes a case is terminated without submission to the jury. The trial judge, either upon his or her own motion or the motion of the defendant, may take the case from the jury when the government's proof is insufficient to sustain a conviction, and enter a verdict for the accused. The issue generally arises upon motion for judgment of acquittal by the defendant.[145] Such a motion is most commonly made after the government puts on its case, and again at the conclusion of all the evidence. Under the prevailing view, a criminal defendant is entitled to acquittal at the hands of the judge's directed verdict when reasonable persons could not conclude that guilt had been proved beyond a reasonable doubt.

## § 6.27    Rebuttal Proof by the Government

After the defense completes its case, the prosecution is entitled to present rebuttal proof designed to controvert evidence presented by the defense or to rebut special defenses advanced by the accused. Police officers frequently appear as witnesses in this phase of the case to correct an error or to contradict the defendant's preceding proof. Rebuttal testimony is not routinely presented, however, and many skillful prosecutors bypass the opportunity to present evidence at this point on the theory that it unduly emphasizes and lends weight to the defense proof, except in extraordinary circumstances.

---

[144]   Buck v. State, 138 P.2d 115 (Okla. Cr. App. 1943), discussed in LADD & CARLSON, note 173 *supra* at 639-48.

[145]   This motion is also called a motion for directed verdict.

## § 6.28  Closing Argument

The prosecutor must be careful in **closing argument** to avoid reference to the fact that the defendant refrained from testifying in cases in which the accused did not take the stand.[146] The prosecutor must also avoid referring to matters not appearing in the record, for proper argument requires that counsel for both sides restrict their comments to the evidence that came up at trial as well as reasonable inferences therefrom.[147] Similarly, an expression of personal belief in the guilt of the accused is improper.

Sometimes prosecutors argue that the jury should convict the defendant in a particular case in order to send a message to the other criminals. "Send a message to David Defendant and all like him that we will not tolerate these sorts of assaults in Calaveras County." While some courts approve the "send a message to the community" sort of argument, others find its invocation to be error. Objection to this sort of argument, particularly in the latter courts, is highly appropriate. See *State v. Holmes.*[148] A related issue involves the prosecutor who argues that there is a "war on crime" going on, or that we are involved in a "war on drugs." The *Holmes* case involved a trial that was marked by references of the latter kind in the closing argument, and the reviewing court reversed.

There is considerable lore on what makes for an effective argument to the jury, and at this point in the trial the attorneys for both sides will attempt to persuade the jury of the accuracy of their position. The Supreme Court has underlined the importance of the final argument, holding that the parties have a constitutional right to present a closing argument even in a nonjury felony trial.[149]

Murder cases and the death penalty sometimes raise special issues relating to the law of closing argument. In several states, the jury in a capital case is required to consider the future dangerousness of the accused. If the defendant poses a likely danger to society, he or she may be an apt candidate for the death penalty, under the statutory scheme. Aggravating factors also play a role, as outlined in § 7.5. Even where state law does not specifically mandate consideration of the defendant's future dangerousness, the issue may nonetheless creep into a case. *Simmons v. South Carolina*[150] illustrates. As the Supreme Court observed in that case, prosecutors in South Carolina "like those in other

---

[146]  Where the prosecutor oversteps legal bounds and mentions this silence, automatic new trial is not necessarily decreed. The issue becomes one of whether the error was prejudicial to the defendant or whether the evidence in the case was so overwhelming that the prosecutor's miscue was "harmless beyond a reasonable doubt." United States v. Hasting, 103 S. Ct. 1974 (1983).

[147]  Ronald L. Carlson, *Argument to the Jury and the Constitutional Right of Confrontation*, 9 CRIM. L. BULL. 293 (1973).

[148]  604 A.2d 987 (N.J. Super. Ct. App. Div. 1992). Reviewing the rules controlling closing argument and errors predicated thereon, see Carlson, *Argument to the Jury: Passion, Persuasion, and Legal Controls*, 33 ST. L.U.L.J. 787 (1989). Notwithstanding the occasional license to plead for community safety, it is highly improper for a prosecutor to turn his argument to the jury into a referendum on the community's crime problem.

[149]  Herring v. New York, 422 U.S. 853, 95 S. Ct. 2550, 45 L. Ed. 2d 593 (1975).

[150]  Simmons v. South Carolina, 114 S. Ct. 2187 (1994).

states that impose the death penalty, frequently emphasize a defendant's future dangerousness in their evidence and argument at the sentencing phase; they urge the jury to sentence the defendant to death so that he will not be a danger to the public if released from prison." Capital cases are often tried in two-stage trials. The first trial, or phase, decides whether the defendant committed the crime. If the answer is "yes" a second phase proceeds, often in front of the same jury. This sentencing phase considers the circumstances of the crime, the defendant's character, prior criminal record, age, background, and future dangerousness as the jury fixes appropriate punishment. Often the choice is between life imprisonment or death.

Unlike capital punishment cases, in most criminal prosecutions the judge fixes the punishment after the jury decides that a defendant is guilty. This will be the approach in the general run of felony cases. In these cases potential length of punishment is not a legitimate object of argument by the attorneys. Were the rule otherwise, prosecutors would argue how little time the defendant might be sentenced to, in order to convince the jury to convict the accused of the highest crime charged. Conversely, defense attorneys would raise the specter of long incarceration, even though the judge may ultimately give probation to a convicted offender. Because sentencing in most states is a judicial function, possible length thereof is normally "off limits" during jury argument.

Capital cases are different. Here, the jury decides the sentence. After conviction, the jury can decide between death and life imprisonment. For this reason, the jury can be told that a life sentence means life without parole, where this statement is accurate. In first degree murder cases about one-half of the states provide for imprisonment without parole as an alternative to capital punishment. A variation on this pattern allows juries, when they decide to sentence the accused to life, to specify whether the defendant should or should not be eligible for parole.[151]

As noted, in most states the judge does the sentencing in noncapital offenses, and in those cases the jury is not informed of the range of available sentences. Jury argument and the court's instructions should be purged of such references in these courts. This rule includes the principle that juries are not usually instructed concerning the consequences of an insanity acquittal. The decision in *Shannon v. United States*[152] explains:

> It is well established that when a jury has no sentencing function, it should be admonished to "reach its verdict without regard to what sentence might be imposed." *Rogers v. United States*, 422 U.S. 35, 40, 95 S. Ct. 2095, 45 L. Ed. 2d 1 (1975). The principle that juries are not to consider the consequences of their verdicts is a reflection of the basic division of labor in our legal system between judge and jury. The jury's function is to find the facts and to decide whether, on those facts, the defendant is guilty of the crime charged. The judge, by contrast, imposes sentence on the defendant after the jury has

---

[151]   E.g., GA. CODE ANN. § 17-10-31.1(a).
[152]   114 S. Ct. 2419 (1994) (footnotes omitted in reprinting).

arrived at a guilty verdict. Information regarding the consequences of a verdict is therefore irrelevant to the jury's task. Moreover, providing jurors sentencing information invites them to ponder matters that are not within their province, distracts them from their fact-finding responsibilities, and creates a strong possibility of confusion.

The Supreme Court applied the foregoing rules to bar a jury instruction in federal cases informing jurors that extended civil commitment might flow from a finding of not guilty by reason of insanity. However, a number of states that have considered the question endorse use of such a jury instruction in state cases involving insanity claims by the defendant.

## § 6.29  Instructions and Verdict

After closing arguments, the judge instructs the jury on the applicable law prior to jury deliberations. In a variation followed in a few courts, instructions are first given by the judge, after which the lawyers argue the case. These **jury instructions** normally cover such matters as the burden of proof in the case, legal elements that must be established before the defendant can be convicted of the crime charged, explanation of lesser offenses of which the jury may convict the defendant, and procedures to be followed in the jury room, including selection of a foreperson. Verdict forms to cover the possible verdicts in the case are given to the jury. The jurors then retire to deliberate, a bailiff or other court officer delivering the exhibits received in evidence to the jury room, and in some states a written copy of the set of instructions given the jury is also delivered. Jury deliberations are private proceedings, with only jurors being present. A unanimous verdict, one in which every juror concurs, is the federal as well as the general rule in felony cases, although some states authorize less-than-unanimous verdicts. In *Apodaca v. Oregon* the Supreme Court allowed Oregon to continue its jury verdict practice, which permitted felony conviction by a 10-2 vote of a 12-member jury.[153] It also approved as constitutional a Louisiana law that permitted 9-3 verdicts in certain serious cases. When the jury is less than 12, unanimity appears to be required.[154]

In most criminal cases a general **verdict** of "guilty" or "not guilty" is returned. Some states also allow a verdict of "not guilty by reason of insanity." However, the court may authorize a special verdict. "A special verdict is one in which the jury reports to the court specific findings upon controlling issues of fact, usually submitted to the jury in the form of factual questions for consideration and determination of evidence. . . . Whether a jury shall be requested or directed to return a special verdict is discretionary with the trial court."[155]

[153]  406 U.S. 404, 92 S. Ct. 1628, 32 L. Ed. 2d 184 (1972). Considering majority verdicts in Louisiana, *see* Johnson v. Louisiana, 406 U.S. 356, 92 S. Ct. 1620, 32 L. Ed. 2d 152 (1972). The unanimity requirement was retained in both states for deciding capital cases.
[154]  Burch v. Louisiana, 441 U.S. 139 (1979). Five-member juries in criminal trials are disallowed. Ballew v. Georgia, 435 U.S. 223 (1978).

If the jury deliberates a very long time, the judge may bring them from the jury room and deliver a verdict-urging instruction intended to assist and expedite the jury's deliberations. This is called an "**Allen**," "**dynamite**" or "**hammer**" **instruction**, which tells those who are in the voting minority on the jury to reexamine their position.[156] It urges the jury to reach agreement, if possible. The court then sends the jury back for further deliberations. When agreement is not reached, a **hung jury** results, and the case must be retried. When a verdict is achieved, however, it is delivered in open court. When the jury's verdict finds the defendant guilty, he or she frequently asks for a poll of the jury, which requires the trial judge to ask each individual juror if he or she concurs in the verdict.[157]

Occasionally misconduct occurs in the jury room. For example, in a recent criminal case, one of the jurors, during jury deliberations, obtained an encyclopedia from which he read to other jurors. In this way, evidence bearing on the case was placed before the jury that was never examined by either side in a trial. When this occurs, the defendant may obtain a new trial based upon juror misconduct. Other examples in which courts have closely scrutinized jury practices include a case in which jurors passed among themselves a newspaper clipping that reported evidence in a criminal trial (the news report was in error),[158] jurors making an unauthorized visit to the crime scene and reenacting it,[159] and one case in which a juror placed a bet on the outcome of the case he was deciding.[160] Fortunately, these seem to be the exceptions and such jury activity is not the general practice in criminal trials.

## § 6.30 Motions Attacking the Verdict

Sometimes after a jury returns a verdict convicting the defendant, defense counsel files a motion asking the court to throw out the decision of the jury. A motion for relief from the jury's verdict is addressed to the trial judge, asking that the judge substitute his or her judgment for that of the jury or otherwise reverse the jury's decision based on some defect in the trial. Grounds for relief occur when the jury's verdict is at odds with the weight of the evidence presented during trial. It is helpful to know the grounds that support these defense motions and the occasions on which the court will grant the defendant relief under them.

---

[155] Cook v. State, 506 S.W.2d 955, 959 (Tenn. Crim. App. 1973).
[156] Huffman v. United States, 297 F.2d 754 (5th Cir. 1962); State v. Lawson, 501 S.W.2d 176 (Mo. App. 1973) (giving of a "hammer" instruction not error).
[157] *See*, e.g., Rule 31, F.R. CR. P.
[158] United States v. Kum Seng Seo, 300 F.2d 623 (3d Cir. 1962). FED. R. EVID. 606(b) (1975) allows inquiry on a motion for new trial into whether "extraneous prejudicial information was improperly brought to the jury's attention. . . ."
[159] People v. DeLucia, 282 N.Y.S.2d 526 (1967).
[160] These cases are collected in LADD & CARLSON, note 90 *supra* at 267.

Two prominent motions used following a jury verdict include a **motion for a new trial** and **motion for judgment notwithstanding the verdict** (judgment N.O.V.).

The latter asks the judge to give the defendant a judgment in his or her favor, i.e., to acquit the defendant, notwithstanding the jury's verdict convicting the defendant.[161] The motion for new trial requests less drastic relief from a jury verdict adverse to the defendant, asking only that the defendant be permitted to run the gauntlet of trial again, this time with a new jury.

While motions for a new trial are routinely filed by the defense, they are granted in only a small percentage of the cases. Under certain circumstances, however, the judge may set aside the verdict and give the defendant another chance to defend against the government's case before a new jury. Situations giving rise to this result include cases in which the original jurors read law books or other texts to each other while deliberating on the case, unknown to the judge; the prosecutor or a government witness talked to a juror about the case outside the courtroom; or the judge believes, upon reflection, that his instructions to the jury on an important point were confusing, misleading, or in error. New evidence that is discovered after the first trial may also give rise to a new trial, if it is highly important and a new trial would probably result in the defendant's acquittal.[162]

These grounds support a motion for a new trial. For a judge to set aside a jury verdict of conviction and enter an order acquitting the defendant (as opposed to simply giving him a new trial), substantially more must be shown by the defendant. Trial defects in the nature of those listed in the preceding paragraph are insufficient. Before obtaining a judgment N.O.V., most jurisdictions require the defendant to demonstrate (1) that the government's evidence was insufficient or lacking on a vital element of the offense charged, or (2) that the indictment or information did not state a criminal offense under the law of the jurisdiction involved.[163]

Motions for either judgment N.O.V. or new trial must generally be filed within a specified period, often within seven days after the jury is discharged. They are usually resisted by the prosecutor, who may file with the deciding judge a memorandum of cases and authorities showing why a new trial or acquittal should not be granted the defendant. The issue is frequently argued at a hearing that does not require the presence of witnesses, because the primary questions are legal ones that do not involve the taking of new evidence in the case.

---

[161] This motion is sometimes referred to as motion for judgment N.O.V. This shorthand description and accompanying letters N.O.V. emanate from the Latin *non obstante veredicto*, "notwithstanding the verdict."

[162] United States v. Bryant, 117 F.3d 1464 (D.C. Cir. 1997). The grounds for new trial motions contained in the text are by no means an exhaustive list, but are illustrative of specific grounds supporting a new trial. For a case discussing guidelines controlling new trials based on jury misconduct, see United States v. Kum Seng Seo, 300 F.2d 623 (3d Cir. 1962).

[163] In federal practice, motions addressed to these two situations are styled motions for judgment of acquittal and motions in arrest of judgment. FED. R. CRIM. P. 29 and 34.

## § 6.31　Motions Attacking the Sentence

The judge who pronounced sentence upon a convicted person allowed a specified period of time to reduce the sentence. Occasionally the judge may decide, upon reflection in the days following sentencing, that he or she was too harsh in the sentence he imposed. In these situations, the defendant who has filed a motion to reduce the sentence may have his or her term of imprisonment reduced. The federal rule on the point provides for correction of a sentence that is determined to have been imposed in violation of law.[164]

## § 6.32　Discovery of New Evidence

What if a defendant discovers a new witness or other evidence relevant to his case after the trial is over? Does he have an automatic right to be retried, and in the new trial to use his newly discovered evidence? The answer is no, and trial courts apply stringent standards to defense requests for a new trial based on newly discovered evidence.

One form of newly discovered evidence is fresh and heretofore unheard testimony from a witness who previously testified against a defendant at trial. Suppose, after a conviction, a witness has a change of heart. The witness originally said the defendant committed the crime; now he or she says that is not true. Will the conviction be thrown out when a prosecution witness repudiates his or her trial testimony? First, in order for the court to reach this result, the witness's evidence must be material. It must be of such nature that a different verdict will likely result if a new trial is granted. This is the standard set forth in numerous cases. However, there is more than one view on when a new trial will be granted. Some courts follow the *Berry* standard, named after a Georgia case, requiring a new trial only where after-discovered evidence would probably change the result. Others follow the *Larrison* standard, requiring a new trial where, without the false testimony, the jury might have reached a different conclusion. A new trial should be granted whenever the judgment against the accused is based chiefly upon evidence supplied by a single prosecuting witness, coupled with a recantation by such a witness. Most federal courts follow the *Berry* standard.[165]

Courts are hesitant to receive new evidence when they believe the recanting witness was coerced into changing his or her testimony. Sometimes pressure caused the witness to do so. In other cases, there may be nothing to contradict the sincerity of the recantation. Particularly compelling are cases in which the recantation is sometimes corroborated by other independent witnesses.

---

[164]　FED. R. CRIM. P. 35.
[165]　Sanders v. Sullivan, 863 F.2d 218 (2d Cir. 1988).

Courts are also hesitant to order new trials when the recantation by the prosecuting witness has been repudiated by him or her. In numerous decisions denying a new trial, the refusal to grant a new trial was grounded in the fact that the witness had subsequently repudiated her recantation.

In summary, courts are understandably cautious when faced with a change in the testimony of a trial witness. That principle does not automatically condemn meritorious post-trial motions, however. Where all factors are present to overturn the jury's verdict, courts have deemed it an abuse of discretion to deny a motion for a new trial.

In *Boyde v. California*,[166] the Supreme Court indicated that in order to receive a new trial based on newly discovered evidence, a defendant must demonstrate that the evidence would more likely than not lead to a different outcome.

Because the discovery of new evidence may take place several months after trial, some legal codes provide a special time dispensation in favor of defense motions based on this ground. See, for example, the Federal Rules of Criminal Procedure. Rule 33 provides that motions for new trial based on the ground of newly discovered evidence may be made within three years after final judgment. A motion for a new trial based on any other grounds shall be made within seven days after verdict or finding of guilty.

## § 6.33  Defendant's Presence in the Courtroom

Rule 43 of the Federal Rules of Criminal Procedure provides that the defendant shall be present at every major stage of the case. However, the case can continue in the defendant's absence if the defendant leaves voluntarily after the trial commences. The personal presence of a defendant is not required in misdemeanors; while the accused is usually present, a misdemeanor defendant sometimes appears by counsel if he or she chooses to absent himself or herself from the proceedings.

For several years there had been significant speculation in legal circles concerning a trial judge's authority to order an unruly defendant to be physically restrained in a courtroom, and to bind and gag him where necessary to maintain order. In an important development the United States Supreme Court spoke on the matter. The case involved persistent disruptions by the defendant at his trial for armed robbery. The Court held that the accused forfeited his right to be present during portions of the proceedings because of his unruly conduct. Mr. Justice Black, writing the majority opinion, indicated that a defendant could be bound and gagged, cited for civil contempt, or removed from the courtroom (the trial continuing without him) until he agreed to behave. The Court found the idea of binding and gagging a defendant a distasteful one, to be used only in extreme cases.[167] Mr. Justice Black concluded:

---

[166]  110 S. Ct. 1190 (1990), citing INS v. Abudu, 485 U.S. 94 (1988).
[167]  Illinois v. Allen, 397 U.S. 337, 90 S. Ct. 1057, 25 L. Ed. 2d 353 (1970).

[O]ur courts, palladiums of liberty as they are, cannot be treated disrespectfully with impunity. Nor can the accused be permitted by his disruptive conduct indefinitely to avoid being tried on the charges brought against him. It would degrade our country and our judicial system to permit our courts to be bullied, insulted, and humiliated and their orderly progress thwarted and obstructed by defendants brought before them charged with crimes. As guardians of the public welfare, our state and federal judicial systems strive to administer equal justice to the rich and the poor, the good and the bad, the native and foreign born of every race, nationality and religion. Being manned by humans, the courts are not perfect and are bound to make some errors. But, if our courts are to remain what the Founders intended, the citadels of justice, their proceedings cannot and must not be infected with the sort of scurrilous, abusive language and conduct paraded before the Illinois trial judge in this case. The record shows that the Illinois judge at all times conducted himself with that dignity, decorum, and patience that befits a judge.

The Federal Rules of Criminal Procedure specifically authorize the continued progress of a trial despite the exclusion of the defendant because of disruptions.[168] Courts have refused to allow defendants to testify in extreme cases of disruptive conduct. On the other hand, due consideration must be given to the question of whether a disruption is the product of disabling mental illness. In *Drope v. Missouri*[169] the Supreme Court held that a defendant did not voluntarily absent himself from the trial so that it could be continued without his presence when he shot himself in the abdomen. There were reports and other evidence that indicated potential mental incompetence of the accused. The Supreme Court found that the correct course would have been to suspend the trial until a psychiatric evaluation could be made.

## § 6.34   Constitutional Considerations

### 1. Publicity

The constitutional guarantee of open criminal trials guarantees that a defendant will not be tried, sentenced, and imprisoned in secret. Occasionally the publicizing of a case becomes a problem, however, and sometimes press coverage of a case imparts such notoriety to the litigation that it is difficult for a defendant to receive a fair trial.

To counteract a buildup of pretrial publicity that will affect a jury adversely against him or her, a defendant will sometimes move to close pretrial evidentiary hearings to the press and public. In some cases this will be effective. In other instances taking the spotlight off the pretrial proceedings may not be enough. In extreme cases the defendant will wish to take the case out of town, where local jurors have not been exposed to prejudicial news stories. Motions

---

[168]   FED. R. CRIM. P. 43.
[169]   420 U.S. 162, 95 S. Ct. 896, 43 L. Ed. 2d 103 (1975).

for **change of venue**, if successful, may require the criminal action to be tried in a different county from that where the crime occurred. On the other hand, some rules of procedure allow the action to be tried in the county of the crime, with the jury being selected in another county and transported to the site of the trial.

More than 45 states allow cameras in the courtroom, including televising of courtroom proceedings. Florida was the first state to allow televising of trials without a defendant's consent. Others require a defendant's consent before televising can proceed. Cameras and microphones continue to be banned from federal criminal courts.[170] Rule 53 of the Federal Rules of Criminal Procedure prohibits the taking of photographs in the courtroom during the progress of federal judicial proceedings. Broadcasting of judicial proceedings from the courtroom is also prohibited.

The Supreme Court has laid down limitations on television in state courtrooms,[171] as well as other deterrents to prejudicial publicity surrounding the trial of a criminal case.[172] Reduction of pretrial publicity helps to prevent a circus atmosphere from developing. It requires the cooperation of law enforcement officers, and judicial orders to prosecutors and police to refrain from releasing certain items for publication in advance of trial may be enforced through citation of violators for contempt of court. Prosecutors are enjoined from making statements to the press or others about a defendant or his case that will create a serious and imminent threat to the impartiality of a jury.

Sometimes the publicity is so pervasive that, to protect jurors from it, they are sequestered and remain together in a hotel during a trial. Newspapers and television may be monitored by court personnel during the hotel stay. One expert observes:

> The jurors in high profile cases pay the greatest price. The chances of sequestration increase to protect jurors from contamination by the nightly analysis of legal pundits. More significantly, televising a high profile case increases the risk that the public will not defer to the jury's resolution of the case. The viewing public becomes the thirteenth juror but is privy to information that the jury has not considered and is not bound by the legal instructions that the jury tries to follow in good faith.[173]

In the area of publicity, the publishing of the names of rape victims, juveniles accused of crimes, and coverage of cases involving abuse of minors are sensitive issues. On the last question, in the *Globe Newspaper* case, the Supreme Court held "that a State's interest in the physical and psychological

---

[170]   76 A.B.A.J. 15 (Aug. 1990).

[171]   Television allowed except where it would materially interfere with the rights of the parties to a fair trial.

[172]   Press Enterprise Co. v. Superior Ct. of California, 106 S. Ct. 2735 (1986); Waller v. Georgia, 467 U.S. 39 (1984).

   Sometimes defendants who complain of prejudicial pretrial publicity in a particular community move the court for a change of venue, seeking trial in a community presumably less affected by the publicity. See § 9.3.

[173]   Peter Aranella, *O.J. Lessons*, 69 S. CAL. L. REV. 2291 (1996).

well-being of a minor victim was sufficiently weighty to justify depriving the press and public of their constitutional right to attend criminal trials, where the trial court makes a case-specific finding that closure of the trial is necessary to protect the welfare of the minor."[174]

In addition to closing the trial, a step that may sometimes occur in exceptional cases, are there other measures that courts can take to protect young children from undue exposure? There is case authority that a trial court can prohibit a reporter from publishing the names of sexually abused minors as a condition for attending a hearing related to the abuse.[175]

Printing names of rape victims may be a different story, at least as far as legal guidelines are concerned. The Supreme Court has held that the media cannot be punished civilly for accurately reporting the name of a rape victim when it was lawfully obtained.[176] Media practice averts legal battles in most instances. While most newspapers maintain a policy of not printing the names of rape victims, there are exceptions. One occurs when the victim's name is printed at the victim's request in instances where the victim comes forward with the story of the attack. Another develops when there are leaks to the press from one side or the other. In the case of basketball star Kobe Bryant for the alleged rape of a young woman in Colorado, public interest was intense. Before long, tabloids published the picture of the woman who complained against Bryant.

Closing a defendant's criminal trial to protect juveniles who are scheduled to appear as witnesses has been mentioned. It is an exceptional, but not unheard of, step to protect the welfare of children. Sometimes the request to close a case comes from another source. Defendants request that trials be closed to the public, and thereby the press, in order to avoid embarrassment or publicity to the defendant. A simple request of this kind is not enough to close a hearing, however, even if unopposed by the prosecutor. The First Amendment bars such closings. A criminal trial will not be closed, absent a demonstration that closure is required to protect the defendant's right to a fair trial or some other overriding consideration. The right of the public and the press to attend criminal trials is implicit in the guarantees of the First Amendment. The right of access to criminal trials also extends to pretrial preliminary hearings.

## 2. Counsel

The Sixth Amendment to the United States Constitution provides: "In all criminal prosecutions, the accused shall enjoy the right to a speedy and public trial . . . and to have the Assistance of Counsel for his defense.

---

[174] The text quote is from *Maryland v. Craig*, 110 S. Ct. 3157, 3167 (1990) referring to the Globe Newspaper case, 102 S. Ct. 2613 1982).

[175] In re a Minor, 595 N.E.2d 1052 (Ill. 1992).

[176] *See* Florida Star v. B.J.F., 109 S. Ct. 2603 (1989).

On the question of counsel at trial, *Gideon v. Wainwright*[177] established the right of a poor person, on trial for a serious offense, to an appointed lawyer. "Governments, both state and federal, quite properly spend vast sums of money to establish machinery to try defendants accused of crime. . . . This noble idea [fairness to both sides in a criminal case] cannot be realized if the poor man charged with a crime has to face his accusers without a lawyer to assist him."[178] The right to counsel means that the defendant is not only entitled to a lawyer, but has a right to effective assistance of counsel. In the view of the courts, this includes adequate investigation of the case by the attorney.[179]

When does the right to counsel start? When the case first begins, or at a subsequent bail hearing? Or only once the trial begins? Rule 44 of the Federal Rules of Criminal Procedure provides that every defendant who is unable to obtain counsel shall be entitled to have counsel assigned to represent that defendant at every stage of the proceedings from initial appearance before the federal magistrate judge or the court through appeal, unless the defendant waives such appointment. Some state codes are not so expansive, with free representation commencing at preliminary hearing, but not before that time.

Along with the idea of restitution for the victim of the crime (see § 7.7) there has been some legal thrust in the direction of requiring reimbursement to the state for costs expended in providing appointed attorneys for defendants, especially in cases in which the financial status of the defendant has improved since the time of counsel's appointment. The Supreme Court of California has upheld such a statute.[180] The statute allowed a trial judge, on conclusion of a proceeding in which the defendant was furnished counsel, to order the defendant to make reimbursement.

What about the right of the defendant to represent himself or herself, if he or she insists on doing so? The United States Supreme Court ruled that this right belonged to the accused in a case from California.[181]

Most defendants, however, elect to go to court with the assistance of a lawyer. The right to counsel for citizens facing charges in an American felony court is clear. What about an enemy combatant captured abroad who is an

---

[177] 372 U.S. 335, 83 S. Ct. 792, 9 L. Ed. 2d 799 (1963). While this chapter of the text is primarily concerned with serious offense trials, it is clear that the right to counsel applies at other stages. See, e.g., § 2.16 (preliminary hearings), § 7.8 (sentencing), § 10.11 (misdemeanors).

[178] 372 U.S. at 344. In many states persons claiming indigency and asking for court-appointed attorneys must fill out a lengthy financial statement, and in some must sign a form authorizing the judge to look at the latest copy of the applicant's income tax return to make sure the accused cannot afford to hire counsel. Falsification of a financial statement can result in a prosecution for perjury. Many communities use an assigned counsel system in these cases; public defender offices have been established in a number of metropolitan areas; and in several jurisdictions a mixed system of public and assigned lawyers handle the duty of appointed counsel for indigents.

[179] Wiggins v. Smith, 539 U.S. 510 (2003). Competency of counsel, *see* Strickland v. Washington, 466 U.S. 668 (1984).

[180] People v. Amor, 523 P.2d 1173 (Cal. 1974). This case involved a court order to a legal secretary earning a salary of $650 per month to pay one-half of the $100 value of public defender services expended in defending her.

[181] Faretta v. California, 422 U.S. 806, 95 S. Ct. 2525, 45 L. Ed. 2d 562 (1975) (waiver of counsel must be voluntary and intelligent, however).

American citizen? Justice O'Connor announced the judgment of the Supreme Court on this question in a 2004 case. First, she framed the issue. "At this difficult time in our Nation's history, we are called upon to consider the legality of the government's detention of a United States citizen on United States soil as an 'enemy combatant' and to address the process that is constitutionally owed to one who seeks to challenge his classification as such." The Court held that a citizen detainee seeking to challenge his classification as an enemy combatant is entitled to notice of the factual basis for this classification by the Government, and a fair opportunity to dispute it. He is also entitled to counsel, including an appointed attorney, if he is without funds, to assist him in these proceedings and hearings.

The defendant was born in Louisiana in 1980. In 2001 the government alleges that he took up arms with the Taliban in Afghanistan. After his capture, he was held at Guantanamo Bay and at a naval brig in Charleston, South Carolina. From 2001 until 2004, the defense claimed, he was held "without access to legal counsel or notice of any charges pending against him." Justice O'Connor's 2004 opinion explained why he was entitled to due process rights. "Striking the proper constitutional balance here is of great importance to the Nation during this period of ongoing combat. But it is equally vital that our calculus not give short shrift to the values that this country holds dear or to the privilege that is American citizenship. It is during our most challenging and uncertain moments that our Nation's commitment to due process is most severely tested; and it is in those times that we must preserve our commitment at home to the principles for which we fight abroad."[182]

### 3. Speedy Trial

The Supreme Court has traced the origins of the right to speedy trial to the time of Magna Carta (1215). This historic right is preserved by the United States Constitution, and currently each of the 50 states guarantees freedom from extended pretrial detention through the right of speedy trial. The Sixth Amendment guarantees that, "[i]n all criminal prosecutions, the accused shall enjoy the right to a speedy and public trial. . . ." Supreme Court cases have qualified the literal sweep of the provision by specifically recognizing the relevance of four separate inquiries: whether delay before trial was uncommonly long, whether the government or the criminal defendant is more to blame for that delay, whether, in due course, the defendant asserted his or her right to a speedy trial, and whether he or she suffered prejudice as a result of the delay.[183]

Failure to demonstrate his or her diligence with respect to these factors will often defeat a defendant's appeal of a conviction based upon denial of a prompt trial. In *Reed v. Farley*[184] the defendant was unsuccessful in his speedy trial claim. He had registered no objection to the late trial date and made no showing of prejudice.

---

[182]    Hamdi v. Rumsfeld, 124 S. Ct. 2633 (2004).

[183]    Doggett v. United States, 112 S. Ct. 2686 (1992).

[184]    114 S. Ct. 2291 (1994) (eight-year delay getting to trial was too much).

The accused's right to a speedy trial, applicable in state as well as federal courts as a matter of constitutional law,[185] has been implemented by statute in several states. For example, some states require a defendant to be tried no more than 120 days after his arrest. Others require the defendant to be tried within 60 days after he or she is indicted. A guiding philosophy that is designed to ensure prompt attention to criminal cases on the trial calendar is recommended in the American Bar Association Report, *Standards Relating to Speedy Trial*:[186]

Part 1. The Trial Calendar

1.1 Priorities in scheduling criminal cases.

To effectuate the right of the accused to a speedy trial and the interest of the public in prompt disposition of criminal cases, insofar as is practicable:

(a) the trial of criminal cases should be given preference over civil cases; and

(b) the trial of defendants in custody and defendants whose pretrial liberty is reasonably believed to present unusual risks should be given preference over other criminal cases.

When a defendant files a demand for speedy trial it is incumbent upon the system to afford him or her a trial with reasonable promptness. Courts have not always stringently enforced the speedy trial concept, and delays of 150 days and longer have sometimes marked the pretrial wait of accused persons in custody before trial is held.[187] This raises an important question for criminal justice administration and one of vital interest for inmates: Is the person who is found guilty and sentenced to prison entitled to have credited against his or her penitentiary sentence the time spent in the city or county jail awaiting trial? While there is authority to the contrary,[188] progressive statutes mandate that such credit be given. The Ohio provision presents an excellent sample:

---

[185] Along with the provision of a speedy trial to the accused, the prosecution must take care to insure the charge is brought within the statute of limitations. "The purpose of a statute of limitations is to limit exposure to criminal prosecution to a certain fixed period of time following the occurrence of those acts the legislature has decided to punish by criminal sanction." Toussie v. United States, 397 U.S. 112, 90 S. Ct. 858, 25 L. Ed. 2d 156 (1970) (other aspects of *Toussie*, portions of which were separate from the quoted passage, were overruled by statute, *see* 50 U.S.C. § 462(d)). States commonly require that felony indictments be filed within three or four years after the commission of the offense, depending on state law. However, there is no limitation on the time within which a murder charge may be brought.

[186] Reprinted with permission; copyright 1968 by the American Bar Association. Recommendations for speeding up the handling of criminal cases also appeared in Standard 4.1, Courts, National Advisory Commission on Criminal Justice Standards and Goals (1973) (time between arrest and felony trial should not exceed 60 days, 30 days or less in misdemeanors).

[187] *See*, e.g., Barker v. Wingo, 407 U.S. 514, 92 S. Ct. 2182, 33 L. Ed. 2d 101 (1972) (16 continuances, accused in jail 10 months before trial).

[188] McGinnis v. Royster, 410 U.S. 263, 93 S. Ct. 1055, 35 L. Ed. 2d 282 (1973) (state statute denying prisoner good conduct time credits for presentence incarceration in county jails held not to violate equal protection clause of Fourteenth Amendment, U.S. Constitution).

§ 2967.191 Credit for confinement awaiting trial and commitment

The adult parole authority shall reduce the minimum and maximum sentence or the definite sentence of a prisoner by the total number of days that the prisoner was confined for any reason arising out of the offense for which he was convicted and sentenced, including confinement in lieu of bail while awaiting trial, confinement for examination to determine his competence to stand trial or sanity, confinement in a community based correctional facility and program or district community based correctional facility and program, and confinement while awaiting transportation to the place where he is to serve his sentence.

What about federal courts? The Federal Speedy Trial Act requires dismissal of charges against a defendant if the accused is not brought to trial within 70 days after an indictment is filed against him or her. In *United States v. Taylor*,[189] the 70-day speedy trial clock ran out on the government, and the District Court dismissed charges with prejudice to reprosecution due to what the court described as the "lackadaisical" attitude on the part of the government. The Court of Appeals characterized the lower court's purpose as sending "a strong message to the government." Upon further review, however, the Supreme Court refused to uphold the dismissal because of the high court's view that the District Court (1) failed to consider lack of prejudice to the defendant from a brief delay in bringing him to trial, and (2) the Speedy Trial Act does not require **dismissal with prejudice** for every violation. Dismissal of the charges without prejudice may be the preferred remedy in many cases, as opposed to the greater deterrent of barring reprosecution. **Dismissal without prejudice** is not a toothless sanction, the Court observed. The Supreme Court pointed out that such a dismissal forces the government to obtain a new indictment if it decides to reprosecute. The speedy trial right exists primarily to protect an individual's liberty interest, to lessen the lengthy incarceration prior to trial, to reduce the lesser (but nevertheless substantial) impairment of liberty imposed on an accused while released on bail, and to shorten disruption of one's life caused by an arrest and presence of unresolved criminal charges.[190]

How much do delays attributable to overcrowded courts weigh in measuring a defendant's speedy trial claims? This issue is discussed in *United States v. Loud Hawk*, as is the question of whether interlocutory appeals by the prosecution count against the government.[191] Absent a showing of bad faith or dilatory purpose on the government's part, no reason existed for according the delays any weight toward the speedy trial claims. Where the prosecutor takes an interim appeal, perhaps on an evidence question deemed to have been erroneously decided by a trial judge, the delay incident to the appeal will be excused. The appeal cannot be a frivolous one to gain the advantage of this rule, however. Government appeals are well grounded where the government's

---

[189]   108 S. Ct. 2413 (1988).
[190]   467 U.S. 180 (1984).
[191]   474 U.S. 302 (1986).

appellate issue is important to the administration of justice; reversal of the trial judge by the Court of Appeals is **prima facie evidence** of the reasonableness of the government's action.

Is there a right to speedy arrest? The usual answer is no, as long as the case is brought within the statute of limitations, unless the defendant can prove unreasonable delay due to the state's intentional attempt to gain a tactical advantage.

Finally, can a prisoner held in jail in State A complain that separate charges against him in State B were not processed rapidly enough and should be dismissed? Is delay by State B excused because "the prisoner is in jail anyway, and we cannot try him until he gets out." Almost all of the states, as well as the federal government, have entered into the Interstate Agreement on Detainers, an interstate compact. The United States Supreme Court explains the procedure: "The Agreement provides for expeditious delivery of the prisoner to the receiving State for trial prior to the termination of his sentence in the sending State." Using the detainer, State B needs to proceed. After rendition of the prisoner by State A, the receiving state has 120 days within which to commence trial of the offender.[192]

## § 6.35   Ethics of Advocacy: Counsel as Witness

May a prosecuting attorney who obtains a confession from a defendant later testify as a witness against him or her and also serve as his or her prosecutor? Courts have expressed their disapproval of such practice. The same approach covers defense counsel. Provisions of legal ethics came into being which rendered it a breach of professional conduct for an attorney to appear as witness in a case in which he is counsel, save for a few exceptions.[193]

## § 6.36   Jury Nullification

What are the ethics of a defense lawyer urging jury nullification? While this does not occur frequently, it may come up in final argument, or at another point in the case. Nullification occurs when a jury finds a defendant not guilty despite the fact that he or she committed the acts charged.[194] The media has speculated about the possible role of jury nullification in the acquittal of O.J. Simpson, both on the part of the jury and in the arguments made by his "dream team" of attorneys. Supporters of jury nullification favor informing

---

[192]   Alabama v. Bozeman, 533 U.S. 146 (2001). Detainers are explained in this text in § 7.11.

[193]   Lawyer may be witness for his or her client as to merely formal matters; on important points, however, except when essential to the ends of justice, a lawyer should avoid testifying in court in behalf of his or her client.

[194]   R. Alex Morgan, *Jury Nullification Should be Made a Routine Part of the Criminal Justice System, but It Won't Be*, 29 Ariz. St. L. J. 1127 (1997).

juries of their right to nullify as a protest against tax laws or drug prosecutions, among others.[195]

Judges oppose jury nullification because it represents a rejection of the sworn duty of jurors to uphold the law. Allowing jurors to substitute their own notion of the law over that given by the court is the equivalent of allowing jurors to declare laws unconstitutional.[196] The United States Supreme Court settled the legal issue more than 100 years ago, in a decision that rejected the jury's right to decide whether or not to follow the law.[197] Although some modern commentators have agitated in the direction of allowing jurors the right to nullify, Supreme Court rejection of the practice remains steadfast.

The advocates of nullification have not always been deterred by court condemnation of the practice. South Dakota voters were asked to adopt a statute that would have allowed jurors to acquit a defendant if they found fault with the law under which he was charged. Proponents of the measure wanted defense attorneys to be able to argue to juries that the defendant should not be convicted under a law that was flawed or carried too harsh a punishment. South Dakota voters rejected the proposed statute by a 4-to-1 vote.

To enforce the doctrine that jurors must follow and apply the law, a California juror was dismissed by the court. During jury deliberations this juror announced that the penal law under which the defendant was charged was so unjust that he would never vote to convict. The judge dismissed the juror, and the defendant was later convicted of statutory rape. The California Supreme Court affirmed the jury verdict. The court ruled that a juror must be able to render a verdict in accordance with the trial court's instructions on the law.

These rules translate into preventing a defense attorney from making a nullification plea in her closing argument. Counsel may not tell the jury that it possesses the power to ignore the law. Counsel should not encourage jurors to violate their oath.[198]

## § 6.37 The Witness in Court

It is the duty of any citizen, including a police officer, to serve as a witness in court when summoned to do so. When testifying, the witness should make every effort to speak clearly, avoid the use of slang, and explain technical terms in an understandable fashion. A witness should always be willing to correct an honest mistake in his or her testimony, and should not approach the experience with bias or prejudice.

---

[195] See discussion in Butler, *Racially Based Jury Nullification: Black Power in the Criminal Justice System*, 105 YALE L.J. 677 (1995).

[196] Andrew D. Leipold, *Rethinking Jury Nullification*, 82 VA. L. REV. 253, 292 (1996).

[197] Sparf v. United States, 156 U.S. 51 (1895).

[198] United States v. Desmarais, 938 F.2d 347, 350 (1st Cir. 1991); Todd E. Pettys, *Evidentiary Relevance, Morally Reasonable Verdicts, and Jury Nullification*, 86 IOWA L. REV. 467, 504, 518 (2001).

Several state and local bar associations promulgate instructions and helpful advice to people who are to be witnesses in trials. One such set of instructions distills numerous pointers advocated by successful trial lawyers, and these suggestions are reproduced here:[199]

### 1. Witness Duty

Lawsuits, as controversies between two or more parties are termed, must be determined on facts alone. In order to produce the facts for the consideration of a jury or judge, people who were present at the time the thing in controversy happened, or who know facts pertinent to the matter, are relied upon to furnish these facts. Such persons are known as witnesses. They are as essential to the outcome of a suit as the judge, the jury, or the lawyers.

For this reason, it is a public duty of any individual who has information about a court action to submit to being a witness cheerfully and willingly. This is really only a common courtesy a person owes another who is in need of information. It is a service you yourself may desperately desire if you become involved in an action in court.

Having performed such service, you should have a sense of satisfaction in having performed an important duty in the administration of justice.

### 2. Method of Securing Facts through Testimony

Truth is the keystone of justice. One of the fundamental rules in the administration of justice, essential in learning the truth, is that both sides of a lawsuit must have an equal opportunity to examine the witness.

This is termed "Examination" and "Cross-Examination." The lawyer for the side of the case who calls on you to testify will ask you questions designed to bring out the facts of which you have knowledge. This is known as the "Direct Examination." After this is completed, the lawyer for the opposing side will then be given opportunity to ask you questions concerning the same information. This is called "Cross-Examination." All of the questions by both lawyers will have only one purpose in mind, to bring out the truth about the facts you know.

### 3. How to Act when a Witness

A. Tell the truth! Nothing else contained in this pamphlet is as important as this one admonition. If you try to color, shade, or change your testimony to help one side or the other, you are headed for trouble. Never become so anxious to help one of the parties that you permit yourself to "take sides." No matter how skillful a lawyer is in cross-examination, he will never confuse or embarrass you if you stick to the truth.

---

[199] *So You're Going to be a Witness*, Iowa State Bar Association.

B. Never lose your temper! If you do, you are lost. If a witness becomes so prejudiced in favor of one side that he loses his temper, when facts that are not favorable to his friend are elicited, he places himself at the mercy of the cross-examiner and makes himself worthless to the side he tries to favor. Judges and juries are not interested in prejudiced testimony, they are interested only in facts. Keep your temper and your service as a witness will be pleasant.

C. Don't be afraid of the lawyers! If you give your information honestly, there is no question a lawyer can ask that will cause you any trouble. It is only when you "cross-examine yourself" that a lawyer can show up your testimony as false. The lawyers are only interested in obtaining the truth. They will be more courteous to you as the character of your testimony merits courtesy.

D. Speak clearly. There is nothing as unpleasant to a court, jury and lawyers as to have a witness who refuses to speak loudly enough to be heard. Such low tone of voice not only detracts from the value of your testimony, but it also tends to make the court and jury think that you are not certain of what you are saying. Everyone in the courtroom is entitled to know what you have to say. There are no secrets in court.

E. If you don't understand a question, ask that it be explained. Many times a witness will not understand a question that has been asked, but will, nevertheless go right ahead and try to answer it. This is confusing to the court, the jury and lawyers. It also extends the time a witness will be on the witness stand because the lawyers must go back and correct any misinformation given by a witness who does not understand the question.

If you do not understand, feel free to say so and ask that the question be explained to you. It will save time and confusion.

F. Answer all questions directly! Too often a witness will be so anxious to tell his story that he will want to get it all told in answer to the first question. Listen to the question. If you can answer it with a "yes" or "no," do so. Never volunteer information the question does not ask for. What you volunteer may be damaging to the side with which you are friendly.

G. Stick to the facts! The only thing that you will be permitted to testify to is what you personally know. Seldom is what someone else told you admissible in the case. What you KNOW is important, what you THINK is unimportant.

H. Don't be apprehensive! There is no reason to fear being called as a witness. To begin with, the lawyers will always be courteous and the judge is there to insure that you will be permitted to tell your story in accordance with the rules of evidence. If you are afraid when you give your testimony, your mind will not be clear and you will probably not be able to tell what you know as clearly as if you were completely composed.

I.   If you don't know, admit it! Some witnesses think they should have an answer to every question asked. No witness knows all the facts but your lawyer may not know every detail of which you have knowledge. It is for this reason that he may ask you questions about things you have no knowledge about. If this is true, tell him that you don't know. It is to your credit to be honest, rather than try to have an answer for everything that is asked you.

J.   Don't try to memorize your story! The administration of justice requires only that a witness tell his story to the best of his ability. No witness is expected to know every detail perfectly. For this reason it is urged that you never try to memorize your story. There is no more certain way to cross yourself than to memorize your story. Discuss your testimony with the lawyer who calls you, before you go into court, if you wish. Sometimes it is essential that you do so. If you do, and are asked about it on the witness stand, do not hesitate to admit it. There is nothing wrong about discussing your testimony with the lawyers.

K.   Don't answer too quickly. Most of the courts in which you will be called to testify as a witness will be what are known as "Courts of Record." This means merely that a record is made by a court reporter of everything that is said by everyone in the court room. In order to make this work easier, you should never answer a question until it is completely finished. Frequently, one of the lawyers will make an objection to a question. You should never try to answer before the objection is completed. Take your time and give the court reporter a chance to do his work and give the lawyers an opportunity to make their objections. Evidence must be legally admissible and the only way in which this can be assured is to permit the lawyers to object when they believe the testimony asked for is improper.

Wait until you are called, tell what you know, in the way you know it, and you will have no trouble.

# Sentencing, Crime and Corrections

# 7

## Chapter Outline

## Key Terms and Concepts

alternative sentencing
bifurcated trial or proceedings
capital punishment
compensation (reparation)
detainer
determinate sentence
deterrence
expungement (expunction) of
   record
incapacitation
indeterminate sentence
mitigation
pardon
parole

parole board
presentence investigation report
   (PSIR)
probation
probation officer
reformation
restitution
sentencing
Sentencing Reform Act of 1984
suspended sentence
verdict of "guilty but mentally ill"
verdict of "guilty but not
   responsible"

## § 7.1   Mechanics of Sentencing

Upon conviction by plea of guilty or as the result of a trial that ends in a guilty verdict, a duty rests upon the court to pronounce sentence. In a serious case, the sentencing judge will order that a presentence investigation be made of the defendant's background.[1] The time needed to complete this investigation and prepare a **presentence investigation report (PSIR)** accounts for some of the necessary delay between the jury's return of a verdict and the passing of sentence. The sentencing judge should be fully apprised of the defendant's prior criminal record, personal situation and characteristics, financial condition, family status, and any other relevant factors essential to the shaping of an intelligent sentence in the case. The job of conducting this investigation and preparing a presentence report generally falls upon the court's **probation officer**.[2]

---

[1]   Misdemeanor courts are sometimes invested with similar authority, but it is much less frequently exercised in petty offense cases.

[2]   Fed. R. Crim. P. 32. On the need to make disclosure of this report to the defendant, see § 7.9 of this chapter. The preparation of such report and submission to the court assumes the customary situation of sentencing by the trial judge. It is this sentencing procedure which will be the primary focus in this chapter. In a minority of states, however, it may be the jury which sets the punishment by its verdict. Jury sentencing is discussed further in § 7.6. With many states moving to mandatory and flat time sentences, judicial discretion to shape the sentence has been trimmed in a number of jurisdictions.

Sentencing the defendant occurs after the court has had an opportunity to review the presentence report. Before imposing sentence, the trial judge hears arguments by defense counsel advancing reasons why the defendant should not be dealt with harshly, and usually the convicted person is given an opportunity to address the judge personally and make a statement on his or her own behalf. In federal courts, the judge must give the defendant an opportunity to make a statement in mitigation of the sentence, and denial of this right is reversible error.[3]

Several alternatives are open to the sentencing judge. The judge has the option of a **suspended sentence**, in which he or she may impose a sentence, then suspend the execution of the term imposed pending good behavior of the defendant. Other options include levying a monetary fine[4] or sentencing the defendant to a term of years in a penal institution.[5] In this latter circumstance, state practice varies. In some, the judge states the minimum and maximum terms to be served by the defendant. In such states, for example, the judge might sentence the defendant to a term not less than 10 nor more than 20 years for burglary. In other jurisdictions felony punishment may be controlled by the **indeterminate sentence** law. In these states the judge may tell the convicted person: "I sentence you to a term of imprisonment in the state penitentiary not to exceed twenty years." A maximum is stated, but no minimum. While some prisoners serve out the entire sentence, inmates are subject to periodic review by the state parole board and most prisoners will be released on parole prior to expiration of the maximum sentence. How early the release occurs depends upon several factors, including the **parole board**'s assessment of the person's prison record and rehabilitation progress.

Finally, supervised freedom may be granted the defendant at sentencing in the form of probation (sometimes called a bench parole). This type of sentence is used when the judge feels the defendant and society will benefit more from conditional release supervised by a probation officer than imprisonment. Because a defendant can be employed during this period, probation allows for the possibility that the victim of the crime may be reimbursed for damages incurred or property lost due to the defendant's crime. Courts frequently make restitution to the victim a condition of the defendant's continuing freedom.[6] The cost factor also plays a role. The expense to society of housing a convicted person in prison costs hundreds of thousands of dollars more than supervising him or her on probation. If employed, the defendant has the opportunity to support his or her dependents, who may become a public burden if he or she is imprisoned.

---

[3]  United States v. Sparrow, 673 F.2d 862 (5th Cir. 1982).

[4]  On the problem of fining indigent defendants, *see* Bearden v. Georgia, 103 S. Ct. 2064 (1983). The fine is used in misdemeanor cases frequently, and the constitutionality of this sanction is discussed in the misdemeanor chapter, § 10.12.

[5]  Confinement of the accused after sentence on a felony will usually be in either a penitentiary or a reformatory. The distinction between these two institutions generally lies in the age or nature of the criminal record of offenders. Young convicts, or those serving time on a first conviction, are prime candidates for reformatory (as opposed to penitentiary) confinement.

[6]  See restitution and compensation of victims discussed in § 7.7.

Legislative attempts have occasionally been made to cut off the possibility of probation in certain offenses. While some decisions approve this approach, efforts to limit probation have not always met with success in the courts. Much depends upon the seriousness of the offense, and some cases have concluded that cruel and unusual punishment was imposed under statutes that precluded parole consideration for people convicted of crimes that did not justify mandatory denial of conditional freedom.

## § 7.2　Sentencing and Corrections: Meeting the Crime Challenge

### 1. Theories of Sentencing

Different principles or theories intersect in the sentencing process. Sentencing in earlier days was based upon the theory that the law should make an example of the criminal defendant. Another view inclined to the position that society should take revenge upon the criminal for his or her crime. Accordingly, sentences were harsh. During the middle decades of the twentieth century, however, a different trend developed. While the exemplary idea remained a factor in sentencing, shaping the sentence to advance rehabilitation of the offender in cases in which he or she was a fit subject became a primary concern. One commentator summarized the idea: "Punishments should be severe enough to impress not only upon the defendant's mind, but upon the public mind, the gravity of society's condemnation of irresponsible behavior. But the ultimate aim of condemning irresponsibility is training for responsibility. . . . Allowance for the possibility of reformation, or formation, of character in the generality of cases becomes at this point, in other words, an overriding consideration."[7]

The 1990s saw a return to more extended punishment, with courts emphasizing the deterrent effect of sentences. Today, deterrence and incapacitation are primary considerations. Reformation of offenders remains an objective, but has been upstaged by a desire to make an example of defendants. There is some emphasis on enhanced prison time for drug dealers or violent offenders, and under some codes, laws mandate life sentences for felons convicted of a third violent crime.

How are the three aims of punishment—**deterrence, incapacitation,** and **reformation**—defined? An oft-quoted court opinion reviewing each of these principles was rendered in *Commonwealth v. Ritter*.[8] The case involved a married man who for several years conducted an affair with a married woman not his wife. On one occasion a spirited argument developed between the two when the man accused the woman of trying to get rid of him after spending all his money and ruining his marriage. The dispute became heated and the man

---

[7]　Harry M. Hart, *The Aims of the Criminal Law*, 23 LAW AND CONTEMPORARY PROBLEMS 401, 426 (1958).

[8]　13 D&C 285 (Pa. 1930) (opinion by Judge Stern, later Chief Justice of the Pennsylvania Supreme Court).

shot and killed the woman, then tried unsuccessfully to kill himself. The man later pled guilty to a charge of murder. Pennsylvania law at the time provided that in cases of guilty pleas, the court should determine whether the crime was murder in the first degree, and then should "at its discretion, impose sentence of death or imprisonment for life."[9] In making a decision between these two punishments, the Pennsylvania court provided a detailed discussion of the various theories in the sentencing field:

> Generally speaking, there have been advanced four theories as the basis upon which society should act in imposing penalties upon those who violate its laws. These are: (1) to bring about the reformation of the evil-doer; (2) to effect retribution or revenge upon him; (3) to restrain him physically, so as to make it impossible for him to commit further crimes; and (4) to deter others from similarly violating the law.

The court observed that while reformation is important in the general run of cases, that principle had no application to the murder defendant before the court. Because he would never be released, there was little purpose in reforming him. "Whichever be the penalty here inflicted, the defendant will not again be in contact with society." The court next observed that "[t]he second theory which has been urged as a basis for the imposition of penalties is that of retribution. This may be regarded as the doctrine of legal revenge, or punishment merely for the sake of punishment. It is to pay back the wrong-doer for his wrong-doing, to make him suffer by way of retaliation even if no benefits result thereby to himself or to others." Modern penology rejects this theory as an inhumane motivation for punishment.

The court found a more respectable basis for sentencing in the concept of incapacitation:

> Rejecting, therefore, the theory of retribution as a proper basis upon which to impose the penalty of law, we come to the third principle which has been advocated, namely, the restraining of the wrongdoer in order to make it impossible for him to commit further crime. Here we arrive not only at a justifiable basis for action but at one which is vital to the protection of society. To permit a man of dangerous criminal tendencies to be in a position where he can give indulgence to such propensities would be a folly which no community should suffer itself to commit, any more than it should allow a wild animal to range at will in the city streets. If, therefore, there is danger that a defendant may again commit crime, society should restrain his liberty until such danger be past, and, in cases similar to the present, if reasonably necessary for that purpose, to terminate his life.

The record of the offender in this case did not make him an apt subject for sentencing under a simple incapacitation theory. Nor was he a candidate for the death penalty. He was no "mad dog" killer, nor a hired hit man. The crime

---

[9]    The death penalty is discussed in this chapter at § 7.5.

was the product of the situation. The court deemed it appropriate to analyze the character of the defendant: "[Examining the record] of the present case from this point of view, in order to determine whether the defendant's continuation in life would be a lurking menace to society, I find nothing in the evidence which would lead to that conclusion. The murder which he committed was the result of many years of entanglement—a terrible tragedy, it is true, but one which was not the result of any bloodthirstiness or lust for crime."

Having reviewed other bases for handing out criminal sentences, the court concluded with a most significant factor. "This brings us to the final and what must be fairly regarded as one of the most important objectives of punishment, namely, the element of deterrence—the theory which regards the penalty as being not an end in itself but the means of attaining an end, namely, the frightening of others who might be tempted to imitate the criminal. From this angle a penalty is a cautionary measure, aimed at the prevention of further crime in the community." With this consideration in mind, the court traced the downward mental spiral of the accused:

> In the present case, the nature of the crime and the psychology of the criminal are clear. For several years the defendant, although a man of mature age, long married and the father of five children, had been embroiled in a love passion for a woman who was not his wife. She, of approximately the same age, and the mother of three children, apparently entered with him upon an illicit relationship. Having, by his business ability, succeeded in achieving a fair degree of material prosperity, he squandered large sums of money upon the woman who had thus come into his life. He developed an extreme jealousy in regard to her and what seems to have been a constant terror that she would desert him, especially when he had arrived at the end of his financial means. He took more and more to drinking and enfeebled his health and mentality to a point where he was obliged to go to a medical institution on two successive occasions a year apart. Finally, he reached so low a depth in the matter of his finances that in order to obtain the very pistol with which he committed the murder he was obliged to pawn his overcoat.

These factors prompted the judge to impose a sentence other than death. "[I]t is not believed that the death penalty in a case such as this would have any effect of deterrence on persons who might commit similar crimes, because offenses of this nature are not the result of calm and thoughtful planning or of rationalized deliberation. . . . The court, therefore, adjudges the defendant to be guilty of murder of the first degree, and imposes upon him the penalty of life imprisonment for and during the term of his natural life."

In other types of cases, the judge indicated that he would consider the death penalty. While it did not fit here, the judge saw its imposition in other cases to be a relevant choice. The court stated: "My own opinion is that the extreme penalty of death works a deterrent effect, and therefore, should be aimed against cases where a murder is committed from what might be called a mental, rather than an emotional, impulse—in other words, where the murder is deliberately planned from a sordid motive or where the likelihood of its occurring is cal-lously ignored by those who commit some other crime which may well give rise to it." Because the homicide in this case was a crime of passion and did not result from cold calculation, the judge did not consider it a death penalty case.

## 2. Modern Trends

Rehabilitation of the offender was accepted by *Commonwealth v. Ritter* to be important "in the general run of cases." For years rehabilitation formed a major goal of modern penology. It is still the aim of many prison administrators today, who favor liberal parole rules. Opponents of this approach argue that prisoners should be held in confinement until the end of their sentences, without parole. Each view will presently be discussed.

The debate about the merits of punishment has reached a high pitch, and the forces in favor of retribution appear to be winning. By 1976, one author concluded, "Today, the 'rehabilitation ideal' lies sprawled on its deathbed."[10]

If a growing number of authorities view prisons as a place for punishment, what has triggered this shift? Several reasons are offered. First, there is the growing fear of crime. In past decades, crime rates multiplied. Along with frightening headlines reporting violent assaults and murders, some citizens and authorities harbored the view that the judicial system had been soft on criminals. When news stories carried captions like "Crime Laid to Timid Judges," conditions proved to be right in some states for a shift away from judicial discretion in sentencing, and the granting of parole.

Finally, dissatisfaction with the American judicial system was coupled with strong feelings in several quarters that attempted rehabilitation of offenders had not worked. One-third to one-half or more of all convicts return to prison after their release, critics point out. Because they see no proof that probation and parole rehabilitate criminals, proponents of punishment argue that the correctional system should be viewed as a system to isolate and punish.

Response to the desire for more stringent punishment took several forms. Frustration over lack of success with other methods for dealing with the problem of drug trafficking and addicts led to the enactment of stiff penalties. The Court of Appeals of New York observed that "drug offenses, concededly, are punished more severely and inflexibly than almost any other offense in the State." The New York court went on to uphold as constitutional drug laws that punished certain narcotics offenses with mandatory life imprisonment. Finding the punishment not disproportionate to the crime, the court explained why flexible sentencing and rehabilitation of offenders had been virtually discarded as goals when dealing with drug traffickers: "Faced with what it found to be a high recidivism rate in drug-related crimes, an inadequate response to less severe punishment, and an insidiously growing drug abuse problem, the Legislature could reasonably shift the emphasis to other penological purposes, namely, isolation and deterrence."[11]

---

[10]    Bennett, *Rehabilitation in Check*, 12 TRIAL MAGAZINE 12 (1976).

[11]    People v. Broadie, 371 N.Y.S.2d 471 (1975). This case was superseded by statute, as recognized in *People v. Askew*, 403 N.Y.S.2d 959 (N.Y. Sup. Ct. 1978).

The United States Supreme Court has ruled in similar fashion. A Michigan defendant was convicted of possession of more than 650 grams of cocaine and was sentenced to a mandatory term of life in prison without possibility of parole. Justice Scalia's Supreme Court opinion ruled that severe mandatory penalties are not unconstitutional for drug defendants. Justice Kennedy's concurring opinion observed that use and distribution of illegal drugs represents "one of the greatest problems affecting the health and welfare of our population."[12]

Other responses to the crime problem revealed a growing "get tough" attitude. California voters adopted Proposition 8, also known as the Gann Initiative. It included a series of steps designed to respond to citizen concerns about crime. Some of the criminal provisions included approval of preventive detention of persons thought to pose a threat to public safety, as well as stringent limitations on plea bargaining in the case of serious felonies.

In Illinois, a system of **determinate sentencing** was instituted, in which "fixed" or "flat time" sentences are handed down. Eliminated is the minimum-maximum sentencing system under which the judge sets a sentence range and a parole board later decides the prison release date.[13] Such laws seek to promote uniformity in sentencing and to eliminate disparity in sentences. They incorporate deterrence and retribution principles and minimize the importance of rehabilitation.[14]

One ramification of the shift to definite sentences is the elimination of traditional parole systems. As the "flat time" sentencing pattern spreads, parole diminishes in significance because of the limitation on early prisoner releases at the discretion of a board. Another result of a system of fixed sentences is the need for new prison construction. With definite sentences and limited paroles, prison populations greatly expanded.[15] One commentator assessed the enthusiasm for more vigorous punishment: "Recent years have been witness to the adoption by state legislatures of statutes increasing the use of mandatory sentences, including the adoption of 'three strikes and you're out' legislation, designed to insure lifetime incarceration for persistent offenders. . . . Chain gangs have returned in many states. The imprisoned population in the United States far outstrips comparable figures in other parts of the industrial world."[16]

The Congressional effort to revolutionize the sentencing of federal offenders reached fruition in the 1980s. The sentencing guideline system that was enacted sought to curtail judicial discretion in sentencing, abolish parole, and mitigate disparities in sentencing. Justice Blackmun's opinion in *Mistretta v.*

---

[12]     Harmelin v. Michigan, 111 S. Ct. 2680 (1991).

[13]     Note, *Determinate Sentencing in California and Illinois*, 1979 WASH. U.L.Q. 551, 558 (1979).

[14]     *Id.* at 557. In Illinois, a system of good conduct credits nonetheless reduces the sentence served. It is different from the traditional parole system, however; before the revised law, an Illinois judge set the maximum period for detention, and the parole board could release the prisoner when rehabilitated and ready for release. Id. at 553.

[15]     In response to this possibility in federal cases, the U.S. Department of Justice has requested substantial appropriations for planning and construction of new prison facilities.

[16]     Robert Cottroll, *Hard Choices and Shifted Burdens: American Crime and American Justice at the End of the Century*, 65 GEO. W. L. REV. 506, 510 (1997).

*United States*[17] remarked that, during the time leading up to enactment of the Sentencing Reform Act, "[r]ehabilitation as a sound penological theory came to be questioned and, in any event, was regarded by some as an unattainable goal." He called attention to the Senate Report preceding the sentencing legislation. The Report referred to the "outmoded rehabilitation model" for federal criminal sentencing, and argued that the efforts of the criminal justice system to achieve rehabilitation of offenders had failed. It criticized the indeterminate sentencing system as having "unjustifi[ed]" and "shameful" consequences: "The first was the great variation among sentences imposed by different judges upon similarly situated offenders. The second was the uncertainty as to the time the offender would spend in prison. Each was a serious impediment to an evenhanded and effective operation of the criminal justice system." The Report went on to note that parole was an inadequate device for overcoming these undesirable consequences.

To remedy these problems the **Sentencing Reform Act of 1984** created the United States Sentencing Commission with the responsibility to distribute to federal judges the sentences to be used in particular cases. It makes all sentences basically determinate, and barred parole for prisoners convicted after the guidelines went into effect. A prisoner is to be released at the completion of his or her sentence—reduced only by any credit earned by good behavior while in custody. A sentence of more than one year can be shortened at the end of each year by 15 percent for good behavior. The Sentencing Reform Act made the Sentencing Commission's guidelines binding on the federal courts, and the *Mistretta* decision held this approach to be constitutional.

In 2005 the Supreme Court modified the rules by making these guidelines advisory, not mandatory. Rather than repealing them, the Court simply downgraded them to advisory status, removing their mandatory nature. Although courts are no longer bound by them, federal judges are still required to consider the guidelines in fixing sentences. Because the guidelines remain active as sentencing guides, it helps to understand how judges use them.

Federal courts begin the sentencing process by applying the sentence applicable to the defendant's offense. Then the judge determines whether any sentencing adjustments apply. A sentence might be reduced for a defendant who played a minor part in the offense or for a defendant who expressed remorse and accepted responsibility for her crime. While these factors help to mitigate or moderate a sentence, the only factor that allows the judge to go below the prescribed statutory sentencing range is the defendant who "substantially assists" government authorities in clearing up crime. On the other

---

[17]  109 S. Ct. 647 (1989) (sentencing guidelines do not violate the separation-of-powers principle). The work of the United States Sentencing Commission has received mixed reviews. For evaluations of the program, *see* Daniel J. Freed, *Federal Sentencing in the Wake of Guidelines: Unacceptable Limits on the Discretion of Sentences,* 101 YALE L.J. 1681 (1992); Symposium, *Making Sense of the Federal Sentencing Guidelines,* 25 U.C. DAVIS L. REV. 563 (1992). Despite the criticism of the federal system, several states have developed similar sentencing guidelines, while others continue their traditional practice of applying indeterminate sentencing patterns. *See generally,* SYMPOSIUM, *A Symposium on Sentencing Reform in the States,* 64 U. COLO. L. REV. 645 (1993).

hand, the judge can enhance the sentence if the crime was committed against a vulnerable victim or the defendant engaged in obstruction of justice. However, after 2004 in state courts and 2005 in federal courts, the factors that justify enhancement must be proved to the jury before they are used by a judge to "up the sentence."

The Federal Sentencing Guidelines that were promulgated in the 1980s spawned imitation in a number of states. In the last two decades or so at least a dozen states adopted sentencing guideline systems not unlike the federal pattern, but often with unique local variations. Under many of these systems the legislature set a standard sentence for a crime, but if a judge determined that an aggravating circumstance occurred during its commission, he or she could adjust the sentence upward.

For example, assume that the customary sentence for armed robbery is seven years. However, if the judge determined that the robbery was committed in order to fund a drug habit, the judge could increase the sentence to eight years. The enhanced prison time is sometimes called an "exceptional" sentence. Prior to 2004 an exceptional sentence could be handed out in appropriate cases. Under a 2004 decision by the United States Supreme Court, however, the option for judges to do so was strictly curtailed. Under *Blakely v. Washington*,[18] a sentence could not be enhanced above normal parameters by a judge unless the facts upon which it was based were heard by a jury.

In the armed robbery example, the judge could not add the extra year of sentence. In similar fashion, a judge is barred from imposing the death penalty after a guilty verdict on first degree murder, if the death penalty is based solely on the judge's finding of an aggravating factor. Suppose a defendant mutilated his victim. In the jurisdiction where the crime was committed, such mutilation is an aggravating factor that authorizes a sentence of death, after a conviction of murder. In modern jurisprudence, the mutilation must be proved to the jury as opposed to simply being noticed by the judge, in order to authorize capital punishment.

In addition to application to individual offenders, federal sentencing guidelines were enacted for business corporations. Effective November 1, 1991, the United States Sentencing Commission activated a series of Guidelines for Sentencing of Organizations. Criminal liability may be imposed on a corporation or other organization on account of the criminal acts of company officers or employees. Punishment of the company may include a substantial fine as well as requiring the organization to remedy any harm caused by the offense. If the organization is operated primarily for a criminal purpose, the fine can be set high enough to divest the organization of its total assets.

The Federal Sentencing Guidelines have resulted in increased incarceration of those convicted of crimes, in an effort to address America's crime problem.

---

[18]    124 S. Ct. 2531 (2004).

At the other end of the spectrum, an opposing view urges that prisons are often graduate schools in crime, and that the less time a person spends there the better it is both for the prisoner and for society. Some suggest that extended incarceration of prisoners has failed to curb crime and, in fact, may have contributed to its increase. The National Advisory Commission on Criminal Justice Standards and Goals suggested that all prison terms be limited to a maximum sentence of five years except in cases of murder or when the defendant is a habitual felony offender.

Along with the issue of rehabilitation of the offender inside the walls, there is the issue of readjustment to society once the prisoner is released. One barrier to reformation of the ex-prisoner are restrictions in state employment and licensing laws relating to ex-offenders. Former inmates are sometimes barred from jobs such as barbering or selling real estate. Because of the kind of job a person holds is a powerful determinant of the kind of life he leads, the President's Commission on Law Enforcement made a plea for states to overhaul state employment restrictions and eliminate irrational barriers. The Commission stated: "Conviction may well be relevant in some cases to the protection of the public through such regulation. It is relevant to the offense they have committed to revoke the license of a lawyer convicted of embezzling the funds of clients or a teamster convicted of vehicular homicide. But it is hard to see why, on the other hand, a man convicted of larceny should not be permitted to cut hair or run a restaurant."[19]

The preceding comment relates to convicted offenders. Sometimes even an arrest that does not result in a conviction can pose an obstacle to employment. One source noted that about 45 percent of major corporate employers in a large eastern city excluded employment candidates with arrest records, and another study found that an even larger percentage of small firms excluded arrestees.[20] In criticizing this business practice, the same commentator suggested that the arrest experience is more widespread than these employers believe. "If employers used polygraph tests rather than arrest records to screen candidates, it would be much more difficult to fill any position. An illustration points up a . . . reason for the inequity of screening employees with arrest records. A personnel audit of a Chicago firm that refused to hire anyone with an arrest record revealed that the vast majority of its most successful employees had in fact been arrested. Though there are justifications for restricted use of arrest records, especially of information regarding uncleared arrests, the blanket application of this employment test seems less justified."

Perhaps in response to such problems, legislatures have enacted expungement statutes that can be used by a person who was arrested on a minor charge, but perhaps was never convicted. In such situations, it is thought that the arrest

---

[19]  TASK FORCE REPORT: CORRECTIONS, p. 33, President's Commission. As stated by one official, "When a releasee is denied the means to make an honest living, every sentence becomes a life sentence." Former U.S. Attorney General John Mitchell, 1971, quoted in Holcomb, *Employment Barriers: The Enduring Consequences of a Brush with the Law*, 54 PUBLIC AFFAIRS COUNCIL NEWS (Aug. 1973).

[20]  Holcomb, note 19 *supra*.

record should not be used to bar employment. The laws operate to expunge or clean up a past record of alleged criminal conduct. Sometimes these laws are restricted to eliminating misdemeanor arrest entries, in other states more serious offenses may be expunged. The next section of the text details how expungement statutes work.

## § 7.3    Expungement of Records and Sentences

Prompted by reasons such as those suggested in the concluding paragraphs of § 7.2, several states have enacted statutes for sealing court records or for **expungement**. Although state statutory patterns vary, the following Ohio statute illustrates one approach. Section 2953.32 of the Ohio Revised Code allows the court, in the case of first offenders who are shown to be rehabilitated, to seal all official records pertaining to the case and dismiss the charges. "The proceedings in the case shall be considered not to have occurred and the conviction or bail forfeiture of the person who is the subject of the proceedings shall be sealed, except that upon conviction of a subsequent offense, the sealed record of prior conviction or bail forfeiture may be considered by the court in determining the sentence or other appropriate disposition . . ."

Expungement should not be misunderstood. It is not designed to provide a routine avenue for hardened, repeat offenders to seal or destroy their criminal records. Ohio restricts the benefit to first-time offenders. A Missouri statute provides for expungement of records of persons arrested but not charged or convicted.[21] And a North Carolina provision reflects a desire to provide expungement privileges for youthful offenders involved in misdemeanor filings. Section 15A-145 of the North Carolina General Statutes provides that such an offender may file a petition "for expunction," and further states:

> If the court, after hearing, finds that the petitioner had remained of good behavior and been free of conviction of any felony or misdemeanor, other than a traffic violation, for two years from the date of conviction of the misdemeanor in question, the petitioner has no outstanding restitution orders or civil judgments representing amounts ordered for restitution entered against him, and (i) petitioner was not 18 years old at the time of conviction in question, or (ii) petitioner was not 21 years old at the time of the conviction of possession of alcohol pursuant to G.S. 18B-302(b)(1), it shall order that person be restored, in the contemplation of the law, to the status he occupied before such arrest or indictment or information. *No person as to whom such order has been entered shall be held thereafter under any provision of any*

---

[21]   MO. REV. STAT. 610.100 (1994). Expungement is defined in REPORT, CRIMINAL JUSTICE COMMITTEE OF BAR ASS'N. OF ST. LOUIS, 55 (1975): "Expungement has been interpreted to require the physical destruction of the record and arrest records are expunged when there is no conviction within a year following the date upon which the records have been closed." Statutes differ considerably as to key variables, such as who is eligible for expungement and when. In some states only arrests are expungeable, in others convictions are included. The statutes referred to in this section of the text illustrate the point.

*laws to be guilty of perjury or otherwise giving a false statement by reason of his failure to recite or acknowledge such arrest, or indictment, information, or trial, or response to any inquiry made of him for any purpose.* (emphasis added)

In *Dickerson v. New Banner Institute, Inc.*[22] the United States Supreme Court noted that "[o]ver half the States have enacted one or more statutes that may be classified as expunction provisions that attempt to conceal prior convictions or to remove some of their collateral or residual effects." The Court observed that expungement statutes vary widely:

These statutes differ, however, in almost every particular. Some are applicable only to young offenders, e.g., Mich.Comp.Laws §§ 780.621 and .622 (1982). Some are available only to persons convicted of certain offenses, e.g., N.J.Stat.Ann § 2C:52-2(b) (West 1982); others, however, permit expunction of a conviction for any crime including murder, e.g., Mass.Gen.Laws Ann., ch. 276, § 100A (West Supp. 1982). Some are confined to first offenders, e.g. Okla.Stat.Tit. 22 § 991(c) (Supp. 1982). Some are discretionary, e.g., Minn.Stat. § 638.02(2) (Supp. 1982), while others provide for automatic expunction under certain circumstances, e.g., Ariz.Rev.Stat.Ann § 13-912 (1978). The statutes vary in the language employed to describe what they do. Some speak of expunging the conviction, others of "sealing" the file or of causing the dismissal of the charge. The statutes also differ in their actual effect. Some are absolute; others are limited. Only a minority address questions such as whether the expunged conviction may be considered in sentencing for a subsequent offense or in setting bail on a later charge, or whether the expunged conviction may be used for impeachment purposes, or whether the convict may deny the fact of his conviction.

## § 7.4  Factors Shaping the Sentence

In sentencing a particular offender, the trial court will consider the nature and seriousness of the offense, the prospect of repetition by the defendant, and the danger to societal safety if the defendant is permitted conditional freedom. The defendant's age, prior criminal record, and any family ties are taken into account. Another factor that may be considered is whether the defendant pled guilty or was convicted after a trial. Some trial judges take the view that lighter sentences are justified for those who plead guilty because (1) the disposition of criminal cases is expedited when defendants plead guilty, and (2) a guilty plea indicates a readiness by the accused to accept responsibility and demonstrates that the offender has taken a first step toward rehabilitation. Arguments to the contrary include the contention that the defendant should not be punished by heavier sentence for simply exercising his constitutional right to trial by jury.

---

[22]   103 S. Ct. 986 (1983), superseded by statute, 18 U.S.C. § 921 (a) (20). *See also* Schaefer, *The Use of Expunged Convictions in Federal Courts*, 35 FED. B.J. 107 (1976).

However, one prominent study approved the practice of granting concessions in appropriate cases when the defendant pleads guilty.[23]

Another factor influencing the sentence may be the number of separate offenses arising out of a single transaction. A single criminal act can violate two or more distinct penal statutes, such as when a person who shoots another with a pistol may be charged with carrying a concealed weapon and attempted murder.[24] In such situations the trial judge can, if the defendant is convicted of both crimes, make the sentences run either consecutively or concurrently. Under the latter approach, the shorter sentence for carrying a concealed weapon would be served during the time the defendant was serving the sentence for attempted murder. However, if the court ordered the sentences to run consecutively, one sentence would begin running upon the expiration of the other, appreciably increasing the maximum confinement faced by the accused.[25] Consecutive sentences are occasionally imposed by the court; however, sentencing in this cumulative way and thus pyramiding penalties in cases where each sentence is for a substantial term of years has been disapproved of by at least one source: "[N]ot more than one sentence for an extended term shall be imposed."[26]

In *Roberts v. United States*,[27] another factor affecting sentence was mentioned. The Supreme Court held that the sentencing judge properly considered, as one of the criteria in imposing consecutive sentences, defendant's refusal to cooperate with police officials investigating a criminal conspiracy to distribute heroin, even though the defendant had admitted his complicity in the heroin ring.

In fashioning the sentence, sometimes judges have sought unusual cures for unique problems. A Los Angeles judge, in sentencing a well-known pickpocket, allowed the man to go free on condition that he wear mittens whenever he was outside his home. The condition was for a six-year period, and the judge specified that the mittens were to be thick enough "to prevent independent movement of the fingers." In another case involving four drug distributors, a Georgia judge told the four that if it were legal he would order them

---

[23] Am. Bar Ass'n, *Standards Relating to Pleas of Guilty*, § 14-1.8 (1979). See § 5.3 of this book. Criticizing this view, *see* People v. Byrd, 162 N.W.2d 777 (Mich. 1968) (Levin, concurring opinion).

[24] For rules respecting the setting forth of two or more offenses in one information see § 4.2 and § 4.5 of this text.

[25] Where the sentencing judge is silent as to concurrent or consecutive effect when defendant is convicted of two offenses with terms imposed on each, rule of concurrent application controls except where consecutive sentences are statutorily mandated. 18 U.S.C. 3584 (a). However, this principle does not apply when the accused is sentenced in one state while under a sentence imposed by a sister state. Herman v. Brewer, 193 N.W.2d 540 (Iowa 1972) (consecutive). *Compare* In re Carey's Petition, 126 N.W.2d 727 (Mich. 1964) (concurrent).

[26] MODEL PENAL CODE § 7.06(1)(d) (2001). For a case disapproving consecutive sentences, see Prince v. United States, 352 U.S. 322, 77 S. Ct. 403, 1 L. Ed. 2d 370 (1957) (20- and 15-year sentences imposed by trial judge to run consecutively). Approving consecutive sentences, see Gore v. United States, 357 U.S. 386, 78 S. Ct. 1280, 2 L. Ed. 2d 1405 (1958) (three sentences of one to five years to run consecutively).

[27] 445 U.S. 552 (1980).

taken to the courthouse lawn and flogged in front of everyone in the country.[28] While most sentences are meted out along more conventional lines, with nonviolent misdemeanor offenders there is some movement to alternatives to conventional jail terms. **Alternative sentencing** programs exist in several states. Judges use weekend sentences to ensure that offenders keep their jobs and family ties. Community service sentences are sometimes given in appropriate cases.

With other types of offenses, there has been a trend toward enhanced punishment. In one kind of case, that term should be longer, some officials contend. The use of handguns has prompted many authorities to urge that a mandatory prison term of 10 years be tacked on to any other sentence given a person who is convicted of a felony in which he or she used a firearm. The aim is punishment of the offender involved in the crime as well as deterrence of others who might be tempted to use a gun while committing an offense.

The broad purpose of the criminal law is to prevent people from doing what society considers undesirable, and in accomplishing this aim criminal law is framed in terms of imposing penalties for bad conduct.[29] This brings us to consideration of the mental state of the offender. Those who are out of touch with reality are deemed to be improper candidates for extended jail confinement. Thus, a final factor affecting the sentence may be judicial consideration of the mental condition of the offender at the time of the crime. When found not guilty by reason of insanity, typically the defendant will be committed to a mental institution. If the offender remains mentally ill, there is no constitutional vice in confining him for a longer period than the maximum prison sentence for the crime charged.[30] Public outcry following acquittal on insanity grounds of would-be presidential assassin John W. Hinckley Jr. led to revision of the law in some places. A verdict of "**guilty but not responsible**" or "guilty but mentally ill," has replaced former verdicts of not guilty by reason of insanity in certain jurisdictions. Where a verdict in the former category is returned, the usual sentencing approach is for the judge to sentence the defendant, then perhaps order his or her commitment to a state mental facility until it is determined that "he is neither a threat to himself nor others." The guilty but mentally ill approach differs from traditional practice in that once a defendant's mental illness is cured, he will not automatically be released. There may be a prison term to complete.[31]

---

[28]   The history of punishments included harsh sentences such as public flogging and old corporal punishments which included severing the hand of a thief.

[29]   LaFave, Criminal Law § 1.2(c) (4th ed. 2003).

[30]   Jones v. United States, 103 S. Ct. 3043 (1983).

[31]   Note, *Guilty But Mentally Ill: A Retreat From the Insanity Defense*, 7 Am. J.L. & Med. 236 (1981). See Note, *Criminal Responsibility: Changes in the Insanity Defense and the "Guilty But Mentally Ill" Response*, 21 Washburn L.J. 515 (1982); Hovenkamp, *Insanity and Criminal Responsibility in Progressive America*, 57 N.D.L. Rev. 541 (1981).

## § 7.5   Capital Punishment

**Capital punishment** has had an uneven history in the United States. During the 1930s, more than 100 people were executed each year under state capital punishment laws. Critics began to challenge the constitutionality of these provisions, and as doubts about the validity of capital punishment grew, the number of executions declined. In 1967 executions stopped so that the Supreme Court could develop jurisprudence regarding the appropriateness of the death penalty. Was capital punishment constitutional?

In *Furman v. Georgia* doubt was cast on the validity of the death penalty when the United States Supreme Court held that the way the death penalty was carried out in the United States constituted cruel and unusual punishment in violation of the United States Constitution. The 5-4 decision of the Court denied the deterrent effect of the death penalty (compare *Commonwealth v. Ritter*, § 7.2) because of the arbitrary way in which it was inflicted. The Court pointed out that of all the persons convicted of crimes such as murder and rape, only a handful are selected for imposition of the death penalty.[32] Justice Brennan emphasized the view that there is no reason to believe that the death penalty serves any penal purpose more effectively than the less severe punishment of imprisonment. Some state court decisions have also taken positions against capital punishment.

Would the death penalty, if inflicted in a more careful and uniform way, be upheld by the high court? After *Furman*, states were uncertain as to how to proceed. Some reasoned that one way around the *Furman* decision would be to make death the mandated penalty, without the possibility of an alternate punishment, for specified heinous crimes. Others set up statutory schemes whereby capital punishment could be imposed only if particularly aggravating circumstances were found to exist in connection with the commission of a murder. The "aggravation" hearing might be held before a judge or jury in proceedings conducted subsequent to the main trial, after the defendant had been found guilty. During the four-year period between *Furman* and the Supreme Court's death penalty cases in 1976, executions were at a standstill. However, state legislatures were busy, and during that time "more change occurred in the law of capital crimes than in any other period in the history of Anglo-American criminal law."[33]

In 1976, in legal decisions having the broadest possible significance, the United States Supreme Court ruled on the constitutionality of the death penalty. The Court ruled in favor of capital punishment when imposed under careful, specific procedures. A majority of the Justices upheld Georgia, Texas, and Florida statutes that provided for bifurcated proceedings before the death penalty was ordered. At the same time, the Court struck down as unconstitutional mandatory

---

[32]   Furman v. Georgia, 408 U.S. 238, 92 S. Ct. 2726, 33 L. Ed. 2d 346 (1972). In the three "death penalty" cases before the court, two involved rape; one defendant, Furman, had been convicted of murder.

[33]   John W. Poulos, *Liability Rules, Sentencing Factors, and the Sixth Amendment Right to a Jury Trial*, 44 MIAMI L. REV. 643, 645 (1990).

death penalty statutes in cases from Louisiana and North Carolina.[34] The Supreme Court continues to emphasize that a mandatory death statute that does not allow consideration of particularized mitigating factors is unconstitutional, even where the crime is the first degree murder of a police officer.[35]

What does a modern death penalty statute look like? Statutes generally call for two trials, often conducted in front of the same jury. After the jury is initially selected, the first trial is held to determine guilt. Did the defendant commit a capital crime, such as premeditated murder? If the answer is yes, the jury sits for another trial right after the first one in order to set the sentence. Here, they consider points for and against the defendant, often called mitigating and aggravating factors. Justice Marshall's opinion in *Stebbing v. Maryland*, dissenting from a denial of certiorari, set forth certain death penalty elements of Maryland law that are presented in several other state statutes.[36] The analysis provides a framework for comparing capital punishment statutes:

> Like most death penalty statutes, the Maryland statute begins by requiring the sentencing authority—either a judge or a jury—first to consider whether the prosecutor has proved, beyond a reasonable doubt, the existence of any of 10 statutory aggravating circumstances. Md. Ann. Code, Art. 27, § 413(d) (1982 and Supp. 1983). If the sentencer does not find at least one aggravating factor, the sentence must be life imprisonment. § 413(f). If the sentencer finds that one or more aggravating factors exist, it then must determine whether the defendant has proven, by a preponderance of the evidence, that any of eight statutory mitigating factors exist. § 413(g) . . . If no mitigating factors are found, the sentencer must impose death. If, instead, the sentencer has found at least one mitigating factor, it must determine, by a preponderance of the evidence, whether the proven mitigating factors outweigh the aggravating circumstances. § 413(h). If they do, the sentencer must impose a life sentence. If the mitigating factors do not outweigh aggravating factors, the jury must impose a death sentence.

If a state has determined that death should be an available penalty for certain crimes, then it must administer that penalty in a way that can rationally distinguish between those individuals for whom death is an appropriate sanction and those for whom it is not. It must allow the sentencer to consider the individual circumstances of the defendant, his background, and his crime. However, every state is not required to copy a particular statutory pattern in drafting its death penalty law. The Eighth Amendment is not violated every time a state reaches a conclusion different from a majority of other jurisdictions over how best to administer its criminal laws.

While the Supreme Court, as noted above, has found that the death penalty is constitutional under certain statutes for the crime of murder, there is still the question of what other crimes can be punished by death. In *Coker v. Georgia*,

---

[34]    Gregg v. Georgia, 428 U.S. 153, 96 S. Ct. 2909, 49 L. Ed. 2d 859 (1976).
[35]    Roberts v. Louisiana, 97 S. Ct. 1993, 52 L. Ed. 2d 637 (1977).
[36]    105 S. Ct. 276 (1984).

the Court held that the sentence of death for the crime of rape of an adult woman was grossly disproportionate and excessive punishment forbidden by the Eighth and Fourteenth Amendments.[37]

Recent terms of the United States Supreme Court gave rise to a large number of interpretations involving the death penalty. In these, the Supreme Court announced a series of important rules:

- Juries, not judges, are empowered to find the specific aggravating factors that justify imposition of the death penalty. The facts supporting capital punishment must be found by a jury, and must not simply be established as a result of fact-finding by a judge alone. *Ring v. Arizona*, 536 U.S. 584 (2002). However, the Ring rule does not apply retroactively to old convictions, and in a 2005 case it did not invalidate a death sentence handed down in a 1980 homicide. *Bell v. Cone*, 125 S. Ct. 845 (2005).

- Imposing the death penalty on a juvenile who was 15 years old or younger when the individual committed a murder is cruel and unusual punishment in violation of the Eighth Amendment to the Constitution, and prohibited. *Thompson v. Oklahoma*, 108 S. Ct. 2687 (1988).

- Death penalty litigation involving juveniles has occupied criminal courts in recent years. Through 2004, many states authorized the death penalty for crimes committed at age 16 and above. The United States Supreme Court revisited the issue in 2005 and determined that the minimum age should be moved up to 18. *Roper v. Simmons*, 125 S. Ct. 1183 (2005).

- Execution of mentally retarded persons is improper under *Atkins v. Virginia*, 122 S. Ct. 2242 (2002). Executing them constitutes cruel and unusual punishment in violation of the Constitution's Eighth Amendment, says the Supreme Court. The Constitution also forbids executing a person who is insane.

- A jury choosing between death and life in prison must be told when a life sentence carries no possibility of parole, when that is the case. *Kelly v. South Carolina*, 534 U.S. 246 (2002).

- The Supreme Court forbids the imposition of the death penalty upon a mere accomplice; there must be a clear finding that the person sentenced to death in fact killed, attempted to kill, or intended to kill. *Cabana v. Bullock*, 474 U.S. 376, 106 S. Ct. 689, 88 L. Ed. 2d 704 (1986). However, the death penalty can be imposed in the absence of an intent to kill if the defendant substantially participated in a felony likely to result in the loss of human life. *Tison v. Arizona*, 107 S. Ct. 1676 (1987).

- Victim impact evidence—testimony by family members as to what the loss of a loved one through homicide meant to the family—has been approved. *See Payne v. Tennessee*, 111 S. Ct. 2597 (1991) (evidence of effect of crime on victim's family allowed).

---

[37]    Coker v. Georgia, 433 U.S. 584, 97 S. Ct. 2861, 53 L. Ed. 2d 982 (1977).

- A murderer who intentionally drives his car over his victim twice arguably commits "gratuitous violence" whether or not he knows that the victim is dead after the first pass, within the meaning of the Arizona capital punishment law. The law provided for consideration in setting the sentence of facts that qualify as an aggravating death penalty factor. Facts that qualify as such are those that show that the crime was committed in an especially heinous, cruel, or depraved manner. Thus, an Arizona sentencer commits no constitutional error by relying on such facts in sentencing the defendant to death. *Richmond v. Lewis*, 113 S. Ct. 528, 121 L. Ed. 2d 411 (1992).

- There is no constitutional requirement that the jury that fixes the punishment at death specify the aggravating factors that permit the imposition of capital punishment. *Clemons v. Mississippi*, 110 S. Ct. 1441 (1990).

Since the founding of the country, beginning with the first execution of a spy by a Virginia firing squad in 1608, there have been more than 14,000 legal executions in America. After the restoration of capital punishment in *Gregg v. Georgia* in 1976, executions began again when convicted murderer Gary Gilmore was killed by a firing squad in Utah in 1977. More than two-thirds of the states have now embraced capital punishment. Lethal injection is the most common form of capital punishment. Some states authorize a second form of death penalty in the event the inmate chooses something different from lethal injection. Other options, depending upon the state, include electrocution, hanging, or firing squad. Federal courts are regularly involved in litigating capital punishment cases. The United States Congress approved a crime bill in 1994 that imposed the death penalty for an enhanced number of federal offenses. Among others, Oklahoma City bomber Timothy McVeigh, as well as drug kingpin Juan Garza, have been high-profile executions carried out within the federal system. The trend of executions makes certain that additional court tests of capital sentencing schemes will continue.

Debate about the death penalty focuses on several issues. Does the death penalty deter potential killers? Is it imposed fairly? Does its impact fall more heavily on racial minorities?[38] Is it cruel and unusual punishment? Opponents say it is cruel. They add that there is a risk of executing someone who is later found to be innocent. Advocates of capital punishment say that it is constitutional, discourages those who might otherwise plan a homicide, and expresses society's outrage over the murder or murders committed by the killer. The debate will continue.

---

[38]   Claims of racial disparity in capital sentencing were struck down in McCleskey v. Kemp, 107 S. Ct. 1756 (1987).

## § 7.6   Reform of the Sentencing System

Several characteristics that presently mark sentencing in the United States
have been singled out for potential reform. Two of these, jury sentencing and
the problem of sentencing disparity, will be discussed in this section.

### 1.  Jury Sentencing

Although a large number of jurisdictions permit the jury to recommend or
fix punishment at life imprisonment in capital cases, a much smaller number
of states go further and permit the jury to determine the type and length of
punishment for several other offenses, including felonies generally. This, some
commentators say, is wrong, and sentencing in general felony and misdemeanor cases is a job for experts. Only the judge should formulate and deliver
the sentence, they say, except in capital cases when there is a special place for
the jury's community voice to be heard on severity of sentence.[39]

Away from the issue of whether jurors or judges should generally be
responsible for fixing the sentence for felonies, there is a distinct place for the
jury to determine disputed facts that are applicable to sentencing. This is true
when a judge contemplates an upward adjustment in the sentence. A jury finding is required when a sentence is contemplated that is above that customarily
given for a crime. Recent years have marked a renewed confidence by the
Supreme Court in the jury performing this function relevant to sentencing.
Other than the fact of a prior conviction, any fact that increases the penalty for
a crime beyond the regular statutory maximum must be submitted to a jury,
and proved beyond a reasonable doubt. In federal practice, such facts must
also be charged in the indictment. For example, assume a robbery conviction
regularly carries a 10-year sentence. Also assume that a judge can add five
years if the robbery was also a hate crime. To be constitutional, a sentence of
15 years requires the hate crime facts to go before the jury, as well as the elements of the robbery claim.

### 2.  Disparity in Sentences

The reduction of arbitrary disparities in sentencing is a goal of several
reform proposals. The problem has been the subject of many studies. In the
federal system, one survey in an earlier period indicated that the average sentence
for forgery in one court was 68 months, in another court sitting in a different
location it was seven months for the same crime. Auto theft brought 47 months
in prison if the prisoner was sentenced in the Southern District of Iowa, but
only 14 months, on the average, in the Northern District of New York.[40] Sim-

---

[39]  *See* United States v. Bishop, 412 U.S. 346 (1973).

[40]  THE TASK FORCE REPORT: THE COURTS 23, President's Commission on Law Enforcement and Administration of Justice (1967). Guidelines promulgated by the U.S. Sentencing Commission are aimed at
reducing disparities in sentence imposed by different judges upon similarly situated defendants. *See*
§ 7.2. Sentencing tables for specific offenses are contained in federal guidelines.

ilar disparities have been noted between states, as well as within states. Sometimes cellmates with comparable prior records are serving strikingly dissimilar sentences for the same offense simply because the two sentencing judges reacted differently to the same crime.

Sentence reform proposals emphasize the need to even out such differences in sentencing. Sometimes extremely severe sentences for a particular crime may be a projection of the value system of a judge, critics say. The President's Commission on Law Enforcement advocated that state appellate courts supervise sentencing across a state to ensure that sentences handed down by individual judges are fair and more uniform than is now the case: "One of the most serious aspects of the disparity problem is the imposition of sentences which are grossly excessive in relation to the seriousness of the crime or the character of the offender. . . . Authority for appellate review of the merits of sentences has been expressly granted by the legislatures of about one-quarter of the States and by Congress for military courts. In addition, the appellate courts of a few States have construed general review statutes as including such authority. . . . The most important contribution of appellate review is the opportunity it provides for the correction of grossly excessive sentences. Although appellate review will not totally eliminate the problem of disparity of sentences, by reducing the peaks of disparity it would narrow the range in which individual differences among judges can affect the length and type of sentences."[41]

In federal courts, the disparities noted in the first paragraph of this section have been leveled out with the inception of the guideline system. The federal sentencing guidelines created minimum prison sentences for most federal offenses. Prior to the guidelines, the federal model vested district judges with wide discretion to impose any sentence the judge deemed appropriate, within the maximum permitted by statute. The United States Parole Commission also had broad discretion to decide when an incarcerated prisoner would be released on parole. Congress decided this system resulted in an unacceptable level of disparity, with defendants convicted of the same crime serving widely divergent sentences. Too much turned on the personal likes and dislikes of the sentencing judge, it was felt. The Sentencing Reform Act of 1984 restructured federal sentencing to eliminate indeterminate sentencing and phase out parole.[42] Today more than 64,000 prisoners are sentenced annually under United States Sentencing Guidelines.

In a dramatic 2005 decision, the United States Supreme Court undercut the formerly mandatory character of federal sentencing guidelines. In *Booker v. United States*,[43] the court ordained that these formerly binding standards

---

[41]   TASK FORCE REPORT at 25, note 40 *supra* (footnotes omitted). Appellate decisions involving disparity in criminal sentences based on the sex of the offender, see United States v. Maples, 501 F.2d 985 (4th Cir. 1974); Comment, 45 TEX. L. REV. 471 (1967). *Compare* Michael M. v. Superior Court of Sonoma County, 101 S. Ct. 1200 (1981). Claims of racial disparity in capital sentencing were struck down in *McCleskey v. Kemp*, 107 S. Ct. 1756 (1987).

[42]   Applying the sentencing guidelines, *see* Koon v. United States, 116 S. Ct. 2035 (1996) (Rodney King beating case).

[43]   United States v. Booker, 125 S. Ct. 738 (2005).

were exactly what they were named to be, guidelines for sentencing only. Federal judges must still consider them in fixing sentences, but they are advisory and judges are no longer bound to follow them. The Court pointed out that by enacting guidelines, Congress sought to provide uniformity and fairness in sentencing. With these two objectives in mind, the Court stated: "The system remaining after [reversal of the mandatory provisions], while lacking the mandatory features that Congress enacted, retains other features that help to further these objectives. As we have said, the Sentencing Commission remains in place, writing Guidelines, collecting information about actual district court sentencing decisions, undertaking research, and revising the Guidelines accordingly."

One impediment to elimination of arbitrary differences in sentences relates to leniency given some defendants because of a defendant's cooperation with the government. The downward departure from established sentences can occur, based on a defendant's assistance to the prosecution. The rate of these downward departures varied dramatically from one judicial district to another. One federal judge called for national standards to make uniform the effect on a sentence of a defendant's assistance and cooperation.[44]

In the last two decades or so at least a dozen states adopted sentencing guideline systems not unlike the federal pattern, but often with unique local variations. Under many of these systems the legislature sets a standard sentence for a crime, but if a judge determines that an aggravating circumstance occurred during its commission, she can adjust the sentence upward.

Federal Sentencing Guidelines are an effort to make federal sentences in various parts of the country more uniform. State jurisdictions have also tried to iron out differences in sentences for local crimes. In an urban area a person convicted of a crime might be sentenced one way, while an individual convicted of the same offense in an urban area might be sentenced quite differently. As noted in § 7.2, one response in some states was to craft statewide sentencing guidelines in the federal pattern. An aspect of these that turned out to be questionable was the right of a judge, either in or out of a guidelines state, to enhance a sentence on her own.

To illustrate, assume that state law in a "guidelines" state provides for a 10-year sentence for the crime of rape. The customary sentence is 10 years for forcible sexual intercourse with a nonconsenting adult female. However, further assume that state law allows the judge to enhance the sentence to 12 years if she finds there was "serious personal injury" inflicted upon the victim during the course of the rape. In other words, the judge could act unilaterally to add two years to the sentence, if the judge discovers the existence of this aggravating factor. Up until 2004, judges were permitted to regularly enhance sentences in this fashion. However, as observed in an earlier section of our text, the 2004 decision in *Blakely v. Washington*[45] changed things. After *Blakely*, judges no longer had a free hand to increase sentences.

---

[44]    Honorable Patti B. Saris, *Below the Radar Screens: Have the Sentencing Guidelines Eliminated Disparity? One Judge's Perspective*, 30 SUFFOLK U.L. REV. 1027 (1997). Congress responded by trying to iron out sentencing differences in 2003, and the Justice Department instituted a reporting system on federal judges who reduce sentences below the guidelines. *See* § 5.4.

[45]    124 S. Ct. 2531 (2004).

In the rape case example posed above, the claim of "serious personal injury" would have to be jury-tested. The facts supporting the additional two years of sentence must be found by a jury in cases in which a jury trial was requested, not simply by a judge.

## § 7.7   Restitution and Compensation of Victims

Concern about the fact that the victim of a crime generally receives nothing for his or her loss has given rise to two ideas in criminal justice administration: **restitution** (making the offender pay or work to restore damage) or, where this is not possible, **compensation** payments from public funds.

### 1. Restitution

Noting that business firms frequently settle thefts by employees privately, one law reform commission urged liberal use of restitution orders as a sentencing tool.[46] The commission first traced the history of restitution in the early law of England:

> As the common law developed, criminal law became a distinct branch of law. Numerous antisocial acts were seen to be "offences against the state" or "crimes" rather than personal wrongs or torts. This tendency to characterize some wrongs as "crimes" was encouraged by the practice under which the lands and property of convicted persons were forfeited to the king or feudal lord; fines, as well, became payable to feudal lords and not to the victim. The natural practice of compensating the victim or his relatives was discouraged by making it an offense to conceal the commission of a felony or convert the crime into a source of profit. In time, fines and property that would have gone in satisfaction of the victim's claims were diverted to the state. . . .

Today, some courts are inclined to require reimbursement to the victim from the defendant who caused the victim's injury or damage. Others are not. One authority suggests that wider use be made of this sentencing tool:

> Restitution should become a central consideration in sentencing and dispositions. The term "central consideration" is used to indicate that restitution would merit foremost, but not exclusive, consideration. What is anticipated is a range of sanctions ranging from relatively light to severe, with restitution receiving consideration in most offenses.

> In many cases, especially those not requiring deprivation of liberty, restitution may be the main sanction. Yet it would hardly be just were the offender merely required to pay back what he had taken. It is fitting that he would be required to pay back more than he took. Consequently, in many cases, a fine would be an appropriate additional sanction in recognition of the harm done to society and the costs involved in upholding values and protecting individual rights. . . .[47]

---

[46] *Restitution and Compensation*, 8-9, 14-15, Law Reform Commission of Canada (1974).
[47] *Ibid.*

Several American cases have viewed the purpose of restitution to be not only reimbursement of the victim, but also rehabilitation of the defendant. This rehabilitative purpose means that the payment ordered should not exceed the defendant's capacity to pay. On the other hand, where rehabilitation is the core idea and the offender is allowed to remain free on condition that he make restitution, the restitution order means the defendant can be required to repay even when the victim was insured.[48]

A restitution award is available in federal court under the Victim and Witness Protection Act for loss caused by the specific conduct of the defendant who is convicted.[49] In addition, in 1996 Congress enacted the Mandatory Victim Restitution Act. This act requires federal judges to impose restitution to victims as a mandatory part of criminal sentences for violent crimes, drug-related offenses, consumer product tampering, and crimes against property.[50]

Victims sometimes need to be aware of the location of offenders, and recent laws have endeavored to address this subject in several ways, with a variety of notification statutes on the books. For example, in a number of states victims are entitled to know that a prisoner who was responsible for their injury is coming up for parole. Others make it mandatory that victims be notified of a decision to release an inmate. Sex offender registration laws are detailed in § 7.13 of this text.

In addition to court-ordered restitution, the crime victim sometimes sues the wrongdoer. An injured party can file a civil suit against the defendant and seek monetary relief through traditional civil litigation. A woman sued basketball star Kobe Bryant for allegedly raping her in Colorado, in addition to the criminal charges that were brought against him. Earlier, the parents of Nicole Simpson and Ron Goldman won a multimillion dollar judgment against O.J. Simpson for their deaths. The conviction of a defendant in criminal courts is not always essential to the success of the civil action. "As demonstrated by the well-reported O.J. Simpson trials, recovery of civil damages requires a less demanding burden of proof [than criminal cases], and substantial awards may be won even after a jury fails to find criminal liability."[51]

## 2. Compensation

Sometimes the identity of an offender is unknown to the injured victim or, if known, the criminal is penniless and cannot pay back the loss. Prospects for substantial restitution are slim, yet there is a need to compensate the victim of a crime. Law reformers urge that the states establish state-financed programs of reparations, especially when the victim has been seriously injured by a crime of violence and is unable to work. Several have done so. The American Bar Association's House of Delegates approved the Uniform Crime Victims

---

[48]   Commonwealth v. Kerr, 444 A.2d 758, 760 (Pa. Super. 1982).

[49]   Hughey v. United States, 110 S. Ct. 1979 (1990).

[50]   18 U.S.C. § 3663A(c)(2004).

[51]   David L. Goldberg, *Civil Remedies for Criminal Conduct*, 30 LITIGATION 32, 34 (Spring 2004).

Reparations Act. One commentator sets forth the assorted reasons for a victim assistance statute:

> Justification for such an act is variously stated. Some persons say the state owes this to victims, having induced citizens to lay down their own arms in reliance on state protection and then having failed to prevent crime. Others urge parity between the expensive concern society lavishes on offenders—constitutional safeguards, free counsel, prison accommodations—and the concern shown their victims. . . .

> Probably the principal explanation for the burgeoning interest in this kind of act is simple humanitarianism—a recognition that we all share an interest in the well-being of our neighbors and an increasing willingness to distribute the cost of catastrophe.[52]

One of the sections of the Uniform Act includes provision for an upward ceiling of compensation to the victim. Money is paid in the amount of the victim's personal injury or death due to "criminally injurious conduct." Injuries to property are excluded. Some states that have reparation laws list certain particular crimes that give rise to compensation, while other jurisdictions allow recovery for "any violent crime."

Under the Uniform Act, when a parent is killed by a criminal (for example, the husband in a family where he is the wage earner) the dependents can collect a compensation award that might include an allowance for funeral and related expenses, as well as recovery for economic loss. The Uniform Act provides for administration by a Crime Victims Reparations Board, a part of the executive branch of the state, which makes the compensation awards. An applicant for an award of reparations must show that the criminal conduct that resulted in injury or death was reported to a law enforcement officer within a limited period after its occurrence.[53]

## § 7.8   Rights of the Accused

In the field of criminal case sentencing, there are several rights that inure to the benefit of accused persons. The double jeopardy provision of the Fifth Amendment to the United States Constitution safeguards against two distinct dangers: multiple prosecution for the same offense and multiple punishment for the same crime. Accordingly, federal cases have disapproved of consecutive sentences when the two offenses in question arose out of the same identical facts and transaction.[54]

---

[52]   Paul F. Rothstein, *How the Uniform Crime Victims Reparations Act Works*, 60 A.B.A.J. 1531, 1533 (1974).

[53]   If not so reported, the claimant must show good cause for failure to report within that time. 11 U.L.A. 40 (1974). Rape trauma syndrome as good cause, *see* White v. Violent Crimes Compensation Bd., 388 A.2d 206 (N.J. 1978).

[54]   *See* Whalen v. United States, 445 U.S. 684, 100 S. Ct. 1432, 63 L. Ed. 2d 715 (1980). The test for determining whether more than one offense has been committed is whether some additional fact is required to prove the second crime. United States v. Sanford, 673 F.2d 1070 (9th Cir. 1982).

In addition, the defendant is entitled to a "reasonable" punishment for the crime—a sentence that is not greatly disproportionate to the offense charged. Punishment for the crime should be graduated and proportioned to the offense. It was not in *Solem v. Helm*,[55] when a South Dakota court sentenced Helm to life imprisonment after conviction for his seventh nonviolent offense. None of the prior convictions involved a crime against the person. The conviction that triggered the life sentence occurred when Helm entered a "no account" check for $100. Because the United States Supreme Court viewed Helm's crime as "one of the most passive felonies a person could commit" involving nonviolence, Helm's life sentence without parole was unconstitutionally harsh. The Supreme Court prohibited the sentence, finding that Helm "has received the penultimate sentence for relatively minor criminal conduct."

Rights to personal participation and to advice of counsel form other aspects of sentencing proceedings. While misdemeanors may be disposed of in the absence of the defendant, in felony cases the defendant is entitled to be personally present at every stage of the trial, including the imposition of sentence. After sentencing, the defendant should be advised by the trial judge both of his or her right to appeal and of the right of a person without funds to appeal as a pauper at public expense.[56] The defendant also has the right to have a lawyer appear with him or her at sentencing to argue on his or her behalf. This includes the right to have an appointed lawyer assist him or her if the defendant is indigent. The state will be represented by the prosecutor at sentencing.

Legal principles guaranteeing the defendant counsel at the sentencing stage were pioneered in the United States Supreme Court case of *Townsend v. Burke*.[57] These principles were again emphasized in *Mempa v. Rhay*,[58] another Supreme Court decision: "There was no occasion in *Gideon* [*v. Wainwright*] to enumerate the various stages in a criminal proceeding at which counsel was required. . . . In particular, *Townsend v. Burke, supra,* illustrates the critical nature of sentencing in a criminal case and might well be considered to support by itself a holding that the right to counsel applies at sentencing."

In addition to a defendant's right to counsel at sentencing, a defendant has the further right to ask the sentencing judge, when he or she is assessing sentence, to disregard prior convictions that are invalid under *Gideon v. Wainwright*.[59] In *United States v. Tucker*,[60] the sentencing judge gave attention to prior convictions achieved many years before when the defendant had been unrepresented by counsel. The government asked the Supreme Court to let Tucker's 25-year prison sentence stand, but the Court disagreed:

---

[55]   103 S. Ct. 3001 (1983). The *Solem* test of disproportionality was limited by Harmelin v. Michigan, 111 S. Ct. 2680 (1991).

[56]   *See* FED. R. CRIM. P. 43 (personal presence of defendant required) and FED. R. CRIM. P. 32 (notification of right to appeal). An exception to the personal presence rule where the defendant is unruly discussed in § 6.33.

[57]   334 U.S. 736, 68 S. Ct. 1252, 92 L. Ed. 1690 (1948).

[58]   389 U.S. 128, 134, 88 S. Ct. 254, 19 L. Ed. 2d 336 (1967).

[59]   372 U.S. 335, 83 S. Ct. 792, 9 L. Ed. 2d 799 (1963) (conviction invalid if indigent defendant not afforded a right to appointed counsel in felony prosecution).

[60]   404 U.S. 443, 92 S. Ct. 589, 30 L. Ed. 2d 592 (1972).

The government is . . . on solid ground in asserting that a sentence imposed by a federal district judge, if within statutory limits, is generally not subject to review. . . .

But these general propositions do not decide the case before us. For we deal here not with a sentence imposed in the informed discretion of a trial judge, but with a sentence founded at least in part upon misinformation of constitutional magnitude. As in *Townsend v. Burke*, 334 U.S. 736, 68 S. Ct. 1252, 92 L. Ed. 1690, "this prisoner was sentenced on the basis of assumptions concerning his criminal record which were materially untrue." The record in the present case makes evident that the sentencing judge gave specific consideration to the respondent's previous convictions before imposing sentence upon him. Yet it is now clear that two of those convictions were wholly unconstitutional under *Gideon v. Wainwright*, 372 U.S. 335, 83 S. Ct. 792.[61]

The Court ordered reevaluation of Tucker's sentence. Similarly, when state law allows a defendant's sentence to be enhanced under recidivist sentencing statutes (frequently requiring jury conviction of the defendant as a habitual offender), the jury may be shown only those prior convictions that were achieved when counsel was present, or when counsel was offered the accused and this right was intelligently waived. "[T]o permit a conviction obtained in violation of *Gideon v. Wainwright* to . . . enhance punishment for another offense . . . is to erode the principle of that case."[62]

Perhaps the one exception to the foregoing principles occurs when the sentencing court considers previous uncounseled misdemeanor convictions in determining the sentence for a subsequent offense. In *Nichols v. United States*,[63] the United States Supreme Court ruled the sentencing use of such a misdemeanor to be proper, as long as the uncounseled conviction did not result in incarceration.

A major question in the right-to-counsel field carries the focus of the discussion from the sentencing stage to the field of revocation of probation for violations of conditional liberty. The details of the revocation process are contained in § 7.10 and will be analyzed there. What is important at this point is whether the right to a lawyer free of charge, available to poor persons at sentencing, spills over into the field of probation revocation.[64] Many states provide by statute for counsel to assist the accused at revocation of probation proceedings, and in a few states such right is extended to parolees facing revocation. The question is, in those states without such provisions in their state law, must the right to counsel be observed in order to comply with the federal Constitution? Does a state probationer have a federal constitutional right to counsel in probation revocation? Several lower court decisions answer this question in the negative, although some confusion was spawned by the

---

[61]   The Court noted that the respondent's convictions occurred years before the *Gideon* case was decided, but the impact of that decision was fully retroactive.

[62]   Burgett v. Texas, 389 U.S. 109, 88 S. Ct. 258, 19 L. Ed. 2d 319 (1967).

[63]   114 S. Ct. 1921 (1994).

[64]   Revocation in federal courts, *see* FED. R. CRIM PROC. 32.1.

Supreme Court's decision in *Mempa v. Rhay*, cited earlier in this section. The *Mempa* case arose under a Washington law in which the sentencing judge who placed felony offenders on probation also deferred any sentence in the case. Under this procedure, in the event conditional release was violated and probation revoked, sentence was imposed at the time of probation revocation. This is what happened to probationer Mempa in *Mempa v. Rhay*, and the Supreme Court ruled that he was entitled to counsel at this stage of the proceedings.

The *Mempa* decision led some authorities to argue that the defendant had an automatic right to counsel whenever probation was revoked. Others pointed out that most states provide for sentencing of the defendant before he or she goes on probation (suspending execution of the announced sentence during defendant's good behavior), and the *Mempa* case was merely another counsel-at-sentencing decision. Thus, the argument went, in most jurisdictions the right to free counsel terminated with completion of the sentencing stage and did not extend thereafter to the point in time when probation was revoked. Those who urged this position pointed to the Supreme Court's statement a year after the *Mempa* case, in which the Court explained the *Mempa* decision: "The right to counsel at *sentencing* must, therefore, be treated like the right to counsel at other stages of adjudication." (emphasis added)[65]

The United States Supreme Court provided needed clarification in *Gagnon v. Scarpelli*.[66] Under *Gagnon*, a free attorney is not automatic in probation revocations. On the other hand, states may not flatly deny attorneys for all probationers. In revocation situations in which it would be fundamentally unfair to a probationer to be unrepresented, the appointment of counsel for poor persons is required. This federal requirement provides at least the minimum standard binding on the states, and must be applied on a case-by-case basis. An example of a case in which appointment of counsel might not be called for under Supreme Court guidelines would be the case of a probationer with skills in law, perhaps college-trained, who is articulate and has had prior experience with such proceedings.

## § 7.9   Probation and Parole

### 1. Probation

Under **probation** the convicted offender is released into the community subject to the control and supervision of a probation agency. Probation is widely used in the United States and is available as a sentencing device in most crimes, although numerous states prohibit the granting of probation in certain very serious offenses such as murder, kidnapping, sale of drugs, or burglary with explosives. Normally, when probation is granted, the defendant is not sent to the penitentiary unless probation is revoked, the period of pro-

---

[65]   McConnell v. Rhay, 393 U.S. 2, 4, 89 S. Ct. 32, 21 L. Ed. 2d 2 (1968).
[66]   411 U.S. 778, 93 S. Ct. 1756, 36 L. Ed. 2d 656 (1973).

bation serving as an alternative to penitentiary confinement. Some states, however, observe the practice of "split" sentencing, authorizing the trial judge to require the defendant to serve a short time in prison prior to release on probation, or as a condition of probation. Probation is a flexible sentencing device; some courts authorize release of a defendant from jail during the working hours of the day but require his or her return at night as a condition of probation.

Whether a defendant will be placed on probation instead of full prison detention depends on several factors, including the potential dangerousness or lack thereof of the offender, the character of the criminal act done by the defendant (whether violent or nonviolent), the defendant's need for institutional treatment, the defendant's willingness to make restitution, and the defendant's history of criminal activity (MODEL PENAL CODE § 7.01).

Responsibility for supervising the probationer generally falls upon the probation service or agency connected with the sentencing court, and it is this agency that has the task of preparing the presentence investigation report. The concept of the PSIR was introduced in § 7.1; it reflects a background investigation of the defendant, his family, prior criminal record, and other matters. From it the judge will glean much information needed in applying probation criteria similar to those illustrated in the Model Penal Code.

Important to the probation agency is the question of whether the defense, prior to sentencing, has a right to see this report. Some jurisdictions require that the presentence report be available for inspection by the offender. In others, however, the report is confidential. Some take a middle course and leave disclosure to the discretion of the trial judge.[67]

In exercising such discretion, judges have been urged by several probation authorities to carefully limit disclosure of the report because (1) disclosure would dry up sources of confidential information, inasmuch as those acquainted with the defendant would be reluctant to talk candidly for fear of retaliation by him or her; and (2) where the defendant is to be supervised on probation by the same officer who compiled the presentence report, disclosure can interfere with the relationship between the two and impede the defendant's progress in those cases where a part of the report was unfavorable to the defendant.

## 2. Parole

**Parole** is a concept distinct from probation. Parole is the conditional release of a defendant who has been sentenced to prison confinement and whose record recommends him or her for release after the prisoner has served a part of the full term of such confinement. Normally, probation operates in lieu of jail confinement, whereas parole applies only after the convicted person has served a portion of his or her time. While probation is granted by the trial judge, the parole decision is made by a parole board or other state agency.

---

[67] FED. R. CRIM. P. 32 (c)(3)(A) (defendant or defendant's counsel entitled to see report except confidential material or information harmful to defendant or others). Capital cases, defendant's right to report, *see* Gardner v. Florida, 430 U.S. 439 (1977).

Parole should also be distinguished from a pardon. A pardon is a distinct concept, with only the chief executive of the jurisdiction having power to grant it.[68] A **pardon** is an act of forgiveness that absolves the defendant of further obligation to the state, while the parolee continues to carry such obligations.

Parole is designed to assist the offender in readjusting to society, with parole officers to help in securing employment and to provide advice and counsel to the prisoner during tentative release. The interposing of halfway houses and prerelease centers between jail and full parole is another option for helping offenders make the transition. Parolees are selected from the prison population after evidencing fitness for parole. Criteria for use by parole boards in making the parole determination include the foreseeability of future harm by the defendant, whether this release will depreciate the seriousness of his or her criminal act, the prisoner's maturity, his or her ability to assume work and family responsibilities, his or her employment and criminal history, the neighborhood in which the prisoner plans to live, and other factors.[69]

Today there is pressure on parole boards from a couple of directions. On the one hand, exploding prison populations lead to overcrowding. Liberal paroles are often considered as a means to reduce prison populations and alleviate the problem. Packed prisons frequently lead to talk of easier paroles. On the other hand, parole boards are loathe to readily parole hardened criminals who have committed serious crimes. In addition, parole boards are restricted from softening policies by get-tough laws that require prisoners to serve at least 90 percent of the sentence handed down by the judge, and to serve that much time before the prisoner qualifies for release. Some have argued that states should narrow the number of crimes that fall under the minimum sentence laws. They claim that laws requiring that the 90 percent minimum—or other similar percentage, depending on the sentencing minimum in any particular state—unduly strain taxpayers' pocket books. The costs of incarceration are high.

In felony cases, the federal system has moved in the direction of straight time sentencing (fewer good conduct credits) and elimination of parole.[70]

## § 7.10   Revoking Conditional Freedom

Probationers and parolees are given their freedom subject to specified conditions. These usually include requirements that the offender refrain from committing a new offense while on probation or parole, refrain from associating with individuals of bad repute, and that he or she report periodically to a

---

[68]   Executive power (vested in state governors; President of United States for federal crimes), can be employed to grant several kinds of relief. Pardon has been mentioned. Other remedies include reprieve (the withdrawing for a time or postponing of execution of a sentence), and commutation of sentence (the reduction of punishment for a specified offense without removing the guilt of the offender). Schick v. Reed, 419 U.S. 256, 95 S. Ct. 379, 42 L. Ed. 2d 430 (1974).

[69]   MODEL PENAL CODE § 7.01.

[70]   See note 16 *supra* and accompanying text.

probation or parole officer. Other conditions may require the defendant to maintain employment, to refrain from leaving a particular state, or to avoid excessive use of alcohol. Careful observance of imposed restrictions during the probationary or parole period will result in the discharge of the offender from these conditions after expiration of a specified period. When the conditions are violated during the trial period, however, the offender may be arrested and his or her freedom terminated.[71]

Some statutes dealing with probation and parole revocation require that an arrest warrant be issued by the revoking authority before revocation proceedings can be initiated. Other states do not require preliminary issuance of an arrest warrant; their view in the parole field is that the parolee technically remains a prisoner even while out on parole, and it is unnecessary for a parole officer to apply for a warrant to arrest one who is at all times during that person's release in the officer's constructive custody.[72]

Two distinct procedural issues arise when revocation takes place. Is the offender who is about to have his or her conditional freedom revoked entitled to a full hearing, with presentation of evidence, before a court order terminating his or her freedom is entered? Is the offender entitled to be represented by a lawyer, and to have one appointed for him or her in the event he or she cannot afford one?

## 1. Probation

Since 1973, the United States Supreme Court has made clear that a probationer is entitled to two hearings: (1) a preliminary hearing at the time of his or her arrest to determine whether there is probable cause to believe he or she has committed a violation of probation, and (2) a somewhat more comprehensive hearing prior to making the final revocation decision. The alleged violator has the right to receive written notice of when and where his or her final revocation hearing will be conducted, and apprising him or her of the particular grounds upon which revocation is sought. The offender is entitled to introduce evidence in his or her behalf, including his or her own testimony. While many states allow representation by a lawyer if the probationer has one, it is less clear whether he or she has the right to have a lawyer appointed if he or she cannot afford to hire one. Some courts have provided free counsel in this situation, others have not. While the Supreme Court has not decreed a general right to counsel for probationers in all states, requirements have been imposed. For states that traditionally denied appointed lawyers in revocation proceed-

---

[71] In probation revocation proceedings, the court may impose sanctions less dramatic than revocation, like issuing the probationer a warning or extending the term of probation.

[72] Several states follow the same approach in probation revocation, either through a theory similar to that advanced in the text or by denominating probation agents as law enforcement officers under state statute.

ings, one point was made clear by the Supreme Court: states cannot deny such rights as a blanket proposition in probation or parole revocation.[73]

Of interest to the probation officer is whether his or her witnesses must appear and testify in order to sustain the officer's recommendation of revocation. Prior to *Morrissey v. Brewer*[74] and the *Gagnon*[75] case, few courts appear to have required confrontation with these government witnesses in probation revocation proceedings. Confidential information that was placed in a recommendation to the court was frequently protected also. Under *Morrissey*, however, people who have given adverse information are to be made available for questioning in the probationer's presence, except in cases in which the hearing officer (usually a judge) determines they would be subject to risk of harm if their identities were known. At the hearing the state must demonstrate the offender's breach of conditional freedom. In so doing, the formal rules of evidence are much relaxed,[76] and the defendant's breach of condition need only be proved by a preponderance of the evidence, or in some states by evidence of "any probative value." The heavier burden of proof in criminal trials that requires proof beyond a reasonable doubt is not exacted here.

In federal practice, Federal Rule of Criminal Procedure 32.1 provides for revocation of probation or supervised release. At the hearing, the probationer is given notice of the hearing and written notice of the alleged violation, an opportunity to question witnesses, and notice of his or her right to be represented by counsel.

In 1983, the Supreme Court added a further development to the law of probation revocation: A state cannot revoke an indigent defendant's probation for failure to pay a fine. Automatic revocation is improper, and in the case in question violated the defendant's equal protection rights under the Fourteenth Amendment. If a probationer cannot pay despite bona fide efforts to do so, Justice O'Connor announced, a court must consider alternative measures other than automatic imprisonment. "Only if alternate measures are not adequate to meet the state's interests in punishment and deterrence may the court imprison a probationer who has made sufficient bona fide efforts to pay."[77]

## 2. Parole

It has been indicated that a right to a hearing exists in probation revocation proceedings. A similar rule has been adopted for parole. "The first [hearing] stage occurs when the parolee is arrested and detained, usually at the

---

[73]   Gagnon v. Scarpelli, note 66 *supra*, and accompanying text, which states that the need for counsel must be decided on a case-by-case basis, and appointed counsel is indicated when the probationer makes a colorable claim that he has not committed the alleged violation or where the prisoner is not capable of speaking effectively for himself.

[74]   408 U.S. 471, 92 S. Ct. 2593, 33 L. Ed. 2d 484 (1972). *Morrissey v. Brewer* deals with parole revocations.

[75]   Note 66 *supra*. *Gagnon* extended the rules established for parole violators to probation violators.

[76]   Some states permit illegally seized evidence to be admitted in probation revocations to show the breach of condition. A similar approach may be used in parole revocations. See note 82 *infra*.

[77]   Bearden v. Georgia, 103 S. Ct. 2064 (1983).

direction of his or her parole officer. The second occurs when parole is formally revoked. There is typically a substantial time lag between the arrest and the eventual determination by the parole board whether parole should be revoked. Additionally, it may be that the parolee is arrested at a place distant from the state institution to which he may be returned before the final decision is made concerning revocation. Given these factors, due process would seem to require that some minimal inquiry be conducted at or reasonably near the place of the alleged parole violation or arrest and as promptly as convenient after arrest while information is fresh and sources are available. Such an inquiry should be seen as in the nature of a preliminary hearing to determine whether there is probable cause or reasonable grounds to believe that the arrested parolee has committed acts that would constitute a violation of parole conditions.[78]

In parole revocations, while a few jurisdictions may place revoking authority in the judge, most states appear to give the parole board authority to conduct these. A common pattern is to provide by rule or statute that after a paroled prisoner is arrested for violation of his or her parole, he or she shall be afforded an appearance before the board. In the past, several states denied the right to counsel at such hearings. Since then, the case-by-case rule of the Supreme Court has been handed down,[79] dictating that in at least some hearings counsel must be appointed. Some states offer counsel at revocations on a regular basis. In certain jurisdictions a rule is maintained that appears to go beyond the Supreme Court's minimum requirements, broadly extending the counsel guarantee to recommitment hearings.[80]

In parole revocations there has not been a general rule rendering revocation reports prepared by the parole officer or other staff members subject to subpoena by the offender. However, *Morrissey v. Brewer* decreed that there is a right on the part of the parolee to cross-examine witnesses from whom the parole officer has obtained information supporting the revocation determination, unless the hearing officer determines that the informant would be subjected to risk of harm if his or her identity were disclosed.[81]

In probation or parole revocation proceedings, does the exclusionary rule apply? A Pennsylvania case enforced the rule when a search turned up evidence of a parole violation. The officer conducting the search did not have any initial information of a violation, so there was a lack of probable cause. The United States Supreme Court reviewed the issue of whether the exclusionary rule was needed to deter illegal searches that are aimed at obtaining evidence of a parole violation in *Pennsylvania Board of Probation and Parole v. Scott.*[82] The United States Supreme Court took a different view than the Pennsylvania Supreme Court, with the U.S. Supreme Court holding that parole boards are not required by federal law to exclude evidence obtained in violation of the Fourth Amendment.

---

[78] Morrissey v. Brewer, note 74 *supra.*
[79] *See* notes 66 and 74 *supra* and accompanying text.
[80] On other developments regarding parole, *see* § 10.20 *infra.*
[81] Morrissey v. Brewer, note 74 *supra.*
[82] 118 S. Ct. 2014 (1998).

Upon revocation of parole, the parolee returns to prison for the unfinished portion of his sentence. Ordinarily, no credit is given for "street time."

## § 7.11   Detainers

Some jurisdictions are now paroling prisoners to detainers from another state, which allows the release of the prisoner from state X while he serves another sentence or answers charges in state Y. A **detainer**, or hold order, may be filed by a prosecutor, police chief, or other official. It is filed with the authorities who have custody of a prisoner, advising the incarcerating authorities that the prisoner is wanted, and requesting that the incarcerating authorities notify the detainer officials near the time when the defendant is scheduled to be released, so that they can arrange to pick him or her up.

Prison officials have frequently criticized detainers, terming them "corrosive" and counter-rehabilitative. The point has been made that a prisoner has little incentive toward self-improvement when at the conclusion of his sentence he will be taken into custody by another state.[83] Prisoners under detainer are sometimes denied privileges given other prisoners, such as serving as a trusty or living in a minimum-security area. Where the detainer state wishes to try the defendant, as opposed to the defendant already having been convicted there, provisions of the interstate detainer compact and the Uniform Mandatory Disposition of Detainer Act require a trial of the defendant in the requesting state within a specified period after the defendant demands it. Such provisions would appear to alleviate some of the prisoner anxiety cited by penologists in the detainer situation, in that the prisoner could move to prompt disposition of the pending case upon proper demand.

## § 7.12   Conditions of Confinement

Prisoner suits and access to the courts are subjects reviewed in detail in §§ 10.19 and 10.20; however, it is important to briefly note in this chapter on sentencing and penology an emerging issue—that of the inmate's right to sue regarding dangerous or inhumane prison conditions. Some of the more significant cases have held that prison facilities must be safe, that minimum medical care must be available,[84] and also that minimum standards of nutrition must be maintained. Overcrowding is another serious problem. Statistics reveal an inmate population explosion. Some two-person cells have been

---

[83]   See this opinion by James V. Bennett, former director of the Federal Bureau of Prisons, writing in Bennett, *The Last Full Ounce*, 23 FEDERAL PROBATION 20, 21 (June, 1959). See also Smith v. Hooey, 393 U.S. 374, 89 S. Ct. 575, 21 L. Ed. 2d 607 (1969).

[84]   On the right to treatment where a patient is confined for mental illness, *see* O'Connor v. Donaldson, 422 U.S. 563, 95 S. Ct. 2486, 45 L. Ed. 2d 396 (1975); Eckerhart v. Hensley, 475 F. Supp. 908 (W.D. Mo. 1979).

occupied by four or five people. One local jail, designed to properly hold only 228 prisoners, was crammed with 810 inmates. Such overcrowding has been stopped by the courts when it reached intolerable limits.

The population in America's prisons is at an all-time high.[85] By 2004, more than 2.1 million people were behind bars. Overcrowding in many facilities is massive, despite new prison construction programs. The challenge of providing a humane and constitutional corrections system in the face of such pressure, and with limited prison capacity, is staggering.

One in every 75 men in the United States is in prison. The number of women in state and federal prisons grows by about five percent each year. State prisons are running out of money and space. Crowding is fueled by get-tough sentences requiring prisoners to remain in jail for a specified amount of their sentence—often 90 percent of the time announced by the sentencing judge. One out of every 11 inmates is serving a life sentence.

Burgeoning prison populations put pressure on wardens and guards to maintain appropriate discipline and protect the safety of those inside the walls, supervisors as well as prisoners. Those administering prisons have been known to separate inmates by race for their first 60 days in the system. This is done to assist prison officials in assessing whether inmates are in gangs and might be prone to racial violence. It has been argued that violence can erupt if white and black gang members are mixed. Courts are in the process of deciding whether this practice is appropriate and constitutional or, on the other hand, whether it violates the Constitution's guarantee of equal protection under the law.[86]

Prison population increases are not the result of more crime. Rather, the responsibility lies with longer mandatory sentences and more restrictive parole policies.

In the face of overwhelming inmate numbers, maintaining discipline within these institutions is a constant challenge. Disciplinary actions against prisoners, such as the use of solitary confinement, must conform to standards of decency. A leading case on this point, *Sostre v. McGinnis*,[87] held that an inmate's lengthy stay in solitary violated due process of law if imposed as a punishment for a prisoner's litigation against state officials. The United States Court of Appeals for the Second Circuit ruled that such disciplinary procedures must be minimally fair, which would mean at least being confronted with the accusation and informed of the evidence.

DNA testing of inmates is on the rise. Detection of crime has been aided by state laws requiring jail inmates to provide DNA samples. Many old crimes have been cleared by determining that a person, now a prisoner on another charge, committed a rape or murder at an earlier time while he was not incarcerated. Many states also have reciprocal provisions for using scientific tech-

---

[85]   There is a need for over 1,000 new prison beds each week.
[86]   Johnson v. California, 125 S Ct. 1141 (2005) (California's policy of segregating by race will not pass equal protection muster unless corrections officials can show, upon remand, that the policy is needed to curb violence caused by racial gangs).
[87]   442 F.2d 178 (2d Cir. 1971).

niques to help to exonerate wrongly convicted prisoners. In these jurisdictions, post-conviction DNA testing of evidence can be requested by the inmate. Such DNA testing sometimes results in exoneration of defendants who were misidentified by eyewitnesses or otherwise falsely convicted.

In October 2004, President Bush signed into law a measure that provides $1 billion over five years to provide greater access to DNA testing. There are provisions to aid victims by helping to solve crimes through DNA techniques. There are measures designed to aid prisoners by improving legal representation in death penalty cases. The legislation also ensures DNA tests for those serving prison sentences, including prisoners on death row.

## § 7.13  Special Treatment of the Sexual Offender: Sexual Psychopath Laws and Sexual Predator Registration

Confinement other than in a penitentiary may result from the operation of particularized sentencing statutes. An example is sexual psychopath legislation that directs commitment of sexually dangerous persons to centers for the mentally ill.

Special statutes in a significant number of states provide for commitment and confinement of dangerous sex offenders. The pattern of these laws allows the prosecutor, when a defendant is charged with a crime, to petition the court to commit the defendant to a mental hospital as a sexually dangerous person. Detention of the defendant is usually indeterminate; release is conditioned upon the detainee's mental condition being corrected to the point that he or she is fit to return to full liberty without danger to the public. Some sexual psychopath laws authorize confinement of the offender for a maximum term that can occupy the person's natural life. These laws reflect a feeling that traditional criminal law penalties are not sufficient to protect society from sexual predator crimes.

During the 1990s, interest was revived in sexual psychopath legislation. New state legislation was enacted during that period. News coverage of sex crimes, often crimes involving children, fueled fresh state enactments.[88] One of those new measures was titled the Sexually Violent Predator Law. In one state, if the state shows beyond a reasonable doubt that the offender is likely to engage in predatory acts of sexual violence, he or she can be confined until it is determined that he or she is prepared for release.[89]

The United States Supreme Court upheld the Kansas Sexually Violent Predator Act in 1997. The act established procedures for the civil commitment of persons who, as the result of a "mental abnormality" or a "personality disorder," were likely to engage in "predatory acts of sexual violence." The defendant in a Kansas case apparently had a history dating back to 1955 of sexually

---

[88]   Deborarh A. Denno, *Life Before the Modern Sex Offender Statutes*, 92 NORTHWESTERN L. REV. 1317, 1385 (1998).

[89]   *See* In re Young, 857 P.2d 989 (Wash. 1993).

molesting children and was repeatedly charged in 1957 and in 1960. Following treatment in a state mental hospital, he was discharged in 1965. By 1967 he was back in prison for molesting an eight-year-old girl and an 11-year-old boy. After another prison stay he was released, whereupon he engaged in molestation again. Again he was imprisoned and served nearly 10 years. Just before his release, the state filed a petition for civil commitment as a sexual predator. He was confined as a predator after a trial. The United States Supreme Court upheld the commitment as constitutional and one that did not violate double jeopardy rules.[90]

Sexual predator registration laws also appeared in some states in the early 1990s. Designed to aid investigators, these statutes generally require that, upon release from prison, a criminal convicted of rape, sodomy, or other sexual misconduct must register with local authorities where he takes up his residence. Sex Offender Registration Acts require that the offender update this registration whenever he changes his address. In addition, some state statutes allow for release of offender registration information to a victim or to the public in order to promote public safety.[91]

By 1998 these statutes, sometimes called "Megan's Laws," had been adopted in one form or another in more than 35 states.[92] Among other jurisdictions, New Jersey passed Megan's Law in an attempt to ensure that its sex offenders will be watched closely.[93] The United States Supreme Court was asked to decide whether the New Jersey provision that requires authorities to tell communities the whereabouts of convicted sex offenders violated double jeopardy laws. Sex offenders in New Jersey as well as New York complained that the notification provisions punished them a second time by holding them up to public scrutiny after they had already served their sentences for sexual crimes. The Supreme Court, acting without comment, rejected the challenges to the New Jersey law as well as to the New York statute, which had been enacted a year after the New Jersey measure.

The Supreme Court reinforced its endorsement of Megan's Law when it ruled that photos of convicted sex offenders may be posted on the Internet. States could use the World Wide Web to inform citizens about potential sexual predators in their neighborhoods. The Court upheld an Alaska law that required former offenders to report to police every 90 days to provide address information.

---

[90]   Kansas v. Hendricks, 117 S. Ct. 2072 (1997).

[91]   Julia A. Houston, Note, *Sex Offender Registration Acts,* 28 GA. L. REV. 729, 730-731 (1994).

[92]   Megan Kanka of New Jersey was raped and murdered by a convicted sexual offender. New Jersey passed a registration law which is codified at N.J. STAT. ANN. § 2C:7-1 to 7:5. There is also a federal registration act.

[93]   Sheila A. Campbell, *Battling Sex Offenders: Is Megan's Law an Effective Means of Achieving Public Safety?* 19 SETON H. LEG. J. 519 (1995). Laws in numerous other states included Connecticut, *see* Connecticut Dept. Pub. Safety v. Doe, 123 S. Ct. 1160 (2003). Alaska, *see* Smith v. Doe, 123 S. Ct. 1140 (2003) (reporting whereabouts to police required).

## § 7.14 Drugs and the Law

The surge in the prison population reported in § 7.12 has been attributed in part to the national strategy designed to punish those convicted of drug-related offenses with long sentences. Crime-fighting dollars have often been targeted for increased prison space. More incarcerations seem certain to come. Mandatory life sentences without parole have become a common, although not universal, statutory pattern for people convicted of possessing significant amounts of certain narcotics.

The war on drugs has a major focus of curtailing the supply of prohibited substances. The effort extends to foreign countries, where search and seizure rights of American drug agents have been expanded. A ruling of the Supreme Court gave United States law enforcement officials broad authority to conduct warrantless searches of non-United States citizens abroad. An international effort is under way. The Colombian government has conducted a war on drug traffickers. Traffickers were blamed for the death of a leading presidential candidate. During the crackdown that followed, traffickers retaliated with a destructive campaign of assassinations and car bombings. The terrorist campaign resulted in the slaying of police, judges, and bystanders. On behalf of the government, army troops and police officers have participated in repeated drug raids. Captured drug bosses have been turned over to United States agents for extradition to the United States.

How will the war on drugs end? While one long-range solution is to drive down demand—one prominent public official has said that victory in the drug war will come only after the American public's insatiable drug habit is brought under control—other short-term measures have been urged. Proposed solutions range from full-scale use of the United States Army and Navy to stop supplies, to legalization. While some hold that strict law enforcement and new laws are the answer, those in favor of legalization urge that we stop filling our jails with drug users. By legalizing drugs, they argue, millions of dollars would be taken away from ruthless drug dealers.

One study provides recommendations for reducing consumption. It decries the effectiveness of law enforcement efforts to intercept illicit drugs, and in the face of illegal substances pouring into the country urges treatment and rehabilitation programs: "The lesson of this study is that the existing federal legislative programs will not reduce the market demand for cocaine. The government continues to devote most federal resources to supply-side law enforcement methods that have a negligible effect on addicts, the people who consume most of the drug. On the demand side, insufficient resources have been devoted to treatment programs that may alter the behaviors of cocaine addicts. . . . To succeed at reducing market demand for cocaine, policymakers must do something different. They must design and fund programs that can remove large numbers of addicts from the population of cocaine users. Unless this goal is accomplished, the 'war on drugs' will remain unwon, and unwinnable."[94]

The debate about national drug policy will continue as the nation struggles to deal with the strain imposed by the drug problem on our police, courts, and prisons.

---

[94]  Morgan Cloud III, *Cocaine Demand and Addiction: A Study of the Possible Convergence of Rational Theory and National Policy*, 42 VAND. L. REV. 725, 817-818 (1989).

# Appeals and
# Habeas Corpus

Chapter Outline

affirm (a case)
appeal
brief
certiorari
clear and convincing evidence
discretionary review
dissenting opinion
habeas corpus
interlocutory appeal
issues of fact
issues of law
opinion of the court

post-conviction remedy
remand (a case)
retroactivity
reverse (a case)
stay of execution
watershed rule
writ of coram nobis
writ of habeas corpus
writ of injunction
writ of mandamus
writ of prohibition

## § 8.1   Appellate Court Structure

In every state as well as in federal cases, a person who is tried and convicted has a right to **appeal** a lower court decision that is adverse to him or her. Serious offense convictions are appealed directly from the trial court to the highest court in the state in a jurisdiction that has a two-tiered court structure. Many states, however, like California and Illinois, as well as the federal system, follow a three-tiered court pattern (e.g., United States District Court—Court of Appeals—Supreme Court, in the federal system). Under the three-tiered approach, felony cases are tried in the district court or other court of general trial jurisdiction, where the defendant has the right to have a jury hear and decide his or her case. Should the jury convict the accused and should the trial judge deny the defendant's post-trial motions (discussed in Chapter 6), an appeal may be taken as of right to the intermediate appellate court. Thereafter, a further appeal may or may not be permitted to the highest appellate court, depending on the merits of the case.

The intermediate appellate courts in the federal system are the United States Court of Appeals, of which there are 13.[1] They review cases from federal district courts located in various states over which they have jurisdiction. For example, the United States Court of Appeals for the Eighth Circuit reviews cases on appeal from federal district courts located in the states of Arkansas,

---

[1]   This figure includes the United States Court of Appeals for the District of Columbia, and for the Federal Circuit.

The Dual Court System: Simplified Flow Chart

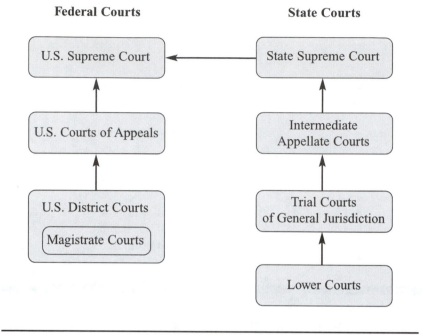

**Geographical Boundaries of U.S. Courts of Appeals and District Courts**

Iowa, Minnesota, Missouri, Nebraska, North Dakota, and South Dakota. State counterparts of this court include the Illinois Appellate Court, the California District Court of Appeals, or the Florida District Court of Appeals.

At the appellate level the case is heard exclusively by judges, and they may vote to **affirm** the decision below, thus leaving the verdict of conviction undisturbed, or overturn it and **reverse** the case. Reversal of the conviction almost always carries with it a **remand** of the case back to the lower court for a new trial. In the event the appellate court affirms, however, the defendant may have one avenue open to him or her in the three-tiered judicial system: the possibility of an additional appeal to the highest appellate court in the jurisdiction. These courts are courts of discretionary jurisdiction in that they pick and choose the cases they will hear. The Supreme Court of the United States is a good example. Outside of a few narrow exceptions, a party has no right to insist upon review of his or her case before such a court. Generally the case must possess sufficient importance, involving broad issues that have far-reaching implications, before it will be reviewed at the top level.

## § 8.2  Supreme Court of the United States

The pinnacle of the American justice system is the United States Supreme Court. The Supreme Court consists of the Chief Justice and eight Associate Justices. The Constitution extends the judicial power of this Court to include review of state court decisions that involve substantial federal questions, in addition to review of federal cases that originate in the federal court system. A major reason behind giving the Supreme Court authority over state as well as federal courts is to ensure that federal constitutional rights of persons will be respected in state trials.

Cases reach the Supreme Court primarily through a procedural device known as **certiorari**. A party who has lost a case in his state supreme court or the United States Court of Appeals may petition the Supreme Court to grant certiorari; that is, to hear and review the decision below. Certiorari will be granted only if at least four of the nine Justices on the Supreme Court vote preliminarily to hear the case. Each Justice studies the application individually and casts his or her vote at a conference of the Justices on whether to review the case as requested by the appellant.[2]

Certiorari is granted very sparingly. In any given year, thousands of litigants may apply to have their claims reviewed by the Supreme Court. The Court will grant review in as few as three or four percent of the cases.[3] The reason for this fine screening was made clear by a former Chief Justice: "To remain effective, the Supreme Court must continue to decide only those cases which present questions whose resolution will have immediate importance far

[2]   C. WRIGHT, LAW OF FEDERAL COURTS, 494 (2d ed. 1970).
[3]   STERN & GRESSMAN, SUPREME COURT PRACTICE, 164 (7th ed. 1993).

beyond the particular facts and parties involved."[4] Reasons that may persuade the Court to grant certiorari involve conflicts between two or more United States Courts of Appeals on the same matter; when a state supreme court has decided a federal question in a way that conflicts with another state's decision or with a decision of a federal court of appeals; or when an important matter of federal law needs to be settled.

A primary purpose in establishing one supreme national tribunal was to secure and preserve national rights in all American courts. Thus, the function of the Supreme Court is to pass upon questions of wide import arising under the United States Constitution, and under federal statutes. "The importance of the issues involved in the case as to which review is sought is of major significance in determining whether the writ of certiorari will issue. . . . Where the writ of certiorari is granted, a combination of factors is usually present to lead the Court to believe that the case is sufficiently important to warrant further review."[5] Selection of cases for review is difficult when more than 6,000 applications are filed in a year, as often occurs. Only about 200 of the 6,000 or so cases that are filed annually are heard in any given year. Important constitutional issues receive priority.[6]

In the 1960s, controversy raged concerning the appropriate role of the Supreme Court, particularly in connection with important criminal law questions arising out of state prosecutions. While that particular debate has subsided, it is important that students of the criminal justice system be aware of the evolution of the Court's judicial philosophy from 1961 through the 2000s. Views critical of the "activist" bent of the Warren Supreme Court were widespread.[7] These critical views were advanced during the heyday of the Warren Court's expansion of criminal procedural rights. The exclusionary rule was broadened to sanction overreaching police searches; *Miranda* imposed warning requirements when police interrogated suspects, and the Court vigorously expanded the rule that prosecutors must refrain from commenting on the failure of an accused to take the stand in a criminal trial.[8] It became important for rank-and-file police officers on the beat to undergo schooling in recent Supreme Court decisions. Charges of "criminal coddling" were aimed at the Court.

Another criticism leveled at the Warren Court was that it made binding on the states a large number of federal criminal procedure rules, smothering state experimentation in the field. Justice Harlan sounded this theme in his dissenting opinion to the Supreme Court decision in *Duncan v. Louisiana*.[9]

---

[4]  Address by Chief Justice Vinson, American Bar Association (Sept. 7, 1949), reprinted in 69 S. Ct. pp. v, vi.

[5]  STERN & GRESSMAN, SUPREME COURT PRACTICE, 184 (7th ed. 1993).

[6]  *Id*. at 185.

[7]  Through 1969 Earl Warren served as Chief Justice of the U.S. Supreme Court and the Court during the 1960s was commonly referred to as the Warren Court because of the name and style of the Chief Justice. Thereafter Warren Burger became Chief Justice, thus the reference to the Burger Court. Finally, Justice William Rehnquist heads the Rehnquist Court.

[8]  Griffin v. California, 380 U.S. 609 (1965).

[9]  391 U.S. 145, 193, 88 S. Ct. 1444, 20 L. Ed. 2d 491 (1968).

We have before us, therefore, an almost perfect example of a situation in which the celebrated dictum of Mr. Justice Brandeis should be invoked. It is, he said, "one of the happy incidents of the federal system that a single courageous State may, if its citizens choose, serve as a laboratory***." New State Ice Company v. Liebmann, 285 U.S. 262, 52 S. Ct. 371, 76 L. Ed. 747 [1932] (dissenting opinion).

This Court, other courts, and the political process are available to correct any experiments in criminal procedure that prove fundamentally unfair to defendants. That is not what is being done today: instead, and quite without reason, the Court has chosen to impose upon every State one means of trying criminal cases; it is a good means, but it is not the only fair means, and it is not demonstrably better than the alternatives States might devise.

In 1969, Earl Warren retired as Chief Justice of the United States Supreme Court, and Justice Warren Burger took over. In its first decade, observers characterized the work of the Burger Court as expanding several procedural rights of the defendant once the case reached court (including extension of the right to counsel in misdemeanor trials and guaranteeing the representative makeup of trial juries), but at the same time sharply increasing the freedom of police to investigate cases and interrogate suspects. Cases on searches, confessions, and lineups were frequently cited as attempts by the Burger Court to provide more flexibility to police. As the Burger Court shifted direction from the course of court decisions taken under Earl Warren, vigorous criticism from several quarters was heard. Civil libertarians were concerned about privacy rights of citizens. One commentator observed: "[C]riminal cases illustrate the Court's support of President Nixon's pledge to strengthen society's 'peace forces' against 'criminal forces'. . . . With respect to criminal procedures, for example, the Burger Court is apparently disposed to minimize or reduce the rights of those interfacing with administrative bureaucracies (police) until litigation is initiated, at which time the Court will apparently uphold traditional constitutional values such as the right to counsel."[10]

Chief Justice William Rehnquist followed Justice Burger, and with a conservative majority, the Court began a steady tack to the right in matters of search and seizure. The Court reined in the exclusionary rule in a number of settings. A commentator supplied this appraisal:

The Supreme Court has dramatically curtailed protection for individual privacy under the Fourth Amendment. Contemporary decisions have restricted the warrant requirement, eased the government's burden of justifying searches and seizures, narrowed the definition of both searches and seizures, and constrained the ability of individuals to challenge government searches.

---

[10]   Lucias J. Barker, *Black Americans and the Burger Court: Implications for the Political System*, 1973, WASH. U.L.Q. 747, 761-64 (1973) (footnotes omitted).

Many academics have decried the Rehnquist Court's assault on privacy, urging more vigorous protection for individuals subject to government searches and seizures. Others have been more accepting [and] have openly welcomed the diminished protection for privacy because of the public's countervailing interest in safety.[11]

Another scholar attributed the harsher light that the Rehnquist Court cast on some Bill of Rights provisions to a change in national philosophy. "Where it was once the received wisdom that the primary, or at least principal, purpose of criminal law and criminology was to bring about the rehabilitation of the offender, that view has been replaced with increased skepticism, if not outright rejection, concerning the prospects of individual reformation. This harsher mood has been accompanied by a new public, legislative, and judicial enthusiasm for punishment."[12]

The appointment by President Clinton of two new Justices, Justice Ginsburg in 1993 followed in 1994 by Justice Breyer, seemed to portend a middle-of-the-road approach to criminal procedure matters in the years immediately ahead. More liberal than many of their colleagues on the Supreme Court bench, Justices Breyer and Ginsberg have frequently been involved in crafting 5-to-4 decisions upholding the Warren Court's criminal procedure innovations. Their presence has also been important in narrowing the application of capital punishment.

The Rehnquist Court has been at the forefront of championing trial by jury, expanding the jury's role in finding facts that are relevant to criminal sentencing. No one can be sentenced to death on a judge's finding alone. A jury verdict of death is essential to imposing capital punishment.

To summarize, the expansion of individual rights during the pretrial process was the benchmark of the Warren Court.[13] The Rehnquist Court, presently dominated by moderates, accepts certain important principles that were originally authored by the Warren Court. Chief among those is the doctrine that the United States Constitution imposes a code of criminal procedure on the states. Accordingly, while the Rehnquist Court has narrowed some of the protections formerly provided under the search and seizure rules, *Miranda*[14] and *Mapp*[15] are here to stay.

State courts are free to expand the rights of criminal suspects beyond those afforded under federal law. "[W]here a state prosecution raises issues of constitutional criminal procedure, a state court may rule in favor of the rights of the defendant without any Supreme Court review, provided it bases its decision, in whole or in part, on a clearly identified independent and adequate state ground. Thus, there has always existed a largely untapped potential in state law

---

[11]  Harold J. Krent, *Of Diaries and Data Banks: Use Restrictions Under the Fourth Amendment*, 74 TEX. L. REV. 49 (1995).

[12]  Robert J. Cottrol, *Hard Choices and Shifted Burdens*, 65 GEO. W. REV. 506, 507 (1997).

[13]  Saleem, *The Age of Unreason*, 50 OKLA. L. REV. 451, 452 (1997).

[14]  Miranda v. Arizona, 384 U.S. 436 (1966) (constitutional warnings are required prior to custodial questioning of an arrestee).

[15]  Mapp v. Ohio, 367 U.S. 693 (1961) (Fourth Amendment bars evidence of incriminating items that were seized from a defendant when the government's search was illegal). The *Mapp* case and the rules excluding illegally seized evidence are reviewed in detail in § 2.2 of this text.

for affording criminal defendants rights above and beyond those provided by federal law. . . . Presently, the conservative impact upon the United States Supreme Court has permitted the laws of several states to surpass federal law in the advancement of the rights of the criminally accused."[16] With the conservative tilt of the Supreme Court, this trend at the state level may continue in several jurisdictions.

The last half of the twentieth century witnessed dramatic changes in Supreme Court law affecting criminal procedure at all levels, including the securing of confessions by police, search and seizure, trial, sentencing, and criminal appeals. Notwithstanding adjustments and modifications by the Rehnquist Court, a major series of constitutional protections remain binding in state and federal prosecutions. In *Albright v Oliver*,[17] the Court lists Bill of Rights guarantees made applicable to the states:

> *Hurtado* [v. California] held that the Due Process Clause did not make applicable to the States the Fifth Amendment's requirement that all prosecutions for an infamous crime be instituted by the indictment of a grand jury. In the more than 100 years which have elapsed since *Hurtado* was decided, the Court has concluded that a number of procedural protections contained in the Bill of Rights were made applicable to the States by the Fourteenth Amendment. See *Mapp v. Ohio*, 367 U.S. 643, 81 S. Ct. 1684, 6 L. Ed. 2d 1081 (1961), overruling *Wolf v. Colorado*, 338 U.S. 25, 69 S. Ct. 1359, 93 L. Ed. 1782 (1949), and holding the Fourth Amendment's exclusionary rule applicable to the States; *Malloy v. Hogan*, 378 U.S. 1, 84 S. Ct. 1489, 12 L. Ed. 2d 653 (1964), overruling *Twining v. New Jersey*, 211 U.S. 78, 29 S. Ct. 14, 53 L. Ed. 97 (1908), and holding the Fifth Amendment's privilege against self-incrimination applicable to the States; *Benton v. Maryland*, 395 U.S. 784, 89 S. Ct. 2056, 23 L. Ed. 2d 707 (1969), overruling *Palko v. Connecticut*, 302 U.S. 319, 58 S. Ct. 149, 82 L. Ed. 288 (1937), and holding the Double Jeopardy Clause of the Fifth Amendment applicable to the States; *Gideon v. Wainwright*, 372 U.S. 335, 83 S. Ct. 792, 9 L. Ed. 2d 799 (1963), overruling *Betts v. Brady*, 316 U.S. 455, 62 S. Ct. 1252, 86 L. Ed. 1595 (1942), and holding that the Sixth Amendment's right to counsel was applicable to the States. See also *Klopfer v. North Carolina*, 386 U.S. 213, 87 S. Ct. 988, 18 L. Ed. 2d 1 (1967) (Sixth Amendment speedy trial right applicable to the States); *Washington v. Texas*, 388 U.S. 14, 87 S. Ct. 1920, 18 L. Ed. 2d 1019 (1967) (Sixth Amendment right to compulsory process applicable to the States); *Duncan v. Louisiana*, 391 U.S. 145, 88 S. Ct. 1444, 20 L. Ed. 2d 491 (1968) (Sixth Amendment right to jury trial applicable to the States).

> This course of decision has substituted, in these areas of criminal procedure, the specific guarantees of the various provisions of the Bill of Rights embodied in the first 10 Amendments to the Constitution for the more generalized language contained in the earlier cases construing the Fourteenth Amendment. It was through these provisions of the Bill of Rights that their Framers sought to restrict the exercise of arbitrary authority by the Government in particular situations.

---

[16]    Kenneth Melilli, *Exclusion of Evidence in Federal Prosecutions on the Basis of State Law*, 22 GA. L. REV. 667, 673, 735 (1988).

[17]    114 S. Ct. 807 (1994).

## § 8.3   Appellate Decision Making

Appellate courts do not ordinarily decide **issues of fact**. These are for determination by the jury at the trial level. The special competence of appeals courts in matters of law renders their review of trial court cases primarily a review of the **issues of law** involved in the case. For example, suppose a police officer took a confession from a defendant without giving the suspect any *Miranda* warnings prior to interrogation. At trial of the case, however, the trial judge erroneously permitted the police officer who obtained the confession to read it to the jury over defense objections. The jury convicted the defendant. On appeal, the defendant argues that the trial judge committed an error of law in letting the jury hear the confession. If the appellate court reverses the conviction (and it might well do so under the assumed facts) it would normally remand the case back to the trial court for a new trial. Included with the remand will be instructions to exclude the confession from the jury in the new trial. A second jury would then hear the evidence in the case, this time without the tainted proof, and render a verdict.

Again, suppose at a robbery trial the defendant presented proof that he was with his friend playing poker at the time of the robbery, and not at the bank as charged by the prosecution. At the close of the evidence a legal definition of the term *alibi* was given to the jury. In the alibi instructions, however, the court added that the accused had the burden of proving he was elsewhere than at the scene of the crime at the time it was committed. The true rule, of course, requires the prosecution to prove that the accused was present at the scene, and the alibi instruction was erroneous when it cast the burden of proof on a vital element in the case on the defendant. This erroneous jury instruction constitutes prejudicial error, and an appellate court reviewing the defendant's conviction will vacate it, remanding the case for new trial.[18]

From such examples twin observations emerge. First, reversal of a conviction by an appellate court generally means a new trial for the accused, not acquittal. Those unaware of the remand process frequently read that a higher court has reversed a conviction and assume that the successful defendant has automatically won his or her freedom. While this may be true in isolated circumstances, what the defendant has won in the vast majority of cases is simply a right to be tried again. For example, in the *Miranda* case, the United States Supreme Court did not free Ernesto Miranda, but remanded his case for retrial. When the case was returned to Arizona for a new trial, Miranda's confession to the crime of rape was excluded from the jury under orders of the United States Supreme Court. He was again convicted and was sentenced to more than 20 years in the Arizona State Penitentiary.[19]

---

[18]   Johnson v. Bennett, 414 F.2d 50 (8th Cir. 1969); Stump v. Bennett, 398 F.2d 111 (8th Cir. 1968). For a discussion of burdens of proof in criminal cases, *see* § 6.25 of this text.

       The examples used here are appeals of trial problems. Defendants who plead guilty may appeal also, attacking the voluntariness of the plea. If the court finds the plea was involuntary it will order the judgment overturned.

[19]   State v. Miranda, 450 P.2d 364 (Ariz. 1969). Ernesto Miranda was ultimately stabbed to death in 1976, the victim of a fight over a $2 card game.

Second, it is to be discerned in the preceding illustrations that reversal is based upon legal errors, not questions of fact. Reversal on legal "technicalities" is antagonistic to some who urge that if evidence of guilt is present, higher courts should not reverse on technical procedural grounds. However, it is precisely the function of the appellate courts to safeguard procedural correctness in criminal trials. Notwithstanding contentions that attention to procedural details is hypertechnical, centuries of legal history teach that sloppy courtroom practices portend unfairness for both sides in an adversary proceeding. The principles of due process of law demand procedural correctness in our criminal courts.

When an appellate court decides a case, it delivers a written opinion explaining and justifying the decision. In this way the higher court explains to the trial judge what he or she did wrong. In addition, the losing party on appeal is not only told that he or she lost, but why he or she lost. Opinion writing by appellate judges also serves to make consistent the approach of lower courts to problems similar to those decided in the case on appeal.

When the judges on the appellate court disagree about the proper decision in a case, it will be decided in accord with the wishes of those in the majority. One of these judges prepares a written opinion that stands as the **opinion of the court**. **Dissenting opinions** may also be prepared by one or more of those judges in the minority. Appellate courts usually consist of an odd number of judges (nine judges in many state supreme courts), which avoids a tie vote. However, when there is a vacancy on the court due to the illness of a judge, retirement of a judge prior to qualification of a successor, or other reason, the possibility of a 4-4 vote exists. In such a situation, the judgment or decision in the court below stands.[20]

## § 8.4   Counsel and Transcript

In cases in which a person had appointed counsel at trial and his or her financial status remains unchanged, or where the expense of trial has depleted the defendant's funds to the point that he or she cannot afford to hire a lawyer to handle the appeal, he or she is entitled to an appointed lawyer. In *Douglas v. California*[21] the defendants requested and were denied appointed counsel when appealing their convictions to the California District Court of Appeals. The Supreme Court of the United States reversed this state appellate court ruling:

> [W]here the merits of the one and only appeal an indigent has as of right are decided without benefit of counsel, we think an unconstitutional line has been drawn between rich and poor. . . . There is lacking that equality demanded by the Fourteenth Amendment where the rich man, who appeals

---

[20]   Charlottesville & Albermarle R. Co. v. Rubin, 60 S.E. 101 (Va. 1908); SUNDERLAND, TRIAL AND APPELLATE PRACTICE, 710 (2d ed. 1941).

[21]   372 U.S. 353, 358, 83 S. Ct. 814, 9 L. Ed. 2d 811(1963).

as of right, enjoys the benefit of counsel's examination into the record, research of the law, and marshalling of the arguments on his behalf, while the indigent, already burdened by a preliminary determination that his case is without merit, is forced to shift for himself. The indigent, where the record is unclear or the errors are hidden, has only the right to a meaningless ritual, while the rich man has a meaningful appeal.

The root idea of *Douglas*, as well as *Griffin v. Illinois*,[22] is that all persons, even if without funds, should be given the opportunity to have a meaningful appeal to an appellate court. In the view of the Supreme Court, a meaningful appeal necessarily implies an attorney to prosecute the appeal for the defendant, as well as a stenographic transcript of the trial proceedings. *Griffin* upheld the defendant's contention that due process and equal protection of law require that poor persons be furnished a transcript. Preparation of appellate briefs and arguments is difficult and sometimes impossible without this word-for-word record of the trial.

> [T]o deny adequate review to the poor means that many of them may lose their life, liberty or property because of unjust convictions which appellate courts would set aside. Many States have recognized this and provided aid for convicted defendants who have a right to appeal and need a transcript but are unable to pay for it. A few have not. Such a denial is a misfit in a country dedicated to affording equal justice to all and special privileges to none in administration of its criminal law. There can be no equal justice where the kind of trial a man gets depends on the amount of money he has. Destitute defendants must be afforded as adequate appellate review as defendants who have money enough to buy transcripts.

If the appeals lawyer believes that there are no meritorious grounds for appeal, it is his duty to the defendant as well as to the court of which he is an officer to refrain from taking an appeal. In the event the defense counsel finds the defendant's appeal to be wholly frivolous, he or she should so advise the appeals court and request permission to withdraw from the case.[23] This request must be supported by a **brief**. Further, the Court of Appeals must make its own examination of the record to determine whether counsel's evaluation of the case as frivolous is a sound one.[24] Of course, if the appeal has merit, law and legal ethics require the lawyer to advocate his client's appeal to the best of his or her ability.

A concluding question in this area concerns ground staked out by the *Douglas* case[25] and reserved for later decision. The *Douglas* decision restricted its ruling on free counsel for poor persons to "the one and only

---

[22]  351 U.S. 12, 19, 76 S. Ct. 585, 100 L. Ed. 891 (1956).
[23]  Anders v. California, 386 U.S. 738, 744, 87 S. Ct. 1396, 18 L. Ed. 2d 493 (1967). *See* Smith v. Robbins, 528 U.S. 259 (2000).
[24]  Penson v. Ohio, 109 S. Ct. 346 (1988).
[25]  Note 21 *supra*.

appeal an indigent has of right." What about appeals beyond the first one? *Ross v. Moffitt*[26] answers this question, and answers it in the negative.

As is the situation in several states, the North Carolina appellate system is multi-tiered, with both an intermediate court of appeals and a supreme court. Under North Carolina law a convicted defendant appealing to the intermediate court of appeals could receive an appointed attorney, but such services were not authorized for defendants who went on to seek discretionary review in the state supreme court. The question before the Court in *Ross* was whether a state could refuse to supply an attorney at this second level of appeal. Mr. Justice Rehnquist delivered the opinion of the United States Supreme Court in *Ross v. Moffitt*: "We do not believe that the Due Process Clause requires North Carolina to provide respondent with counsel on his discretionary appeal to the State Supreme Court." A similar disposition was made by Justice Rehnquist of the claim that an indigent person is entitled to free counsel to prepare a petition for certiorari to the United States Supreme Court: "Much of the discussion . . . is equally relevant to the question of whether a State must provide counsel for a defendant seeking review of his conviction in this Court. . . . The suggestion that a State is responsible for providing counsel to one petitioning this Court simply because it initiated the prosecution which led to the judgment sought to be reviewed is unsupported by either reason or authority."

The foregoing discussion in this section observes that a free lawyer must be made available to a penniless defendant who loses at trial and wants a lawyer for his first appeal. The discussion presumes that the defendant's trial effort was a losing one, and the defendant needs a lawyer to help her on appeal. What if she pled guilty, instead of having a trial? While appeals from guilty pleas are not nearly as common as appeals from trials, they do occasionally occur. Is a defendant who pled guilty entitled to a free lawyer when she appeals, if she cannot otherwise afford an attorney? Should there be a difference in whether a defendant is eligible for a free appellate lawyer depending upon whether the accused was tried, or pled guilty? Courts are presently considering the issue of whether states can deny free legal services to defendants who plead guilty and want to appeal a conviction entered on the guilty plea.

## § 8.5 Appeal by State

Prosecutors are specifically permitted to seek review of lower court decisions.[27] The case of *Warden v. Hayden*[28] is an example in point. The United States Court of Appeals for the Fourth Circuit first ruled against the state of Maryland, which had earlier obtained a conviction of the defendant in a Maryland trial court on a charge of armed robbery. The basis upon which the United States Court of Appeals set aside the conviction was that at the time of arrest,

---

[26]   417 U.S. 600, 94 S. Ct. 2437, 41 L. Ed. 2d 341 (1974).
[27]   *See*, e.g., 18 U.S.C.A. § 3731.
[28]   387 U.S. 294, 87 S. Ct. 1642, 18 L. Ed. 2d 782 (1967).

police officers seized items of evidentiary value from the defendant. Under established Supreme Court rules this evidence was not properly subject to seizure, and the federal Court of Appeals so held. Disputing the decision, the Maryland attorney general applied for certiorari in the Supreme Court of the United States. The Supreme Court granted certiorari, and after hearing arguments on the "mere evidence" rule, the Supreme Court changed the law, reversed the Court of Appeals and reinstated the conviction.[29]

From the trial court level, two kinds of appeals are allowed to the prosecutor. In the first, prosecutors are entitled to appeal to the state appellate court even though the defendant has been acquitted at the trial level. This may occur when the prosecutor believes the trial judge made an error adverse to the state. The appellate court can find that the trial court did make an error and instruct on the proper procedure for future cases. However, the defendant who was acquitted in the particular case that was appealed cannot be retried, because of the double jeopardy clause.

For this reason, there has been marked statutory movement in the states in recent years to give the prosecutor a right to appeal before the jury hears the case. This appeal, frequently termed an **interlocutory appeal**, is extremely helpful when a trial judge holds a pretrial hearing on the admissibility of a confession or an item of physical evidence that police have seized. Where the trial judge suppresses the confession or physical evidence, but the prosecutor feels his or her decision is in error, the prosecutor can take the suppression decision to the appellate court for review and possible reversal before the entire case goes to trial. Trial of the case will be stayed pending such an appeal. Several code revision commissions have recommended giving the prosecution this right to appeal pretrial evidentiary rulings. It has been correctly remarked that the government has little incentive to appeal after a not guilty verdict because the accused may not be retried. On the other hand, an interlocutory appeal, particularly an effort to correct an adverse search and seizure decision, comes at a point in the case when the desire to set the law straight is very high.

## § 8.6  Habeas Corpus: Historical Background

The root of the **writ of habeas corpus** is that in a civilized society, government must always be accountable to the judiciary for a person's imprisonment.[30] For this reason, if a prisoner who is held in a state penitentiary claims he or she was illegally convicted because his or her constitutional rights were violated at trial, the prisoner may air his or her claims before a habeas corpus judge.

---

[29] For discussion of articles subject to seizure by police officers, see § 2.2(1).
[30] Fay v. Noia, 372 U.S. 391, 83 S. Ct. 822, 9 L. Ed. 2d 837 (1983). The *Fay* case was limited by Stone v. Powell, 428 U.S. 465 (1976).

The writ of habeas corpus dates from the early years of the English common law, and was received into our own law during the colonial period. It was incorporated into the United States Constitution, Article 1, § 9. From the era of John Marshall, Chief Justice of the United States Supreme Court in the early 1800s, to the present, habeas corpus has been called the "Great Writ." Habeas corpus relief extends to cases where a person's conviction was achieved in disregard of one of the basic rights of the person, and if the habeas corpus judge so finds, he or she may order the discharge of the prisoner. As in the case of a reversal where the defendant has won on appeal, however, the normal mode of disposition of a prisoner who is successful in habeas corpus is to give the state the option to retry him or her.[31]

In contrast to the case of appeals, in many states a petition for habeas corpus need not be filed by a prisoner within any set time limit after conviction.[32] In one case from 1963, the United States Supreme Court ruled that a habeas corpus application could be made by a prisoner who had been convicted in 1942.[33] For this reason, if a prisoner turns up important new evidence in his case even long after the conviction and appeal processes are completed, he may petition for review of the conviction in habeas corpus.

Federal cases may be different, particularly after 1996. It is to be noted that habeas actions may be brought by state prisoners in their own state courts. Subject to close restrictions, such prisoners can also file claims in federal tribunals. Also, federal prisoners who were convicted of offenses in United States District Courts are required to bring their claims before federal judges. In federal courts prior to 1996, if the habeas corpus petition was not filed until many years after conviction, that was of no consequence. However, 1996 legislation changed this. Congress adopted a general time limitation for filing a habeas corpus petition of one year after the direct appeal in the case was concluded, and a shorter period for capital cases.[34]

## § 8.7   Grounds for Habeas Relief

While habeas corpus applies in certain noncriminal situations, of significance to this discussion are cases in which the writ is sought to test the detention of persons held in custody after criminal conviction.[35] The prisoner starts the case by filing a petition for habeas corpus with the appropriate court of general trial jurisdiction, naming the warden or superintendent of the penal

---

[31]   See § 8.3, supra; Stump v. Bennett, 398 F.2d 111 (8th Cir. 1968).

[32]   Appeal from a trial court to a court of appeals is taken by filing with the clerk of the trial court a notice of appeal. Notice of appeal must be filed within a specific period after conviction and judgment, ranging from 10 to perhaps 60 or 90 days (the time varies from state to state). If not done within the stipulated period, the right to appeal may be lost.

[33]   Fay v. Noia, 372 U.S. 391, 83 S. Ct. 822, 9 L. Ed. 2d 837 (1963).

[34]   Antiterrorism and Effective Death Penalty Act, 28 U.S.C. 2244. Other provisions of this 1996 act appear in § 8.7.

[35]   Habeas corpus may also be confronted prior to conviction in criminal cases, as where the accused in the custody of the sheriff uses the writ to come into court and demand speedy trial.

institution as the defendant. The court may order a hearing, and at such hearing a police officer may be called upon to provide testimony in resistance to the petition.

Grounds for granting habeas corpus relief are varied, but several representative grounds are listed for illustrative purposes:

- Prejudicial publicity prevented a fair trial when the defendant was tried, in violation of due process of law.

- Denial of counsel at preliminary hearing, trial, or appeal.

- Incompetent or ineffective counsel.

- Knowing use by the prosecution of false evidence.

- Insanity of the defendant at the time he or she pled guilty or was tried.

- Extraction and use by authorities of an involuntary confession.

- State failure to disclose evidence favorable to an accused (suppression of evidence).

While many habeas corpus petitions are filed with state judges, it is also possible for state prisoners to file for habeas corpus relief in the federal district court having territorial jurisdiction over the state penal institution where the filing prisoner is incarcerated. Federal courts receive such petitions when: (1) state remedies have been exhausted (the state courts having passed on the questions involved, either on appeal or in state habeas corpus), and/or (2) the prisoner makes a claim that his or her state trial or appeal involved a denial of federal constitutional rights.

Federal habeas corpus courts sit to ensure that individuals are not imprisoned in violation of the U.S. Constitution. In *Herrera v. Collins*,[36] a number of legal protections for accused persons are listed:

> A person when first charged with a crime is entitled to a presumption of innocence, and may insist that his guilt be established beyond a reasonable doubt. *In re Winship,* 397 U.S. 358, 90 S. Ct. 1068, 25 L. Ed. 2d 368 (1970). Other constitutional provisions also have the effect of ensuring against the risk of convicting an innocent person. See, *e.g., Coy v. Iowa,* 487 U.S. 1012, 108 S. Ct. 2798, 101 L. Ed. 2d 857 (1988) (right to confront adverse witnesses); *Taylor v. Illinois,* 484 U.S. 400, 108 S. Ct. 646, 98 L. Ed. 2d 798 (1988) (right to compulsory process); *Strickland v. Washington,* 466 U.S. 668, 104 S. Ct. 2052, 80 L. Ed.2d 674 (1984) (right to effective assistance of counsel); *Winship, supra* (prosecution must prove guilt beyond a reasonable doubt); *Duncan v. Louisiana,* 391 U.S. 145, 88 S. Ct. 1444, 20 L. Ed. 2d 491 (1968) (right to jury trial); *Brady v. Maryland,* 373 U.S. 83, 83 S. Ct. 1194, 10 L. Ed. 2d 215 (1963) (prosecution must disclose exculpatory evidence); *Gideon v. Wainwright,* 372 U.S. 133, 136, 75 S. Ct. 623, 625, 99 L. Ed. 942 (1955) (right to "fair trial in a fair tribunal"). In capital cases, we have

---

[36]  113 S. Ct. 853 (1993).

required additional protections because of the nature of the penalty at stake. See *e.g.*, *Beck v. Alabama*, 447 U.S. 625, 100 S. Ct. 2382, 65 L. Ed. 2d 392 (1980) (jury must be given option of convicting the defendant of a lesser offense). All of these constitutional safeguards, of course, make it more difficult for the State to rebut and finally overturn the presumption of innocence which attaches to every criminal defendant. But we have also observed that "[d]ue process does not require that every conceivable step be taken, at whatever cost, to eliminate the possibility of convicting an innocent person." *Patterson v. New York,* 432 U.S. 197, 208, 97 S. Ct. 2319, 2326, 53 L. Ed. 2d 281 (1977).

To conclude otherwise would all but paralyze our system for enforcement of the criminal law.

Once a defendant has been afforded a fair trial and convicted of the offense for which it was charged, the presumption of innocence disappears. *Cf. Ross v. Moffitt,* 417 U.S. 600, 610, 94 S. Ct. 2437, 2444, 41 L. Ed. 2d 341 (1974) ("The purpose of the trial stage from the State's point of view is to convert a criminal defendant from a person presumed innocent to one found guilty beyond a reasonable doubt").

Whether alleged search and seizure violations by city or state police could be litigated in federal habeas corpus has come under Supreme Court scrutiny. In *Stone v. Powell*[37] the Supreme Court held that prisoners had only a very limited right to bring these claims into federal courts for judicial relief. Earlier in the year the Supreme Court had allowed a state prisoner to attack his own plea of guilty to murder because the sentencing judge had not explained the elements of second-degree murder, the Court invalidating the conviction in federal habeas corpus.[38] But *Stone v. Powell* reflects a desire to constrict access to federal courts in certain kinds of prisoner claims. Additional decisions of the latter kind could impede the flow of habeas corpus petitions into federal courts, where the burden of these has become a cause for concern on the part of judges and administrators.

Another doctrine that cuts down the flow of habeas petitions is nonretroactivity of newly announced constitutional protections. Jury instructions in murder and voluntary manslaughter cases can be important. In *Gilmore v. Taylor*,[39] the accused was charged with the murder of his former wife's boyfriend. At an Illinois trial, the defendant claimed he was acting under sudden passion. The judge gave jury instructions that were criticized by the accused on the following basis: Because the murder instructions preceded the voluntary manslaughter instructions and lacked certain guiding limitations, it

---

[37] 428 U.S. 465 (1976). Other aspects of this case are noted in § 10.18. *Stone's* rule excluding search and seizure claims was not extended to a state prisoner's claim that his conviction rested on statements obtained in violation of *Miranda.* Withrow v. Williams, 113 S. Ct. 1745 (1993).

[38] Henderson v. Morgan, 426 U.S. 637, 96 S. Ct. 2253, 49 L. Ed. 2d 108 (1976).

[39] 124 L. Ed. 2d 306 (1993). Successive claims in habeas corpus, *see* Sawyer v. Whitley, 112 S. Ct. 2514 (1992).

was possible for the jury to find that the defendant was guilty of murder without even considering whether the defendant committed only the lesser offense of voluntary manslaughter. Although the jury instruction was disapproved and struck down in other cases *after* the time of the defendant's trial, he could not take advantage of the new rule disapproving this jury charge. The instruction comported with prevailing law at the time of the prisoner's trial and he could not gain federal habeas corpus relief. The defect in the instruction—even though one of constitutional dimension—did not fall into the small core of issues that are "implicit in the concept of ordered liberty." Retroactive application belongs only to those watershed rules of criminal procedure implicating the fundamental fairness and accuracy of criminal proceedings, according to Justice Rehnquist. This did not.

Most newly announced constitutional rules do not qualify as "watershed rules"—truly significant changes in law—so in most cases a prisoner convicted many years before the new rule cannot take advantage of it to win a new trial. As opposed to a modest change in practice, a **watershed rule** alters our understanding of basic, bedrock procedural elements essential to a fair proceeding. The right to counsel is such a rule. For much of the last century that right was guaranteed to accused persons in federal and most state courts. However, a few states lagged behind in affording a free lawyer to a defendant who was without funds. Eventually the United States Supreme Court stepped in. The high court ruled that poor prisoners must be provided a lawyer when facing serious charges. All states were required to follow this rule. When the Supreme Court announced this principle and then made it binding in all state courts, this was a watershed rule. Even prisoners convicted five, six, or 10 years before the Court's announcement in formerly noncomplying jurisdictions could raise the lack of counsel claim in a habeas corpus action and win a new trial. If the defendant was without funds when he was first tried, and was forced to go to trial without counsel, he was entitled to relief in the form of a new trial with counsel.

A further restriction on habeas applicants is the insistence that a petitioner make a showing of some significant probability that he or she would have been acquitted had it not been for the error in his or her trial. A reasonable probability of this kind has been described as a probability sufficient to undermine confidence in the trial's outcome. Habeas courts increasingly require a demonstration by the petitioner that he or she is innocent of the crime charged, along with pointing to a constitutional error in the proceedings against him or her. Where the alleged constitutional error in a defendant's trial resulted in the failure of the jury to see and hear important defense evidence, the habeas petitioner must show that it is likely that no reasonable juror would have convicted him or her in light of the new evidence.[40] With some claims, courts have demanded that prisoners show their innocence by **clear and convincing evidence**.

---

[40]    Schlup v. Delo, 513 U.S. 298 (1995).

Federal courts have instituted restrictions on prisoners seeking to file repetitive constitutional claims, such as the inmate who files seven or eight writs in a three-year period. The "successive petitions" problem was addressed in the Federal Antiterrorism and Effective Death Penalty Act of 1996. Any claim already raised in a federal habeas corpus action is barred in a subsequent action, and the later claim that simply repeats earlier grievances will be dismissed. "If the petitioner has previously filed a federal habeas and is now raising an issue for the first time in a successive federal petition, the only way in which the federal courts will be permitted to hear the successive petition is if the petitioner proves that his or her claim rests on a previously unavailable rule of constitutional law that the Supreme Court has made retroactive to cases on collateral review or, alternatively, that its factual predicate could not have been discovered earlier by the exercise of due diligence, and that the facts underlying the claim, if proven and viewed in light of the evidence as a whole, would be sufficient to establish by clear and convincing evidence that, but for constitutional error, no reasonable fact finder would have found the applicant guilty of the underlying offense."[41]

In addition, the 1996 federal act places a one-year limitation on federal habeas actions. Prisoners are required to file their petitions for relief within one year from the completion of direct review. They are also required to be in custody, locked up in jail or prison, at the time the petition for habeas corpus is filed. If a prisoner is released before his or her habeas case is decided, it does not render the case moot as long as he or she was incarcerated when the action was filed.[42]

To summarize, federal habeas corpus is hedged with a number of restrictions. However, for the state or federal prisoner who has suffered a significant constitutional violation during the proceedings against him or her, habeas corpus remains a bulwark for litigating injustices. Habeas review is available to check violations of criminal law when the error in a defendant's trial qualifies as a fundamental defect that results in a miscarriage of justice or an omission inconsistent with fair procedure.[43]

## § 8.8 Constitutional Rights

### 1. Transcript

When a penitentiary inmate's claim is reviewed by the hearing judge (normally no jury participates in habeas corpus decision-making), the judge may grant relief or may deny the request. In the latter event, the inmate has a right to appeal the judge's decision, just as he or she earlier had the right to appeal

---

[41] Snider, *After the Antiterrorism and Effective Death Penalty Act of 1996*, 3 GEORGIA B.J. 20, No. 2 (Oct. 1997).

[42] Spencer v. Kemna, 118 S. Ct. 978 (1998).

[43] Reed v. Farley, 114 S. Ct. 2291 (1994).

from a jury's verdict that convicted him or her in the first place. To make such habeas corpus appeals meaningful, it may be necessary to have a stenographic transcript of the testimony that was taken by the judge at the habeas hearing. The United States Supreme Court decision in *Long v. District Court*[44] established the right of a prisoner to receive a copy of the court reporter's record of the habeas corpus hearing for use on appeal, and to have it provided without charge if the prisoner lacks funds to purchase one. The decision in the *Long* case is an example of equal protection of the laws in post-conviction proceedings.

## 2. Counsel

In *Douglas v. California* (see § 8.4) the Supreme Court of the United States mandated counsel for indigent defendants on direct appeals from convictions. However, the Court has not expanded this rule to habeas corpus petitions. There is no Supreme Court requirement that attorneys be provided to indigent applicants for habeas relief. This point was reconfirmed after *Douglas* in *Coleman v. Thompson*.[45] However, several states by statute provide counsel to poor prisoners seeking a post-conviction remedy.

## 3. Preparation Assistance

A major case decided by the Supreme Court laid down the rules that permit penitentiary inmates to assist each other in drawing up habeas corpus petitions. The case arose in Tennessee. Like many states, Tennessee had a prison regulation that provided: "No inmate will advise, assist or otherwise contract to aid another, either with or without a fee, to prepare Writs or other legal matters." Prisoner William Joe Johnson was a lifer who had been in solitary confinement for the greater part of three years because of his refusal to comply with this regulation. Johnson claimed the right to assist other prisoners with writ applications, and when he raised the question in habeas corpus in federal court, the United States Supreme Court was ultimately required to lay down rules concerning the prison "writ writer."

The Court ruled that states could not bar inmates from furnishing legal assistance to other prisoners, unless and until they instituted an alternative plan for legal assistance. Alternatives in the form of public defenders assigned to the prison, use of senior law students, or a voluntary program of the bar association were mentioned by the Court. Even without a legal aid plan, prisons can prohibit the exchange of money or other considerations for legal help between prisoners. But in the absence of a legal aid plan, states cannot completely prohibit mutual assistance among inmates in the preparation of writ applications.[46] A later Supreme Court case held that the fundamental constitu-

---

[44] 385 U.S. 192, 87 S. Ct. 362, 17 L. Ed. 2d 290 (1966).

[45] 501 U.S. 722 (1991). An exception exists for state or federal death row inmates pursuing federal habeas corpus. WILKES, FEDERAL POSTCONVICTION REMEDIES AND RELIEF HANDBOOK § 2:2 (2004).

[46] Johnson v. Avery, 393 U.S. 483, 89 S. Ct. 747, 21 L. Ed. 2d 718 (1969). For further discussion on the prisoner's right to access to the courts, see § 10.20.

tional right of access to the courts requires prison authorities to assist inmates in the preparation of meaningful legal papers by providing prisoners either with adequate law libraries or with adequate assistance from persons trained in the law.[47] However, the research materials can be restricted to the "tools" that inmates need to attack their sentences or challenge conditions of confinement. Materials for other sorts of litigation or unrelated legal problems are not a constitutional requirement.[48]

## § 8.9    Standard for Granting Relief

Where false or perjured evidence played a role in convicting the defendant and this is established in habeas corpus, will the defendant receive a new trial? It has been held that proof that false evidence was used by the government may alone be insufficient. False evidence that will trigger a new trial must be of an extraordinary nature. It must leave the court with a firm belief that, but for the perjured testimony, the defendant most likely would not have been convicted.

In *Sanders v Sullivan*,[49] the defendant was convicted of murder on the basis of testimony by witness Perez and his common-law wife. After the defendant was in the penitentiary, the witness's wife died, and the witness recanted his testimony. It was his wife, not the defendant, who shot and killed the deceased, he said. An issue arose as to whether, in order to receive a new trial, the defendant had to prove that the prosecutor had knowledge of any perjury. The court said no, and added:

> We are not alone in believing that our holding today is in step with the spirit of the Constitution. Academic commentary has long supported our position. Nearly twenty years ago, one observer concluded:
>
> > The established standard of certain courts, to the effect that a conviction based on false evidence is unassailable unless the defendant can prove a knowing use by the prosecution, appears inadvisable. Judicial concern in these cases should concentrate on vouchsafing the right of a fair trial to the convicted person. Hedged with the appropriate standards requiring the defendant to demonstrate materiality of the tainted evidence, the more liberal approach advocated here would threaten only those final judgments which merit unsettlement.
> >
> > Carlson, *False or Suppressed Evidence: Why a Need for the Prosecutorial Tie?* 1969 DUKE L.J. 1171, 1187-88 (footnote omitted).

In this case, Judge Kaufman found that the recantation of testimony by the witness "would most likely change the outcome of the trial." In granting relief, he concluded: "In this case, allowing the conviction to stand violates due process."

---

[47]   Bounds v. Smith, 430 U.S. 817 (1977).

[48]   Lewis v. Casey, 116 S. Ct. 2174 (1996).

[49]   863 F.2d 218 (2d Cir. 1988).

*Banks v. Dretke*[50] is another case in which the ruling was in favor of the defendant. The United States Supreme Court reviewed the record and then questioned whether Banks received a fair trial. The State had failed to disclose a statement made by an informant, which was favorable to the defense. State suppression of evidence that is helpful to an accused person was noted in § 8.7 of this text as an accepted ground for a convicted defendant to seek habeas relief. On the basis of such a claim, Banks was successful in attacking his conviction and the Supreme Court ruled in his favor.

## § 8.10   Special Writs and Remedies

While habeas corpus is the most widespread form of **post-conviction remedy** available to prisoners in the United States, certain others should be mentioned. Some states operate under a general post-conviction procedure act, in lieu of habeas corpus.[51] Correction of improper judgments is sometimes sought under a **writ of coram nobis**.[52] Other remedies are also available. In federal tribunals, a defendant may move for correction of a sentence that was imposed as a result of "arithmetical, technical, or other clear error."[53] Further, within one year of conviction and sentence, the court, on motion of the government, may reduce a sentence to reflect a defendant's substantial assistance to the prosecution in an ongoing criminal investigation. In cases of very strong cooperation, Rule 35(b) of the Federal Rules of Criminal Procedure further provides that "the court may reduce the sentence to a level below the minimum sentence established by statute."

Special actions that may be taken by courts in processing and disposing of cases are listed hereafter and briefly described.

### 1.  Mandamus

The **writ of mandamus** is sought to compel a lower court to do something it has refused to do. For example, if a lower court that is ordered to retry a defendant has failed to do so, application can be made to the appellate court

---

[50]   124 S. Ct. 1256 (2004).

[51]   Under the Uniform Post-Conviction Procedure Act, petitions for post-conviction relief are filed in the sentencing court. The Act also provides for counsel in post-conviction proceedings, and a free transcript in post-conviction appeals in the case of poor persons. The Uniform Post-Conviction Procedure Act was drafted by the National Conference of Commissioners on Uniform State Laws and has been enacted into law in several states.

[52]   Writ of coram nobis is available in some states to permit a court which entered a judgment to correct it after rendition. It is also available in federal court to vacate a faulty federal conviction. United States v. Johnson, 237 F.3d 751 (6th Cir. 2001) (*coram nobis* may sometimes be used to vacate a federal conviction, even including cases in which the petitioner has already served his sentence, in cases in which his fundamental rights were violated).

[53]   FED. R. CRIM. P. 35.

for a writ of mandamus to force the lower court to comply. A **writ of prohibition** is a corollary writ, and it prohibits a court from doing something beyond its authority.[54]

### 2. Stay of Execution

When a case is appealed to a higher court, this does not necessarily prohibit the carrying out of the sentence imposed on a defendant. Especially in capital punishment cases, in which delay in execution of the sentence can have life or death significance, an application for **stay of execution** may be made to stay proceedings until the appellate processes have been completed. The presence of irreparable injury (not deemed present in most felonies) if the sentence is carried out will move the appellate court to grant a stay.

Rule 38, Federal Rules of Criminal Procedure, provides that a sentence of death shall be automatically stayed in federal courts whenever an appeal is taken. Sentences of imprisonment are stayed if an appeal is taken and the defendant is admitted to bail. As discussed in the bail section, bail will be denied on appeal if any one of four circumstances is present: (1) the appeal is frivolous, (2) the appeal is taken for delay, (3) the imposition of regular reporting requirements and other conditions of release will not assure non-flight by the defendant; or (4) the defendant poses a danger to any other person or the community.

### 3. Injunction

**Writs of injunction** may be issued by a court commanding persons to refrain from doing particular acts. An injunction frequently is issued during the pendency of legal proceedings to protect property or other rights until in-court proceedings are completed. This is a temporary injunction, and it may be made final if the court finds the enjoined party should be controlled in the future by the terms of the injunction.

---

[54]　STERN & GRESSMAN, SUPREME COURT PRACTICE (7th ed. 1993). Mandamus may be used where the lower court has neglected a duty, but may not be employed to force action when nonaction is within the proper discretion of the lower court. For example, a writ of mandamus will not apply to compel a magistrate to issue a search warrant based on the affidavits presented to him, in the view of one authority. It is the magistrate's duty to hear and decide the matter, however, and when he or she refuses to make any decisions at all, a writ of mandamus may be issued to compel him or her to take action, although the magistrate cannot be told to grant or deny the request for a warrant. *See* 4 WHARTON, CRIMINAL LAW AND PROCEDURE 234 (1957).

# Special Problems:

## Location of Trial
## and Double Jeopardy

# 9

## Chapter Outline

## § 9.1  Location of Trial: Constitutional Basis

The Sixth Amendment to the United States Constitution provides that in all criminal prosecutions "the accused shall enjoy the right to a speedy and public trial, by an impartial jury of the State and district wherein the crime shall have been committed, which district shall have been previously ascertained by law . . ." The guarantee of a trial in the appropriate state and district is implemented in federal cases by the existence of United States District Courts, which have territorial jurisdiction over federal offenses committed within the states. These courts have jurisdiction over some or all of a state, depending on the size of the state.[1] Here we should clarify the differences between jurisdiction and venue, which are distinctly different. Jurisdiction refers to a court's inherent power to decide a case; it is established by the laws that establish the court and limit its powers. Venue designates the particular county or city in which a court with jurisdiction may hear and determine the case; in criminal cases the venue for trial is generally the place where the crime was committed.

State courts are also guided by the territorial principle, with state constitutions and statutes providing that persons are liable to prosecution for public offenses committed in whole or significant part within the boundaries of the prosecuting state, whether the defendant is a resident of the state or any other state or country. Jurisdiction is thus asserted over crimes that occur within the state. Most states also identify the specific place of trial under venue statutes

---

[1]  Iowa, for example, is divided into two federal districts, northern and southern. Thus, if a person commits robbery of a federally insured bank in the city of Des Moines (the state capital), he or she may be tried under the federal bank robbery statute in the United States District Court for the Southern District of Iowa. The federal case reporter system published by West Publishing Company contains in the opening portions of its federal case reports (Federal 3d Reporter, Federal Supplement, Federal Rules Decision) a chart showing the thirteen federal judicial circuits as well as lists of all United States Courts of Appeals and District Court judges, specifying the federal judicial district in which each of the latter are assigned. A federal judicial circuit chart also appears in § 8.1 of this text.

that direct that the defendant be tried in the county where the crime was committed. Venue may be in more than one county, in cases in which the offense crosses county boundaries. For example, if a person is kidnapped in one county and held for ransom in another, prosecution under the state kidnapping law may proceed in either county.

In a Kentucky case,[2] the defendants were charged with raping three young girls and were sentenced to life in prison. According to one of the victims, she was abducted in Jefferson County, Kentucky, and taken to Oldham County in the same state, where she was raped. Because the trial was held in Jefferson County, it was argued by the defendants that venue was improper, that any trial should have been held in Oldham County, and that the rape convictions should therefore be set aside. The Kentucky Court of Appeals denied the claims made by referring to the principle that different acts may constitute part of the same crime:

> KRS 452.550 provides: "Where an offense is committed partly in one and partly in another county, or if acts and their effects constituting an offense occur in different counties, the prosecution may be in either county in which any of such acts occurs." The initial abduction was a sequential part of carrying out the purpose of having carnal knowledge of their victim. Accordingly venue was in either Jefferson County or Oldham County.

In similar fashion, the United States Supreme Court has established that when a crime consists of distinct parts that have different localities, the main offense may be tried where any part can be proved to have been done.[3]

Frequently venue is a fact that must be established by the prosecutor in criminal trials. Some codes require the defendant to make a timely objection to the prosecution's failure to properly establish venue in order to trigger the issue. Many others simply view it as part of the case that the prosecutor must prove at trial, along with the other elements of the crime.[4] In *United States v. Davis*,[5] several important points relevant to federal court jurisdiction are made. "The right of criminal defendants to be tried in the state and district in which the crime was committed is guaranteed by Article III and the Sixth Amendment to the United States Constitution and Rule 18 of the Federal Rules of Criminal Procedure." The burden of proving that the crime occurred in the district of trial is squarely on the prosecution, but in establishing same, the prosecution is not invariably required to meet the reasonable doubt standard applicable to all substantive elements of the offense. Rather, federal cases take the view that the prosecution need only show by a preponderance of the evidence that the trial is in the same district as the criminal offense. Although a number of states follow the federal courts, other states disagree and require proof of venue beyond a reasonable doubt. Can venue be proved by circumstantial evidence? Some cases say yes, although one of these decisions reversed a conviction because of the failure of the government to prove that venue was properly laid in the trial district.[6]

---

2    Moore v. Commonwealth, 523 S.W.2d 635 (Ky. 1975).
3    United States v. Rodriguez-Moreno, 526 U.S. 275 (1999).
4    KAMISAR, LAFAVE, ISRAEL, AND KING, MODERN CRIMINAL PROCEDURE 1015 (10th ed. 2002).
5    666 F.2d 195 (5th Cir. 1982) (footnotes omitted).
6    *Ibid.*

## § 9.2   Commission of an Offense

The question of whether an offense is committed within the boundaries of a state for the purpose of jurisdiction to prosecute the perpetrator can raise interesting issues. In the case of numerous felonies (robbery, larceny, arson) there may be no difficulty in fixing the place of the crime. But states frequently deem it within their jurisdictional authority to prosecute more complicated offenses that begin in another state and are completed in the trial state, as well as crimes that begin in the trial state and are completed in another jurisdiction. For example, in *People v. Botkin*[7] the California Supreme Court held that a person could be prosecuted for murder in California when she prepared and mailed a box of poisoned candy in San Francisco, addressed to the victim in Dover, Delaware, where the addressee received, consumed, and expired from the poisoned candy. California Penal Code § 27(1) applied to persons who committed "in whole or in part, any crime within this state." The "in part" portion of the formula contained here and in similar state statutes in other jurisdictions is frequently applied for purposes of conspiracy prosecutions, when meetings of the conspirators as well as overt acts to advance the purpose of the conspiracy take place in various states.[8] Questions of location of prosecution can arise in bizarre shooting situations when the bullet crosses a state line. What if a man shoots another some distance away, and the victim is hit and dies across the state boundary line in another state? Is jurisdiction in the state where the shot is fired, the state where the victim is hit, or both?[9]

---

[7] 64 P. 286 (Cal. 1901). State v. Harrington, 260 A.2d 692 (Vt. 1970), cites *Botkin* with approval and holds: "Where the crime is composed of an interstate series of acts, it is jurisdictionally competent for a state to attach legal consequences to any overt act committed within its boundaries, even though the final impact and injury may occur elsewhere."

[8] On conspiracy prosecution where the agreement occurs in another state followed by a conspirator's overt act in the forum state, *see* People v. Perry, 177 N.E.2d 323, 327-328 (Ill. 1961). Under the theory that a conspiracy trial may be had in every state where acts in furtherance of the conspiracy take place, multiple state prosecutions can be had over the same series of transactions. In federal court, however, a trial at one location in the case of a conspiracy generally can be pleaded to bar another prosecution concerning the same agreement.

[9] In Simpson v. State, 17 S.E. 984 (Ga. 1893), the accused, standing in South Carolina, fired twice at another person, the latter being in Georgia. Prosecution for the offense was instituted in Georgia, and the defendant was convicted. The Georgia Supreme Court held that the crime occurred in Georgia, ruling that "a crime is committed where the criminal act takes effect." The court strongly intimated that prosecution of the accused could have been had in either Georgia or South Carolina. However, in another shooting case, State v. Hall, 19 S.E. 602 (N.C. 1894), the defendant was standing in North Carolina and shot a man across the border in Tennessee. Prosecution of the defendant was had in North Carolina. Holding that a state cannot punish offenses committed in another state, the North Carolina Supreme Court ruled that the murder charge could not be prosecuted in North Carolina, although a use of deadly weapons charge might be proper in that state.

Several states have enacted "state of death" statutes that promote the notion that the place where a crime takes effect has jurisdiction to prosecution. In the situation where the defendant stabs his victim in State X but the victim later dies in State Y where he was taken for hospitalization, there is considered to be murder in the state where the wound was given, and is also murder under these statutes in State Y, the place where the victim died. Concurrent jurisdiction to try the case exists, and the defendant may be liable for murder prosecution in either state. George, *Extraterritorial Application of Penal Legislation*, 64 MICH. L. REV. 609, 622 (1966). *See also* CAL. PENAL CODE § 778 (jurisdiction in California to try offenses commenced without the state but consummated within its boundaries).

Other cases have posed knotty jurisdiction and venue questions. In witness intimidation cases, if a witness is to testify in a proceeding in state A but is threatened by friends of the defendant in state B, does the crime of tampering with a witness occur in State A or State B? When a pornographer distributes obscene materials through the mails, does he commit an offense where he mailed the materials, or where they were received? Or both? Case law provides responses to these questions. In witness intimidation cases, one decision ruled that a trial about threats made to the witness could properly be had at the place of the judicial proceedings where the witness was slated to testify. A proper situs for trial of those who threatened the witness would be the location of the original trial, which they sought to disrupt.[10] As to the shipment of pornography, another opinion indicated that interstate shipment of obscene materials constitutes a continuous offense that occurs in every district the material touches.[11]

In federal cases some special problems have occurred, particularly in the field of criminal conduct connected with use of the United States mails. In *Travis v. United States*,[12] the defendant was charged with making and filing a false affidavit. Under a federal statute the affidavit was required to be sent to a government agency, and the defendant mailed it in Colorado addressed to the agency in Washington, D.C. The defendant was later prosecuted and convicted in federal court in Colorado. Bearing in mind the federal constitutional provision that criminal trials shall be held in the state and district where the crime is committed, the question in the case was whether the trial should have taken place in Colorado or the District of Columbia. A majority of the United States Supreme Court reversed the defendant's conviction and ruled that venue lay only in Washington, D.C., despite sharp criticism from three dissenting judges.

As recently as 1998 the Supreme Court has demonstrated its willingness to support dismissal of criminal charges against defendants where the prosecution has commenced charges in the wrong place. In *United States v. Cabrales*,[13] a defendant was indicted for money laundering. Although cash was generated by unlawful distribution of cocaine in Missouri, the laundering occurred entirely in Florida. The Court pointed out that proper venue in criminal proceedings was a matter of concern to the nation's founders. "Their complaints against the King of Great Britain, listed in the Declaration of Independence, included his transportation of colonists beyond Seas to be tried." Because the Constitution safeguards the defendant's venue right, the government's efforts to try Vickie Cabrales in Missouri were misdirected. She was not charged with assisting in the Missouri drug trafficking, nor with conspiracy. She was charged with money laundering "after the fact" of the drug dealing, transactions that began and were completed in Florida. For this reason, the charges against her in Missouri were correctly dismissed. Missouri was not a place of proper venue for the money laundering offense.

---

[10]   United States v. Kiblen, 667 F.2d 452 (4th Cir. 1982).
[11]   United States v. Bagrell, 679 F.2d 826 (11th Cir. 1982).
[12]   364 U.S. 631, 81 S. Ct. 358, 5 L. Ed. 2d 340 (1961). FED. R. CRIM. P. 18, provides for prosecution "in a district in which the offense was committed."
[13]   118 S. Ct. 1772 (1998).

## § 9.3    Change of Venue

The right of the defendant to be tried in the county (in state prosecutions) or the district (in federal cases) where the crime occurred is not inconsistent with his or her right to ask for a change of venue in certain circumstances. Occasionally a defendant may feel that advance publicity or other causes have created an atmosphere not conducive to a fair trial in the location where the offense took place. A defendant will frequently desire transfer of the case to another location in these circumstances, and a **motion for change of venue** may be employed to accomplish this. Appropriate grounds must be shown before the court will change venue, however. For example, under Rule 21 of the Federal Rules of Criminal Procedure, the defendant must establish (1) that there exists in the place where the prosecution is pending so great a prejudice against the defendant that he or she cannot obtain a fair and impartial trial there; or (2) another location is much more convenient for the parties and witnesses than the intended place of trial, and the interests of justice require a transfer of location. Numerous states have similar provisions.

Changes of venue usually require the criminal action to be tried in a different location from that where the crime occurred. However, some states provide an alternative possibility. Their rules of procedure allow the action to be tried in the county of the crime, with the jury being selected in another county and transported to the site of the trial.[14]

Sometimes a change of judge, as opposed to change of venue, is requested. A federal statute requires a judge to disqualify himself or herself in any proceeding in which the judge's impartiality might reasonably be questioned.[15] Where there is evidence that a judge is biased, defendants have moved for **recusal** of the judge from defendant's hearing or trial. However, to force a judge from a case, a party's showing must be a strong one. A Supreme Court case observes: "[J]udicial remarks during the course of a trial that are critical or disapproving of, or even hostile to, counsel, the parties, or their cases, ordinarily do not support a bias or partiality challenge. They may do so if they reveal an opinion that derives from an extrajudicial source; and they will do so if they reveal such a high degree of favoritism or antagonism as to make fair judgment impossible."[16]

## § 9.4    Extradition and Transfer of Custody for Trial

### 1.  Interstate Extradition

The Uniform Criminal Extradition Act, adopted in the vast majority of states, provides that it is the duty of a state governor to deliver up a person from his or her state to another state when that person has fled the other state

---

[14]   Rule 19.2, GA. UNIF. SUP. CT. R.
[15]   28 U.S.C. § 455, *construed in* Demjanjuk v. Petrovsky, 776 F.2d 571 (6th Cir. 1985).
[16]   Liteky v. United States, 114 S. Ct. 1147 (1994).

to avoid prosecution. Delivery of the fugitive to the executive authority of the state that desires custody of such person is appropriate when the defendant is charged with "treason, felony, or other crime."[17] Demand for **extradition** must be written and must be accompanied by a copy of an indictment, information warrant, or magistrate's affidavit, which charges the demanded person with a crime. If the defendant escaped from confinement in the demanding state, a copy of a judgment of conviction or any sentence imposed must accompany the demand.

When the governor of the state where the defendant is located decides the demand should be complied with, he or she signs a warrant of arrest directed to a peace officer for execution. After arrest of the named person on the fugitive warrant, such person is taken before a judge of a court of record who must inform him or her of the demand made for his or her surrender and of the crime charged in the demanding state. Advice as to legal rights (right to counsel, hearing) should be given at this time. When requested by the accused, a hearing will be set, with notice to the prosecuting officer of the county in which the arrest was made as well as the agent of the demanding state. This hearing is designed to inquire into whether the person is a fugitive subject to extradition. It is frequently waived by the accused.[18]

A Supreme Court opinion aptly summarized the philosophy of criminal extradition. In *Michigan v. Doran*,[19] the governor of Michigan decided to send Robert W. Doran to Arizona to face charges that he stole a truck. The governor ordered extradition. Doran resisted, petitioning in the Michigan courts for a writ of habeas corpus. He won a decision granting his freedom; however, the United States Supreme Court reversed the decision of the Michigan Supreme Court that had mandated Doran's release. The United States Supreme Court stated:

> The Extradition Clause was intended to enable each state to bring offenders to trial as swiftly as possible in the state where the alleged offense was committed. . . . The purpose of the Clause was to preclude any state from becom-

---

[17]  Under an expansive reading of the term "fugitive," modern extradition acts have done away with the requirement that in order to be subject to extradition, every defendant must have fled from justice. Thus, David who lives in State B and conspired to commit an offense in State A might be extradited to State A for trial even though he never lived there and did not "flee from justice" in that state. See 11 U.L.A. § 6 (1974) (Governor of state may surrender accused to another state where crime committed even though accused was not in that state at time of commission of crime.).

[18]  *See* Uniform Criminal Extradition Act, 11 U.L.A. 290 (1974). Many states have adopted reciprocal arrangements on detainers under the detainer compact, captioned the Interstate Agreement on Detainers, to expedite trial of prisoners held in custody in other jurisdictions. *See also* the Uniform Mandatory Disposition of Detainer Act, 11 U.L.A. 321 (1974).

Interstate extradition has a constitutional base. The United States Constitution provides that "a person charged in any state with treason, felony, or other crime who shall flee from justice and be found in another state, shall on demand of the executive authority of the state from which he fled, be delivered up to be removed to the state having jurisdiction of the crime." Art. 4 § 2. To the effect that the word *crime* in this context includes a misdemeanor, rendering it an extraditable offense, *see* Ex parte Reggel, 114 U.S. 642, 5 S. Ct. 1148, 29 L. Ed. 250 (1885).

For a list of the countries with which the United States has entered into treaties of extradition, *see* 18 U.S.C. § 3181. The federal extradition statute appears at 18 U.S.C. §§ 3181 to 3195.

[19]  99 S. Ct. 530 (1978). In accord with *Doran*, *see* Pacileo v. Walker, 449 U.S. 86 (1980).

ing a sanctuary for fugitives from the justice of another state and thus "balkanize" the administration of criminal justice among the several states.

Governors are required to cooperate with each other in surrendering prisoners. When the papers from the demanding state are in order and a proper identification of the defendant has been made, the governor of the asylum state (the place to which the defendant has fled) must comply. It is not only the governor whose actions are circumscribed, however. The *courts* of the asylum state may not pose unreasonable obstacles to the process by setting the defendant free. The *Doran* case explains:

> [When the governor of the state where the person is found, the asylum state, grants extradition, such] grant of extradition is prima facie evidence that the constitutional and statutory requirements have been met. Cf. Bassing v. Cady, 208 U.S. 386, 392, 28 S.Ct. 392, 393, 52 L.Ed. 540 (1908). Once the governor has granted extradition, a court considering release on habeas corpus can do no more than decide (1) whether the extradition documents on their face are in order; (b) whether the petitioner has been charged with a crime in the demanding state; (c) whether the petitioner is the person named in the request for extradition; and (d) whether the petitioner is a fugitive. These are historic facts readily verifiable.

Neither the governor of the asylum state nor its courts have the power to interfere with and stymie transfer of a fugitive. The governor of the asylum state no longer has the discretion not to extradite.[20] It is no defense to extradition that the defendant claims that he fled the state where the crime occurred under duress. In *New Mexico ex rel. Ortiz v. Reed*,[21] the Supreme Court held that the state of New Mexico was required to return a fugitive to Ohio. Responding to the defendant's fear that he faced physical harm if sent to an Ohio prison, the Court held that "what may be expected to happen in the demanding state when the fugitive returns [is an issue] that must be tried in the Courts of that State, and not in those of the asylum State."

Notwithstanding the language of *Doran* that interstate extradition was intended to be a summary proceeding, many state laws have developed numerous ponderous steps in the process, once a fugitive refuses to waive extradition. This poses special difficulties for prosecutors in cities that border another state. For example, many communities are located along rivers that separate two states, and sprawling urban areas commonly spread across state boundaries. A thief can steal a car and by driving it to another part of the urban area, or by crossing a river (and thereby removing himself to another state), successfully trigger the operation of substantial procedural steps required to secure extradition. With modern emphasis on reducing pretrial delays and making the delivery of justice more effective, proposals to overhaul interstate extradition of fugitives have appeared. One such suggestion, an interstate

---

[20]    Puerto Rico v. Branstad, 107 S. Ct. 2802 (1987).
[21]    118 S. Ct. 1860 (1998).

extradition compact, would simplify the multiple procedural steps presently required in a simple extradition case. One of the features of the suggested compact allows extradition to be requested by the prosecutor of the city where the crime occurred and granted by the prosecutor where the fugitive is apprehended. In situations of interstate flight by criminals, the proposed compact eliminates the need to involve the governor of the demanding state and the surrendering state.[22]

In addition to extradition, a federal statute is designed to assist state prosecutions and deter those intending to flee jurisdictions in order to frustrate the administration of justice. The statute makes it a felony to travel in interstate commerce to avoid prosecution or the giving of testimony, and provides as follows:

§ 1073. Flight to avoid prosecution or giving testimony

Whoever moves or travels in interstate or foreign commerce with intent either (1) to avoid prosecution, or custody or confinement after conviction, under the laws of the place from which he flees, for a crime, or an attempt to commit a crime, punishable by death or which is a felony under the laws of the place from which the fugitive flees, or (2) to avoid giving testimony in any criminal proceedings in such place in which the commission of an offense punishable by death or which is a felony under the laws of said State, is charged, or (3) to avoid service of, or contempt proceedings for alleged disobedience of, lawful process requiring attendance and the giving of testimony or the production of documentary evidence before an agency of a State empowered by the law of such State to conduct investigations of alleged criminal activities, shall be fined under this title or imprisoned not more than five years, or both.

. . .

Violations of this section may be prosecuted only in the Federal judicial district in which the original crime was alleged to have been committed, or in which the person was held in custody or confinement, or in which an avoidance of service of process or a contempt referred to in clause (3) of the first paragraph of this section is alleged to have been committed, and only upon formal approval in writing by the Attorney General, the Deputy Attorney General, the Associate Attorney General, or an Assistant Attorney General of the United States, which function of approving prosecutions may not be delegated.[23]

The federal statute just cited provides for the transfer of witnesses from one jurisdiction to another. To further combat problems in producing witness testimony, most states have enacted reciprocal legislation patterned after the Uniform Act to Secure the Attendance of Witnesses from Without a State in Criminal Proceedings. These laws operate between and among participating states and provide legal machinery whereby the state in which the criminal

---

[22]   IOWA CODE ch. 818 (1998).

[23]   18 U.S.C. § 1073. By a 1980 addition to this section, Congress expressly declared its intent that section 1073 of title 18, United States Code, apply to cases involving parental kidnapping and interstate or international flight to avoid prosecution under applicable state felony statutes.

proceeding is being held can obtain the testimony of an unwilling witness who is a nonresident or has fled the state. The Supreme Court upheld the power of a state to order a witness to appear in another state in *New York v. O'Neill*.[24] By holding such statutes constitutional, the Supreme Court furthered the administration of justice by enabling defendants as well as state prosecutors to obtain witnesses who might otherwise be difficult to reach.

## 2. Forcible Transfer of Defendants

It is a general rule of law that an accused person can be brought within the territorial jurisdiction where he or she is charged, and the right of the local court to proceed with trial is not impaired by the fact that his or her presence was secured by kidnapping, deception, or abduction. An accused person usually has no defense to a state or federal criminal prosecution on the ground that he or she was illegally arrested or forcibly brought within the territory of the court.

Often it is a private bail bondsman who seizes the accused in State A and brings him or her to State B for trial, without the benefit of legal process. However, sometimes the participation of government agents in the process is relatively direct. One case involved efforts to bring a Mexican doctor to the United States for trial. Mexican authorities would not assist in a legal extradition. Federal agents believed the doctor had participated in the torture of a captured DEA agent. Mexican bounty hunters were hired to apprehend the doctor and force him to come to the United States. The bounty hunters took the doctor from his home in Mexico for this purpose. The doctor later sued the U.S. government for violating international law. His claims were rejected.[25]

## 3. International Extradition

What about securing the presence of a defendant in an American trial from a foreign country? How is this handled when, for example, a United States court wants to try a citizen of Colombia for conspiracy to commit drug crimes in an American jurisdiction? What about the converse of this situation? Can an American court send a United States citizen to a foreign nation for trial?

The last question arose in a dramatic case, the extradition of John Demjanjuk from northern Ohio to the State of Israel. Demjanjuk was a native of the Ukraine, one of the republics of the Soviet Union. After World War II he came to the United States and became a naturalized citizen in 1958. The district court found that Demjanjuk was conscripted into the Soviet Army in 1940

---

[24]   359 U.S. 1, 79 S. Ct. 564, 3 L. Ed. 2d 585 (1959). The uniform act on witnesses has been widely adopted.

[25]   *See* United States v. Alvarez-Machain, 124 S. Ct. 821, 159 L. Ed. 2d 718 (2003). Frisbie v. Collins, 342 U.S. 519, 522, 72 S. Ct. 509, 96 L. Ed. 541 (1952) ("the power of a court to try a person for crime is not impaired by the fact that he had been brought within the court's jurisdiction by reason of a 'forcible abduction'. . .").

and was captured by the Germans in 1942. Although he steadfastly denied it, the district court further found that Demjanjuk became a guard for the Germans at the Treblinka concentration camp in Poland. Five Treblinka survivors and one former German guard identified him as the Ukrainian guard at the camp who was known as "Ivan the Terrible."

The State of Israel filed a request for extradition with the United States Department of State. Following a hearing in federal court in Ohio, the district court ordered Demjanjuk extradited for trial in Israel pursuant to a treaty of extradition between the United States and Israel. The treaty provided that each contracting party (the U.S. and Israel) would deliver people found in its territory for prosecution in the other country when they have been charged in the requesting country with crimes like murder, manslaughter, or inflicting grievous bodily harm.

The United States Court of Appeals approved extradition. "It is a fundamental requirement for international extradition that the crime for which extradition is sought be one provided for by the treaty between the requesting and the requested nation." Because an offense is extraditable only if the acts charged are criminal by the laws of both countries, the court ruled: "Murder is a crime in every state of the United States. The fact that there is no separate offense of mass murder or murder of tens of thousands of Jews in this country is beside the point. The act of unlawfully killing one or more persons with the requisite malice is punishable as murder. That is the test. The acts charged are criminal both in Israel and throughout the United States, including Ohio."[26]

The principle of double criminality is the key to international extradition. It holds that an offense is not extraditable unless it constitutes a crime in the country where the defendant is found, as well as in the requesting country.[27] Hence the emphasis on this point in the Demjanjuk litigation. Ultimately, the case against the defendant was dismissed. John Demjanjuk was released by Israel's Supreme Court upon a finding of reasonable doubt as to guilt.

International extradition requires a treaty with the cooperating country. The United States cannot extradite someone to another country in the absence of a valid treaty. The United States has extradition treaties with numerous countries, and there are currently a number of active extradition cases involving fugitives in the United States who are wanted by other countries who are in America as well as cases involving criminals wanted in the United States who are living abroad.[27]

---

[26]    Demjanjuk v. Petrovsky, 776 F.2d 571, 580 (6th Cir. 1985). Bernholz and Herman, *Problems of Double Criminality,* 21 TRIAL 58 (Jan. 1985).

[27]    For a list of countries with which the United States has extradition treaties, *see* 18 U.S.C. § 3181-3195.

## § 9.5 Double Jeopardy: Application to States

After years of controversy over the point, the United States Supreme Court ruled in *Benton v. Maryland* in 1969 that the double jeopardy provision of the United States Constitution applied to the states.[28] In extending the federal guarantee, the Supreme Court cited the fundamental character of double jeopardy protection to the American scheme of justice. The decision that accomplished this result overruled the earlier landmark case of *Palko v. Connecticut*,[29] in which the Court in 1937 had refused to make the federal double jeopardy provision applicable in state trials. In *Benton*, the defendant had been originally charged with both burglary and larceny. Upon trial by jury he was acquitted of the larceny but convicted of the burglary. He appealed the burglary conviction to the Maryland Court of Appeals, won, and the case was remanded to the trial court for a new trial. The defendant argued to the trial court that he had run the gauntlet of trial on the larceny charge, had been acquitted, and was thus immune from reprosecution for that offense. The trial judge disagreed and the defendant was charged again with both burglary and larceny. This time he was convicted of both offenses. Upon review, the United States Supreme Court ruled the larceny conviction could not stand:

> The fundamental nature of the guarantee against double jeopardy can hardly be obtained. Its origins can be traced to Greek and Roman times, and it became established in the common law of England long before this Nation's independence. See *Bartkus v. Illinois*, 359 U.S. 121, 151-155, 79 S.Ct. 676, 697, 3 L.Ed.2d. 684 (1959) (Black, J. dissenting). As with many other elements of the common law, it was carried into the jurisprudence of this Country through the medium of Blackstone, who codified the doctrine in his Commentaries. "[T]he plea of autrefois acquit, or a former acquittal," he wrote, "is grounded on this universal maxim of the common law of England, that no man is to be brought into jeopardy of his life more than once for the same offense." Today, every State incorporates some form of the prohibition in its constitution or common law. As this Court put it in *Green v. United States*, 355 U.S. 184, 187-88, 78 S.Ct. 221, 223, 2 L.Ed.2d 199 (1957), "[t]he underlying idea, one that is deeply ingrained in at least the Anglo-American system of jurisprudence, is that the State with all its resources and power should not be allowed to make repeated attempts to convict an individual for an alleged offense, thereby subjecting him to embarrassment, expense and ordeal and compelling him to live in a continuing state of anxiety and insecurity, as well as enhancing the possibility that even though innocent he may be found guilty." This underlying notion has from the very beginning been part of our constitutional tradition. Like the right to trial by jury, it is clearly

---

[28] Benton v. Maryland, 395 U.S. 784, 89 S. Ct. 2056, 23 L. Ed. 2d 707 (1969). *Benton* was followed by Price v. Georgia, 398 U.S. 323, 90 S. Ct. 1757, 26 L. Ed. 2d 300 (1970). The Supreme Court held it unconstitutional for a state to retry a defendant for an offense that was rejected in the first trial, the jury having convicted the defendant of the lesser of two offenses upon first trial of the case. Retrial could only be had of the lesser offense, the conviction that the defendant had appealed.

[29] 302 U.S. 319, 58 S. Ct. 149, 82 L. Ed. 288 (1937).

"fundamental to the American scheme of justice." The validity of petitioner's larceny conviction must be judged not by the watered-down standards enunciated in *Palko*, but under this Court's interpretations of the Fifth Amendment double jeopardy provision.

While virtually every state has its own statutory or constitutional provision on double jeopardy,[30] the federal clause is considerably more stringent than many of the state prohibitions. For example, some states provide that jeopardy attaches to bar retrial of a person only upon that person's conviction or acquittal of a particular charge. Suppose a criminal trial begins, and that the prosecutor declares midway through the government's case that he or she has discovered that a key prosecution witness has left on vacation and is absent from the state. In these circumstances he or she might request that a mistrial be declared by the trial judge, the prosecutor's intent being to begin trial anew upon this witness's return. Older cases in some jurisdictions have held that the defendant might be put on trial again because the first case had been terminated prior to conviction or acquittal, and jeopardy had not yet attached. However, in a federal court a contrary result would almost certainly prevail because of the federal view that jeopardy attaches in a jury case once the jurors have been empaneled and sworn.[31] Because of the 1969 application of the federal jeopardy clause to the states, the more stringent federal standard concerning the time when jeopardy attaches controls state trials also.[32]

The double jeopardy clause prevents both double jeopardy prosecutions as well as double punishments for the same crime. The protection against multiple punishments prohibits the government from punishing a person twice for the same offense.

The United States Supreme Court has found no double punishments in connection with a number of modern sanctions against lawbreakers. First, there was the question of forfeiting a defendant's property after he had suffered a criminal court conviction. Civil forfeiture laws are designed to strip defendants of proceeds of crime, such as money obtained from drug trafficking. Property purchased by crime profits may be confiscated under laws requiring disgorgement of the fruits of illegal conduct. Is it double jeopardy to both punish a defendant for a criminal offense and forfeit his property for that same offense in a separate civil proceeding? No, said the Supreme Court in *United States v. Ursery*.[33] Vehicles used in criminal enterprises may also be forfeited. The theory is that when an owner of property uses it to commit crimes, the owner can be held accountable for the misuse of the property. As Justice Kennedy points out in *Ursery,* the same rationale enables forfeiture of

---

[30]   E.g., O.C.G.A. § 16-1-6 (2004)(Georgia).

[31]   Serfass v. United States, 420 U.S. 377, 95 S. Ct. 1055, 43 L. Ed. 2d 265 (1975). In a nonjury trial jeopardy attaches when the court begins to hear evidence. For review of state rules on when jeopardy attaches, *see* Annotation, *When Does Jeopardy Attach in a Nonjury Trial?*, 49 A.L.R.3D 1039 (1973).

[32]   State v. Moriwake, 647 P.2d 705 (Haw. 1982).

[33]   116 S. Ct. 2135 (1996) (civil forfeiture does not constitute punishment for double jeopardy purposes.).

currency used to facilitate a criminal offense. Forfeiture punishes an owner by taking property involved in a crime, and it often happens that the owner is also the wrongdoer charged with a criminal offense.

In other sorts of situations the court also found no impermissible double punishment. After a sexual offender completes his or her prison term, he or she can be confined further in a civil commitment under sexual predator laws. Such a commitment does not violate double jeopardy rules.[34] Nor does a law that requires authorities to tell communities the whereabouts of a convicted sexual offender when one moves into the neighborhood. Sexual offenders in New Jersey and New York complained that the notification provisions punished them a second time by holding them up to public humiliation after they had served their criminal sentences. The Supreme Court disagreed.

## § 9.6   Retrial of the Accused: When Permitted

Where two separate criminal convictions are involved, even if they come under two distinct statutory provisions, double jeopardy bars double convictions unless each statutory provision requires proof of a fact that the other does not. Where the underlying conduct for which defendant is punished is exactly the same under both statutes, one of the convictions must be vacated.[35] In so holding, the Supreme Court reaffirmed the long-standing *Blockburger* test, which ordains that two statutes on a related topic define different offenses only if "each provision requires proof of a fact which the other does not."[36]

Occasionally unforeseen circumstances arise during a trial, making its completion impossible. A case involving this problem reached the Supreme Court, raising the question of whether jeopardy attaches when this occurs. In *United States v. Jorn*[37] the defendant was charged with willfully assisting taxpayers to prepare fraudulent income tax returns in violation of the United States Code. He came to trial before a jury in the United States District Court for the District of Utah. After the jury was selected and sworn, the first government witness testified. This was an Internal Revenue Service official. Thereafter the first of a series of individual taxpayers whom the defendant allegedly assisted in preparing false returns took the stand on behalf of the prosecution. After this witness was sworn, counsel for the accused interjected that each of the taxpayer witnesses should be warned as to their constitutional rights. Following this request, the trial judge addressed the witness on the stand and informed him of his right to consult counsel before testifying and of his right to remain silent. The witness, referring to himself and his wife, responded to the judge that "our returns have information in them that we know is wrong, and we have admitted this, and I would admit it farther in this court."

---

[34]   Selig v. Yount, 531 U.S. 250 (2001); Kansas v. Hendricks, 117 S. Ct. 2072 (1997).

[35]   Rutledge v United States, 116 S. Ct. 1241 (1996).

[36]   Blockburger v. United States, 284 U.S. 299 (1932).

[37]   400 U.S. 470, 91 S. Ct. 547, 27 L. Ed. 2d 543 (1971).

The judge dismissed the witness ("I am not going to let you admit it any further in this court.") and instructed him to step down. The trial judge then asked the Assistant United States Attorney whether the taxpayer witnesses had been given warnings as to their constitutional rights. Subsequent to the ensuing dialogue on this question the court indicated doubt that the taxpayers had been appropriately warned by the government, dismissed the jury, and vacated the case, then called the taxpayer witnesses before him and advised them to consult counsel before deciding to testify. When the case was scheduled for a new trial thereafter, the defendant moved to dismiss on the ground of double jeopardy. The defendant's motion was granted and the government's case against the defendant was dismissed by the trial judge. The government prosecuted an appeal to the Supreme Court of the United States, which affirmed the dismissal.

A critical question involved in the case centers on the ability of the government to put to trial an accused person who has already been tried on a prior occasion, but which trial was aborted before completion. Certain federal cases determining whether the accused must undergo a second trial in such circumstances have fallen into distinct patterns. If the first trial was interrupted and terminated before completion because of some omission by the government, the defendant was entitled to his or her freedom. If the second trial was necessitated by some activity of the accused, he or she could be retried. An example of the latter situation occurs when the defendant pleads that a mistrial be declared because his or her star witness, yet to testify in the case, has become seriously ill. Suppose the judge stops the proceedings and declares a mistrial? Retrial may be later initiated without legal difficulty upon recovery of this witness.

Retrial is also permitted when a convicted person attacks his conviction on appeal or in habeas corpus and wins, perhaps because the trial jury was improperly selected or because of an erroneous trial court ruling on a point of evidence. In such situations, the accused may be prosecuted again, under the general rule, and the Supreme Court has so held.[38] A similar rule holds that reprosecution may be had where the trial judge deems it necessary to expel the defendant's attorney for misconduct during the opening statement and a mistrial is thereafter declared upon defendant's motion. When circumstances develop that are not attributable to prosecutorial or judicial overreaching, a motion by the defendant for mistrial is ordinarily assumed to remove any barrier to reprosecution.[39]

Assume that after a case is fully tried and given to the jury to decide, they deadlock and cannot agree on a verdict. Has jeopardy attached in such a case? When the first trial ends in a hung jury, retrial is permitted.[40]

As is apparent, a number of circumstances can cause the first trial of a defendant to end without a verdict. Equally apparent is the conclusion that

[38] United States v. Tateo, 377 U.S. 463, 84 S. Ct. 1587, 12 L. Ed. 2d 448 (1964).
[39] United States v. Dinitz, 424 U.S. 600, 96 S. Ct. 1075, 47 L. Ed. 2d 267 (1976).
[40] United States v. Perez, 22 U.S. (9 Wheat.) 579 (1824); Walters v. State, 503 S.W.2d 895 (Ark. 1974).

many of these unresolved or prematurely terminated cases may be retried.[41] Retrial is permissible after a conviction is reversed on appeal.[42] Some court decisions emphasize that reprosecution is not barred unless the appellate reversal was based on a finding that the evidence did not authorize a verdict— insufficiency of the evidence is a key. Where, for example, the ground for reversal was the trial court's instructional error, defendant's objection to retrial (which objection was contained in a **motion in autrefois convict** and plea of former jeopardy) was denied.[43] Incorrect receipt or rejection of evidence, incorrect instructions, or other trial error that is not grounded in insufficiency of the evidence may result in reversal of defendant's original conviction, but does not bar readjudication of guilt in a proceeding free from error.[44]

Conversely, where the prosecution fails to prove an essential element of an offense in achieving a conviction and the case is reversed on appeal, retrial is prohibited. "Unless the evidence at the first trial is sufficient to authorize the verdict of guilty, a second prosecution is barred."[45] A similar result obtains if, at the close of the prosecution's case-in-chief at a bench trial, the trial court dismisses or grants a directed verdict because the evidence is legally insufficient to sustain a guilty verdict.[46]

Other decisions have spelled out additional details of the double jeopardy rule. In *Breed v. Jones*,[47] Justice Burger announced the rule that a prisoner who is tried first as a juvenile in a full adjudication proceeding cannot be retried for the same offense as an adult. The Supreme Court has also adjudicated the right of the state to retry a defendant after the first trial was aborted in consequence of a prosecutor's improper question. In *Oregon v. Kennedy*,[48] the prosecutor asked a witness if he had ever done business with the defendant. When the witness replied that he had not, the prosecutor inquired: "Is that because he is a crook?" The defendant asked for a mistrial based on the prosecutor's remark, and the trial judge granted it. On retrial, the trial court rejected the defendant's double jeopardy objection. The United States Supreme Court upheld this approach.

When the defendant moves for a mistrial and the judge grants it, the defendant cannot complain when the case is retried. There is a narrow exception to this rule that occurs when a prosecutor behaves so badly that a defendant is virtually forced to ask for a mistrial. These are cases in which the prosecutor's bad acts "were done 'in order to goad the [defendant] into requesting a mistrial.'" The prosecutor's actions in *Oregon v. Kennedy* did not fall into this category. The Supreme Court could find no malicious intent on

---

[41]   Illinois v. Somerville, 410 U.S. 458, 93 S. Ct. 1066, 35 L. Ed. 2d 425 (1973). The Somerville approach was followed in United States v. Sanford, 429 U.S. 14, 97 S. Ct. 20, 50 L. Ed. 2d 17 (1976).

[42]   Montana v. Hall, 107 S. Ct. 1825 (1987).

[43]   Price v. State, 370 S.E.2d 6 (Ga. App. 1988).

[44]   Lockhart v. Nelson, 109 S. Ct. 285 (1988).

[45]   Holcomb v. Peachtree City, 370 S.E.2d 23 (Ga. App. 1988). *See* Hudson v. Louisiana, 450 U.S. 40 (1981) (retrial barred where conviction set aside because of insufficient evidence).

[46]   Smalis v. Pennsylvania, 476 U.S. 140 (1986).

[47]   421 U.S. 519, 95 S. Ct. 1779, 44 L. Ed. 2d 346 (1975). *See* § 10.4 infra.

[48]   456 U.S. 667 (1982).

the part of the prosecutor to elicit a mistrial request from the defendant. In the absence of any finding that the prosecutor engaged in extreme bad faith misconduct, the court upheld Kennedy's theft conviction.

## § 9.7  Heavier Sentence Upon Retrial

Absent extraordinary circumstances, it is held that the accused may be tried for a second time for the same offense as that for which he or she was originally convicted when his or her prior conviction has been set aside at defendant's own initiative.[49] A problem may arise when a defendant is reconvicted on the second trial, but this time the judge imposes a harsher sentence upon him or her. For example, suppose state law permits the sentencing judge to impose a fixed maximum term ranging from 10 years to life imprisonment in cases where a defendant is convicted of second degree murder. The defendant is so convicted and is sentenced to 20 years by the trial judge. He appeals, wins, and the first conviction and sentence are vacated. Upon retrial the defendant is again convicted of second degree murder, but this time he is sentenced to life imprisonment.

Does this prisoner have grounds for a constitutional objection because of the new sentence? Probably so, under the Supreme Court decision in *North Carolina v. Pearce*.[50] On facts similar to those set forth in the example above, the United States Supreme Court ruled that more severe punishment could only be imposed by the judge at resentencing if based upon conduct occurring between the time of the first and second sentence. In cases in which there is no identifiable conduct during this period that justifies a harsher sentence, and fresh information has not surfaced that would justify the increased sentence, a more severe sentence is barred as unconstitutional. And the trial judge who does increase upon a second conviction must explain his or her reasons at the time of imposing same, placing the factual data upon which the increased sentence is based in the trial court record.[51]

Later cases have expanded the material upon which an enhanced sentence may be based. Along with misconduct by the accused after the first trial, the sentencing judge in the second case can also consider new information that only became available to the court at or near the time of the second sentencing proceeding. This information might relate to much earlier conduct by the defendant. In the absence of objective information justifying it, an enhanced second sentence is presumed to be vindictive. The Supreme Court remarked:

---

[49] KLOTTER, KANOVITZ, AND KANOVITZ, CONSTITUTIONAL LAW 395 (10th ed. 2005).

[50] 395 U.S. 711, 89 S. Ct. 2072, 23 L. Ed. 2d 656 (1969). The *Pearce* doctrine has removed the major obstacle that prevents a defendant who received a moderate sentence from appealing his first conviction.

[51] In Ashman, *The Prisoner's Dilemma: Harsher Punishment Upon Retrial*, 55 A.B.A.J. 928 (1969), the author states that "without question" North Carolina v. Pearce has removed most of the obstacles which deter a defendant from attacking his first conviction. *See* United States v. Tucker, 581 F.2d 602 (7th Cir. 1978).

As we explained in *Texas v. McCullough*, [475 U.S. at 138], "the evil the [*Pearce*] Court sought to prevent" was not the imposition of "enlarged sentences after a new trial" but "vindictiveness of a sentencing judge." *Ibid.* See also *Chaffin v. Stynchcombe*, 412 U.S. 17, 25, 93 S. Ct. 1977, 1982, 36 L.Ed. 2d 714 (1973) (the *Pearce* presumption was not designed to prevent the imposition of an increased sentence on retrial "for some valid reason associated with the need for flexibility and discretion in the sentencing process," but was "premised on the apparent need to guard against vindictiveness in the resentencing process").[52]

What about retrial of a capital case? Can a second trial end in the death penalty for a defendant after the first litigation resulted in a sentence of life imprisonment? An early case on the point, which applied *Pearce* principles, was the decision of the Pennsylvania Supreme Court in *Commonwealth v. Littlejohn*.[53] In an opinion by Justice Roberts, that court ruled it improper for the Commonwealth to seek the death penalty on retrial in cases in which defendants had been found guilty of murder in the first degree and sentenced to life imprisonment on the first trial, then successfully attacked the conviction on appeal and won a new trial. Without such a rule, a defendant would face the dilemma of choosing between serving out a sentence imposed after trial in which error was committed or running the risk of the death penalty if he or she attacks it, a choice that would place an unconstitutional burden on the prisoner, in the view of the court.[54]

When the United States Supreme Court addressed the *Littlejohn* problem, they decided it the same way. In *Bullington v. Missouri*,[55] the prosecution was barred from seeking imposition of the death penalty upon retrial of Bullington for capital murder. Bullington was convicted of murder in his first trial, and the jury fixed his punishment at life imprisonment. After the trial, Bullington complained because of the improper makeup of the trial jury; his claim was deemed meritorious and he won a new trial. As the case was readied for the second trial, an issue arose as to whether the state could seek the death penalty, or whether the most severe potential sentence was life imprisonment. The Supreme Court ruled that where the first jury had rejected death, it could not be imposed in the second trial because of the double jeopardy clause. As will be seen, however, a different rule applies to noncapital crimes.

Even the *Bullington* rule has an important qualification for capital case defendants. In *Bullington,* the jury entered a life sentence against defendant Bullington. That decision controlled Bullington's retrial. The maximum sen-

---

[52]   Alabama v. Smith, 109 S. Ct. 2201 (1989).

[53]   250 A.2d 811 (Pa. 1969).

[54]   The court likened such a choice to that faced by defendants charged under the Federal Kidnapping Act; if a defendant chose to be tried by a jury he was subject to the death penalty, but if he was tried by the court alone he was not exposed to capital punishment. In United States v. Jackson, 390 U.S. 570, 88 S. Ct. 1209, 20 L. Ed. 2d 138 (1968), the Supreme Court struck down this feature of the Federal Act, ruling that the invalidated provision unconstitutionally chilled the free exercise of a defendant's right to trial by jury.

[55]   101 S. Ct. 1853 (1981). *Accord*, Arizona v. Rumsey, 467 U.S. 203 (1984).

tence was limited to life. What if, instead of clearly deciding the issue, there was a hung jury as to the severity of the sentence when the murder jury was deliberating? A 2003 Supreme Court decision involved a hopelessly deadlocked jury. The trial judge discharged the jury without receiving a sentencing verdict from them. The court entered a sentence of life imprisonment, as provided by law. On appeal, the defendant's first-degree murder conviction was reversed. The case was sent back to the trial court for a new trial. This time a fresh jury fixed the punishment at death, after the defendant was convicted of murder again. The United States Supreme Court affirmed that decision, holding double jeopardy does not preclude a second jury's consideration of the death penalty.[56] The key was that the first jury had not decided on a punishment.

In the years since *North Carolina v. Pearce* was announced in 1969, the United States Supreme Court has answered several questions raised by the *Pearce* decision. For example, what about states where the jury fixes the sentence in noncapital felonies? What if the jury fixes a higher sentence when a defendant is tried a second time than that fixed by the original jury? There is authority that would allow a jury to fix a 20-year sentence on retrial of a robbery charge (where that is the maximum) in a case in which the defendant was originally convicted and sentenced to 10 years, appealed, and won a retrial. In *Chaffin v. Stynchcombe*,[57] for example, the Supreme Court upheld a higher sentence imposed by a jury that had not been informed of the defendant's prior sentence.

In misdemeanor cases defendants may typically appeal petty offense convictions, taking the case on appeal from a magistrate's court to a circuit or district court for **trial de novo**.[58] The court of general trial jurisdiction (district, superior, or circuit court) could give a heavier sentence than that given by the magistrate.[59] Why doesn't this rule disturb the *Pearce* principle? Some hairsplitting has been done by the Supreme Court. What the defendant is getting in these circumstances is a completely new misdemeanor trial, subject to a fresh view on the imposition of punishment. Further, although trial courts may increase the sentence following trial de novo and second conviction of the same misdemeanor, separate rules control prosecutors who attempt to file different, heavier charges. *Blackledge v. Perry*[60] illustrates the point. There, a North Carolina defendant was convicted of a misdemeanor arising out of a fight in which the defendant had engaged. He decided to appeal his assault conviction and filed a notice of appeal to have his case heard de novo in the County Superior Court. While the appeal was pending, the prosecutor obtained an indictment from the grand jury charging the defendant with a serious felony. This indictment for felonious assault covered the same conduct for which the defendant had been convicted in the preceding misdemeanor trial.

56 Sattazahn v. Pennsylvania, 537 U.S. 101 (2003).
57 412 U.S. 17, 93 S. Ct. 1977, 36 L. Ed. 2d 714 (1973).
58 Trial *de novo* means that a fresh determination of guilt or innocence will be made in the second trial, unaffected by the result in the first trial.
59 Colten v. Kentucky, 407 U.S. 104, 92 S. Ct. 1953, 32 L. Ed. 2d 584 (1972).
60 417 U.S. 21, 94 S. Ct. 2098, 40 L. Ed. 2d 628 (1974).

The Supreme Court disallowed the new charge because it violated the *Pearce* doctrine: "A person convicted of an offense is entitled to pursue his statutory right to a trial de novo, without apprehension that the State will retaliate by substituting a more serious charge for the original one thus subjecting him to a significantly increased potential period of incarceration."[61]

In summary, although the *Pearce* principle has been distinguished as inapplicable in a number of procedural settings arising since the decision was originally announced, its core philosophy remains. A prosecutor may not seek a higher penalty in retrial of case simply to punish the accused for pursuing his constitutional rights.

## § 9.8    Different Victims or Sovereigns

Exploration of the full meaning of the double jeopardy concept has been a major focus of the United States Supreme Court since federal jeopardy protection was made applicable in state prosecutions. In *Ashe v. Swenson*,[62] the Supreme Court analyzed **collateral estoppel**, the concept that provides that when a defendant has been adjudged not guilty under a particular set of facts, he or she may not be retried on the same facts in any future lawsuit between the same plaintiff and defendant. An armed robbery defendant was tried for participating in the robbery of one victim of a poker game stickup, and found not guilty. Six weeks later he was brought to trial again, this time for the robbery of another participant in the same poker game. On the new trial he was convicted and sentenced to a 35-year term in the state penitentiary. This conviction was ultimately upset in the United States Supreme Court, which held that after the first jury had determined by its verdict that the petitioner was not one of the robbers (or at least there was reasonable doubt that he was), the state could not constitutionally hale him before a new jury to litigate that issue again. Collateral estoppel is embodied in the double jeopardy guarantee.[63]

In another important decision, the Supreme Court ruled that the double jeopardy clause prohibited a state from trying the defendant for grand larceny following his conviction under two city ordinances, the municipal ordinance violations being based upon the same acts that gave rise to the felony charge. The Supreme Court unanimously rejected the state's theory that state and municipal prosecutions are brought by separate sovereigns, and that the defendant may thus be tried on separate charges arising from the same criminal activity. Unlike the rule applicable to successive federal-state trials over the same facts, the court pointed out that state and municipal courts are merely separate arms of the same sovereign, and the double jeopardy clause prohibits the state's felony trial when the city has already prosecuted on the same facts.[64]

---

[61]  However, not all "upping" of charges will be deemed vindictive and improper. *See* United States v. Goodwin, 457 U.S. 368 (1982).

[62]  397 U.S. 436, 90 S. Ct. 1189, 25 L. Ed. 2d 469 (1970).

[63]  Following *Ashe, see* Harris v. Washington, 404 U.S. 55, 92 S. Ct. 183, 30 L. Ed. 2d 212 (1971).

[64]  Waller v. Florida, 397 U.S. 387, 90 S. Ct. 1184, 25 L. Ed. 2d 435 (1970).

Separate charges filed by the city and state within the same jurisdiction are treated differently from state and federal prosecutions for the same conduct. Federal and state governments often exercise concurrent jurisdiction over criminal acts arising from a single transaction. Suppose a person robs a federally insured bank in a particular state. Prosecution of a defendant by the state for bank robbery after the defendant had been tried and acquitted of the same crime in federal court was approved in *Bartkus v. Illinois*.[65]

Today, as a matter of policy, numerous states decline the *Bartkus* invitation to try a suspect who has been tried for the same transaction in federal court. Over half the states prohibit state prosecution following federal prosecution covering the same offense.[66] Oklahoma is apparently not one of these. Terry Nichols was first tried and convicted in federal court for helping to bomb a federal building, and given a life sentence. Local prosecutors in the state of Oklahoma wanted to make him suffer the death penalty, so they brought state charges.

The case was a serious one. Terry Nichols was accused of collaborating with Timothy McVeigh in planning the blast that killed 168 people and injured more than 500 others. McVeigh was the one who actually carried out the bombing of the Murrah Federal Building in Oklahoma City. "Had [McVeigh] had his way, the death toll would have been much higher. It was purely and simply a fortuity not in any way creditable to him that more people were not killed when he detonated the bomb outside the Murrah Federal Building. When asked if he had any regrets, McVeigh replied that his only regret was that the building had not collapsed completely. Before the events of September 11,[2001], McVeigh's malicious and premeditated crime was frequently referred to as 'the deadliest act of terrorism ever committed on American soil.'"[66] Nichols was convicted by Oklahoma jurors of helping McVeigh acquire components for the bomb, but they did not condemn him to death.

As noted, the Oklahoma pattern illustrated in the *Nichols* case runs counter to the general rule. States do not usually prosecute after a defendant has been sent to federal prison. The general rule also controls the reverse situation, in which federal authorities are asked to pursue charges after state officials have fully tried a defendant. Their usual answer to this request is "no." The federal pattern is explained in *State v. Rogers*.[67]

> *United States v. Watts*, 505 F.2d 951 (Cir. 1974), affirmed a federal conviction after a prior acquittal in Georgia. The United States Supreme Court vacated the conviction at the request of the Solicitor General. The conviction was not vacated because the conviction was barred by legal doctrine; it was vacated because the conviction did not conform to Department of Justice policy of not prosecuting individuals previously tried in state court unless compelling reasons existed for such a prosecution. *Watts v. United States*, 422 U.S. 1032, 45 L.Ed.2d 688, 95 S.Ct. 2648 (1975).

[65] 359 U.S. 121, 79 S. Ct. 676, 3 L. Ed. 2d 684 (1959). On successive state-federal prosecutions, *see* Pope v. Thone, 671 F.2d 298 (8th Cir. 1982); Annotation, 18 A.L.R. FED. 393 (1974).
[66] Sharon Davies, *Profiling Terror*, 1 OH. ST. J. OF CR. L. 45, 78 (2003).
[67] 90 N.M. 673, 568 P.2d 199 (1977).

In *State v. Rogers*, a federal jury had found Rogers not guilty of charges similar to those brought subsequently by the State of New Mexico, the state court dismissed the New Mexico prosecution for kidnapping.

The federal policy of declining to prosecute state prisoners who are involved in state trials is often referred to as the *Petite* policy.[68] "The rationale for the *Petite* policy is to vindicate substantial federal interests through appropriate federal prosecutions, to protect persons charged with criminal conduct from the burdens associated with multiple prosecutions and punishments for substantially the same act(s) or transaction(s), to promote efficient utilization of Department resources, and to promote coordination and cooperation between federal and state prosecutors."[69] Despite general policy, federal prosecutors occasionally proceed with federal criminal cases based on substantially the same conduct, after a state prosecution. Such federal litigation is limited to exceptional cases.

What are the "compelling reasons" that might prompt federal authorities to prosecute a state court defendant who has already run the gauntlet of a criminal trial in state court? Civil rights cases have sometimes prompted a successive federal prosecution. During the early morning hours of March 3, 1991, Rodney King led officers on a high-speed chase in California. He was on parole after serving a one-year sentence for armed robbery. After King was out of his car, he was struck several times by officers with batons. Some of the officers involved in the apprehension of King were charged with use of excessive force. The jury in the state trial acquitted all defendants except officer Powell; the jury hung on one of the assault charges against him.

Riots followed, and a federal grand jury returned an indictment against four officers for federal civil rights violations drawn from the incident. The federal trial jury found two of the defendant officers guilty and acquitted the other two.

Prosecution of the officers was not without its critics. The American Civil Liberties Union (ACLU) studied the issue and concluded that the officers had been twice put in jeopardy for the same offense. The organization was critical of the dual sovereignty doctrine, explained earlier in this section. A member of the ACLU National Board of Directors also observed that the prosecution was unprecedented. Sergeant Stacey Koon had been originally acquitted. Until this federal case "[t]he Supreme Court has never held that reprosecution following an acquittal is permissible under the Double Jeopardy Clause."[70]

It should be noted that historically the federal prosecution of state prisoners has been the exception, not the rule. Notwithstanding occasional exceptions, the states under our system have historically shouldered the primary

---

[68]  Petite v. United States, 361 U.S. 529 (1960) (*Petite* policy); Rinaldi v. United States, 434 U.S. 22 (1977).

[69]  Ellen Podgor, *Department of Justice Guidelines*, 13 CORNELL J. OF LAW & PUB. POL'Y 167, 179 (2004).

[70]  Susan Herman, *Double Jeopardy All Over Again*, 41 U.C.L.A. L. REV. 609, 610 (1994). *See* further discussion in Laurie Levinson, *The Future of State and Federal Civil Rights Prosecutions: The Lessons of the Rodney King Trial*, 41 U.C.L.A. L. REV. 509, 532 (1994); Akhil Amar and Jonathan Marcus, *Double Jeopardy Law After Rodney King*, 95 COLUMBIA L. REV. 1 (1995).

responsibility for defining and prosecuting crime, especially street crime. However, that may be changing. There is a trend toward federalization of crime, and with the change an enhanced need arises to determine whether a defendant will be prosecuted in state or federal court, or both.

Several prosecutors, judges, and attorneys have sounded an alarm regarding this trend, visible in the federal crime bill of 1994. Juvenile offenders who possess a firearm during a crime of violence are now subject to federal jurisdiction. Carjackings that result in a homicide can now go to federal court. "Similar reprehensible offenses that result in death but traditionally have been prosecuted on the local level are also federalized, such as drive-by shootings, murder-for-hire, sexual exploitation of children, and torture. Other new federal crimes include disposal of firearms or receipt of firearms by persons who have committed domestic abuse, and committing a crime of violence against a spouse or intimate partner if the offender traveled across state lines to make contact with that person. The release of personal information on motor vehicle records by state motor vehicle department employees is subject to federal criminal fines and redress through civil action."[71] The federal death penalty was extended to cover more than 60 additional crimes.

One federal judge and his coauthor observed that while the United States Constitution originally mentioned only three federal crimes "there are now over three thousand federal crimes and the list is growing."[72]

What is wrong with having two sovereigns available to prosecute essentially the same criminal act, on a wholesale basis? Objections are raised on the following grounds. Violent street crime has always been dealt with by local prosecutors. Critics urge that too much power is being shifted into the hands of the central government and away from the states. There are concerns that, in a desperate effort to control the modern crime crisis, Congress's shift of responsibility will overload federal resources and raise a host of legal concerns. "Incentives to refer state cases to federal court include the expenses a state saves by transferring from the state to the federal government the cost of processing, trying, and imprisoning defendants. In some cases both state and federal governments may have to pay these expenses. As the Rodney King beating cases illustrated, criminal defendants may be prosecuted first in state court, then in federal court, for the same conduct made criminal by separate state and federal statutes. New double jeopardy problems probably will arise as a result of criminalizing the federal courts."[73]

When the question does not involve federal and state governments seeking separate trials, but rather one state's attempt to try a defendant after trial in another state for the same offense, the case of *State v. Glover*[74] holds that there

---

[71]  Smith, *Closing In on Crime Bill 1994*, CRIMINAL JUSTICE 38, 39-40 (Summer 1994). The bill is captioned the Violent Crime Control and Law Enforcement Act of 1994.

[72]  Carrigan and Lee, *Criminalizing the Federal Courts*, TRIAL 50, 51 (June 1994).

[73]  *Id.* at 52. The 1994 crime bill added many new federal offenses and broadened existing ones, resulting in a total of more than 3,000 federal crimes. Beale, *Too Many and Yet Too Few*, 46 HASTINGS L. J. 979 (1995).

[74]  500 S.W.2d 271 (Mo. App. 1973).

may be successive prosecutions where the transaction violates the laws of both jurisdictions. As noted earlier, some crimes have multi-state aspects.[75] The general rule holds that conviction or acquittal in one state is not a bar to prosecution in another state, in the absence of a statute.[76] The Supreme Court confirmed reprosecution by a different sovereign in *Heath v. Alabama*.[77] The defendant, a resident of Alabama, met with two accomplices in Georgia, just over the border from the defendant's Alabama home. They conspired to kill the defendant's wife. The defendant led them to his home, then left the premises. The other two kidnapped the defendant's wife. A car with her body inside was later found on the side of a road in Troup County, Georgia. The cause of death was a gunshot wound to the head. Georgia and Alabama authorities pursued dual investigations. The grand jury of Troup County, Georgia, indicted the defendant for the offense of "malice" murder. Defendant pled guilty and was sentenced to life imprisonment. Thereafter, an Alabama grand jury returned an indictment for the capital offense of murder. Before trial, the defendant entered a plea of former jeopardy. The judge ruled that double jeopardy did not bar successive prosecutions by two different states for the same act. Upon trial the Alabama jury convicted the defendant, and he was sentenced to death. The United States Supreme Court upheld the right of Alabama to try and sentence the defendant in its own way, observing: "To deny a State its power to enforce its criminal laws because another State has won the race to the courthouse 'would be a shocking and untoward deprivation of the historic right and obligation of the States to maintain peace and order within their confines.'"

---

[75]   *See* note 8 *supra*.

[76]   Some states have statutes barring such prosecutions.

[77]   474 U.S. 82 (1985).

# Miscellaneous Proceedings:

## Juvenile Justice, Misdemeanor Trials, Damage Suits Against Police, Prisoner Rights

## Chapter Outline

Section

# A. JUVENILE JUSTICE

## § 10.1   Juvenile Proceedings: Historical Setting

The problem dealt with in this and succeeding sections is broad in scope and serious in nature. The President's Commission on Law Enforcement reported that one of every six young men in America will be referred to a juvenile court for an act of delinquency before his eighteenth birthday. In the words of the Commission, juvenile criminality has become "the single most pressing and threatening aspect of the crime problem in the United States." The juvenile court is the primary judicial agency for dealing with this problem.

The first juvenile court in this country was established in Illinois under an 1899 act that provided that the child offender was not to be punished in a criminal sense, but was to be provided treatment under the control of the juvenile court.[1] The concept behind the law was that rehabilitative supervision was preferable to confinement in an adult jail, and held the best hope for reform of the youthful offender. Earlier common law rules had afforded some protection of minors, but reformers urged that a comprehensive system of juvenile justice was essential to the goal of rehabilitation.

---

[1]   State v. Monahan, 104 A.2d 21 (N.J. 1954); President's Commission on Law Enforcement and Administration of Justice, *Task Force Report: Juvenile Delinquency and Youth Crime*, 3 (1967).

The principle of removing or mitigating the criminal responsibility of children has ancient origins. In the early case of *State v. Aaron*, 4 N.J.L. 231, 244 [Reprint 269, 277] (Sup. Ct. 1818), Chief Justice Kirkpatrick restated the settled common law doctrine, adapted from earlier Roman law, that since a child under seven "cannot have discretion to discern between good and evil" he is incapable of committing crime; between the ages of seven and 14 he is subject to a rebuttable presumption of incapacity; and after 14 he is presumptively capable. Although the common law rule precluded criminal convictions of many young offenders, there are instances in which it failed to do so, with shocking consequences. Blackstone cites cases in which children of very tender age were drastically condemned as adult criminals; he refers to the hanging of an eight-year-old for maliciously burning some barns; to the hanging of a ten-year-old who had killed one of his companions; and to the burning of a girl of 13 who had killed her mistress. 4 Bl. Comm. (13th ed. 1800), 23. Similar illustrations in our own State are not lacking. In 1818 a boy of 11 was tried for murder (*State v. Aaron*, supra), and in 1828 a boy of 13 was hanged for an offense which he committed when he was 12. *State v. Guild*, 10 N.J.L. 163 (Sup. Ct. 1828). During most of the Nineteenth Century, child and adult offenders were treated alike although intermittent steps were taken towards their separate confinement. It was not until the turn of the century that modern concepts really began to take form; they embodied the upward movement in the child's age of criminal responsibility, the extended recognition of society's obligation as parens patriae to care for delinquent children, and the creation of independent juvenile courts.[2]

During the first two-thirds of the last century, the idea of rehabilitation of juveniles reached full flower. The past 20 years, however, have witnessed a decidedly different trend. Due to a perceived rise in juvenile crime, legislatures have moved increasingly in the direction of enhancing criminal penalties for juveniles. This "get tough" attitude has resulted in harsher punishment for juveniles and confinement for more extended periods in juvenile detention facilities. It has made it easier to transfer juveniles to adult criminal courts, particularly when violent crimes are involved. Two commentators assess the current situation. "Juvenile justice has come full circle in this century [1900-1999]. With the creation of juvenile courts 100 years ago, reformers achieved their objective of removing juveniles from the harsh, punishment-oriented criminal justice system. Now, juvenile justice is once again embracing criminal court handling of certain juvenile offenders and diminishing the role of the juvenile court."[3]

---

[2]    State v. Monahan, 104 A.2d 21, 22 (N.J. 1954). Recognition of special treatment for youthful offenders, *see* discussion in Eddings v. Oklahoma, 102 S. Ct. 869 (1982); Thompson v. Oklahoma, 108 S. Ct. 2687 (1988).

[3]    Richard Redding and James Howell, *Blended Sentencing in American Juvenile Courts.* In FAGAN AND ZIMRING, THE CHANGING BORDERS OF JUVENILE JUSTICE 145 (2000).

## § 10.2   Age Limits on Juvenile Prosecution

In the years following enactment of the Illinois Juvenile Court Act of 1899, many states adopted the pattern of establishing courts to deal with juvenile matters. Today there is legislation on the subject in every American jurisdiction. As the movement toward special treatment of juveniles expanded, a Standard Juvenile Court Act was prepared for the National Probation Association by a committee of judges from various states. This Act formed a model for legislation in several states and, following its promulgation, numerous jurisdictions enacted comprehensive supplements to their juvenile justice systems.

Juvenile courts exercise jurisdiction over people who are below a designated age (varying between ages 16 and 21, depending on the state.) Under early provisions of the Standard Juvenile Court Act, as amended, exclusive jurisdiction was vested in the juvenile court in cases involving child offenders under 16 years of age. For youths between 16 and 18 years old the juvenile court also had jurisdiction; however, where persons in this age group were involved in very serious offenses or constituted problem offenders, the juvenile court could certify such youths to an adult trial court for regular criminal proceedings.[4] Those 18 years of age and older were subject to criminal court proceedings.

Several questions have arisen in terms of the age cut-offs listed in the previous paragraph. First, if a youth commits a burglary at age 17, then turns 18 while awaiting a juvenile court hearing, should he or she be tried as a juvenile or as an adult? Suppose a minor of 15 participates with adults in a robbery that results in the death of the robbery victim: Should the minor be tried for murder as an adult, even though he or she did not pull the trigger of the gun that caused the homicide? Is the commission of certain serious offenses by a minor a circumstance that divests the juvenile court of jurisdiction over him or her?

In response to these questions, it is to be noted that several states have dealt with the first problem, that of the 17-year-old who commits an offense and who celebrates his eighteenth birthday in custody (or perhaps free on conditional liberty) pending adjudication of juvenile proceedings against him. A number of decisions favor considering the date of the court proceedings as decisive, and not the age of the youth at the time of the law violation. Thus, the juvenile court would lose jurisdiction in many states under such facts.

The next issue involves the minor who participates in a robbery that results in a homicide. In the case of adult offenders, the felony-murder rule will apply if the jurisdiction is one of those that has this type of homicide statute. Under the felony-murder rule, the premeditated intent to commit the felony (e.g., a robbery) is transferred from that offense to the homicide actually committed, and provides the elements of willfulness and premeditation essential to first degree murder. Thus, a person may be guilty of murder even

---

[4]   National Probation & Parole Ass'n., Standard Juvenile Court Act. For similar transfer provisions in the case of youths between 16 and 18 years old, see Uniform Juvenile Court Act § 34 (petition for transfer, hearing required).

though he does not pull the trigger, as long as someone in his or her robbery gang kills during the course of the crime.[5] Arguably, then, a minor who participates in a robbery in which an adult accomplice kills someone could be charged with murder and tried in criminal court for that offense. In the New York case of *People v. Roper*[6] the prosecutor suggested a similar theory in an effort to uphold the first degree murder conviction of a 15-year-old who participated in the robbery of a restaurant with another person. In the course of the robbery a customer of the restaurant was killed. However, the appellate court ruled that because a minor of 15 could not be tried for the adult felony of robbery in consequence of the Juvenile Court Act (which rendered all children under age 16 immune from adult prosecution save for murder), there could by law be no felonious intent on the part of the minor. Without the necessary mental element of felonious intent, eliminated by operation of the juvenile law, an element essential to the crime of murder was lacking. Accordingly, the New York Court of Appeals reversed the conviction of the 15-year-old.

Where there is proof that the minor himself or herself directly committed a homicide, however, felony court prosecution often occurs. Suppose the youthful offender shot or stabbed a victim. Such a juvenile might be tried in criminal court like an adult even if he or she is under 16. Some jurisdictions vest the juvenile court with primary dominion over offenses committed by persons under age 16, but limited exemptions are carved out for very serious crimes. The exceptions to juvenile jurisdiction may be murders committed by minors, as well as violent sexual offenses. Some jurisdictions, for example, have provided that a child under 16 who committed an offense was not to be deemed guilty of any crime but was to be treated as a juvenile offender, except where the crime was punishable by death or life imprisonment. Of course, under Supreme Court law decided in the late 1980s, even though a juvenile may be tried as an adult for first degree murder, he or she cannot be executed. Cases developed in § 7.5 establish that imposing the death penalty on juveniles who were 15 years old or younger when the crime was committed is prohibited. A different rule on the death penalty may prevail if an older juvenile commits a homicide.[7]

Episodes of youth violence in the late 1990s renewed controversy about trying juvenile offenders as adults. In Jonesboro, Arkansas, two boys of 11 and 13 years of age were charged with murdering four schoolmates and a teacher with rifles. Arkansas law provided that children under 14 could not be tried as adults. Cases like this have triggered legislative debate. Many states continue to impose age limits below which juveniles cannot be tried as adults even for very serious crimes, with the minimum age for transfer having been lowered to 14 in many cases; other states allow children under 14 to be tried as adults. Courts have split over which approach is proper. In an earlier decision, the majority ruled that a teenager could not be tried for murder in criminal court.

---

[5]  *See* People v. Cabaltero, 87 P.2d 364 (Cal. App. 1939).
[6]  181 N.E. 88 (N.Y. 1932).
[7]  State v. Monahan, 104 A.2d 21, 27 (N.J. 1954).

A dissenting judge objected that the majority decision allowed ". . . maraud-ing gangs of little hoodlums armed with guns, knives, switch knives or other lethal weapons . . . to be considered as a matter of law incapable of commit-ting the crime of murder." The majority opinion emphasized that America's national hopes and destinies rest with its youth. "Centuries of history indicate that the pathway lies not in unrelenting and vengeful punishment, but in per-sistently seeking and uprooting the causes of juvenile delinquency and in widening and strengthening the reformative process through socially enlight-ened movements."

## § 10.3   Power of Disposition

The point is frequently made that juvenile courts have constitutional power to exercise control and dominion over the offender only during his or her minority (until 18 years of age in most states). This might limit detention or confinement for serious offenses to a shorter period than the public expects the offender to serve, given the damage inflicted by the juvenile's criminal conduct. However, institutionalizing an offender in a youth detention facility for longer than the offender's minority is barred in several jurisdictions. Thus, in these states, the juvenile court judge is limited regarding the number of years of confinement to which the juvenile can be sentenced. For this reason, juvenile courts can waive jurisdiction of minors between the ages of 14 and 18 to the criminal court in serious cases, and criminal courts have the power to institutionalize for longer than minority.[8]

Sending a juvenile to adult court for trial occurs in a significant number of cases. In the federal system, when a juvenile 15 years or older commits a felonious act that is a crime of violence, full criminal prosecution may be requested by the prosecutor. However, transfer is allowed for youths as young as 13 committing certain violent crimes. The general dividing line between adult and juvenile prosecutions in the federal system is 18 years of age.[9]

In one state's practice, the juvenile courts have jurisdiction over all chil-dren under age 13 as well as older children, in the case of most crimes, between the ages of 13 and 17. Minority ends at 17. Outside of a few desig-nated "adult" felonies, juvenile court jurisdiction controls. However, adult trial courts are given exclusive jurisdiction over juveniles between the ages of 13 and 17 who commit seven enumerated crimes: murder, voluntary manslaugh-

---

[8]    In felonies, where the offender is over 16 but still of juvenile age, he or she can be waived to criminal court under the STANDARD JUVENILE COURT ACT. Similar transfer provisions in the UNIFORM JUVENILE COURT ACT are noted in this chapter at note 4 *supra*. The age at which a person becomes eligible for waiver differs among the states, however, ranging from 13 to 16 under various state laws. Some states impose no minimum age for adult prosecution.

         Where the juvenile court retains jurisdiction in a nontransfer case it has been noted that some states allow the juvenile judge to sentence the offender to confinement only during his or her minority. How-ever, variations occur. In some places other than those described in the text a juvenile who is convicted or held responsible can be confined until 21 years of age.

[9]    18 U.S.C. § 5032.

ter, rape, aggravated sodomy, aggravated child molestation, aggravated sexual battery, and armed robbery committed with a firearm.[10] Juveniles committing these crimes will be transferred to adult court. Evidence-gathering will be intensified in such cases. In connection with the prosecution of any of these offenses, the juvenile's confession often plays a role.[11] Details on how the confession is handled appear in § 10.4(6) of this text. When there is a conviction of a juvenile involved in a very serious offense (outside of the short list of adult felonies) this exposes the offender to a potential five-year sentence at the hands of the juvenile court judge.

As noted in § 10.2, some jurisdictions bar adult trials of very youthful offenders, and courts in those states will not try them as adults even for extremely brutal crimes. For example, children under 13 may never be tried as adults in one state. This is not the case in all courts, however. Today, some states allow 12-year-olds to be tried as adults for murder.

Where a murder is not involved and the juvenile court judge hears the case, a finding of delinquency may result. After the judge so decides, the court may order commitment of the offender. When a juvenile is institutionalized for a period in the state training school (or industrial school), this facility comprises a place of confinement separate from adult criminal offenders.

> [J]uveniles sixteen and under would seem to have some potential for rehabilitation; this potential is best protected by preventing institutionalization in an adult penitentiary. Further, even lacking such potential, the inhumanity of sentencing children of this age group to a system where they are subject to physical and psychological abuse by older inmates requires their segregation from adult criminals.[12]

Frequently a disposition short of commitment to a training school is an appropriate resolution of the juvenile case. The court also has power to dictate various sanctions short of confinement, including the imposition of a fine, requiring restitution, or commitment of the child to the care or supervision of a probation officer or public agency. The court may separate children from their parents when such action appears to be in the best interests of the child. It should be noted that dispositions are frequently made of juvenile cases without full hearing before the juvenile judge. The President's Commission on Law Enforcement reported examples of pre-judicial handling methods operative in juvenile justice—police station "adjustment" of the juvenile case; diversion of alleged delinquents to clinics and community agencies; and unofficial handling of the matter by the juvenile judge, perhaps by giving a warning to the offender.

---

[10]  Georgia, for example, follows this pattern of sending juveniles to adult court for designated crimes. O.C.G.A. § 15-11-5(b)(2).
[11]  Yarborough v. Alvarado, 124 S. Ct. 2140 (2004).
[12]  Herman, *Scope and Purposes of Juvenile Court Jurisdiction*, 48 J. CRIM. L., C. & P.S. 590, 604 (1958). On the right of confined juveniles to rehabilitative treatment, *see* § 10.5.

## § 10.4  Trials and Hearings

In a few states separate juvenile courts are not created by the jurisdiction's juvenile court act, juvenile cases being handled by ordinary criminal and civil courts, which maintain separate dockets and records for juvenile matters. In many other states, however, there has been established separate family or juvenile courts whose judges deal exclusively with juvenile matters. The term "**juvenile court**" is used to include both of these systems.

When a complaint is received concerning the conduct of a juvenile, an intake officer frequently investigates and either informally adjusts the case or authorizes the filing of a petition. The hearing jurisdiction of the juvenile court is invoked when a petition is filed alleging that a minor is **delinquent**, dependent, or neglected. Where the anticipated disposition of the case is something short of detention of the minor in a training school, a **summary proceeding** may be employed to dispose of the case. In such a proceeding an informal hearing before the juvenile judge may be held, usually one in which the strict rules of evidence are not applied and hearsay may be admitted. Where a finding of delinquency based on an offense or a series of offenses is sought by the authorities, however, and institutionalization of the offender looms as a possibility, certain constitutional safeguards must attend the proceeding.

The Supreme Court emphasized this point in 1967 in *In re Gault*.[13] A 15-year-old boy had been committed as a juvenile to the Arizona State Industrial School. He was originally taken into custody as a result of a verbal complaint from a woman that she had received an offensive telephone call. At the time he was picked up for this offense, the boy's mother and father were at work, and no notice that the boy was being taken into custody was left at the home. The boy's mother discovered his whereabouts after she returned home from work. A hearing was scheduled in juvenile court the following day. The mother appeared at the hearing along with the boy, but the complaining witness was not there, no transcript of the proceeding was made, and no copy of the petition filed by the deputy probation officer was served on the boy or his parents. The boy was examined by the judge, who at the conclusion of the hearing indicated that he would think about disposition of the case. At a further hearing held a week later, the judge committed the boy as a juvenile delinquent to the State Industrial School "for the period of his minority [that is, until 21], unless sooner discharged by due process of law." The United States Supreme Court invalidated this disposition of the case and ruled that enumerated constitutional rights must be observed before a juvenile is ordered to institutional commitment. The status of certain major features of constitutional protection in cases involving juveniles following the *Gault* decision are listed below.

---

[13]    387 U.S. 1, 87 S. Ct. 1428, 18 L. Ed. 2d 527 (1967).

## 1. Counsel

The Supreme Court established in *Gault* that in specified juvenile proceedings the juvenile has the right to the assistance of counsel, including the right to an appointed attorney if his or her family has insufficient funds to retain one. The following points were made:

1. In proceedings to determine delinquency that may result in commitment to an institution, the child and his parents are entitled to be notified of the child's right to be represented by counsel retained by them.

2. If they are unable to afford counsel, they should be notified that counsel may be appointed to represent the child.[14]

Juveniles have a right to waive counsel, but the waiver must be knowing and voluntary. Several states wisely require that there be consultation with a parent or guardian before the juvenile's waiver is effective.

## 2. Notice

Advance notice must be given to the child and his or her parents of a scheduled delinquency proceeding so that opportunity to prepare will be afforded. The notice or petition should be served on these parties and must set forth the juvenile's alleged misconduct with particularity. As stated in the *Gault* case, due process of law "does not allow a hearing to be held in which a youth's freedom and his parent's right to his custody are at stake without giving them timely notice, in advance of the hearing, of the specific issues they must meet."[15]

## 3. Privilege to Refrain from Testifying

The *Gault* case held that the constitutional privilege against self-incrimination is applicable to juveniles. This apparently means that a juvenile can refuse to testify at a hearing, and is entitled to be advised of this right by the judge before testifying, at least in the absence of representation of the juvenile by defense counsel.[16] Must the juvenile be informed concerning his or her right to silence before the case gets to court? It is generally the rule that for cases heard in juvenile court, *Miranda* warnings are not constitutionally mandated.[17] However, the previous section of this text noted the modern trend of sending juveniles to adult criminal courts for trial of violent crimes, where

---

[14] However, appointed lawyers are not automatically required to be provided in every parental status termination proceeding involving indigent parents. Lassiter v. Department of Social Services, 452 U.S. 18 (1981).

[15] The *Gault* notice requirements were codified in the 1974 Juvenile Justice and Delinquency Prevention Act, 18 U.S.C. § 5033.

[16] *See* Crisp v. Mayabb, 668 F.2d 1127 (10th Cir. 1982).

[17] State law can exceed minimum protections afforded under the United States Constitution. As a result, some jurisdictions may require constitutional warnings in juvenile interrogations as a matter of *state* law.

*Miranda* fully applies. Accordingly, during the evidence-gathering phase of the case it may be prudent for the authorities to warn the accused that he or she has a right to counsel and a right to remain silent, especially in the case of serious violations.

### 4. Confrontation

Absent a valid confession by the juvenile, a finding of delinquency cannot be upheld unless the juvenile is confronted by witnesses against him or her at the hearing and an opportunity is afforded the juvenile or his or her counsel to cross-examine.

### 5. Jury Trial

Jury trial is routinely available in a few jurisdictions (but fewer-than-12-member juries may be provided). However, in most states trial is before the judge. Whether juveniles have a right to trial by jury was a question left to state decisions and was not made a federal requirement by the *Gault* case. A subsequent Supreme Court decision confirmed that states are free to require jury trials in serious juvenile adjudications, but these are not required under federal constitutional law.[18]

### 6. *Miranda* Warnings

The issue of *Miranda* warning requirements was left open in *Gault* when the Court stated "we are not here concerned with the procedures or constitutional rights applicable to the pre-judicial stages of the juvenile process . . ." *Miranda's* application to juvenile cases has been uneven. Some states have required all or part of the *Miranda* warnings in juvenile cases, while others have not.

In 1979, in *Fare v. Michael C.*, the Supreme Court analyzed interrogation of a juvenile who had been fully advised of his *Miranda* rights.[19] His statements to police were deemed voluntary and admissible, even though he asked: "Can I have my probation officer here?" This request was denied. The Supreme Court held that a request to see a probation officer was not the same as asking to see a lawyer. In the latter case, had the suspect done so, the interrogators would have been required to stop. Apparently a request to see a parent will often be treated like the probation officer request in the *Fare* case. It is not the equivalent of a request to seek advice of counsel nor will it be deemed an assertion of the right to silence.[20]

---

[18] McKeiver v. Pennsylvania, 403 U.S. 528, 91 S. Ct. 1976, 29 L. Ed. 2d 647 (1971).

[19] Fare v. Michael C., 442 U.S. 707 (1979).

[20] United States v. White Bear, 668 F.2d 409, 412 (8th Cir. 1982) (juvenile can waive his or her rights without parent or attorney present); United States ex rel. Riley v. Franzen, 653 F.2d 1153, 1558-1559 (7th Cir. 1981) (request to speak with father not an invocation of right to an attorney or right to remain silent).

The Supreme Court revisited juvenile confessions in 2004. Often confessions of juveniles are used against them when they are tried as adults. In the 2004 case, the parents of a 17-year-old brought him to the station house at the request of police. He was taken by police to an interview room and questioned for two hours. His parents were not permitted to join him and he was not given *Miranda* warnings. The defendant made damaging admissions during the questioning session, and was charged with murder and attempted robbery. The trial judge decided that the defendant was not confined when he was with the police nor was he technically "in custody" when he was questioned. Accordingly, his declarations were voluntary and admissible. The detective who interrogated the juvenile had twice asked the defendant if he wanted to take a break during the questioning. At the end of the interview the defendant went home. These facts suggested to the United States Supreme Court that this was not a custodial interrogation requiring *Miranda* warnings, notwithstanding the juvenile status of the offender.[21]

## 7. Confidentiality of Records

Although the use of a juvenile record against a person several years later in a criminal trial was not dealt with in the *Gault* case, there are numerous lower court decisions on the point. Because the proceedings against a juvenile are not deemed to be criminal, under many decisions they cannot be shown in a later prosecution of the offender when he or she is an adult. A major deviation from this rule occurs when it is not the defendant on trial who has a prior juvenile record, but a witness called by the government. The juvenile record of a witness can be shown if the judge deems it necessary to a fair trial.[22] In similar fashion, under limited circumstances the government may be allowed to impeach a witness called by the defendant by using such witness's juvenile record. Thus, although his or her juvenile record cannot be used against an adult defendant when he or she takes the stand in a criminal prosecution, other witnesses may have their juvenile records exposed, in the discretion of the criminal trial judge. The drafters of the Federal Rules of Evidence noted the general policy against the use of juvenile records, then cited the exceptional case: "[T]he importance of a given witness may be so great as to require the overriding of general policy in the interests of particular justice."[23]

Outside of the exceptional case in adult courts, for other purposes juvenile records are typically treated as confidential matters and are not publicized to the general public. A juvenile court rule in one state illustrates the general policy:[24]

---

[21]  Yarborough v. Alvarado, 124 S. Ct. 2140 (2004).
[22]  FED. R. EVID. 609. *See* Davis v. Alaska, 415 U.S. 308, 94 S. Ct. 1105, 39 L. Ed. 2d 347 (1974).
[23]  Advisory Committee Note, FED. R. EVID. 609.
[24]  Rule 122.02, MO. JUV. CT. RULES (2004).

122.02 Juvenile Court Records to be Confidential

The records of the juvenile court as well as all information obtained and social records prepared in the discharge of official duty for the court shall be kept confidential and shall be open to inspection only by order of the judge of the juvenile court or as otherwise provided by statute.

The Federal Juvenile Delinquency Act embraces a similar policy. Except in specified cases, information about sealed records may not be released. Unless a juvenile who is taken into custody is prosecuted as an adult, neither the name nor picture of any juvenile can be made public in connection with a juvenile delinquency proceeding.[25]

In addition, rules in several states authorize the sealing (and in some cases even the destruction) of juvenile records after the juvenile reaches adulthood.

## 8. Burden of Proof

To justify a court finding against a juvenile at a delinquency hearing, the prevailing burden-of-proof test in most American courts prior to 1970 required the judge to be persuaded by a preponderance of the evidence that the juvenile committed the alleged delinquent act. A few states indicated, at least when the alleged act of delinquency would have constituted a crime if done by an adult, that there had to be proof beyond a reasonable doubt before such an act could be made the basis for an adjudication of delinquency. A Supreme Court decision settled the question by making the latter standard, proof beyond a reasonable doubt, binding in such cases on a national basis.[26]

After presentation of the evidence and the conclusion of the adjudication hearing, the judge will enter an order deciding the merits of the case. If it is proved that the minor committed the offense, the judge frequently couches the language of his or her decree in terms of finding the youth "involved" in the wrongful act, as opposed to finding him or her guilty.[27] A second hearing may be necessary in some circumstances to assess proper supervision, confinement, or detention of the minor.

## 9. Double Jeopardy

*Gault* did not decide whether the protection of the double jeopardy clause extended to juvenile delinquency adjudications. Some states ruled that double jeopardy applied. In Texas, a juvenile's case was heard and the juvenile was committed to the Texas Youth Council upon a finding of delinquency. After the juvenile became 17, he was indicted for the same offense and the prosecutor sought to try him as an adult in criminal court. The Texas Court of Criminal

---

[25]    18 U.S.C. § 5038(e); 22 FED. PROC. L. ED. § 2282.
[26]    In re Winship, 397 U.S. 358, 90 S. Ct. 1068, 25 L. Ed. 2d 368 (1970).
[27]    CIPES, CRIMINAL DEFENSE TECHNIQUES, § 60.01[2].

Appeals held this a violation of the youth's constitutional rights.[28] A juvenile cannot be adjudged a delinquent and held in custody as such, said the court, and then be indicted, tried, and convicted of the identical offense after he reaches the age of 17.

Because of a conflict between the states on the question, the United States Supreme Court reviewed the problem in *Breed v. Jones*.[29] The Court ruled unanimously that a juvenile cannot be tried twice for the same crime, first in the juvenile court and again as an adult. Chief Justice Warren Burger, writing for the Court, said that juveniles have the same constitutional protection against being held in double jeopardy as adults.

This approach prevents multiple trials of a juvenile for the same offense. It does not abrogate the right of the juvenile judge to hold a transfer hearing. When the juvenile court is initially involved in a violent crime case involving a teenager, the primary responsibility of the juvenile judge may be limited to simply exploring the facts of the case that are relevant to transfer of the juvenile to adult court. In these situations, sometimes a defendant claims this transfer hearing amounts to a prior "trial" in juvenile court. He then claims double jeopardy. Not so, says the United States Supreme Court.[30] When the juvenile proceeding is in the nature of a transfer inquiry, this does not constitute a trial so as to permit the defendant to claim double jeopardy when tried in adult criminal court.

## 10. Bail

While some courts have extended pretrial release guarantees to juvenile cases, many have not. Under the general approach that the Supreme Court has used in determining what rights of adult defendants also apply in juvenile proceedings, it may be concluded that there is no unqualified right to bail for a juvenile.[31] This is reflected in the fact that the Supreme Court in *Schall v. Martin*[32] upheld a preventive detention statute applicable to juvenile court cases.

When a juvenile is confined prior to disposition of his or her case, separation from the general jail population is the rule. In federal practice, a juvenile alleged to be delinquent may be detained only in a juvenile facility and not with adults who are charged with crimes.[33]

[28] Garza v. State, 369 S.W.2d 36 (Tex. Civ. App. 1963). The same view was affirmed in State v. Marshall, 503 S.W.2d 875 (Tex. Cr. App. 1973).
[29] 421 U.S. 519, 95 S. Ct. 1779, 44 L. Ed. 2d 346 (1975).
[30] Distinguishing *Breed*, the Supreme Court ruled that Maryland's method of submitting juvenile cases to a master in order to develop recommendations for the Juvenile Court did not violate double jeopardy. Swisher v. Brady, 438 U.S. 204 (1978).
[31] LAFAVE & ISRAEL, CRIMINAL PROCEDURE 615 (2d ed. 1992).
[32] 467 U.S. 253 (1984).
[33] 18 U.S.C. § 5035.

## § 10.5  Beyond *Gault*

The *Gault*, *Winship*, and *Breed* cases have designated required safeguards applicable to serious delinquency proceedings. The requirements established by these cases have been set forth. These, however, constitute "minimum" standards imposed under the United States Constitution, and several courts go beyond these standards and extend additional rights to juveniles.[34]

One expanding area of rights concerns the method of confining juveniles who are found to be delinquent by the juvenile judge. Modern court decisions have increasingly focused on conditions of confinement.[35] In one case, a federal court held that minors civilly committed to state youth camps after being found delinquent were entitled to assert their right to minimum wages under the Fair Labor Standards Act. The court viewed as serious the allegation that some of the youths had worked as many as 12 hours a day but that youthful workers were not paid proper wages.[36] Further, pretrial detention of juveniles (as opposed to post-adjudication confinement) has come under court scrutiny. It may constitute a denial of juvenile rights to hold juveniles in the same cells with adult offenders. The effect of hardened offenders on youthful detainees may be devastating, and courts have struck down the practice of mixing them.[37]

There seems to be popular support for separate confinement of juveniles. As we have seen, the manner of detention of juveniles has come under court scrutiny, particularly when officials mix youthful offenders with adults. However, in another area of juvenile justice, the public seems to have an opposite reaction. This is when youths involved in violent crimes are transferred out of the juvenile justice system and into the adult correctional process. Generally, there is little public outcry when violent juvenile offenders are sent to adult criminal court. If anything, popular momentum frequently favors full criminal trials, with stiff punishments. The "get tough" approach to juvenile crime favors trying violent offenders as adults. As Richard Redding has remarked: "The new consensus has returned the juvenile justice system to its original purpose of providing rehabilitation for minor offenders while punishing serious offenders in the criminal justice system." He notes that most states have lowered the minimum age for transfer to adult courts to 14, and at least a few states "now allow children of any age to be transferred for any crime."

The increasing frequency of transfer often reflects a desire to ensure incarceration in difficult cases beyond the age of majority of the offender. To address this problem, Redding proposes that juvenile courts be empowered to impose adult sentences on minors, and to supervise rehabilitation or probation into adulthood. "Some may argue that the juvenile court system is irrelevant if the juvenile court can sentence in the same manner as an adult court. How-

---

[34]   Speedy trial rights, *see* 18 U.S.C. § 5036; United States v. Wong, 40 F.3d 1347 (2d Cir. 1994).

[35]   *See* § 10.20 of this text.

[36]   King v. Carey, 405 F. Supp. 41 (W.D.N.Y. 1975).

[37]   *See* Swansey v. Elrod, 386 F. Supp. 1138 (N.D. Ill. 1975) (improper to hold minors awaiting adult trials with older offenders in Cook County Jail). Federal practice, *see* note 33 *supra*.

ever, juvenile court judges are far more experienced in juvenile justice and have a greater understanding of the unique developmental and mental health needs and deficits of juveniles."[38]

## B. MISDEMEANOR TRIALS

## § 10.6  Misdemeanors: Classification of Offenses

Major crimes include **felonies** and serious **misdemeanors**. Petty offenses include misdemeanors of a minor nature and local law ordinance violations. Thus, a misdemeanor can constitute either a major or a petty offense.[39] The line separating the major-petty division is established by the amount of penalty involved. Under one common formula, a petty offense is one that does not exceed imprisonment for six months or a fine of not more than $500.[40] In many states, the great bulk of the misdemeanors on the statute books carry an authorized penalty of 30 days imprisonment, well within the petty offense category.

Whether the offense is major or petty makes a significant difference in terms of the procedural steps that must be followed in processing the case under modern practice. These procedural distinctions were unknown in the early common law. The common law required that every offense, including a minor one, be prosecuted on grand jury indictment, with a right of jury trial. This ultimately resulted in intolerable delay, inconvenience, and clogging of court calendars with minor cases. The notion developed that it was unnecessary to employ this ponderous legal machinery for every minute offense, and more expeditious procedures were adopted in the statutes to handle petty misdemeanors.[41] This revised approach continues in our criminal law today.

Felonies, which are tried in courts of general jurisdiction, are typically defined in state laws as offenses punishable by death or imprisonment for a term exceeding one year. The Uniform Arrest Act defines a felony as any crime that may be punished by death or imprisonment in a state prison. "Offenses punishable by death or a prison term (usually of one year or more) are classified as felonies, while those punishable by a jail sentence (usually less than one year) or a fine are misdemeanors."[42]

---

[38] Richard Redding, *Juveniles Transferred to Criminal Court: Legal Reform Proposals Based on Social Science Research*, 1997 UTAH L. REV. 709.
[39] PERKINS, CRIMINAL LAW, 16 (1957).
[40] Some magistrates have jurisdiction to try minor offenses that carry up to a year's imprisonment. Jurisdiction of United States Magistrates in the federal system, *see* 18 U.S.C. § 3401(f).
[41] PERKINS, CRIMINAL LAW, 14 (1957).
[42] KLOTTER, KANOVITZ, AND KANOVITZ, CONSTITUTIONAL LAW § 3.17(B)(10th ed. 2005).

Misdemeanors, as previously noted, may be divided into two categories. Most states have a few major misdemeanors that are variously designated as high, indictable, or gross misdemeanors. These serious offenses might carry up to one year maximum imprisonment. Drunk driving and certain larcenies might be examples in this category of offense, depending on state law. However, ordinarily misdemeanors are petty offenses, carrying a substantially less severe maximum penalty (e.g., 30 days) and are commonly resolved in court by payment of a fine. Driving offenses (speeding, failure to have vehicle under control) are examples in this category. Violations of a city building code, and actions violative of a municipal disorderly conduct ordinance are examples of local law ordinance violations. While many ordinance violations carry the same level of sanction as petty misdemeanors (e.g., 30 days/$100), some ordinances authorize a fine alone upon proof of violation. Procedurally, these ordinance cases are characteristically handled in court in the same manner as minor misdemeanors.

Petty misdemeanors are commonly disposed of in courts with more limited jurisdiction than those that handle felonies. In federal practice the judicial officers with jurisdiction over petty offenses are the United States Magistrates (formerly Commissioners). In state practice the misdemeanor court has sundry titles—municipal court, police court, magistrate's court, mayor's court, or justice of the peace. The hearing jurisdiction of these courts in felony cases is generally limited to conducting preliminary appearances and hearings.

## § 10.7   Misdemeanor and Felony Procedure Compared

Because felony prosecutions threaten serious loss of liberty, they are attended with more complex procedural features than misdemeanor litigation. The chart in § 1.5 tracing the felony case process illustrates the point. This is not to say, however, that great similarities do not exist between felony and misdemeanor trials. Numerous features have common application to both types of proceedings. For example, the rules of evidence covered in Chapter 6 should be followed in both felony and petty misdemeanor trials. However, because there are certain distinctions, it is important to highlight the points of criminal trial practice that distinguish felony cases from misdemeanor cases.

As indicated in § 10.6, prosecution by grand jury indictment and the common law right of trial by jury are dispensed with in petty misdemeanor adjudications. However, some states by statute provide a jury trial in specified misdemeanors, frequently limiting the jury size to six jurors. Because grand jury indictment or formal information is not required, the complaint upon which an arrest warrant is issued serves in numerous lower courts as the official statement of the charge against the defendant. Defendants arrested without warrant will have an information or complaint lodged against them on evidence supplied by the arresting officer or a complaining witness who saw the misdemeanor occur.[43] In petty misdemeanors there is no arraignment in

---

[43]   *See* § 2.4 and § 10.8 of this text.

the same sense that one is formally held in felony cases. Because the complaint functions as the charging vehicle in misdemeanor court, the defendant's first appearance before the magistrate is usually the point when the defendant enters his or her plea, and this appearance thus serves as the arraignment in the misdemeanor case.

In cases involving petty offenses, a forfeiture of collateral security often disposes of the matter in lieu of appearance of the defendant. Especially in connection with motor vehicle rules-of-the-road violations, defendants are sometimes authorized by state law to post collateral with the court in a pre-established amount depending on the violation, waive appearance before the magistrate, and consent to forfeiture of the collateral to resolve the case.[44]

Some state codes authorize the accused to litigate misdemeanor cases by counsel; that is, in the absence of the accused with only his or her counsel being present.[45] This is in stark contrast to felony cases, in which the accused is to be personally present at all stages of the proceedings in court.

## § 10.8   Misdemeanor Practice and Procedure

Several state codes prescribe the form to be followed in preparing minor offense charges for presentation to the magistrate. A written charge is usually required in misdemeanor cases, verified by the complainant. Case law indicates that a complaint charging a crime should inform the defendant of the nature of the charge and the acts constituting it. In minor misdemeanors a simplified form is frequently authorized. An Ohio form of citation illustrates, drawn from illustrative forms appended to the Ohio Rules of Criminal Procedure:

---

FORM XIV
FRANKLIN COUNTY MUNICIPAL COURT
FRANKLIN COUNTY, OHIO

State of Ohio                         Citation No. _____

/City of Columbus/                    Case No. _____

v.                                    MINOR MISDEMEANOR
                                              CITATION
_____

name of defendant

_____      (Rule 4.1)

address

_____

age

---

[44]   The collateral may be collected by a designated police officer or court clerk in the absence of the magistrate, in many jurisdictions.

[45]   IOWA R. CRIM. P. 2.27 (2003) provides: "In felony cases the defendant shall be present . . . at the initial appearance, arraignment and plea . . . at every stage of the trial. . . . In other cases the defendant may appear by counsel."

TO DEFENDANT:

On _____, 20_____, at _____

_____

_____

You _____

describe the offense charged and state the

_____

numerical designation of the applicable statute or ordinance

_____

_____

_____

_____

You are ordered to appear at _____

time, day, date, room

Franklin County Municipal Court, 120 West Gay Street, Columbus, Ohio 43215, /before the Franklin County Juvenile Court, 50 East Mound Street, Columbus, Ohio 43215, at the time and place ordered by that court./

If you wish to contest this matter you must appear at the above time and place. In lieu of appearing at the above time and place, you may, within the time stated above, appear personally at 120 West Gay Street, Columbus, Ohio 43215, Room 120 sign the guilty plea and waiver of trial which appear in this form, and pay a fine of $_____ and court costs of $_____.

If you fail to appear at the time and place stated above you may be arrested.

This citation was served personally on defendant.

_____

Signature of Issuing Law
Enforcement Officer

Being duly sworn the issuing law enforcement officer states that he has read the citation and that it is true.

_____

Issuing Officer

Sworn to and subscribed before me by _____

on _____, 20_____.

/ Judge / Clerk / Deputy Clerk / _____

Notary Public,
My Commission expires
_____, 20___
Franklin County / State
of Ohio /

A defendant who wishes to do so can execute a written guilty plea, waiver of trial and payment of fines and costs agreement located at the end of the form.

## § 10.9    Rules of Practice

In federal courts a series of detailed rules control trial of federal misdemeanor cases. These rules set forth federal misdemeanor procedure and illustrate several features common to state misdemeanor practice as well. Rule 58(b)(1) of the Federal Rules of Criminal Procedure authorizes the initiation of a petty offense prosecution when a law enforcement officer prepares and files a complaint with the magistrate. Where this written statement of the charge provides probable cause, the magistrate may issue an arrest warrant for the defendant. Short of arrest, the magistrate may issue a notice for the defendant to appear or a summons for his or her appearance. The movement on the part of the legal system to the use of the summons, especially in petty offense cases, has been covered previously.[46] The aim is to carry out a policy against unnecessary detention of defendants prior to trial. The summons directs the defendant to appear before the United States Magistrate at a stated time and place. If the defendant fails to appear in response to this summons, an arrest warrant is then issued.[47]

As noted earlier, in cases in which the defendant appears in court in response to a summons or an arrest warrant, the complaint already exists. Where the arrest is without a warrant and the defendant is taken into custody, the complaint should be prepared forthwith by the officer. In both types of cases, the defendant must be informed of the complaint against him or her at or before his first appearance before the magistrate, because in minor misdemeanor cases the complaint frequently serves as the official statement of the charge. The magistrate who handles the case then takes the defendant's plea to the charge that is set forth in the complaint. Like felony cases, permissible pleas to federal misdemeanor charges include pleas of guilty, not guilty, or nolo contendere. Provision for taking the plea at first appearance is contained in Rule 58(b)(3) of the Federal Rules, this appearance serving as the arraignment in the misdemeanor case.

When the defendant pleads not guilty, trial can be held immediately if agreeable to the parties, but more commonly is set for one week to 10 days after first appearance to allow a reasonable opportunity for preparation of evidence. Federal misdemeanor trial procedure follows a pattern similar to that of felony cases tried before a judge when the jury is waived. The magistrate makes authoritative resolution of both the law and the facts applicable to the case. If the magistrate finds the defendant guilty, the magistrate's dispositional alternatives include imposition of a fine or a fine with court costs, imprisonment, or probation. As in the case of felonies, the magistrate may direct the probation service of the court to conduct a presentence investigation and render a report to the magistrate prior to the imposition of sentence.

---

[46]    *See* § 2.1(3) and § 3.4 of this text.
[47]    FED. R. CRIM. P. 58(d)(3).

An appeal from a judgment of conviction will stay a sentence of imprisonment, but only in the event that the defendant is admitted to bail pending appeal.[48] An appeal must be taken within 10 days of the judgment to be effective, and is taken to the United States District Court. A similar appeals pattern is seen in the procedures established in numerous states, with judgments from petty offense courts going to courts of general trial jurisdiction for review. One interesting distinction exists here, however. In many states a trial *de novo* is held on the appealed case in the court of general jurisdiction.[49] In federal cases, the trial court's review of the misdemeanor conviction is more limited.[50]

## § 10.10    Rules of Practice: Forfeiture of Collateral

Forfeiture of a fixed sum in lieu of appearance is authorized in federal practice. This procedure is particularly useful in dealing with minor traffic cases. The district court to which the magistrate is answerable must authorize this disposition, and frequently lists the specific cases that may be resolved by forfeiture procedure. A list of violations for which collateral can be posted and the amount in each case (e.g., entering restricted road on federal land—$30; reckless driving on roadways in a federal arsenal—$75) is distributed to the magistrates in the district. When an arrest is made and the violation falls within the list of designated offenses, the defendant may dispose of the matter by posting the specified collateral. After forfeiture, further recourse against defendant is foreclosed respecting the subject offense. Rule 58(d)(1) of the Federal Rules of Criminal Procedure provides: "If the court has a local rule governing forfeiture of collateral, the court may accept a fixed-sum payment in lieu of the defendant's appearance and end the case."

## § 10.11    Counsel

Under the federal rules detailed in the immediately preceding sections, the magistrate must allow the defendant reasonable time and opportunity to consult counsel. An interesting question is raised for both state and federal courts. Does an indigent defendant facing a misdemeanor charge have a right to a free lawyer, similar to the right to counsel guaranteed felony defendants under the United States Constitution?

Under *Argersinger v. Hamlin*,[51] the Supreme Court ruled that there could be no imprisonment of a defendant for even minor offenses unless the state complied with the right to counsel. In the case of indigent defendants, *Argersinger* thus prevents incarceration when a misdemeanor is tried, unless the

---

[48]   Bail on appeal, see the controlling rules contained in 18 U.S.C. § 3143 and § 3.2 of this text.
[49]   Definitions and illustrations are contained in § 9.7 *supra*.
[50]   FED. R. CRIM. P. 58(g)(2)(d).
[51]   407 U.S. 25, 92 S. Ct. 2006, 32 L. Ed. 2d 530 (1972).

defendant is first offered an appointed attorney. When a judge hears such a misdemeanor case without offering to appoint counsel, *Argersinger* limits the sentence to the imposition of a fine.[52] As stated by Justice Douglas: "Under the rule we announce today, every judge will know when the trial of a misdemeanor starts that no imprisonment may be imposed, even though local law permits it, unless the accused is represented by counsel."

At first blush, *Argersinger* appears to impose an impossible burden on misdemeanor courts with its requirement of free lawyers in potential jail cases. But it should be noted that this right of defendants is subject to waiver, softening the impact of the case on the court system. After the misdemeanor judge explains his or her rights to a defendant, a defendant may relinquish the right to an attorney and handle the case without counsel. Many defendants do so. In addition, a 1979 decision confirmed *Argersinger's* message that where the punishment is a fine, the right to counsel is not triggered.[53] Finally, *Argersinger* has no application to minor traffic violations or other similar petty offenses. Federal Rule of Criminal Procedure 58(b)(2)(c) states that petty offenses do not trigger the appointment of counsel, and another provision of the rule defines a petty offense as one "for which no sentence of imprisonment will be imposed."

A related issue is whether a defendant should be given *Miranda* warnings in misdemeanor cases. In *Berkemer v. McCarty*[54] the Supreme Court held that *Miranda* applied to all instances of custodial interrogation regardless of the gravity of the offense. This included custodial interrogation for a misdemeanor traffic offense. However, questioning in the station house may be different than on-the-scene interrogation. In *Pennsylvania v. Bruder*,[55] the Supreme Court ruled that an ordinary traffic stop does not involve "custody" for purposes of the *Miranda* rule. In this case, statements that a driver made during roadside questioning were admissible:

> The facts in this record, which Bruder does not contest, reveal the same noncoercive aspects as the *Berkemer* detention: "a single police officer ask[ing] respondent a modest number of questions and request[ing] him to perform a simple balancing test at a location visible to passing motorists." 468 U.S., at 442, 104 S.Ct., at 3151 (footnote omitted). Accordingly, *Berkemer's* rule, that ordinary traffic stops do not involve custody for purposes of *Miranda*, governs this case. The judgment of the Pennsylvania Superior Court that evidence was inadmissible for lack of *Miranda* warnings is reversed. (footnotes omitted)

A suggestion is advanced by one author to relieve the sometimes desperate load of cases. He recommends that this be done by decriminalizing many minor offenses that clog the courts today.[56] Offenses that are now defined as

---

[52]  On the methods available to the state for collection of a fine, *see* § 10.12.

[53]  Scott v. Illinois, 440 U.S. 367 (1979) ($50 fine for shoplifting).

[54]  104 S. Ct. 3138 (1984).

[55]  109 S. Ct. 205 (1988).

[56]  Froyd, 62 A.B.A.J. 1154, 1157 (1976). The author concludes: "Until the reach of the criminal law is sharply cut back, the system of criminal justice will continue to suffer."

misdemeanors, such as public drunkenness, private consensual sexual activities, and domestic disputes short of physical assaults, continue to clutter the courts needlessly, he urges. Extending the right to a free lawyer when misdemeanor cases involve a bit of jail time adds further impetus to a need for a solution. The last section of this portion of the text addresses potential remedies for the burdens facing misdemeanor courts.[57]

## § 10.12   Constitutional Considerations: Jury Trials, Transcripts, and Fines

### 1.  Jury Trials

When does a misdemeanant have a right to insist on a trial by jury as a matter of federal constitutional law? Whenever the authorized prison term for the misdemeanor exceeds six months, in the view of the United States Supreme Court, and this rule applies to state as well as federal misdemeanants. In *Baldwin v. New York*[58] the defendant was arrested and charged with "jostling," a Class A misdemeanor in New York, punishable by a maximum term of imprisonment of one year. He was brought to trial in the New York City Criminal Court. Section 40 of the New York Criminal Court Act declared that all trials in that court should be without a jury. The defendant requested a jury trial, the request was denied, and the defendant was convicted on the testimony of the arresting officer. The United States Supreme Court reversed this conviction. The six-months line of demarcation for determining when the right to trial by jury attached was explained in the opinion of Mr. Justice White. Justice White announced the judgment of the court, and delivered an opinion in which Mr. Justice Brennan and Mr. Justice Marshall joined:

> [W]e long ago declared that the Sixth Amendment right to jury trial "is not to be construed as relating only to felonies, or offenses punishable by confinement in the penitentiary. It embraces as well some class of misdemeanors, the punishment of which involves or may involve the deprivation of liberty of the citizen." *Callan v. Wilson*, 127 U.S. 540, 549 (1888).
>
> A better guide "[i]n determining whether the length of the authorized prison term or the seriousness of other punishment is enough in itself to require a jury trial" is disclosed by "the existing laws and practices in the Nation." *Duncan v. Louisiana*, [391 U.S. 145] at 161. In the federal system, as we noted in *Duncan*, petty offenses have been defined as those punishable by no more than six months in prison and a $500 fine. And, with a few exceptions, crimes triable without a jury in the American States since the late 18th century were also generally punishable by no more than a six-month prison term.

---

[57]   *See* § 10.13 *infra*.

[58]   399 U.S. 66, 90 S. Ct. 1886, 26 L. Ed. 2d 437 (1970). On the massing of minor offenses where the total or aggregate punishment arising out of one transaction exceeds six months, *see* § 6.4.

The Supreme Court engrafted a special refinement on the *Baldwin* rule in succeeding years. Apparently a person can be denied his or her right to trial by jury where the conviction carries as much as a one-year sentence if the defendant can get a full jury trial on appeal from such a conviction. The issue arises in states where nonjury trials in municipal court may be appealed, and the appeal results in a *de novo* trial in a district or superior court. Of course, where no such special appeal to a jury exists, the *Baldwin* six-months rule controls the important question of whether the criminal charge is originally triable before a jury.

In a related decision the court held that trial by a six-member jury satisfied the Sixth Amendment requirement of jury trial.[59] In a number of states, the jury provided in serious misdemeanor cases consists of less than the traditional 12-person, unanimous verdict jury panel. Florida, the state in which the question of jury size arose, provided for a 12-person jury in capital cases, but in all other criminal cases (including felonies) a six-member jury was the rule. A robbery defendant convicted by a six-member jury claimed that the constitutional guarantee of trial by jury meant a trial before 12 persons. The Supreme Court rebuffed this claim: "We hold that the twelve-man panel is not a necessary ingredient of trial by jury . . ."

## 2. Transcripts

In *Mayer v. Chicago*[60] the Supreme Court handed down rules relevant to appeal procedures in misdemeanor cases. When appealing misdemeanor or ordinance violations to an appellate court,[61] a poor person without funds to purchase a transcript is entitled to a verbatim transcript of his or her trial or other record sufficiently complete to make the appeal meaningful. A meaningful "transcript substitute" might include a statement based on the magistrate's minutes of evidence or a partial transcript, as the case requires. Thus, rules similar to those treated in § 8.4 of this text have been incorporated into minor offense prosecutions.

## 3. Fines

Misdemeanors sometimes are resolved by the imposition of a sentence involving both imprisonment and a fine. *Williams v. Illinois*[62] was such a case. The defendant was convicted of petty theft and received the maximum sen-

---

[59] Williams v. Florida, 399 U.S. 902, 90 S. Ct. 1893, 26 L. Ed. 2d 446 (1970). Mr. Justice Harlan, in an appendix to his concurring opinion in Williams v. Florida, lists numerous states which provide a 6-person jury for misdemeanor trials. On less-than-unanimous verdicts, these were approved in Apodaca v. Oregon, 406 U.S. 404, 92 S. Ct. 1628, 32 L. Ed. 2d 184 (1972) (conviction of Oregon defendants by 11-1 and 10-2 jury votes approved).

[60] 404 U.S. 189, 92 S. Ct. 410, 30 L. Ed. 2d 372 (1971). Misdemeanor appeals are discussed in § 10.9.

[61] There is a distinction between a true appeal of a lower court decision versus a trial *de novo* in a case taken from a misdemeanor court to a court of general trial jurisdiction; in such *de novo* trials, some states which have this procedure deny free transcripts of the original trial.

[62] 399 U.S. 235, 90 S. Ct. 2018, 26 L. Ed. 2d 586 (1970).

tence provided by state law: one year imprisonment and a $500 fine. Under an Illinois statute, the defendant could be kept in jail to work off the fine at $5 per day if it remained unpaid at the expiration of the sentence. After serving his year, the defendant was retained as an inmate in the county jail beyond the maximum period of confinement fixed by the statute for the subject offense as a result of his inability to pay the fine. The United States Supreme Court ruled this illegal, asserting that it worked an invidious discrimination on an indigent prisoner solely because of his financial inability to pay the fine. Mr. Chief Justice Burger, who delivered the opinion of the Court, was careful to limit the decision to extensions of jail sentences due to nonpayment of fines. The decision appears to avoid the question of original incarceration for non-payment.

The question reserved in *Williams v. Illinois* was answered in *Tate v. Short*.[63] *Williams* dealt with fines unpaid after expiration of a jail term; Tate dealt with an original sentence of a fine only. Because the defendant could not pay it, the Texas court required him to serve time in jail at a specified rate per day until the monetary amount accumulated by this method equaled the amount of the fine. The United States Supreme Court invalidated this procedure. The Supreme Court reasoned that it was inconsistent with equal protection of the laws to allow persons with funds to satisfy the state's penal interest by paying a fine, while converting the fine into a prison term for individuals with no accumulated assets.[64]

Another fine case was handed down by the Supreme Court. In *Bearden v. Georgia*,[65] the Court held that probation could not be revoked for failure to pay a fine if the defendant was "broke" but had tried to raise the money. Danny Bearden had paid a portion of his fine; then he was laid off his job. "Petitioner, who has only a ninth grade education and cannot read, tried repeatedly to find other work but was unable to do so." The trial court revoked probation for Bearden's failure to pay the balance of the fine and restitution (original conviction for theft). The United States Supreme Court, sensitive to economic conditions, reversed the decision of the sentencing court. "[I]t is fundamentally unfair to revoke probation automatically [and send defendant to jail] without considering whether adequate alternative methods of punishing the defendant are available."

---

[63] 401 U.S. 395, 91 S. Ct. 668, 28 L. Ed. 2d 130 (1971). Tate had accumulated $425 of traffic fines on nine convictions in Houston, Texas. He was sent to jail to work out the fine at the rate of $5 per day, meaning he would have to serve 85 days.

[64] On alternatives available to the sentencing judge, see § 10.9. The court might impose a probation requirement that an indigent do specified work during the day to satisfy the fine.

[65] 103 S. Ct. 2064 (1983).

## § 10.13　Magistrate Courts: Ability to Try Misdemeanor Cases

In some magistrate courts, the crush of business is overwhelming, and court officials worry about keeping up with the caseload. Urban courts are often overworked to the point that cases become lost in the shuffle, and solutions to critical docket crowding are sought. A proposal has been urged by one commentator to relieve the volume of cases. This authority recommends decriminalizing petty offenses that needlessly tie up magistrate courts. The proposal would streamline the docket and relieve the burden of appointing a lawyer in numerous misdemeanors as well. Offenses like public intoxication, consensual sexual activities, and disputes between neighbors could be handled informally or administratively, and kept out of the court system. The author points to docket samples indicating that approximately one-fourth of the Boston Municipal Court criminal complaints are for prostitution. "The estimated annual cost of the fruitless efforts to suppress streetwalking in Boston is half a million dollars."[66] Another authority criticizes society's "pre-occupation with victimless crimes" and points out: "One-half of all criminal arrests in the United States are for drunkenness, disorderly conduct, vagrancy and gambling."[67]

## C. DAMAGE SUITS AGAINST POLICE

## § 10.14　Police Tort Liability Generally

**Civil damages** may be recovered by private citizens injured by police misconduct, and because of this circumstance it is essential that the law enforcement officer understand the basic outlines of the tort liability to which he is exposed. Basically, grounds for suit may be generated when the officer is negligent in the conduct of his duties, commits a willful wrong, or when he violates the constitutional rights of the plaintiff.

A lawsuit for money damages begins when an injured party files a complaint (in some states the civil pleading is called a petition) against the defendant, usually in a court of general trial jurisdiction. The petition sets forth the grounds relied upon by the plaintiff, which allegedly justify monetary recovery, identifies the injury suffered by the plaintiff, and concludes with a request for a specific sum of money to compensate the plaintiff for his or her injury.

Law enforcement officers may be named as defendants in damage cases, even where the officer's employer (state, county or municipality) is also sued. When the police officer is acting within the scope of his or her employment and negligently injures another, the employer is frequently held to respond in damages. This is under the ancient **principle of respondeat superior**. This

---

[66]　Froyd, 62 A.B.A.J. 1154, 1157 (1976).
[67]　Rosenblatt, *Why Can't Courts Fight Crime?* 58 JUDICATURE 466 (1975).

principle requires the master to answer for the harm done by its servant. Where the police officer and employer are held jointly liable, the amount of the plaintiff's recovery may be collected against the officer to the extent of his or her non-exempt resources, or from the employer.

Some state laws place a **shield of immunity** in front of municipalities, barring suits against them. Such immunity is a fading feature of state law today.[68] When such municipal tort immunity is retained, however, the police officer will probably be the sole defendant in a damage action alleging negligence by the officer in the execution of his or her duties. An officer's personal financial exposure in such a suit may be limited by a police officer's official indemnity bond or other insurance plan. In some jurisdictions such a bond is statutorily required to protect the police officer. As well as shielding the police officer's savings from being used to satisfy any money judgment obtained by the plaintiff, such bond may also discharge the costs of defense; that is, the defendant officer's attorney fees. These can be substantial in an extended suit. Other jurisdictions have indemnity statutes whereby the governmental unit for whom the officer works indemnifies him or her for damages assessed against the officer as a result of acts done in the performance of the officer's duties.

## § 10.15  Misuse of Weapons, Suits Concerning Arrest and Search, Operation of Vehicles

### 1. Weapons

The basic grounds for liability in connection with the use of firearms are summarized by one commentator:[69]

> The cases brought against police officers for injuries sustained as a result of negligence in the use of weaponry fall into two broad categories: (1) where the subject of an arrest or an attempted apprehension is injured as the result of the use of excessive force by the police officer; (2) where an innocent bystander is injured as the result of the careless aim or ricocheting of an officer's bullet aimed at a fugitive, or as the result of the officer heedlessly "fooling" with his weapon, or where the weapon is discharged accidentally during cleaning or repair.

---

[68]  With constitutional torts, federal claims are not barred by any local doctrine of immunity, although state-based causes of action may be limited by immunity rules. See Monell v. Department of Social Services, 436 U.S. 658 (1978) that extended liability for constitutional torts to include cities as well as individual police officers. The *Monell* decision overruled prior case law. Older cases held that Congress did not intend to hold municipalities liable under the Civil Rights Act for the actions of their employees. Under *Monell* whenever a constitutional injury is inflicted by police because of some city policy or custom (e.g., failure to adequately supervise or train the police) the city may be liable for that injury. *See* Note, *The Civil Rights* Litigant, 42 U.S.C. § 1983, and Local Government Immunity, 33 ARK. L. REV. 529 (1980).

[69]  Herbert E. Greenstone, *Liability of Police Officers for Misuse of Their Weapons*, 16 CLEV.-MAR. L. REV. 397, 400 (1967).

The need to use a certain amount of force in effecting an arrest has been recognized in every jurisdiction, but the officer must employ no more than is reasonably necessary to accomplish his or her lawful purpose. Here the seriousness of the offense for which the arrest is made plays a role. **Deadly force** may not be used to prevent commission of a misdemeanor or to make a misdemeanor arrest, but substantial force may be employed in felonies where necessary to protect the officer or the public. Deadly force, such as shooting the suspect, is not permitted to prevent escape in a non-violent felony. The Supreme Court barred such use of force when a fleeing burglary suspect was killed as he attempted to climb over a fence to elude an officer who was pursuing him.[70] In the misdemeanor situation, substantial force may be used in only a limited number of situations, as where the officer is threatened with bodily harm, or when assaulted by one resisting arrest.

The question of **excessive force** to arrest has been a controversial topic. In one federal case, the United States District Court entered judgment for defendant police officers. The court held that the force used was not disproportionate to the situation, where the court found the plaintiff flagrantly, repeatedly, and dangerously refused to yield to police officers in a vehicle and foot pursuit, where he struggled violently as long as he was physically able and attempted to grab an officer's pistol, and where four men were finally required to subdue the plaintiff, despite the blows he had received.[71] Some cases have gone the other way, as the Rodney King beating case illustrates, as detailed in § 9.8 of this text.

What if it is not the person who is arrested who is injured, but a bystander? Suits by injured bystanders frequently raise the question of whether an officer exercised reasonable prudence when he or she used his or her weapon to apprehend a suspect, considering existing traffic and other attendant circumstances. Officers have been held negligent for firing their revolvers in the middle of busy shopping districts or other areas where heavy pedestrian traffic threatened injury or death of innocent bystanders.

### 2. Suits Concerning Arrest and Search

Liability of the law enforcement officer for civil damages is somewhat limited under the **false arrest** theory. If the officer acts with a reasonable belief that the defendant committed a public offense, he or she is protected from liability under the general rule. The law officer need not be correct in his or her judgment; the defendant may be innocent of the suspected crime. But if

---

[70] Tennessee v. Garner, 471 U.S. 1 (1985). *See* Comment, *The Unconstitutional Use of Deadly Force Against Nonviolent Fleeing Felons: Garner v. Memphis Police Department*, 18 GA. L. REV. 137 (1983), cited in Davis v. Little, 851 F.2d 605 (2d Cir. 1988); and Carter v. City of Chattanooga, 850 F.2d 1119 (6th Cir. 1988).

[71] Melton v. Shivers, 496 F. Supp. 781 (M.D. Ala. 1980). See 60 A.L.R. FED. 204, which discusses the question of when a police officer's use of force during arrest becomes so excessive as to constitute violation of constitutional rights, imposing liability under Federal Civil Rights Act of 1871 (42 U.S.C.S. § 1983).

the officer used the judgment of a reasonable person before he or she made the arrest, if a reasonable person would have proceeded as the officer did, the officer cannot be held liable for civil damages.

A few states take the position that the plaintiff must prove malice in order to recover for **false imprisonment**; that is, the plaintiff must prove that the officer bore particular ill-will for him or her, and that the imprisonment resulted from this unwholesome motivation. Under the general view, however, malice is not an essential element. The tort of false imprisonment is established under the general rule when the plaintiff proves: (1) the detention or restraint was against the person's will, and (2) it was unlawful. A tort law authority comments on the burdens of proof in the companion torts of **malicious prosecution** (the groundless institution of criminal proceedings against the person).[72] A criminal prosecution is based upon probable cause, and the instigator of the prosecution (often a police officer) is absolved of malicious prosecution liability, when: "(1) the instigator believes the accused is guilty, and (2) this belief is based on reasonable grounds. Even though known facts would convince a reasonably prudent and cautious man of accused's guilt, the instigator does not have probable cause unless he believes the accused is guilty."

Searches can also give rise to citizen suits. The New York Court of Claims awarded damages totaling $14,000 to a man and his wife who allegedly suffered fear, shock, and depression as the result of an early morning "no-knock" search. The court held that the state police were negligent in obtaining and executing the search warrant on the wrong parties at the wrong house. The husband was entitled to damages in the amount of $10,000 and the wife $4,000. Liability attached to the state under the doctrine of respondeat superior.[73]

A decision of the United States Supreme Court dealt with claims by the respondent that he had been the victim of an overenthusiastic police search. The search of his apartment led to seizure of a controlled substance, and the respondent pled guilty to manufacturing same. He was sentenced to 25 years imprisonment. The question in *Haring v. Prosise*[74] was whether the guilty plea extinguished the right of Prosise to bring a civil damage suit against Officer Haring and other members of the police department who had participated in the search of his apartment. The Supreme Court held it did not, and that Prosise could pursue his civil claims.

Special duties of care arise when an arrestee is taken into custody and placed in jail. "The Restatement and case law also recognize that persons who take others into their custody, for example peace officers who arrest persons suspected of crime, owe a special duty to aid and protect them. Restatement (Second) of Torts § 314A(4) (1965) (see *Smith v. Miller*, 241 Iowa 625, 628-

---

[72]  MORRIS, TORTS, 313, 316 (1953).

[73]  Herman v. State, 357 N.Y.S.2d 811 (1974).

[74]  103 S. Ct. 2368 (1983). In a related area of the law, sometimes prisoners seek to set aside sentences following pleas of guilty, claiming earlier illegal searches. While the Fourth Amendment claims may not ordinarily be raised in a habeas corpus proceeding following a plea of guilty, see Tollet v. Henderson, 411 U.S. 258, there are some exceptions. Lefkowitz v. Newsome, 420 U.S. 283 (1975). *See also* Menna v. New York, 423 U.S. 61 (1975) (double jeopardy may be raised following state plea).

31, 40 N.W.2d 597, 598-600 (1950) (sheriff owed duty of reasonable care to protect jail inmate from harm caused by fire.))[75]

### 3. Operation of Vehicles

Under ordinary circumstances of routine police patrol, police officers are held to the same standard of care as other drivers. Officers must avoid negligence in the operation of their vehicles. **Negligence** is defined as a failure to exercise the care of an ordinarily prudent person; negligence in the operation of police vehicles will render the officer liable in damages for injuries inflicted by his or her lack of due care. Frequently such suits are lodged against the officer's employer, the municipality.

The standard of negligence, when applied to a police driver where such officer is responding to an emergency situation or is answering an emergency call, is considerably altered. "The police officer, however, due to the exigencies of an emergency may take risks, particularly as to the speed of travel, which, if undertaken by the ordinary driver, would amount to negligence."[76]

State codes provide that speed limits do not apply to vehicles operated under the direction of police in the chase of violators of the law or when responding to emergency calls. To the extent that observance of precautions is possible in these circumstances, however, these must be followed. Emergency conditions do not relieve the driver of an emergency vehicle from the duty to drive with due regard for the safety of other persons.[77]

The approach sometimes taken in statutes is to grant immunity to members of the police department, sheriff's department, or highway patrol when they are responding to an emergency call. Laws may exempt public employees from liability for civil damages resulting from the operation, in the line of duty, of an authorized emergency vehicle. However, the same laws may require that the officer must be reacting to specified situations in order to fall within the exemption from liability: (1) responding to an emergency call, (2) in the immediate pursuit of an actual or suspected law violator, or (3) responding to (but not returning from) a fire alarm.

The United States Supreme Court reflected upon the difficulties faced by officers in high-speed chase situations. On the one hand, the officer needs to stop the suspect. On the other, the officer must balance the high-speed threat to everyone within stopping range—be they suspects, their passengers, other drivers, or bystanders. As long as the officer does not chase with an intent to harm suspects physically, the Court imposes no federal constitutional liability on officers for injuries incurred in the chase. These rules were articulated in the context of a decision involving a high-speed police chase of a speeding motorcyclist. The chase resulted in the death of the motorcyclist's passenger.[78]

[75]  Hildenbrand v. Cox, 369 N.W.2d 411 (Iowa 1985).
[76]  Morrison, *Negligent Operation of a Police Vehicle*, 16 CLEV.-MAR. L. REV. 442 (1967).
[77]  *See* Dillenbeck v. Los Angeles, 446 P.2d 129 (Cal. 1968). In Lingo v. Hoekstra, 200 N.E.2d 325 (Ohio 1964), the court held that a police officer who was following a suspected speeder was liable to a plaintiff, a passenger in another vehicle, struck in an intersection by the officer.
[78]  County of Sacramento v. Lewis, 118 S. Ct. 1708 (1998).

## § 10.16   Wrongful Death

In *Grudt v. City of Los Angeles*[79] the California Supreme Court set forth the operative facts. A 55-year-old man was observed by two plainclothes police officers as they drove an unmarked sedan. It was 12:15 A.M. Grudt was traveling at about 35 to 40 miles per hour in a high-crime neighborhood and narrowly missed running down two women in a crosswalk. The officers determined to stop him for questioning. They pulled alongside Grudt's car and one shouted "Police officer. Pull over." Later testimony developed that Grudt was slightly hard of hearing. He continued driving with the police officers in pursuit. Two other plainclothes officers responded to a police broadcast and arrived with their vehicle in the vicinity of the chase. The man's car had come to a stop. One of the later-arriving officers alighted from his vehicle and loaded a double-barreled shotgun as he approached Grudt's car. Although the evidence was conflicting on precisely what occurred, there was police testimony that this officer tapped on the closed left front window of the man's car with the muzzle of the shotgun, lifted the shotgun in the air to dispel the driver's fears, and leaned forward and pointed to his badge. He further testified that the driver thereupon accelerated the car, and the officer feared it would strike his partner, who was now standing in the vicinity. He fired the shotgun through the left rear window of the vehicle, and the other officer fired his revolver. The driver died within seconds of the shooting, and the death was attributable to the shotgun blast, according to a medical witness whose testimony is reported in the court opinion.

Grudt's widow brought a wrongful death action for monetary damages against the two police officers who fired their weapons, and against the City of Los Angeles. In her complaint she alleged that the officers intentionally and wrongfully shot her husband, and that the city was negligent in continuing to employ the officers after it knew or should have known that they were dangerous and violent officers, prone to the use of unnecessary physical force. The trial judge struck this latter allegation, and a jury verdict was returned for the defendants upon trial of the case. However, on appeal the California Supreme Court reversed this judgment. The court ruled that the widow was entitled to present evidence to sustain the theory stricken by the trial judge, and also to argue to the jury that the officers were negligent in their conduct. The trial judge had excluded the question of the officers' negligence from the jury. The California Supreme Court concluded:

> At the very least, the evidence favorable to plaintiff raised a reasonable doubt whether the police officers acted in a manner consistent with their duty of due care when they originally decided to apprehend Grudt, when they approached his vehicle with drawn weapons, and when they shot him to death. "[T]he actor's conduct must always be gauged in relation to all the other material circumstances surrounding it and if such other circumstances

---

[79]   86 Cal. Rptr. 465 (1970).

admit of a reasonable doubt as to whether such questioned conduct falls within or without the bounds of ordinary care then such doubt must be resolved as a matter of fact rather than of law." Therefore, the trial judge should have instructed the jury on both negligence and intentional tort theories and left it to their judgment to decide which, if either, was factually established.

## § 10.17   Constitutional Tort

Under the federal Civil Rights Act (42 U.S.C. § 1983 and related provisions) a police officer is liable when, acting under color of law, he or she deprives a person of his or her constitutional rights, privileges, or immunities. Appreciation of the fact that police officers arrest more than 10 million people every year enhances the expectation that suits over civil rights violations will increase in the future. Compensatory damages that reimburse the plaintiff for his or her actual injuries are recoverable under the Civil Rights Act, as well as exemplary damages in cases in which the plaintiff proves that the officer acted maliciously. The theory underlying these exemplary or **punitive damages** is that such damages have a beneficial deterrent effect upon the future conduct of the defendant officer involved in the particular case at hand, as well as upon other officers who might otherwise be inclined to act in a similarly unconstitutional manner.

Examples of cases in which plaintiffs successfully sued police and others for civil rights violations are listed below.

- *Rogers v. City of Little Rock*, 152 F.3d 790 (8th Cir. 1998). An officer stopped the plaintiff's car, offered to follow her home to get her insurance papers, and coerced her into having sex. The U.S. Court of Appeals for the Eighth Circuit upheld a $100,000 judgment against the officer, as well as the district court's finding that his conduct "shocked the conscience" in violation of substantive due process.

- An arrestee was awarded $30,000 for an ankle injury when a police car door was slammed on his ankle, $5,000 for a knee injury when he was dragged across the street while unconscious, and $400,000 for a head injury, which included permanent brain damage, resulting from a police officer's alleged use of excessive force. He was also awarded $62,760 in rehabilitation expenses and $122,098 to ensure that he would be able to afford assistance in managing his grocery store. *Braud v Painter*, 730 F. Supp. 1 (M.D. La. 1990).

- *Johnson v. Cannon*, 947 F. Supp. 1567 (M.D. Fla. 1996). A deputy sheriff stopped a woman for traffic violations. He gave her two traffic citations, then asked her if she was "willing to negotiate the tickets?" He threatened to arrest her and have her children removed by a public agency if she refused to "negotiate" with him. The deputy then proceeded to the woman's residence, at which time he sexually assaulted her. She sued under 42 U.S.C. § 1983 and the court ruled she had a valid cause of action because the officer's misconduct occurred during the performance of his police duties.

- *Spell v. McDaniel*, 824 F.2d 1380 (4th Cir. 1987), *cert. denied*, 108 S. Ct. 752, 98 L. Ed. 2d 765. A municipality is liable for a police beating if the brutality is either the result of municipal policy or if the city condoned it. Theories advanced by the plaintiff included one of municipal policy based on police training practices. In addition, witnesses testified that police brutality was common in Fayetteville, North Carolina. A jury awarded $900,000 in compensatory damages against McDaniel and the city, jointly and severally.

- *Culver v. Fowler*, 862 F. Supp. 369 (M.D. Ga. 1994). A police officer who had control of a prisoner was charged with kneeing him in the groin. The United States District Court awarded the plaintiff $25,000 general compensatory damages, $6,012 special damages for medical expenses, and $25,000 punitive damages. The court stated that kneeing a prisoner in the groin is a barbaric and cruel means of control.

- *Bogan v. Stroud*, 958 F.2d 180 (7th Cir. 1992). The United States Court of Appeals for the Seventh Circuit found that correction officers beat, stabbed, and kicked a prisoner who had been disarmed and knocked to the ground. A damage award of $5,000 against one officer and $1,000 against two others was justified, in the view of the court.

- *Davis v. Moss*, 841 F. Supp. 1193 (M.D. Ga. 1994). When a prisoner was shoved down a flight of metal stairs, the court awarded him $25,000 in punitive damages to deter the defendant corrections officer and others from "using unnecessary and malicious force against inmates."

- *Palmer v. Hall*, 517 F.2d 705 (5th Cir. 1975). A city police officer was sued as a result of a 12-year-old boy being shot in the leg. The injured plaintiff recovered $35,000 in compensatory and $15,000 in punitive damages in a civil rights action after he was shot by the police officer who had mistaken the youngster's BB gun for a rifle. The boy was apparently fleeing when the officer fired his .357 Magnum pistol.

While civil suits arising out of police actions have been on the rise in recent years,[80] they are not routinely successful. Statistically, verdicts and judgments are rendered against the officers in substantially less than one-half the cases. The United States Supreme Court has ruled that a civil cause of action does not lie against an officer for giving allegedly perjured testimony.[81] However, police do not have total immunity to suit, as the cases in this section

[80] A comprehensive list of federal Civil Rights Act damage actions, with dispositions, is located in 15 AM. JUR. Trials 555, 580 (1968). It should be noted that the fact that a person is ultimately proved guilty of the crime for which he was arrested does not justify a post-arrest deprivation of rights. His or her right to collect damages based upon official misconduct is not destroyed by proof of his or her criminal guilt. Jackson v. Martin, 261 F. Supp. 902 (N.D. Miss. 1966).

[81] Briscoe v. Lahue, 103 S. Ct. 1108 (1983).

disclose.[82] One commentator summarizes the situation: "The *Malley* [*v. Briggs*] case, therefore, makes clear that under no circumstances, will the Court extend the 'absolute immunity' defense (available to judges, prosecutors, and legislators) to police officers. The only exception is when the officer is testifying in a criminal trial. This means that officers enjoy only qualified immunity, but that they will not be liable if they act in an objectively reasonable manner."[83]

A breakdown in municipal immunity allows cities to be sued for **constitutional torts**, under current law. However, as a general rule, a single act of police misconduct that injures a plaintiff will not usually result in municipal liability. There must be an ongoing policy of rough or inappropriate action that is promoted or tolerated by a city department in order to place liability on the city.[84] Failure to properly train police may serve as the basis for liability under § 1983. To prevail, the injured plaintiff must show that the deficiency in the training program is closely related to the injury suffered.[85]

Can a civil action for money damages be successfully maintained against a law enforcement officer for her failure to give the suspect *Miranda* warnings? The question arose in a 2003 decision of the United States Supreme Court. In a scuffle with police, the officers said a defendant named Martinez grabbed for the gun of one officer. The officer's partner shot Martinez numerous times. One of her shots blinded him, and other bullets paralyzed him from the waist down. Martinez was never charged with a crime.

The legal issue over the right to bring a § 1983 action arose after Martinez was questioned intensively during the time he was in the hospital receiving emergency medical treatment for his bullet wounds. The police questioner was trying to get Martinez to admit that he took a gun from the officer's holster. At no point during the interview was Martinez given *Miranda* warnings. When Martinez sued over this omission, the Court ruled that a simple failure to give a *Miranda* warning does not establish a constitutional violation sufficient to provide grounds for a civil action against the investigating officer.[86]

## § 10.18 Damage Suits: Alternative to the Exclusionary Rule?

As indicated previously in this chapter, searches by police may give rise to damage suits. If the police were careless or clumsy in making the search or if they made an unwarranted entry into a home to search, many authorities urge that the police and their employer should be subject to suit. But that should be the sole remedy open to the citizen, these critics argue. Under their

[82] *See* Malley v. Briggs, 475 U.S. 335 (1986).
[83] DEL CARMEN AND WALKER, BRIEFS OF LEADING CASES IN LAW ENFORCEMENT 246 (3d ed. 1997).
[84] *See* Monell v. Department of Social Services, 436 U.S. 658 (1978) (not liable under respondeat superior, but when constitutional deprivation arises from governmental custom).
[85] City of Canton v. Harris, 109 S. Ct. 1197 (1989).
[86] Chavez v. Martinez, 123 S. Ct. 1994 (2003).

view, contraband that the police find, even in a clumsy search, should not be excluded from evidence in a criminal prosecution of the citizen. The exclusionary rule is the subject of wide-ranging debate, with many urging its judicial revision or repeal to assist in meeting the crime challenge. In the case of *Illinois v. Gates*,[87] the United States Supreme Court declined to abandon the exclusionary rule. However, Justice White's concurring opinion gave his view that the rule should be overturned. When police act in good faith, their searches should never be thrown out, he urged: "I continue to believe that the exclusionary rule is an inappropriate remedy where law enforcement officials act in the reasonable belief that a search and seizure was consistent with the Fourth Amendment." There are, of course, forceful counter-arguments. Many legal authorities urge that the exclusionary rule is the only really effective way to protect the privacy of our citizens as well as Fourth Amendment rights. Supporters of the rule contend that the drafters of the Fourth Amendment recognized that some of the guilty would go unpunished in order to uphold the dignity, freedom and right of privacy of the individual.[88]

For the moment, we turn to the contentions of those who argue that the exclusionary rule should be abandoned. Why, some people ask, should the criminal "go free because the constable has blundered?"[89] However, many of these same critics recognize a companion need to retain some control over abuse of police authority, and they suggest that it rests in the sanction discussed in this area of the text—the civil damage suit.

Under one view, a primary thrust of such suits would operate against the governmental unit (city, state) employing the officer. Because the plaintiff could collect damages for an illegal search and seizure from the city, there is no need to exclude wrongfully seized evidence from the trial. This argument suggests that the threat of such tort suits will provide an effective incentive for administrators and city councils to institute policies to deter police misconduct.

A study by the American Bar Association listed sanctions currently available to redress abuse of police authority. Among others, it listed: (1) suits against individual officers, (2) actions against departments or municipalities, (3) federal Civil Rights Act suits, (4) injunctions, (5) internal and external review (civilian review boards, etc.), and (6) the exclusionary rule. The ABA report proposed strengthening the tort remedy by repealing municipal tort immunity where such immunity currently exists, and rendering municipalities fully liable for the actions of police officers who are acting within the scope of their employment as municipal employees.[90]

Two commentators suggest yet another resolution of the dilemma of enforcing proper investigative procedure without jeopardizing successful prosecution of criminals: decertification of police officers. These writers ini-

[87] 426 U.S. 213, 103 S. Ct. 2317 (1983), discussed in § 2.2 of this text.
[88] Peterson, *Will the Fourth Amendment Stand?* 59 JUDICATURE 370 (1976).
[89] People v. Defore, 242 N.Y. 13, 150 N.E. 585 (1926) (Cardozo, J.). Several views on the exclusionary rule appear in § 6.3(3).
[90] ABA Report, *Standards Relating to the Urban Police Function*, 5.5 (1972). The ABA report called for broad abolition of governmental immunity.

tially tracked the erosion of the exclusionary rule. "In 1984, the Court ruled that the exclusionary rule does not apply to evidence obtained by police relying in good faith on an invalid search warrant.[91] More recently, the Court refused to exclude illegally obtained evidence from use in civil deportation proceedings. The premise of both majority opinions was that the deterrence achieved could not, under the circumstances, justify the exclusion of the evidence. A further erosion of Fourth Amendment protection need not be inevitable. As an alternative to, or even as a complement of, the exclusionary rule, states can deter police misconduct by decertification of the officer—that is, by revoking the officer's state certification for constitutional violations in evidence gathering. Almost all the states have boards or commissions, commonly called Peace Officer Standards and Training (P.O.S.T.) Boards, which have the authority to set training and selection standards. Without a certificate, an individual cannot be employed as a police officer in that state."[92]

This text has not endorsed this or any other specific modification of the exclusionary rule. Rather, an effort has been made here to expose the reader to a number of suggestions that have been advanced in the criminal procedure field. The immediately foregoing one, stripping an officer of his position, is strong medicine for Fourth Amendment violations.

## D. PRISONER RIGHTS

## § 10.19  Suits Against Penitentiary Personnel

Like law enforcement officers, prison guards, administrators, and supervisory personnel are subject to civil suit under certain circumstances. The right of the penitentiary inmate to sue for money damages has been succinctly outlined:[93]

> A means to enforce the rights granted to prisoners is the federal civil rights acts. These acts provide remedies for anyone deprived of any constitutional rights by someone acting under color of law. Misuse of power by a state official has been held to constitute action under color of law, and the acts have been held applicable to permit individual prisoners to bring actions against prison officials. The acts enable a prisoner to seek an injunction to prevent further infringement of his rights, and this action is not limited by the exhaustion [of remedies] doctrine. Prison officials may be subjected to rather stiff criminal penalties or civil actions for damages. Of all the remedies available to prisoners whose rights have been violated while in prison, the civil rights acts appear to be the most readily available.

---

[91]  United States v. Leon and Massachusetts v. Sheppard are discussed in § 6.3 of this text.

[92]  Roger Goldman and Steven Puro, *Decertification of Police: An Alternative to Traditional Remedies for Police Misconduct*, 15 HASTINGS CONST. L. Q. 45 (1987).

[93]  Note, *The Problems of Modern Penology: Prison Life and Prisoners' Rights*, 53 IOWA L. REV. 671, 702-703, (1967). Prisoner's right to medical treatment, *see* Revere v. Mass. General Hospital, 103 S. Ct. 2979 (1983).

In a novel application of some of the foregoing principles, an inmate sued the state for failure to furnish the prisoner with a bland diet. The Louisiana First Circuit Court of Appeals affirmed a damage award of $75,000 assessed against the state of Louisiana on proof that, after a prison inmate was prescribed a bland diet as part of his medical treatment for a serious acidic stomach condition, prison authorities failed to provide such a diet. The prisoner developed three ulcers that required surgical removal of 70 percent of his stomach.[94]

While some suits by prisoners have met with success in the courts, many others have been thrown out as meritless. Recently, the Prison Litigation Reform Act (PLRA) was passed by Congress to stanch the flow of frivolous prisoner suits and appeals. The number of inmate suits had grown to more than 56,000 per year by the mid-1990s. Dismissal of meritless actions was facilitated by the new legislation. For example, the PLRA allowed court dismissal of a 42 U.S.C. § 1983 claim brought by inmates for emotional distress because they felt they might have been exposed to asbestos while working in the prison kitchen. The PLRA seeks to narrow the role of courts in overseeing the day-to-day operation of prisons, while at the same time retaining access to courts for prisoners with meritorious claims.

## § 10.20  Prisoner Rights

Much current writing has been dedicated to the subject of the right of penitentiary inmates to bring lawsuits, and to the developing legal rights of prisoners generally. In this section, a few selected areas of prisoner rights will be discussed to illustrate the trend of court decisions. Some areas of current litigation include the rights of prisoners to protection against attacks and injury; freedom of communication, including access to courts; and prisoner rights in transfer, release, and disciplinary proceedings.

The rights of inmates to sue for specified injuries were noted in the preceding section of this text. The United States District Court for the Northern District of Texas held that this right included a right to enforce protection against certain injuries inflicted by other inmates. A prison inmate held in a federal prison was allowed to recover under the Federal Tort Claims Act[95] when he was injured after another inmate hurled a "Molotov cocktail" into his cell. The court held that the prison officials negligent in several particulars, including the failure of prison authorities to take precautionary action when, prior to the incident, the assailant was observed tampering with the deadlock system that controlled the cell doors, and in storing flammable liquids where they were accessible to inmates. The plaintiff in the case was burned, and recovered $40,000 against the United States. In another suit, a federal judge in Alabama criticized the "rampant violence and jungle atmosphere" in Alabama prisons.[96]

94  Brown v. State Through Dept. 8 Corrections, 354 So. 2d 633 (La. App. 1977).

95  Bourgeois v. United States, 375 F. Supp. 133 (N.D. Tex. 1974).

96  Pugh v. Locke, 406 F. Supp. 318 (M.D. Ala. 1976), aff'd, 559 F.2d 283, modified, 438 U.S. 781, cert. denied, 438 U.S. 915.

Freedom of communication for prisoners has been expanded by court decisions. As stated in one opinion, "There is no iron curtain drawn between the Constitution and the prisons of this country."[97] Traditionally, prison officials have been allowed to censor mail coming into the prison on the ground that they must be concerned with prison security. *Procunier v. Martinez*[98] recognized the need to maintain security, but imposed certain restrictions on prison censorship. After *Procunier*, an inmate was entitled to be notified of the rejection of a letter sent to the prisoner, and the sender of the letter must be allowed to protest the rejection and secure review by a prison official other than the original censor. In one example from California, when mail left the penitentiary, California mail censorship regulations had banned inmate correspondence when the correspondence unduly complained about the prison or expressed inflammatory political or religious views. This was ruled unconstitutional under the First Amendment (freedom of speech). The Procunier decision explained: "The wife of a prison inmate who is not permitted to read all that her husband wanted to say to her has suffered an abridgment of her [First and Fourteenth Amendment rights]." The Court recognized the right of officials not to send or deliver letters concerning escape plans or proposed criminal activity, but the California regulations were overbroad: "Prison officials may not censor inmate correspondence simply to eliminate unflattering or unwelcome opinions."

Outgoing correspondence was the primary focus of *Procunier*. The correspondence limitations imposed by *Procunier* were limited to outgoing mail by a different case. Incoming correspondence—items sent from the outside to prisoners—will be governed by a more flexible standard. The United States Supreme Court clarified the right of prison authorities to reject incoming publications if the warden found the publication to be "detrimental to the security, good order, or discipline of the [jail or penitentiary] or if it might facilitate criminal activity."[99]

What kinds of incoming mail are outside the range of privacy? A state court decision presented one example. It held that a pretrial detainee did not have a reasonable expectation of privacy in a particular item of mail received at the jail. A defendant named Ruan was being held in jail. The following message was written on the back of an envelope addressed to defendant Ruan from his sister: "For Bob Ruan only, not for you coppers to read, so forget it! (Ha Ha)" The jailer opened and read the letter. It referred to a ring in the writer's possession, stolen by the defendant. Based on the letter and Ruan's own incriminating statements, the police obtained a search warrant, searched Mary Ruan's residence, and seized the stolen ring. Defendant's theft conviction was affirmed.[100]

---

[97]　Wolff v. McDonnell, 418 U.S. 539, 94 S. Ct. 2963, 41 L. Ed. 2d 935 (1974).
[98]　416 U.S. 396 (1974).
[99]　Thornburgh v. Abbott, 490 U.S. 401 (1989).
[100]　State v. Ruan, 419 N.W.2d 734 (Iowa App. 1987).

The *Procunier* ruling dealt not only with correspondence but also with jail visits. It rejected a California regulation that banned the use by attorneys of law students to interview inmate clients:

> The remoteness of many California penal institutions makes a personal visit to an inmate client a time-consuming undertaking. . . . Allowing law students and paraprofessionals to interview inmates might well reduce the cost of legal representation for prisoners. The District Court therefore concluded that the regulation imposed a substantial burden on the right of access to the courts. . . . This result is mandated by our decision in *Johnson v. Avery*, 393 U.S., 483, 89 S.Ct. 747, 21 L.Ed.2d 718 (1969). There the Court struck down a prison regulation prohibiting any inmate from advising or assisting another in the preparation of legal documents. Given the inadequacy of alternative sources of legal assistance, the rule had the effect of denying to illiterate or poorly-educated inmates any opportunity to vindicate possible valid constitutional claims. The Court found that the regulation impermissibly burdened the right of access to all courts. . . .[101]

Suppose a family member arrives at the penitentiary to visit an inmate. Can a prison visitor be strip-searched? In *Hunter v. Auger*,[102] because general strip searches of prison visitors were not incident to arrest, were done even though the visitors' activities were not suspicious, and were based solely on uncorroborated anonymous tips that visitors would attempt to smuggle drugs to inmates, the court found that the strip searches were conducted without probable cause and were an unreasonable infringement of the visitor's Fourth Amendment rights.

This text has noted the challenge to prison administrators when managing crowded penal facilities. Administrators sometimes employ penalties of various kinds to deter bad inmate conduct. Sanctions are taken against inmates who obtain and use illegal drugs inside the walls. Prison visitation policies that ban family visits for a period of time in the case of inmates who commit multiple substance-abuse violations is a proper management policy, say the courts.[103] Such court decisions confirm the general authority of corrections officials to run the nation's prisons, and permits them to make the decisions necessary for the orderly administration of penitentiaries.

While many prison policies have generally enjoyed a "hands off" policy by the courts, procedures used to place an inmate in a mental institution have prompted court intervention. When authorities decide a prisoner should be shifted from the penitentiary to a place for confinement of the mentally ill, this

---

[101] 416 U.S. 396 (1974). On the need for a prison to maintain an adequate law library, *see* Bounds v. Smith, 430 U.S. 817 (1977).

[102] 672 F.2d 668 (8th Cir. 1982). Where probable cause or reasonable suspicion exists, the prison can take protective measures. The Supreme Court addressed strip searches of prisoners in Bell v. Wolfish, 441 U.S. 520 (1979) (prisoners, as opposed to incoming family members, may be strip-searched after contact visits with outsiders).

[103] Overton v. Bazzetta, 123 S. Ct. 2162 (2003).

step requires notice to the prisoner and a hearing, according to the United States Supreme Court.[104] Similarly, before a prison disciplinary committee deprives a prisoner of good-time credits for violation of prison regulations, the inmate is entitled to 24-hour notice of the charges and a written statement of the reasons for disciplinary action.[105] Whether an indigent prisoner is entitled generally to an appointed lawyer to assist his or her challenge at such hearings appeared to be in question for a time, but in 1976 the Supreme Court made clear that the answer was no.[106]

Transfer and release proceedings pose related questions. While some have argued that transfer of a prisoner from a less secure to a more secure detention facility requires a full hearing with the prisoner present, the Supreme Court has held against such hearing rights. At least where the transfer is for disciplinary reasons as opposed to "administrative" transfers, nothing in the federal due process clause forbids transfer of a prison inmate from one prison to another.[107] In one case, a prisoner was transferred from a medium-security institution to a maximum-security prison after a series of serious fires at the medium-security institution. Approving the right to transfer without a full adversary hearing, the Court distinguished *Wolff v. McDonnell* (right to notice and hearing before loss of good-time credits) on the basis that the state is empowered to confine the prisoner at any of its prisons.[108]

Parole eligibility proceedings present yet another issue for prison administration. Although case law has frequently denied the inmate the right to an appointed attorney at hearings before the parole board, some courts have indicated that state parole boards should furnish prisoners with a statement of the reasons for denial of parole. Other courts have not required that a parole board announce findings upon which it bases its decisions to grant or deny parole. The question has been raised in the Supreme Court,[109] which approved the practice of parole boards communicating reasons for denial "as a guide to the inmate for his future behavior," but did not require the board to provide a summary of the evidence.

To summarize, in the broad sweep of day-to-day prison life the courts have avoided interference with the administration of prisons. The discretionary powers vested in prison officials have only been subjected to outside review when courts decided that the officials engaged in arbitrary action. When such occurs, or when prison conditions fall to such a level that confinement may be termed cruel and inhumane punishment, judicial intervention is a possibility.

---

[104]   Vitek v. Jones, 445 U.S. 480 (1980).
[105]   Wolff v. McDonnell, note 97 *supra*.
[106]   Baxter v. Palmigiano, 425 U.S. 308, 96 S. Ct. 1551, 47 L. Ed. 2d 810 (1976).
[107]   Montanye v. Haymes, 427 U.S. 236, 96 S. Ct. 2543, 49 L. Ed. 2d 466 (1976).
[108]   Meacham v. Fano, 427 U.S. 328, 96 S. Ct. 2532, 49 L. Ed. 2d 451 (1976) (transfer preceded by hearing before prison classification board, but prisoner was not present during warden's testimony). *See* Olim v. Wakinekona, 103 S. Ct. 1741 (1983) (no vested right in place of confinement).
[109]   *See* Greenholtz v. Nebraska Penal Inmates, 99 S. Ct. 2100 (1979) (nothing requires parole board to specify particular evidence on which it rests discretionary determination.)

As a norm, however, the "hands off" doctrine holds sway. Notwithstanding some movement in the direction of expanding prisoner rights in fields like communication policy or transfers to a mental health facility, other aspects of prison life remain unchanged. An example is the right of corrections officers to search for weapons or implements that might be used to injure officers or make an escape. A commentator explains: "Fourth Amendment rights for inmates do not mirror the rights afforded to individuals outside of prison walls. For example, prisoners have virtually no recourse under this amendment when their prison cells are searched. Inmates are subject to searches of their persons and belongings despite there being no showing of a particularized need. Courts always find that security within prisons trumps the typical Fourth Amendment rights provided to other citizens."[110]

---

[110]   Ellen Podgor, *Government Surveillance of Attorney-Client Communications*, 17 GEORGETOWN J. LEG. ETHICS 145, 155 (2003).

# The Adversary System

Decency, security and liberty alike demand that government officials shall be subjected to the same rules of conduct that are commands to the citizen. In a government of laws, existence of the
government will be imperiled if it fails to observe the law scrupu-
lously. Our government is the potent, the omnipresent teacher. For
good or for ill, it teaches the whole people by its example.

Mr. Justice Brandeis*

We know that a trial based on false or suppressed evidence is not
trial at all. False or suppressed evidence can neither convict nor
condemn.

United States ex rel.
Hough v. Maroney**

---

\*      Olmstead v. United States, 277 U.S. 438, 485, 48 S. Ct. 564, 72 L. Ed. 944 (1928) (dissenting opinion).
\*\*   247 F. Supp. 767, 779 (W.D. Pa. 1965).

# 11

Chapter Outline

## § 11.1  Defense of the System

Trial by law courts is the successor to personal force, community lynching, trial by ordeal, and trial by combat.[1] One of the fundamental defenses made of resolving disputes in the courtroom is that there is no better method for the termination of controversies that cannot be settled by negotiation. Occasionally the treatment experienced by a law enforcement officer in a trial causes the officer frustration or discouragement with the adversary process. Being the recipient of an antagonistic or unfair cross-examination sometimes tempts one to condemn the entire legal system, and when this occurs it is well to reflect upon the desirability of the alternatives to court process listed in the first sentence of this paragraph.

Nine hundred years ago in England, a landowner unjustly deprived of his property had five days to round up an army and retake his property by storm. If the landowner failed, his land became the lawful property of the usurper. As late as the 1600s in the United States, those accused of crimes were sometimes thrown, with hands and feet bound, into tanks of water. If they floated, they were judged guilty and hanged. If they sank, they were declared innocent and, of course, drowned. Barbaric? Unfair? Most people probably did not think so then.[2] Modern notions of justice are quite different.

## § 11.2  Responsibility of Advocates

A perceptive commentator observed: "The adversarial component of the litigation process is the cornerstone of the American justice system. Ideally, if two equally matched attorneys zealously and competently represent their clients within the bounds of the ethical rules and the law, the correct result will

---

[1]   Abram, The Challenge of the Courtroom: Reflections on the Adversary System, 11 U. Chi. Law School-Record 1, 4 (1963).

[2]   Statement of American Bar Association, Law Day U.S.A., May 1, 1983.

ultimately be reached."[3] Under our law, the success of the trial system depends upon both sides being represented by contentious opposing **advocates**. The principle that leads to spirited give-and-take in criminal prosecutions is one upon which our American theory of trial is based—that of an **"adversary" or "contentious" justice system**.

This system is based on the assumption that the truth of any controversy will come out best when each side (the defendant as well as the state) vigorously presents its evidence and presses the theory of law supporting its case.[4] Thus, the defense lawyer only does his or her duty to the client and the legal system when he or she conducts the client's cause with devotion, zeal, and professionalism.[5]

## § 11.3   Role of the Defense Attorney

Ethical rules prohibit an attorney from knowingly using perjured testimony or offering evidence the attorney knows to be false. A lawyer should preserve the confidences and secrets of his or her client. A **defense attorney** has the duty to advise the client, but it is for the client to decide whether to plead guilty. If the client pleads "not guilty" it is the responsibility of counsel to vigorously pursue the defense through trial of the case.

One observer has commented that attorneys representing defendants differ from other members of the profession and the general public—not because of any professional or moral superiority, but because they play a unique and essential institutional role in our criminal justice system. "They serve as the necessary advocates of defendants' rights. By fulfilling that role, they vindicate limits the Constitution imposes upon government power, and assure that the adversary justice system functions correctly. Recognition of defense counsel's dual roles suggests that Sixth Amendment theory should do more than simply guarantee the right of individual defendants to a lawyer. It should also protect the ability of attorneys, individually and collectively, to provide that representation."[6]

Commentators have urged that of all the rights that an accused person has, the right to representation by a trained lawyer is the most important. "Only the adversarial system can effectuate the search for the truth. The alternative is a nonadversarial society whereby one being accused is the equivalent of one being convicted. If criminal defense lawyers do not 'put the government to its proof whenever necessary or whenever the client requires it, then we are close to those totalitarian states where accusation equals guilt [and] the criminal

---

3    Lonnie Brown, *Ending Illegitimate Advocacy*, 62 OH. ST. L. J. 1555, 1616 (2001).

4    Edward Barrett, *The Adversary System and the Ethics of Advocacy*, 37 NOTRE DAME LAWYER 479 (1962); Jackson, *Are All Laws Technicalities?* JURIS DOCTOR 16 (Nov. 1974) (urging that defense counsel's role is one of law enforcement; the enforcement of those laws protecting the individual against society).

5    *See* Ronald Carlson, *Competency and Professionalism in Modern Litigation*, 23 GA. L. REV. 689 (1989).

6    Morgan Cloud, *Forfeiting Defense Attorneys Fees*, 1987 WIS. L. REV. 1.

defense lawyers are but an adjunct prosecutor expected to make the client confess and aid in his or her rehabilitation.' Hence, if criminal defendants are not represented, the foundation of the judicial system is eroded."[7]

## § 11.4   Role of the Prosecutor

The most famous and frequently quoted statement on the role of the **prosecutor** appears in *Berger v. United States*:

> The United States Attorney is the representative not of an ordinary party to a controversy, but of a sovereignty whose obligation to govern impartially is as compelling as its obligation to govern at all; and whose interest, therefore, in a criminal prosecution is not that it shall win a case, but that justice shall be done. As such, he is in a peculiar and very definite sense the servant of the law, the twofold aim of which is that guilt shall not escape or innocence suffer. He may prosecute with earnestness and vigor—indeed, he should do so. But, while he may strike hard blows, he is not at liberty to strike foul ones. It is as much his duty to refrain from improper methods calculated to produce a wrongful conviction as it is to use every legitimate means to bring about a just one.[8]

Just as a witness has a responsibility to the truth and to correct the record, points detailed in the next section of the text, so does the prosecutor. When knowledge comes to a prosecutor that perjurious testimony has been used on behalf of the state, the prosecutor has a duty to correct it.

## § 11.5   Responsibility of Police Officers

Police officers are singularly important persons in the adversary process. Frequently they are the chief witnesses for the government, and much of the zeal of the defense is spent on them. How a police officer reacts to this pressure in court will determine to a large extent whether the integrity of the legal process will be maintained. It is helpful to keep this in mind, and to resist in the heat of battle any temptation to win by foul means. When the officer is in court, he or she should never refrain from correcting his or her testimony when an honest error has been made. The matter should be brought to the attention of the court as soon as the mistake is realized, for it is improper to leave inaccurate testimony standing in the record. While the law enforcement officer is naturally interested in successful prosecutions, he or she must also guard against showing a specific interest in gaining a conviction. Respect is lost

---

[7]   Stephen Jones, *A Lawyer's Ethical Duty to Represent the Unpopular Client*, 1 Chapman L. Rev. 105, 107 (1998), quoting from J. Hall, Professional Responsibility of the Criminal Lawyer § 9:12 (2d ed. 1996).

[8]   295 U.S. 78 (1935).

when a jury perceives a tenacious desire on an officer's part to achieve conviction at any cost. Telling the truth is of paramount importance. If testimony is shaded to help the prosecution, it will likely rebound to the detriment of the government, either in the trial itself or later in habeas corpus. "Fairness in our system, and the appearance of fairness, is essential if the system is to win the respect and cooperation of all citizens, without which crime cannot be controlled."[9]

The government wins in a criminal case only when justice is done. This means that both the police and the prosecutor have a particular responsibility to make certain that fair tactics and truthful evidence prevail in criminal trials. The following statement is as true today as when it was initially made in 1935: "It is as much his [the prosecutor's] duty to refrain from improper methods calculated to produce a wrongful conviction as it is to use every legitimate means to bring about a just one."[10]

## § 11.6  Responsibility of Judges

Whether the judge is accepting a guilty plea, presiding at a jury trial, or hearing a case without a jury, impartiality is essential. Particularly sensitive are cases in which the judge decides the case without a jury, conducting a **bench trial** in which the court sits as the sole trier of both the facts and the law:

> When sitting as a trier of facts, a judge, like a jury, must be careful to exclude all considerations except those arising from the evidence before him. Anything less, even if it has no part in the ultimate decision, leaves the unsuccessful litigant convinced he has not had fair treatment. It is almost as important to avoid this appearance of unfairness as it is to avoid unfairness itself.[11]

The judge faces a difficult task. If the trial judge wields her power arbitrarily in favor of the prosecution, the defendant and his or her family will think the defendant "got railroaded." At the other extreme, partiality in favor of a defendant will be scrutinized, and judicial handling of criminal cases has sometimes engendered public resentment when a prosecution was dismissed or a sentence was viewed as "soft." In such sensitive times, it is critical that trial judges handling criminal cases do so with deftness and with fairness to both sides in the process. In meting out justice the judge must display "cold neutrality," in the words of Edmund Burke. In his classic definition of a good judge, Socrates cited the need for the jurist to hear courteously, consider soberly, and decide impartially. These principles were reviewed in a case

---

[9]  REPORT, LAW ENFORCEMENT TASK FORCE, NATIONAL COMMISSION ON THE CAUSES AND PREVENTION OF VIOLENCE, 482 (1969).

[10]  Berger v. United States, 295 U.S. 78 (1935). See CODE OF PROFESSIONAL RESPONSIBILITY EC 7-13, Am. Bar Assn.

[11]  Hall v. State, 325 N.W.2d 752 (Iowa 1982). See State v. Glanton, 231 N.W.2d 31 (Iowa 1975). Iowa Supreme Court Justice David Harris provides an excellent profile of what constitutes an impartial jurist in this court opinion, drawing upon historical thinkers such as Sir Francis Bacon.

involving actions by a trial judge when a defendant was tried on charges flowing from a drug deal that had fatal consequences. The defendant believed a person named Rowe owed her money for drugs she had supplied to Rowe. The defendant enlisted Arnold, Walton, and Turnipseed to assist in recovering the debt. When one of them said he intended to kill Rowe, the defendant replied: "I didn't tell y'all to kill nobody. [I] told you to go over there and whip his ass and take my money and take my dope."

While the defendant's threesome was searching Rowe's house, a friend of Rowe entered Rowe's home. Arnold shot him in the chest and killed him. The defendant was charged with conspiracy to commit armed robbery and felony murder. She was given a new trial because of the actions of the trial judge. A description of the judge's conduct is detailed in the state supreme court opinion, and is outlined hereafter.

During jury selection, the defense attorney rose from his chair, presumably to address the judge. "According to a witness who was in the courtroom, however, before counsel could speak, the trial judge spoke in a loud, harsh and condemning voice, telling counsel to 'sit down and shut up.'"[12] The state supreme court, which reversed the defendant's conviction, spotted another error that the appellate justices deemed to be a glaring one. When the defense attorney objected to a question asked by the prosecutor, the judge warned the defense lawyer not to "interrupt the [State's witness examination] again" by raising objections. "Conversely, while defense counsel was cross-examining a different witness, the judge interposed his own objection to the questions being posed, even though the prosecutor had raised no objection on behalf of the State."

Finally, after a number of such incidents, the defense attorney asked the judge to remove himself from the bench because the judge had assisted the prosecutor in making the State's case before the jury. The trial judge responded by denying the defense motion, then warned the defense counsel that if he sought again to bring discredit upon the court, the court would cite him for contempt. In view of this record, the state supreme court had grave doubts about whether the defendant was convicted in a fair trial. The reviewing court stated:

> We are mindful of the extraordinary pressures attending a criminal trial of this magnitude. On the one hand, defense counsel is obligated to vigorously defend his client against all charges brought by the State. Likewise, prosecutors must effectively present the State's case to the jury. At the same time, the trial judge is charged with ensuring that the rules of evidence and procedure are followed, and that the proceedings are both orderly and fair. When these several interests come together in the courtroom during trial, we believe that occasional, brief disagreements between the bench and bar are to be expected.

> The instances discussed above, however, represent more than mere friction between zealous counsel and a diligent jurist. The judge's conduct, as discussed above, created the impression that he harbored an inclination to be

---

12    Johnson v. State, 278 Ga. 344, 602 S.E.2d 623 (2004).

biased against [the defendant] and partial toward the prosecution. . . . Because the trial judge's impartiality was questionable, it was error for him to deny appellant's motion for recusal. Because we cannot say it is likely that the incidents discussed above had no impact on the jury's disposition of this matter, we must reverse the judgments of conviction.

Other authorities point out that a judge should not sneer at a witness's testimony nor laugh derisively at a lawyer's question. A trial judge should not "telegraph to a jury, by purposeful exclamations, gestures or facial expressions, his approval or disapproval, belief or disbelief, in the testimony of witnesses or arguments of counsel." Above all else, the trial court should not exhibit a hostile attitude toward any party in any case before the bench.[13]

## § 11.7  Need for Support and Reform of System

Enforcement of the law, like the laws themselves, requires public assistance and cooperation.[14] In addition to his or her attitude toward the trial process as previously noted, the relationship of the law officer to the court system as a whole is very important. The court system needs our support, as well as our responsible criticism. The latter assists in catalyzing needed revisions and reforms. Those working in the criminal justice system are in an excellent position to provide both. Bill of Rights provisions, sometimes vigorously enforced by the courts to the detriment of the police, do indeed make it more difficult to secure convictions. But this is one of the prices we pay for living in a free society. Another need is that of society to provide adequate resources to assure efficient and responsible administration of the criminal laws. A task force report to the National Violence Commission has suggested that the public could assist the police in a much more meaningful way. "For it is clear that we could be of greater assistance to our police by appropriating the necessary funds to finance crime laboratories, adequate prosecutorial staffs, and proper correctional treatment."[14]

---

[13] *See* discussion of this point in Long v. Broadlawns Med. Cntr., 656 N.W.2d 71 (Iowa 2002).
[14] REPORT, note 10 at 499.

# Glossary

**abandoned property doctrine** For purposes of seizure of evidence outside Fourth Amendment protection, an officer is permitted to pick up property dropped or abandoned by a suspect, examine it, and retain it as evidence if useful.

**acquittal** A finding of not guilty in a criminal trial.

**adjudication** The formal judgment, decree or determination.

**admission** A defendant's statement that she committed the crime, or his or her declaration that he or she did an act that contributed to the offense.

**adversary system** A system of law whereby opposing parties contend against one another in front of an impartial deciding body.

**advocate** One who assists, defends or pleads for another.

**affirm (a case)** To confirm; in appellate courts, to affirm a judgment, decree or order is to confirm that it is valid and that it stands as correct.

**"Allen" instruction** Derived from *Allen v. United States*, 164 U.S. 492, 17 S. Ct. 154, 41 L. Ed. 528, where such an instruction was approved, it refers to an instruction given to jurors when they report an inability to agree on a verdict advising jurors to listen to each other's views with a willingness to be convinced by each other's arguments; (also referred to as a "dynamite" or "hammer" instruction).

**alternative sentencing** Nontraditional sentences that allow for alternatives to conventional jail terms.

**American Law Institute test** Combining the *M'Naghten* and "irresistible impulse" tests for insanity, under this most commonly used test an accused person is not held criminally responsible if proven that as a result of mental disease or defect at the time of the offense the accused lacked the ability to appreciate the wrongfulness of the act or the ability to conduct himself or herself according to the law—it does not require a complete lack of knowledge of the wrongness of the criminal act, only the lack of capacity to understand right from wrong or to conform conduct to the law; (see also M'Naghten Rule and irresistible impulse test).

**appeal** Resort to a higher (appellate) court for review of a trial court; in the federal system an appeal can go to an intermediate appellate court and then to the Supreme Court.

**arraignment** Procedure where the accused is brought before the court to plead to the criminal charge in an indictment or information; n the federal system the charge is read to the accused and he or she must plead "guilty," "not guilty" or, where permitted, "nolo contendere".

**arrest** To deprive a person of liberty by legal authority; taking a person into custody or detention to answer to criminal charges.

**arrest warrant** A written order based on a complaint commanding a law enforcement official to arrest a person and bring him or her before a magistrate.

**bail** The surety or sureties put forth by a party to obtain release of a person under arrest by becoming responsible for the person's appearance at the time and place designated by the court. Cash bail bond is a sum of money designated by the court posted by defendant or another person to the court with the understanding that it will be forfeited if defendant does not comply with court appearance instructions. Unsecured bail bond is a bail bond for which defendant is liable upon failure to comply with court appearance instructions but which is not secured by deposit of funds.

**bailable offense** An offense for which a prisoner may be admitted to bail.

**bench trial** A trial held before a judge without a jury.

**bifurcated trial or proceedings** Two-part proceedings, such as separate trials to determine guilt and to set sentence; death penalty trials are bifurcated in this manner.

**bind over** Whereby a court or magistrate requires a person to appear for trial; also refers to the act of a lower court transferring a case to higher court or grand jury after finding of probable cause that defendant committed the crime.

**booking a suspect** An administrative procedure by which an arrested person at the police station is put on the police "blotter," including information such as the person's name, crime for which arrested and other facts; may also include photographing and fingerprinting the suspect.

**brief** A written document; that summarizes the legal arguments of a party; in criminal practice, both the prosecutor as well as the defense counsel usually file competing briefs when a defendant moves to dismiss the government's case.

**burden of proof** In the law of evidence, it is the burden of one party of proving a fact or facts in dispute.

**capital punishment** Punishment by death for capital crimes.

**certiorari** A writ issued by a superior court to an inferior court requiring the court to provide a certified record of a particular case so that the court who issued the writ can inspect the proceedings for irregularities.

**challenge for cause** During voir dire, a request to the judge that a prospective juror be released from the jury because of specific cause or reason (see also peremptory challenge); when a challenge for cause is granted, a juror is disqualified without the party who asserted the challenge needing to spend a peremptory challenge.

**change of venue** The transfer of a suit begun in one geographic area to another.

**charge** To indict or formally accuse.

**citation** An order form issued by the police or the court for a person to appear before a magistrate or judge at a specified time and date.

**civil damages** Monetary recovery collected by a plaintiff following trial in a civil court in which plaintiff must show specific injury and request compensation for such injury.

**clear and convincing evidence** Generally this means proof to a high level of certainty, certainly more than a preponderance of the evidence, but somewhat less than proof beyond a reasonable doubt.

**closing argument (also final argument or summation)** The final statements by the attorneys to the jury or court; each side summarizes the evidence they believe they have established and what they feel the other side has failed to establish; in federal criminal cases, the prosecution goes first, the defense replies, and then the prosecution is allowed to reply.

**collateral estoppel doctrine** When an issue of fact has been determined by a valid judgment, it cannot be litigated again by the same parties.

**collective entity rule** Under this rule, because corporations are collective entities, their records are not private and not protected by the Fifth Amendment.

**common law** As opposed to law created by legislatures, common law is the law established over time by custom and usage; it begins with the ancient, unwritten law of England and includes statutory and case law of the American colonies.

**compensation (also reparation)** Payment of damages; making amends.

**complainant** The person who instigates prosecution or applies to the courts for legal redress by filing a complaint (i.e., plaintiff).

**complaint** The original pleading which initiates an action; it is a written statement of the essential facts of the offense charged (in some jurisdictions "complaint" is the equivalent of "information").

**consent search** A search made by police after the subject of the search has agreed to the search, or when the occupant of the premises lets police in to search the place.

**consolidation of cases or actions** The act of uniting several actions into one trial and judgment, by order of a court, where all actions are by the same parties, or against the same party, when a legal basis for employer liability is established pending in the same court, and involving essentially the same matters and issues.

**constitutional torts** Municipalities can be sued for deprivation of any rights, privileges or immunities secured by the Constitution and law, and they are liable to injured parties.

**contemporaneous searches** Dealing with the timeliness of searches, this refers to the rule that a search must follow an arrest as soon as reasonably possible, the more immediate the better.

**conviction** The result of a criminal trial which ends with the defendant being found guilty as charged.

**coram nobis relief** (see writ of coram nobis)

**count** Each separate and independent claim—a civil petition or a criminal indictment may contain several counts; "count" and "charge" referring to allegations in an indictment or information are synonymous.

**critical stage** The stages of a criminal case in which the right to counsel attaches; the defendant is entitled to have a lawyer represent him or her at all critical stages of the case, including preliminary hearing and trial.

**cross-examination** The examination of a witness by the opposing party that called him or her; generally the scope of examination is limited to matters covered on direct examination.

**custody** The confinement or control of a thing or person; being "in custody" refers to restraint of liberty, and custodial interrogation of the accused takes place when the defendant is not free to leave the interrogation room.

**deadly force** Force likely or intended to cause death or great bodily harm.

**defendant** The person defending or denying criminal responsibility; the accused person or the party against whom relief or recovery is sought.

**defense attorney** The lawyer who represents the accused/defendant.

**delinquent** One who is a juvenile and is guilty of a crime or offense.

**deposition** Testimony of a witness taken in writing during questioning; the deposition is taken under oath, not in open court, but often in an attorney's office.

**derivative evidence** Evidence which is derived from other illegally obtained evidence is inadmissible because of the taint on the original evidence (see "fruit of the poisonous tree" doctrine).

**detainer** The document that alerts authorities who have a prisoner in confinement in State A that the prisoner is needed in State B for trial on another charge.

**determinate sentence** Sentence to confinement for a fixed period of time as specified by statute.

**deterrence** Impeding or tending to prevent, often by setting an example.

**directed verdict** (see motion for judgment of acquittal)

**direct examination (also examination in chief)** The first interrogation or examination of a witness by the person who called the witness to the stand.

**discretionary review** Form of appellate review that is not required but is a matter of choice; for example, the Supreme Court chooses its cases for review and is not required to review matters on appeal.

**dismissal with prejudice** An adjudication on the merits and final disposition, it bars the right to bring or maintain an action of the same claim or cause.

**dismissal without prejudice** Refers to a dismissal or finding that extinguishes a legal action, but which allows the disappointed party to bring the action again at a later time.

**disposition** In criminal procedure, refers to the sentencing or other final finding in the case.

**dissenting opinion** Most commonly refers to the opinion provided by one or more judges of a court that expresses explicit disagreement with the decision handed down by the majority; a dissent may or may not be accompanied by a written opinion.

**diversion** Referring to alternative sentencing measures, it is a disposition of a criminal defendant where the court directs defendant to participate in some form of program or other alternative to traditional incarceration.

**double jeopardy** Refers to being subject to prosecution more than once for the same offense; the Fifth Amendment of the Constitution prohibits a second prosecution after a first trial for the same offense.

**dual sovereignty** Federal and state governments are each sovereign in their own right, so in some cases a person can be tried twice for the same act or acts because the crime violated both state and federal laws; thus, double jeopardy does not apply because it refers to more than one prosecution by the same sovereign jurisdiction for the same offense.

**Durham test** The irresistible impulse test of criminal responsibility resulting from Durham v. United States, C.A.D.C., 214 F.2d 862, 875. Under the Durham Rule, to find a defendant not guilty by reason of insanity of mental irresponsibility, the jury must find that defendant was suffering from the mental disease at the time of the commission of the act and that there was causal relation between the disease and the act.

**"dynamite" instruction** (see "Allen" instruction)

**evidence** Any court materials or proof, such as witness testimony, documents, exhibits, physical items or objects, etc.

**excessive force** Any amount of force beyond what is necessary and justifiable, given the particulars of the events and the people involved.

**exclusionary rule** Under the exclusionary rule, any evidence that has been obtained in violation of the privileges guaranteed by the U.S. Constitution must be excluded at trial.

**exculpatory evidence** Evidence that clears or tends to clear the defendant.

**exigent circumstances** These emergency or emergency-like circumstances may provide permission by police to make warrantless entry or warrantless search and seizure because delay may pose a danger to persons or allow destruction of evidence.

**expert witness** A person who through education or experience has specialized or superior knowledge about a given subject, who will be provide guidance to the jury on technical matters through direct and cross-examination as a witness.

**expungement (expunction) of record** The court-imposed destruction or sealing of a criminal conviction record after a set amount of time.

**extradition** The surrender by one state or country to another of a person accused or convicted in the other territory, which territory then demands the surrender of that person.

**false arrest** An arrest without proper legal authority, resulting in unlawful restraint of a person's liberty.

**false imprisonment** Because an arrest restrains the liberty of a person, false arrest is also false imprisonment, whereby a person unlawfully loses his or her liberty.

**felony** Contrasted with misdemeanor, felony is a more serious offense, usually characterized as an offense that is punishable by death or imprisonment in a state prison (versus imprisonment in a local jail), or a crime for which the term of imprisonment is more than year.

**"fruit of the poisonous tree" doctrine** Evidence which is obtained from , or is discovered as a result of an illegal search or is generally inadmissible against the defendant because it is tainted by being a product of a bad initial search.

**good faith exception** This exception to the exclusionary rule allows the admission into court of evidence obtained with error or mistake as long as the error or mistake was honest and reasonable.

**grand jury** A group of citizens, the number of which may vary by state, who are gathered to determine whether probable cause exists that a crime has been committed and whether an indictment (true bill) should be returned against the accused; its purpose is merely to determine if the case will go to trial and not to determine whether the accused is guilty; grand jury proceedings are not public proceedings.

**guilty plea** Formal admission of guilt in court by the defendant, only admissible if the defendant has been fully advised of rights, understands those rights and makes the plea voluntarily.

**habeas corpus** (see writ of habeas corpus)

**habitual offender laws** Under such laws, jurors may convict a defendant not only of the principal crime in the case but of being a habitual criminal after proof of previous crimes has been introduced at trial; such conviction usually leads to an enhanced sentence.

**"hammer" instruction** (see "Allen" instruction)

**hearings** Formal proceedings, usually public, but less formal than a trial, with issues of fact or law; frequently describes any proceedings before magistrates sitting without a jury; generally introduction and admissibility of evidence is less stringent in hearings than in trials.

**hearsay evidence** Testimony in court of a statement made out of court by someone other than the person testifying; it does not come from personal knowledge of the witness who is on the stand but from something the witness heard others say; use of hearsay evidence is strictly limited.

**hot pursuit** Also known as fresh pursuit, refers to the right of law enforcement officials to chase a suspect and even cross jurisdictional lines (in jurisdictions which allow it) in pursuit of a felon in order to arrest the person for a crime committed in the first jurisdiction.

**hung jury** A jury divided in opinion and unable to come to a unanimous verdict after lengthy attempts (see "Allen" instruction).

**immunity from prosecution** If granted by the prosecution, a witness may be protected from being prosecuted pursuant to his or her testimony; "use immunity" prohibits the use of the witness's compelled testimony from being used in any subsequent criminal prosecution of the witness; when a witness testifies about a crime under the protection of "transactional immunity," any later prosecution of the witness for that crime is prohibited after the person gives his or her immunized testimony.

**impeachment of witness** To call into question the truthfulness of a witness by means of evidence meant to show that the witness may not be completely believable; done through means such as proof of inconsistent statements, contradiction of facts, bias, or proof of questionable character.

***in camera*** In chambers, private; may refer to proceedings before a judge in private chambers or when all spectators are barred from the courtroom.

**incompetence** Severe mental disability or impairment; lacking understanding or ability to make or communicate responsible decisions.

**indeterminate sentence** A sentence of imprisonment that is not fixed by the court but left to penal authorities: minimum and maximum time limits may be set by the court, leaving discretion to grant early release by a parole board or other supervisory authority.

**indictment** An accusation in writing originating with a prosecutor and issued by a grand jury charging a person with a crime—referred to as a "true bill;" failure to indict is a "no bill" (see information).

**information** An accusation against a person for a crime, presented by a public officer such as a prosecutor (as opposed to an indictment, which is handed down by the grand jury); in many states may be used in place of a grand jury indictment to bring a person to trial.

**interlocutory appeal** An interim appeal, not appealing the final disposition of the case but of some step or decision along the way that affects the process and possibly the final adjudication of the case.

**"irresistible impulse" test** As used in an insanity defense, refers to an impulse on the part of the accused that he or she is incapable of resisting due to mental disease that affects the person's self-control and choice of actions; this test is broader than the M'Naghten test because under the irresistible impulse test the person may avoid responsibility even though he or she understood the nature of the act and its wrongness; (see also American Law Institute Test and M'Naghten Rule).

**issues of fact** Arises when a fact is maintained by one party and denied by the other party; issues of fact are determined by the jury at the trial level.

**issues of law** Arises when matters of law in a case are in question; appeals courts review issues of law.

***Jackson v. Denno* hearing** A pretrial hearing addressing a defendant's Miranda or voluntariness objections to validity of a confession. The court will hear evidence to determine whether the trial jury will get to hear and see the confession.

**Jencks Act** A criminal defendant in federal court is entitled to access to government documents for assistance in cross-examination of witnesses in order to impeach for prior inconsistent statements; Jencks v. U.S., 353 U.S. 657, 77 S. Ct. 1007, 1 L. Ed. 2d 1103, leading to federal statute 18 U.S.C.A. § 3500.

**joinder** Joining two things together, such as uniting one person with another in some legal proceeding; two or more persons may be joined for trial or indictment in order to facilitate judicial economy, where the pair joined together in committing a crime.

**joint indictment** When several offenders are included in the same indictment.

**joint trial** The trial of two or more persons for the same or similar offenses.

**judgment N.O.V.** (see motion for judgment notwithstanding the verdict)

**jurisdiction** The authority or inherent power by which courts and judicial officers decide cases; distinguished from venue, which refers to the geographic place of the trial.

**jurisprudence** The philosophy or science of law, ascertaining the principles on which legal rules are based.

**jurist** A person who is skilled in the law, often used to refer to a person who is officially qualified to decide legal matters, such as a magistrate, judge, or a justice.

**jury** A specified number of men and women selected and sworn to determine matters of fact and decide the truth of the evidence presented to them.

**jury instructions** A direction given by the judge to the jury concerning the law of the case, informing the jury of the law applicable to the case and the rules or principles of law that the jurors are bound to accept and apply.

**jury nullification** Jury nullification occurs when the jury's verdict is at odds with the weight of the evidence presented at trial. , particularly when jurors affirmatively decide not to follow the law; jurors who nullify have decided to substitute their own notion of law over that given by the court, although the Supreme Court rejects the practice of juries in effect declaring laws unconstitutional.

**juvenile court** A court having special jurisdiction over delinquent, dependent and neglected children.

**"knock-and-announce" rule** A rule requiring officers to let householders know that they are there to arrest or search; in specified cases a peace officer, whether with a warrant or on probable cause without a warrant, may after announcement of authority and purpose break through a door to gain admittance to a dwelling.

**leave of court** Permission granted by a court to do something which normally would not be allowable.

**lineup** A police identification procedure by which the suspect in a crime is exhibited before the victim or witness; a number of individuals are lined up, from which the witness may then make an identification; the procedure must meet certain standards and be free of suggestion as to the suspect; (see showup).

**M'Naghten Rule** A widely used and long-established test to be applied for the defense of insanity under which the accused is not criminally responsible if at the time of committing the act he or she suffered such a defect of reason or mental disease that he or she did not know the nature and quality of the act or did not understand that the act was wrong; M'Naghten's Case, 8 Eng. Rep. 718 (1843); (see also American Law Institute test and irresistible impulse test).

**magistrate** A public officer with judicial power.

**malicious prosecution** Prosecution that is malicious in nature and without probable cause.

*Miranda* **warning** Prior to any custodial interrogation in which a person is deprived of his or her freedom in any significant way, the person must be warned that he or she: (1) has the right to remain silent; (2) that any statement made may be used as evidence against him or her; (3) that he or she has the right to an attorney; (4) that if he or she cannot afford an attorney, one will be appointed prior to any questions if so desired. Administration of these warnings or waiver of them must be demonstrated for any evidence obtained during interrogation to be admissible in court.

**misdemeanor** Contrasted with felony, misdemeanor is a less serious offense, generally punishable by fine or imprisonment in local jail as opposed to state penitentiary; certain states have various classes of misdemeanors.

**mitigation** Alleviation, reduction, abatement or diminution of a penalty or punishment imposed by law.

**motion** An application to a court or judge to obtain a ruling or order.

**motion for a new trial** Following the verdict, a request that the judge set aside the judgment and order a new trial on the basis that the trial was improper or unfair due to specified prejudicial errors.

**motion for change of venue** A motion made by defendant to transfer the case to a different location, usually on the grounds that an atmosphere exists that prevents a fair trial in the original location.

**motion for judgment of acquittal** Also called a motion for a directed verdict, it asks the judge to throw out the prosecutor's case without letting it go to the jury because the government case is defective and flawed.

**motion for judgment notwithstanding the verdict (also judgment N.O.V.)** Following the verdict, a motion that judgment be entered in favor of the defendant notwithstanding the verdict actually returned by the jury.

**motion in autrefois convict** A motion by defendant to the court objecting to retrial because defendant was already convicted for the same crime. Success of the motion is dependant on the reason why the prior conviction was reversed.

**motion in limine** A written motion for a protective order against prejudicial questions and statements, to avoid admittance into trial of irrelevant and inadmissible matters.

**motion to suppress** A motion to bar evidence from the trial that has either been illegally obtained or that is viewed as irrelevant and/or prejudicial to the case.

**motion to vacate judgment** A motion for the judgment to be set aside on grounds that it was issued improperly, whether purposefully or by mistake.

**negligence** Failure to use the care that any reasonable and careful person would use, characterized by inadvertence, thoughtlessness, and inattention.

**nolo contendere plea** Literally, "I will not contest it." A plea in a criminal case which has a similar legal effect to pleading guilty except that the plea of nolo contendere cannot be used against the defendant in a civil action as an admission of guilt; this plea is only allowed with consent of the court.

**"no-knock" statutes** These quick-entry statutes enacted in some jurisdictions aim to prevent destruction of evidence and to increase officer safety by allowing unannounced forcible entry in some circumstances, under judicial authorization, with approval for action being given beforehand and included in the search warrant.

**opening statement** Statement made by counsel at the start of a trial that outlines or summarizes the nature of the case and the anticipated proof, to advise the jury of facts and issues involved and to give the jury a general picture of the case at trial.

**opinion of the court** The statement by a judge or court of the decision reached, outlining the law applied to the case and detailing the reasoning behind the judgment.

**ordinary witness** A witness who is a nonexpert, such as a bystander witness, testifying to facts and not opinions.

**pardon** An act from a governing power that mitigates the punishment instituted; at the state level, the power to pardon generally rests with the governor while the President of the United States has the power to pardon federal offenses.

**parole** A conditional release of a prisoner, generally under the supervision of a parole officer, from jail or prison after the prisoner has served part of the sentence.

**parole board** The administrative body that determines whether inmates shall be conditionally released before completion of their sentences.

**peremptory challenge** During voir dire, a request to the judge that a prospective juror be released from the jury; no reason or cause need be given; the number of peremptory challenges is a set number determined by statute or court rule (see also challenge for cause).

**plain view doctrine** During search and seizure situations, objects that are in plain view of the peace officer who has the right to be in that particular place are subject to seizure without a warrant and may be admitted into evidence.

**plea** The answer the defendant gives to the prosecutor's accusation.

**plea bargaining** The process in which the prosecutor and the defendant come to an agreement on the disposition of the case subject to court approval; it usually means that defendant pleads guilty to a lesser charge or only one of several charges in return for a sentence that is lighter than that possible or likely for the more serious or numerous charges.

**post-conviction remedy** A procedure allowing a prisoner to challenge the constitutionality of his or her sentence, moving the court to vacate, set aside or correct the original verdict or imposed sentence.

**preclusion sanction** A party to an action my be sanctioned or prevented from introducing evidence if he or she fails to comply with the rules of discovery.

**preliminary hearing (also preliminary examination)** A hearing by a judge to determine whether a person charged with a crime should be held for trial; in felony cases it is prior to indictment and the state must prove evidence to establish probable cause that a crime has been committed by the defendant.

**preponderance of evidence** Evidence of greater weight or more convincing than the evidence which is offered in opposition to it; it shows that the fact it is meant to prove is more probable than not.

**presentence investigation report (PSIR)** A report of the background of a convicted offender designed to assist the judge in determining the sentence against the offender; it not only includes personal background information but resources available to assist the offender, the probation officer's view of the offender's motivations and ambitions, and recommendation for sentencing.

**pretrial conference** A conference called at the discretion of the court that brings opposing counsel together with the purpose of narrowing the issues to be tried, establishing guidelines for matters and evidence to be presented, and other steps to help disposition of the case.

**pretrial discovery** Opportunities available to both parties of a case prior to trial that aid in the gathering of information and evidence, including interrogatories, depositions, requests for admission of fact, etc., provided under rules of procedure and statutes.

**preventive detention laws** Confinement of a defendant while awaiting trial in order to protect others.

**prima facie evidence** Evidence that is sufficient to establish a fact and which, if not contradicted, will remain sufficient to sustain a judgment in favor of the issue it supports, until contradicted by other evidence.

**probable cause** A reasonable ground for belief in the existence of a fact; probable cause for an arrest occurs when a prudent person would reasonably conclude that a crime was committed and the defendant committed it.

**probation** A sentence releasing the defendant into the community under the supervision of a probation officer; release by the court before any prison sentence has begun.

**probative value** That which furnishes, establishes or contributes a decision on disputed facts in a case. Evidence that has probative value helps to decide the case.

**proof beyond a reasonable doubt** Proof that is wholly consistent with the defendant's guilt and inconsistent with any other rational conclusion.

**prosecution** A proceeding initiated by the governing body before a judge or jury to determine the guilt or innocence of a person charged with a crime.

**prosecutor** The person acting on the part of the governing body who initiates and takes charge of a case and serves as the trial lawyer for the people.

**punitive damages** These damages are awarded in civil cases and are above and beyond what will compensate a plaintiff for loss due to the aggravated conduct of the defendant; meant as additional compensation to the plaintiff and as additional punishment for the defendant.

**real evidence** Evidence provided by items themselves as opposed to descriptions of the evidence; in criminal cases, guns or knives or drugs are examples of real evidence, as opposed to oral testimony from human witnesses.

**reasonable grounds** For the purposes of arrest without warrant, having reasonable grounds refers to having probable cause.

**recidivist** A repeat offender.

**recusal** When a judge is disqualified (or disqualifies himself or herself) from hearing a case due to interest or prejudice.

**re-direct** An examination of a witness by the direct examiner following the cross-examination.

**release on own recognizance** When an accused person is released without monetary bail, usually because of strong ties to the community and there is every reason to believe that he or she will appear for trial.

**remand (a case)** When an appellate court sends a case back to the original court for the purpose of having it looked at again or for having some action taken.

**res gestae statements** Considered exceptions to the hearsay rule, certain acts and declarations are admissible because of their inherently credible and spontaneous nature because of their occurrence during or concurrent to the event in question; they must be so closely connected to the event in time and substance as to be a part of the happening.

**restitution** The act of making good or repaying for the act committed.

**respondeat superior** Literally, "Let the master answer." Means that a "master" is liable in certain cases for the wrongful acts of a "servant" toward those to whom the master owes a duty to use care and when the wrongful act occurred in the course of the servant's employment under legitimate authority.

**retroactivity** When the Supreme Court announces a new rule of criminal procedure, a decision must be made about whether it inures to the benefit of defendants in earlier cases (many of whom are incarcerated); some new rules are prospective only, applying exclusively to help defendants in future cases; others in the nature of basic rights are given retroactive application.

**reverse (a case or judgment)** To overturn the decision made.

**reversible error** An error that warrants the appellate court to reverse the judgment below; it is a substantial error that may have prejudiced the appealing party.

**right to counsel** As guaranteed by the Sixth and Fourteenth Amendments to the U.S. Constitution as well as by court rule and statute, it is the right of a criminal defendant to be represented at critical stages of a case by his or her own lawyer, or by a court-appointed attorney if he or she cannot afford to hire one.

**rules of evidence** The rules of the court that govern the admissibility of evidence at trials and hearings, such as the Federal Rules of Evidence, the Uniform Rules of Evidence, and state rules of evidence.

**screening** A way of disposing of a case at some point prior to prosecution, such as when police or prosecutors dismiss a charge or an officer makes a decision not to formally charge a suspect.

**search warrant** An order, based on probable cause and issued by a magistrate or justice, that directs a law enforcement officer to search for and seize property or evidence that is being or has been used in connection with a crime.

**searches incident to lawful arrest** A law enforcement officer who has lawfully arrested a person has the right to search that person and the immediate area of the arrest for weapons.

**sentencing** The postconviction part of the criminal justice process in which the defendant is administered the punishment following his or her conviction; usually imposed by the judge, but in some cases determined by a jury.

**Sentencing Reform Act of 1984** This Act created the United States Sentencing Commission, with the responsibility of establishing determinate sentences and distributing them to federal judges.

**sequestration** The isolation of jurors from contact with others during the course of a sensational trial.

**severance** Dividing defendants who have been jointly indicted into separate cases for trial; when accused persons committed crimes together and are joined in an indictment, a successful defense motion to sever gives one of the defendants his or her own individual trial.

**shield of immunity** Some states have shield of immunity laws that protect municipalities from civil suits.

**showup** A type of pretrial identification procedure in which a suspect is brought before a victim or witness to a crime; less formal than a lineup but serving the same purpose; the procedure must meet certain standards to be admissible in court; (see lineup).

**"silver platter" doctrine** This rule no longer applies—in the past evidence that was illegally obtained by state officers was admissible in federal prosecutions because no federal official had violated the defendant's rights.

**special hearing on bail** In more serious cases, magistrates may conduct this hearing because predetermined formulas for bond are not appropriate for the case at hand, which requires individualized determination of bail.

**spoliation** An obstruction of justice, it refers to the destruction or significant alteration of evidence.

**station-house bail** Prior to initial appearance before a magistrate, defendants in custody for misdemeanors at police headquarters may post bail in an amount set by a police officer based on a pre-set bail schedule.

**statutory law** The body of law created by the legislature in contrast to laws created by judicial opinions and administrative bodies.

**stay of execution** The stopping of execution of judgment; may also refer to the stopping of the execution of capital punishment to permit further appeals.

**stop-and-frisk** The temporary seizure and "patting down" of a person who raises suspicion and appears to be armed; an officer is not required to have full probable cause that a person poses the threat of crime, but the stop cannot be based on hunch alone; the scope of the search is limited to that justified by the circumstances that led the officer to stop the person.

**subpoena** A command to appear at a certain time and place to give testimony about a particular matter.

**subpoena duces tecum** A command to produce certain documents at trial pertinent to the case.

**summary proceeding** A short and simple proceeding; any proceeding that settles or disposes of a case promptly without presentment or indictment or aid of a jury.

**summons** A written instrument designed to give notification to a person of an action against him or her in court and the requirement to appear at a given date and time to answer the complaint.

**suppression hearing** A pretrial proceeding where the defendant attempts to block the admission of particular evidence from being introduced at trial because it has been illegally obtained or is irrelevant and/or prejudicial.

**suspended sentence** A sentence after conviction for a crime that is formally given but not actually required to be served.

**tort** A private or civil wrong or injury, for which the remedy sought is a civil action for damages; three elements of a tort action are the existence of legal duty from defendant to plaintiff, breach of duty, and damage as a result of the breach.

**"totality of circumstances" test** In *Illinois v. Gates*, the Supreme Court allowed that even though one piece of evidence standing alone might not provide probable cause for a search, a collection of evidence corroborated by police follow-up can provide a totality of circumstances that substantiate a search warrant.

**trial** A judicial review and determination of issues between parties in a lawsuit; this review may be by the judge alone in a bench trial, or by a jury in a jury trial.

**trial de novo** A new trial or retrial in which the whole case is begun anew as if no previous trial existed.

**trial errors versus structural defects** Trial errors refer to relatively minor errors of a court in matters of criminal procedure, whereas structural defects are defects in the process that require automatic reversal because they infect the entire trial process.

**"true bill" of indictment** The endorsement made by a grand jury following a bill of indictment where they find that there is sufficient evidence to support a criminal charge.

**venire** Literally, "to come; to appear in court." The list of jurors summoned to serve for a particular time.

**venue** The particular county or geographic area in which a court with jurisdiction may hear and determine a case; it relates only to place; it differs from jurisdiction, which refers to the power to decide a case.

**verdict** The formal decision or finding that resolves the case, either by jury or judge.

**verdict of "guilty but mentally ill"** Under this verdict, the defendant is not automatically released upon recovering from mental illness; there may be a prison term to complete.

**verdict of "guilty but not responsible"** Under this verdict, the judge usually sentences the defendant to a state mental facility until he or she can safely be released as no threat to himself or herself or others.

**voir dire** Literally, "to speak the truth." The preliminary examination of jurors by both parties to the action in order to determine competency, biases, etc., providing an opportunity for both parties to object to a certain number of jurors; (see challenge for cause and peremptory challenge).

**waiver** Sometimes defendants waive, or voluntarily relinquish, certain of their constitutional or statutory rights. For example, defendants sometimes waive their right to a preliminary hearing; defendants can also waive their right to silence during police interrogations and talk with the officers about the crime under investigation.

**writ of coram nobis** Addressed to the court which rendered the judgment, as opposed to appeals, which are directed to another court; it is meant to bring the court's attention to or obtain relief from errors of fact that were not presented to the court during the trial because of excusable mistake and which may have affected the outcome of the decision; the writ of coram nobis asks the judge to correct the original erroneous judgment.

**writ of habeas corpus** Habeas corpus literally means "you have the body." Refers to writs whose purpose is to bring a person before a court or judge; the primary function is to release a person from unlawful imprisonment; it does not declare a person's guilt or innocence but is intended to keep a prisoner from being improperly restrained of liberty.

**writ of injunction** A writ granted by the court that is directed to a particular party, forbidding the person from doing a particular thing or requiring the person to refrain from a certain act.

**writ of mandamus** Literally, "we command." A writ issued by a court instructing an inferior court, board, corporation or person to perform a ministerial act or mandatory duty; it is traditionally used to deal with abuses of judicial power, however it is a drastic remedy used in extraordinary situations.

**writ of prohibition** The counterpart to the writ of mandamus, it prohibits an inferior court or judicial body from taking improper action or exceeding its jurisdiction.

# Table of Cases

# Index

Home search, 35-36
Hospital records, 182
Hot pursuit, 24, 43-44, 43n69
Hung jury, 205
Husband-wife privilege, 189
Hypnosis, in crime detection, 177

Immediate vicinity, 35
Immunity
　of police officers or their employers, 337, 340
　from prosecution, for witnesses, 116
　qualified, of police officers, 343-344
Impeachment
　bias examination, 193
　character proof, 193
　of criminal defendant, 194-196
　felony query, 194
　*Miranda*-tainted confessions and, 160
　by prior inconsistent statement, 193
　protection of defendant, 196
Imprisonment, for non-payment of fine, 335
*In camera*, 86, 135, 190
Incapacitation, 225, 226
Indemnification, 337
Indeterminate sentence law, 224
Indictment, 15
　arraignment, 123
　constitutional considerations, 107-110
　eliminates preliminary hearing, 67
　explained, 10
　form, 118-119
　grand jury procedure, 112-118
　joinder and severance of defendants, 120-122
　for misdemeanors, unnecessary, 327
　waiver of, 122
Information, 15, 68
　arraignment, 123
　choice of charge, 110-111
　constitutional considerations, 107-110
　explained, 10
　form, 111-112
　for misdemeanors, 327
　preliminary, 64
　right of state to prosecute on, 107-108
Informers, 190
Initial (preliminary) appearance, 63
　arraignment distinguished from, 64
Injunction
　against police action, 345
　writs of, 283
Inmates. *See* Prisoners

Insanity defense, 185-186
Instructions to jury. *See* Jury instructions
Interlocutory appeal, 274
Interrogation, of suspects, 28-29
Interstate Agreement on Detainers, 216, 292n18
In the officer's presence, 20
Intoxication defense, 185
Investigatory stop, 9
Irresistible impulse test, 186
Issues of fact, 270
Issues of law, 270

*Jackson v. Denno* hearing, 163-164
Jail visits, 349
Jencks Act, 193
Joinder of offenses or defendants, 120-122, 165
Joint indictment, 120
Joint trials, 120
Judges
　recusal of, 291
　role of, in adversary system, 358-360
　witness examination by, 192-193
Jurisdiction, 289. *See also* Location of trial
　concurrent, 289n9, 306
　defined, 287
　territorial, 287, 295
　venue distinguished from, 287-288
Jurors
　capital cases and, 167-168, 239
　excused for cause, 167
Jury, 6
　in habeas corpus appeal (none), 279
　hung jury, 205
　sequestering of, 167
　viewing of scene of the crime, 173-174
Jury deliberations, 204-205
Jury instructions, 12, 204
　erroneous, 270
　habeas corpus appeals and, 277
Jury misconduct, 205
Jury nullification, 216-217
Jury selection
　alternate jurors, 167n
　challenge for cause, 166
　challenges, 166-167
　group of citizens in pool, 168
　number of jurors needed, 167, 334
　peremptory challenges, 166-167, 169
　racial and gender discrimination in, 169
　venire members, 167-168
　voir dire examination, 166, 168